CA Proficiency 1

Taxation 1 (RoI)

2016–2017

Chartered
Accountants
Ireland

Published in 2016 by
Chartered Accountants Ireland
Chartered Accountants House
47–49 Pearse Street
Dublin 2

ISBN 978-1-910374-50-4

Typeset by Deanta Global Publishing Services
Printed and bound by CPI Group (UK) Ltd, Croydon, CR0 4YY

Contents

Chartered Accountants Regulatory Board *Code of Ethics*

The Chartered Accountants Regulatory Board *Code of Ethics* applies to all aspects of a Chartered Accountant's professional life, including dealing with income tax issues, corporation tax issues, capital gains tax issues, capital acquisitions tax issues and stamp duty issues. The *Code of Ethics* outlines the principles that should guide a Chartered Accountant, namely:

- Integrity
- Objectivity
- Professional Competence and Due Care
- Confidentiality
- Professional Behaviour

As a Chartered Accountant, you will have to ensure that your dealings with the tax aspects of your professional life are in compliance with these fundamental principles. Set out in **Appendix 3** is further information regarding these principles and their importance in guiding you on how to deal with issues which may arise throughout your professional life, including giving tax advice and preparing tax computations.

Overview of Tax System

Learning Objectives

In this chapter you will learn:

- how the administration of our tax system is structured and the role of the Revenue Commissioners;
- how different types of taxpayer are identified;
- how different types of income are classified;
- some key definitions; and
- essential data on income tax rates and bands.

1.1 Introduction

The main taxes levied in Ireland may be classified as **taxes on income**, **taxes on transactions** and **taxes on capital**.

The main taxes on **income** are income tax and corporation tax. The main taxes on **transactions** include value-added tax, Customs & Excise duties, stamp duty, capital gains tax and capital acquisitions tax. The main tax on **capital** is local property tax.

A further distinction is also made between **direct taxes, indirect taxes** and **social contributions**.

Direct taxes are typically taxes on earned income or wealth, e.g. income tax, corporation tax, capital gains tax, capital acquisitions tax and local property tax.

Indirect taxes are typically taxes or levies on transactions or production, e.g. VAT, stamp duty, Customs and Excise duties and carbon tax.

Social contributions are levies that are paid into social security funds or schemes.

Irish income tax is generally assessed on the **worldwide income** of **Irish resident** persons. Non-residents are, in general, liable only to the extent that they have income arising in Ireland. Irish corporation tax is levied on the worldwide income of companies resident in Ireland for tax purposes and on the trading income of non-resident companies to the extent that it arises in Ireland. A non-resident company is liable to **income tax** on **Irish source income** if it is not trading in the State through a branch or an agency.

1.2 Legislation

Income and corporation tax law is based on legislation contained mainly in the **Taxes Consolidation Act 1997 (TCA 1997)** and the annual **Finance Acts (FA)**. Certain tax rules relating to the legislation are set out in regulations or Statutory Instruments that are issued by the Revenue Commissioners under powers conferred by the foregoing legislation. Relevant tax case law and tax practice also play an important role in putting tax legislation into effect. Decisions from the **Court of Justice of the European Union (CJEU)** and **EU Directives** are also influential. EU consent is also required where tax measures support an industry sector or region.

1.3   The Revenue Commissioners, Appeal Commissioners and Collector-General

Responsibility for the care and management of the Irish tax system rests with the Office of the Revenue Commissioners. This is a division within the Department of Finance and overall control rests with the Minister for Finance.

- The board of the **Revenue Commissioners** consists of three Commissioners, one of whom is chairman, appointed by An Taoiseach.
- **Inspectors of Taxes** are appointed by the Revenue Commissioners and are deployed throughout the country in four regional divisions and a separate Large Cases Division. They are responsible for the efficient operation of the Irish tax system by issuing tax returns and other forms for completion, by issuing assessments to taxation, examining tax returns completed by taxpayers and agreeing taxpayers' liabilities.
- The **Collector-General** is appointed by the Revenue Commissioners and is responsible for the efficient collection of taxes, including the pursuance of unpaid taxes.
- **Appeal Commissioners** are appointed by the Minister for Finance and adjudicate between Revenue and taxpayers on matters of disagreement.

1.3.1   Revenue Divisions

The country is divided into four regional divisions as follows:

1. **Border, Midlands, West,** which covers Galway, Sligo, Leitrim, Donegal, Louth, Monaghan, Cavan, Mayo, Westmeath, Offaly, Longford and Roscommon.
2. **Dublin**, which includes Dublin City and County.
3. **East & South East,** which covers Meath, Kildare, Wicklow, Wexford, Carlow, Waterford, Tipperary, Kilkenny and Laois.
4. **South West,** which covers Cork, Limerick, Kerry and Clare.

Each region looks after all tax aspects of the taxpayers in their region. Business taxpayers are generally dealt with in the district where their business is managed and controlled. Non-business taxpayers are dealt with in the region where they live. Each region is further divided up into Revenue districts covering different geographical areas.

The **Large Cases Division** is a separate division that deals with large companies and very wealthy individuals regardless of where they are living or where their businesses are located. There are also a number of other divisions within Revenue as follows:

- Investigations and Prosecutions Division
- Four Revenue Legislation Service Divisions
- Planning Division
- Corporate Services & Accountant General's Division

- Corporate Affairs & Customs Division
- Revenue Solicitor's Division
- Information, Communications Technology and Logistics Division.

1.3.2 Appeal Commissioners

Where assessments to tax cannot be finalised due to a dispute between Revenue and the taxpayer, from **21 March 2016** an appeal can be made directly to the Tax Appeals Commissioner (TAC) who will have the sole responsibility for accepting or refusing the appeal. Under the **Finance (Tax Appeals) Act 2015** all appeal hearings are held in public, unless a party seeks a direction from the Commissioners that a hearing or part thereof is held *in camera*.

Decisions of the Appeal Commissioners are final and conclusive. However, an appeal to the High Court is possible in situations where either party considers that the Appeal Commissioners erred in their determinations on a **point of law** only. See **Chapter 10** for more detail.

1.4 Classes of Taxpayer

Income tax is assessed on the following persons (the term "person" for tax purposes includes individuals, corporate bodies and trusts):

1. Individuals.
2. Individuals in partnerships.
3. Trusts.
4. Non-resident companies are liable to income tax on certain types of income, such as rents arising in Ireland.

Income tax is levied on income applicable to the above classes of taxpayer. It may be assessed by **direct self-assessment** (i.e. profits of a sole trader) or by **deduction at source** from an individual's income (i.e. employees under the PAYE system).

1.5 Classification of Income

If a person's income is assessed directly, it must first be **classified according to the source** from which it arises under the Schedule system used by the Irish Revenue. For example, an individual's total income may be categorised as "trading income", "employment income" and "investment income". Special rules apply for calculating the taxable income from **each** source and for determining the **timing** of the tax charge.

Under the Schedule system the various sources of income are classified as follows:

Schedule D
- **Case I**   Trading income.
- **Case II**   Income from vocations and professions.
- **Case III**   Investment income and income from foreign employments and possessions, provided they have not suffered Irish standard rate income tax at source.
- **Case IV**   Republic of Ireland deposit interest that has suffered deposit interest retention tax (DIRT). Income not taxed specifically under Schedule E or F or under any other Case of Schedule D and income received under deduction of Irish income tax at the 20% standard rate.
- **Case V**   Rents and income from property in the Republic of Ireland.

Schedule E
Income derived from employments, directorships and pensions arising in Ireland.

Schedule F
This applies to dividends and other distributions paid by Irish resident companies.

1.6 Definitions

Income tax year   The tax year is a **calendar** year.

Year of assessment   Income tax is charged for a **year** of assessment.

Basis of assessment   Income is assessable to income tax on a **current year basis** (i.e. income earned in 2016 is assessable to tax in the 2016 tax year).

Self-assessment   Individuals must file a return of income for each tax year not later than 31 October in the year following the tax year.

   Where returns are filed and taxes paid **electronically** through the Revenue On-line Service (ROS), the deadline is extended by up to two weeks. For 2015 income tax returns the extended date to "pay and file" is **10 November 2016**. Since **1 January 2015**, all new registered or re-registered individuals for income tax must file their tax returns electronically.

Tax-adjusted profits   Net profit per the trader's accounts, less any adjustments required for tax purposes.

Total income   This is total income from all sources as computed in accordance with the provisions of TCA 1997.

Taxable income   This is total income less allowances, reliefs and deductions.

Tax credits   These are reliefs that are given as a deduction from tax payable and not by way of a deduction from income.

Standard rate of tax   This is the lower rate of income tax, currently 20% for year 2016.

Marginal/higher rate of tax   This is the higher rate of tax, currently 40% for year 2016.

1.7 Income Tax Rates and Bands

Tax Year 2016	Tax Rate	Single/ Widowed/Surviving Civil Partner	One Parent Family	Married Couple/ Civil Partnership – One Income	Married Couple/ Civil Partnership – Two Incomes
Taxable	20%	€33,800	€37,800	€42,800	€67,600*
Income	40%	Balance	Balance	Balance	Balance

Transferable between spouses/civil partners up to a maximum of €42,800 for any one spouse/civil partner.

1.8   Simple Income Tax Computation Layout

Income Tax Computation of _____	for 2016	
Total Income		X
TAX PAYABLE: €33,800 @ 20% (Single Person)	X	
Balance @ 40%	X	
Gross Income Tax Liability		X
Less: Tax Credits		(X)
Net Tax Due		X

Example 1.1
John is single and his income for 2016 was €46,000. His tax credits were €2,200. Compute his income tax liability for 2016.

Income Tax Computation of John for 2016

	€	€
Total Income		46,000
TAX PAYABLE: €33,800 @ 20% Balance (Single Person) €12,200 @ 40%	6,760 4,880	
Gross Income Tax Liability	11,640	
Less: Tax Credits	(2,200)	
Net Tax Due	9,440	

Example 1.2
Martin and Mary are married and jointly assessed for 2016. Martin's income is €7,000 and Mary's income is €48,000. Their tax credits are €5,500. Compute their income tax liability for 2016.

Income Tax Computation of Martin and Mary for 2016

	Martin €	Mary €	Total €
Total Income	7,000	48,000	55,000
TAX PAYABLE: Mary – first €42,800 @ 20% (Married Persons) Martin – total €7,000 @ 20% Mary – balance €5,200 @ 40%	1,400	8,560 2,080	8,560 1,400 2,080
Gross Income Tax Liability	1,400	10,640	12,040
Less: Tax Credits			(5,500)
Net Tax Due			6,540

Questions

Review Questions

(See Suggested Solutions to Review Questions at the end of this textbook.)

Question 1.1

Pat's income for 2016 is €15,000 and he is married to Una, whose income is €47,000. They are jointly assessed and their tax credits are €6,600.

Requirement
Compute their income tax liability for 2016.

Question 1.2

Paul and Jason are civil partners and jointly assessed for 2016. Paul's income is €47,000 and Jason's income is €41,000. Their tax credits are €4,400.

Requirement
Compute their income tax liability for 2016.

Question 1.3

Seán earned €88,000 in 2016 and is married to Norah, who is a home carer with no income. Their tax credits are €5,950.

Requirement
Compute their income tax liability for 2016.

Residence and Domicile

2.1   Introduction

The extent to which an individual's income is liable to Irish income tax depends on three criteria:

1. the individual's **residence**;
2. the individual's **ordinary residence**; and
3. the individual's **domicile**.

In simple terms, an Irish tax resident is liable to Irish income tax on their worldwide income. A non-resident is liable to Irish income tax on their Irish income only.

Before looking at the tax implications of the above in detail, it is necessary to examine the meaning of the terms "residence", "ordinary residence" and "domicile".

2.2   Residence

An individual's tax residence is determined for **each tax year separately**. Generally, an individual will be **resident** in Ireland for a tax year if he/she is either:

- present in Ireland for a total of **183 days or more** during that tax year; *or*
- present in Ireland for a total of **280 days or more** in the **current and previous** tax years,

provided that where an individual is present in the State (i.e. Republic of Ireland) for only **30 days or** less in a tax year,

■ they will not be Irish resident in that year; *and*

■ no account will be taken of that period in calculating the aggregate of 280 days or more over two tax years.

An individual is present in Ireland for a day if he or she is in Ireland at **any time during that day**. The tests to establish residency are summarised in **Figure 2.1**.

FIGURE 2.1: TEST TO ESTABLISH IRISH RESIDENCY (OTHER THAN ELECTION)

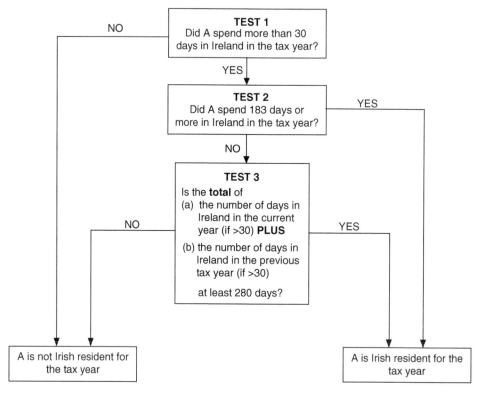

2.3   Election to be Resident

An individual may **elect to be** Irish resident for a tax year if:

■ they are not resident in Ireland in the tax year; *and*

■ they satisfy Revenue that they are in Ireland with the intention and in such circumstances that they will be resident in Ireland for the next tax year.

An individual might elect to be Irish tax resident for the following reasons:

■ to qualify for full tax credits;

■ to avail of Ireland's network of double taxation agreements; *or*

■ to qualify for joint assessment. The Irish Revenue's view is that **both** the individual and their spouse must be Irish resident to qualify; however, each case will be examined on an individual basis.

Example 2.1

Anne jets between her home in Barbados and her retreat in West Cork. She spends the following number of days in Ireland over the following tax years:

Year	Days
2013	Nil
2014	100
2015	125
2016	165

YEAR 2014

Test 1:	Does Anne spend more than 30 days in Ireland in 2014?
Answer:	Yes, therefore go to Test 2.
Test 2:	Does Anne spend 183 days or more in Ireland in 2014?
Answer:	No, therefore go to Test 3.
Test 3:	Is Anne's total number of days in Ireland in 2014 and 2013 greater than 279?
Answer:	100 days in 2014 and 0 days in 2013. No, not greater than 279 days. Anne is not resident in 2014.

YEAR 2015

Test 1:	Does Anne spend more than 30 days in Ireland in 2015?
Answer:	Yes, therefore go to Test 2.
Test 2:	Does Anne spend 183 days or more in Ireland in 2015?
Answer:	No, therefore go to Test 3.
Test 3:	Is Anne's total number of days in Ireland in 2015 and 2014 greater than 279?
Answer:	125 days in 2015 **plus** 100 days in 2014. Total days in Ireland 2015 and 2014 = 225. No, not greater than 279 days. Anne is not resident in 2015.

YEAR 2016

Test 1:	Does Anne spend more than 30 days in Ireland in 2016?
Answer:	Yes, therefore go to Test 2.
Test 2:	Does Anne spend 183 days or more in Ireland in 2016?
Answer:	No, therefore go to Test 3.
Test 3:	Is Anne's total number of days in Ireland in 2016 and 2015 greater than 279?
Answer:	165 days in 2016 **plus** 125 days in 2015. Total days in Ireland 2016 and 2015 = 290. Yes, greater than 279 days. Anne is Irish resident for 2016.

2.4 Ordinary Residence

An individual's ordinary residence refers to an individual's pattern of residence over a number of tax years and is determined for each tax year separately. An individual is ordinarily resident in Ireland for a tax year if he has been resident in Ireland for each of the **last three consecutive tax years**.

An individual does not stop being ordinarily resident in Ireland unless he has been **non-resident** for the preceding **three consecutive tax years**.

Example 2.2

Tom comes to live in Ireland from the US on 1 May 2012. He leaves permanently on 28 January 2016.

Tax Year	Resident	Ordinarily Resident
2012	Yes > 183 days	No
2013	Yes > 183 days	No
2014	Yes > 183 days	No
2015	Yes > 183 days	Yes (resident for previous three years)
2016	No – fails 30-day test	Yes

Tom will continue, until 2018, to be ordinarily resident in Ireland. He will cease to be ordinarily resident when he has been non-resident for three years, i.e. 2019.

2.5   Domicile

Domicile is a legal term. The main idea underlying the concept is **home**, the permanent home. Generally a person is domiciled in the country of which he is a national and in which he spends his life. However, the equating of domicile to home must be treated with care as, in certain circumstances, a person may be domiciled in a country which is not and never has been his home. A person can have two homes but can only have **one domicile** at any one time.

2.5.1   Domicile of Origin

An individual is **born** with a domicile known as the domicile of origin. A child at birth acquires the domicile of the father. If the parents are not married, the domicile of the mother is acquired instead. An individual can **reject** their domicile of origin and **acquire** a new domicile. In order to abandon the domicile of origin, the individual must prove conclusively that they have **severed all links** with the country in which the domicile of origin lies. A domicile of origin cannot be lost by a mere abandonment, it can only be lost by the acquisition of a domicile of choice.

2.5.2   Domicile of Choice

A domicile of choice is the domicile that any independent person (e.g. an individual who has attained 18 years of age) can acquire by a combination of **residence** and **intention**. To acquire a domicile of choice, an individual must establish a physical presence in the new jurisdiction and have an intention to reside there indefinitely. A domicile of choice can be abandoned. This will involve either the acquisition of a new domicile of choice or the revival of the domicile of origin.

2.5.3   Domicile of Dependence

The domicile of dependent persons (children less than 18 years or incapacitated persons) is **dependent** on the domicile of someone else other than themselves.

Three general points regarding domicile require special attention:

1. a person cannot be without a domicile;
2. a person cannot possess more than one domicile at any time; and
3. an existing domicile is presumed to continue until it is proved that a new domicile of choice has been acquired.

2.6   Impact of Residence, Ordinary Residence and Domicile

2.6.1   Resident and Domiciled

Individuals who are resident and domiciled are liable to Irish income tax on their **worldwide personal income**, irrespective of where it is earned and whether or not it is remitted to Ireland.

Example 2.3

Pat, a single man, has the following sources of income in 2016:

	€
Salary paid by Irish company	75,000
Dividends from Spanish company	10,000
Rent received from USA (not remitted)	5,200
Total income	90,200

Pat is resident and domiciled in Ireland. Therefore, he is liable to income tax on his worldwide income of €90,200 regardless of where it arises or whether it is remitted into Ireland.

2.6.2   Resident and Domiciled but Not Ordinarily Resident

An Irish domiciled individual who is resident but not ordinarily resident in Ireland (e.g. an Irish citizen who has been living abroad for many years and who has returned) is liable to income tax on:

1.   any income arising in Ireland; **and**
2.   foreign sourced income, whether remitted to the State or not – essentially their worldwide income.

Example 2.4

Patrick, an Irish citizen, returned to Dublin in May 2016 after a five-year secondment to his employer's parent company in Dubai. He has the following sources of income in 2016:

	€
Salary paid by Dubai parent company (to May 2016)	60,000
Salary paid by Irish company (June to Dec 2016)	40,000
Rent received on Dubai apartment (June to Dec) (remitted)	9,000
Dubai deposit interest (paid Oct 2016) (not remitted)	4,000

Patrick is domiciled (Irish citizen) and resident (>183 days) in Ireland for 2016, but is not ordinarily resident (as he was non-resident for 2015, 2014 and 2013). As Patrick qualifies for split-year residence (see **Section 2.8**), he is therefore liable on:

	€
Salary paid by Irish company (June to Dec 2016)	40,000
Dubai rent	9,000
Dubai deposit interest	4,000

2.6.3   Resident but Not Domiciled

An individual who is resident but not domiciled in Ireland is liable to income tax in full on:

1.   any income arising in Ireland; ***and***
2.   other income (excluding employment income) arising outside of Ireland **but only** to the extent that it is **remitted into** Ireland; ***and***
3.   income from an office or employment, insofar as that income relates to the performance, **in the State**, of the duties of that office or employment (irrespective of where it is paid or whether it is remitted into Ireland or not).

2.6.4   Not Resident and Not Ordinarily Resident

An individual who is not resident in Ireland is liable to income tax only on income arising in Ireland. In addition, a non-resident individual is not generally entitled to tax credits and reliefs (but see **Section 2.6.6**). The domicile of such a person is not relevant.

2.6.5 Not Resident but Ordinarily Resident

An individual who is not resident in Ireland but is ordinarily resident in Ireland is liable to Irish tax on their worldwide income **except for**:

1. income from a trade or profession, no part of which is carried on in Ireland;
2. employment that is carried on outside the State (incidental duties may be carried on in the State); and
3. other foreign income which in any year of assessment **does not exceed €3,810**.

Example 2.5

Mary Rose, an Irish citizen, who is single, emigrated to Canada in May 2014. Apart from an annual two-week holiday she has not returned to Ireland. She has the following sources of income in 2016.

	€
Salary paid by her Canadian employer	90,000
Rent received from letting her house in Canada (not remitted)	15,000

She is non-resident for 2014 and 2015, but is still ordinarily resident for 2016. Therefore she is liable to income tax on the Canadian rent since it is in excess of €3,810 but not on her Canadian salary as the employment was exercised wholly outside Ireland.

2.6.6 Non-resident Individual Entitlement to Tax Credits

In general, non-resident individuals are not entitled to tax credits. However, there are two exceptions to this:

1. citizens or nationals of an EU Member State – full tax credits are granted on a cumulative basis if 75% of the worldwide income is taxable in Ireland. A portion of tax credits may be due if Irish income is less than 75%; or
2. citizens of a country with which there is a double taxation agreement – full tax credits are allowable on a cumulative basis where the person's only source of income is Irish. Where the person has non-Irish source income in addition to Irish income, a portion of tax credits may be due.

2.7 Split-year Residence

As outlined above, an individual is Irish resident or non-resident, as the case may be, for a full tax year. **Section 822 TCA 1997** provides that an individual can be treated as Irish resident for **part** of a year only in certain circumstances.

2.7.1 Year of Arrival

As far as **employment income** is concerned, an individual who:

1. has not been resident in Ireland in the preceding tax year,
2. arrives in Ireland in the current tax year,
3. is resident in Ireland in the current tax year (i.e. 183 days or more), and
4. satisfies Revenue that he is in Ireland with the intention of and in such circumstances that he will be Irish tax resident in the following tax year,

will be treated as Irish resident only from **the date of his arrival** in the State. There is no apportionment of tax credits, allowances or tax bands.

Example 2.6

Simon, a single man, has lived in London all his life. His employer sends him on a three-year secondment to Ireland. He arrives on 1 June 2016. His salary from his UK employer is his only income. In 2016, his salary was €66,000 and was paid to him in the UK.

His basic personal tax credit was €1,650 and his employee tax credit was €1,650 for 2016.

Will Simon qualify for split-year residence?

Q. Is he resident in 2015?
A. No.

Q. Did he arrive in 2016?
A. Yes.

Q. Is he resident in 2016?
A. Yes, under the 183-day rule.

Q. Does he intend to be resident in 2017?
A. Yes.

Simon therefore qualifies for the split-year residence: he will be treated as resident from 1 June 2016. His Irish income tax liability will be as follows:

Schedule D Case III

€66,000 × 7/12ths	€38,500
Tax payable:	
€33,800 @ 20%	€6,760
€4,700 @ 40%	€1,880
	€8,640
Deduct tax credits:	

Basic personal tax credit	€1,650	
Employee tax credit	€1,650	(€3,300)
Net tax liability		€5,340

2.7.2 Year of Departure

For **employment income only**, an individual who is:

1. resident in the current tax year, **and**
2. satisfies Revenue that he is leaving the State, other than for a temporary purpose, with the intention and in such circumstances that he will not be resident in the next tax year,

will be treated as resident only up to **the date of departure**.

Example 2.7

Brian, a single man from Dublin, leaves to work in Boston on 1 May 2016. He has signed a three-year employment contract with a US firm.

His basic personal tax credit was €1,650 and his employee tax credit was €1,650 for 2016.

His income in 2016 is as follows:

Irish salary	€18,500
PAYE deducted	€3,530
US salary	€30,000

continued overleaf

Will Brian qualify for split-year residence?

Q. Is he resident in 2016?
A. Yes, under the 280-day rule.

Q. Is he leaving Ireland for other than a temporary purpose?
A. Yes.

Q. Does he intend and is it likely, given the circumstances of his departure to the US, that he will not be resident in 2017?
A. Yes.

Brian therefore qualifies for the split-year concession. His Irish income tax liability for 2016 will be as follows:

Schedule E

Irish salary		€18,500
Tax @ 20%		€3,700
Deduct tax credits:		
Basic personal tax credit	€1,650	
Employee tax credit	€1,650	(€3,300)
Net tax liability		€400
Less: PAYE deducted		(€3,530)
Tax refund due		(€3,130)

Brian is not taxed on his US employment income and receives full personal tax credits.

2.8 Special Assignee Relief Programme (SARP)

In 2009 the **Special Assignee Relief Programme (SARP)** for higher paid executives coming to work in Ireland for the first time was introduced. This has been amended a few times since its introduction and significant changes to the relief were introduced by Finance Act 2014, which came into effect from 1 January 2015.

The relief, contained in section 825C TCA 1997, provides that where a "relevant employee":

1. is resident in the State for tax purposes, **and**
2. performs in the State the duties of his or her employment with a "relevant employer" or "associated company", **and**
3. has "relevant income" from his relevant employer or associated company that is not less than €75,000,

then the relevant employee, on making a claim, will be entitled to claim for a **deduction** of a "**specified amount**" for the **first five years** from the income, gains or profit of the employment with the relevant employer or associated company.

The **specified amount** is calculated at **30% of income over €75,000 (annualised)** and consequently **exempts this amount from income tax, but not from PRSI and USC.**

2.8.1 Definitions

Relevant Employee

A "relevant employee" is a person who:

1. was a full-time employee of the "relevant employer" for the whole of the six months immediately before his or her arrival in the State and exercised their duties of employment for that relevant employer **outside** the State, *and*
2. arrives in the State in any of the tax years **2015, 2016** or **2017**, at the request of the relevant employer, to:
   (a) perform in the State the duties of his or her employment for that employer, *or*
   (b) to take up employment in the State with an associated company, *and*
3. performs their duties of employment in the State for a **minimum** period of **12 consecutive months** from the date he or she first performed those duties in the State;
4. was **not resident** in the State for the **five tax years** immediately **preceding** the tax year in which he or she first arrives in the State for the purposes of the employment, **and**
5. in respect of whom the relevant employer certifies with Revenue the employee's compliance with conditions 1–3 above, within 30 days from the employee's arrival in the State.

Relevant Employer

"Relevant employer" means a company that is incorporated and tax resident in a country with which Ireland has a double taxation agreement, or an information-sharing agreement.

Associated Company

"Associated company" means a company that is associated with the relevant employer. Under section 432 TCA 1997, a company shall be treated as another company's associated company at a particular time if, at that time or at any time within the previous year, either company has control over the other, or both companies are under the control of the same person or persons.

Relevant Income

While all income and emoluments are subject to income tax, the "relevant income" definition assesses whether a person can **qualify** for SARP by having **relevant income of not less than €75,000** (annual amount). Relevant income includes all the relevant employee's income, profits and gains from the employment, but excludes the following:

1. benefits in kind and perquisites;
2. any bonus, commission or other similar payments (whether contractual or not);
3. termination payments;
4. shares or share-based remuneration; and
5. payments in relation to restrictive covenants.

In effect, **relevant income will be the base salary**.

Note that the "relevant income" definition is **only** for the purposes of assessing whether the person can qualify for SARP and is **not relevant in calculating the actual relief**, i.e. the "specified amount".

Example 2.8

Mary Watson, an American citizen, was sent to work in the State in January 2016 by a relevant employer and had the following sources of income in 2016:

	€
Salary paid by US parent	150,000
Bonus paid by US parent	70,000
Benefit in kind	4,000
Total income	224,000
Less: tax deducted under the PAYE system	(81,500)
After tax income	142,500

SARP relief:

(a) Relevant Income ⩾ €75,000
  Salary €150,000 ⩾ €75,000 ⇨ eligible for SARP relief
(b) Calculation of **specified amount**:

Total income:	224,000
Less: lower threshold	(75,000)
	149,000
Specified amount @ 30%	**44,700**
Total income	224,000
Less: specified amount	(44,700)
Taxable income	179,300

Ms Watson will need to make a claim for a tax repayment of €17,880 (€44,700 @ 40%).

Section 825C TCA 1997 requires the relevant employer to notify Revenue of an employee's entitlement to SARP within **30 days** of the employee's arrival in Ireland. Failure to meet this condition may mean that an employee cannot avail of the relief.

2.9 Domicile Levy

Section 531AA TCA 1997 introduced a levy, from 1 January 2010, to ensure that individuals who are domiciled in Ireland make a contribution to the Exchequer irrespective of their residence status. The individual is not required to be a "citizen of Ireland".

The domicile levy applies to an individual:

1. who is domiciled in Ireland in that tax year;
2. whose worldwide income for the tax year is greater than €1 million;
3. whose final Irish income tax liability is less than €200,000; **and**
4. who has Irish property with a market value exceeding €5 million at 31 December.

The amount of the levy is **€200,000**. Irish income tax paid by an individual will be allowed as a credit against the domicile levy. However, taxes paid overseas on the worldwide income are not allowed as a credit. Irish property does not include shares in a company (or a holding company) **carrying on a trade**, but includes all property **situated in Ireland** to which the individual is beneficially entitled in possession at 31 December. The market value is the price at which the property would sell on the open market and does not take into account any charges or mortgages taken out against the property.

The levy operates on an individual basis, i.e. if jointly-assessed spouses both meet the conditions above, the levy is payable by both spouses. The tax is payable on a self-assessment basis on or before 31 October in the year following the valuation date, i.e. 31 December each year.

This section also empowers Revenue to request any person it believes to be a relevant person to deliver a full and true return of all particulars in relation to the determination of the domicile levy, together with payment of same within 30 days of the request.

Questions

Review Questions
(See Suggested Solutions to Review Questions at the end of this textbook.)

Question 2.1

Hank is a US citizen seconded to work in Ireland for two years. He arrives on 19 May 2014 and leaves on 1 May 2016. He does not leave the country during that period.

Requirement
Establish Hank's residence status for each year.

Question 2.2

Kenji is a Japanese citizen seconded to work in Ireland for a two-year period. He arrives on 17 December 2013 and leaves on 16 January 2016. He does not leave the country during the period of his secondment.

Requirement
What is Kenji's residence status for each year?

Question 2.3

Aurore is a French woman who has been seconded from France to work in Ireland for three years. She arrives on 1 February 2015 and leaves on 10 January 2018. Her French employer continues to pay her salary in France of €3,000 per month and an additional €2,000 per month in Ireland.

Requirement
What is Aurore's residence status for each year? What advice would you give Aurore and her employer in connection with her residence status and salary payment?

Question 2.4

Mr Harris is married and has the following sources of income for 2016:

	€
Irish rents	37,000
US dividends	4,000

Tax was deducted by the lessee of €7,400 on the gross rent received of €37,000 in 2016. Mr Harris is not Irish domiciled and is not resident or ordinarily resident in Ireland.

Requirement
Calculate Mr Harris's income tax liability for 2016.

Question 2.5

Mr Klaus, a German citizen, was sent to work in Ireland on 1 May 2016 by his company, Flow GmbH. He had the following sources of income in 2016:

	€
Salary paid by German parent from 1 May 2016	250,000
Benefit in kind	2,500
Bonus payment	20,000

Requirement
Calculate Mr Klaus's entitlement to relief under SARP.

Classification of Income

Learning Objectives

In this chapter you will learn:

- how income is classified for tax purposes according to its source;
- how to distinguish between the different types of income and, in particular, self-employed income versus employment income;
- the basis of assessment for each of the different types of income;
- the special rules associated with the commencement, cessation of trading and change of accounting date in a year of assessment;
- the distinctions between and classification of unearned and passive income, e.g. bank interest, dividends and rental income; and
- the definition of employment and the rules regarding the assessment to tax of employment income, benefits in kind, commencement, termination and retirement payments.

3.1   Cases I and II, Schedule D

3.1.1   Introduction

Income tax is charged on profits or gains arising from any **trade** (Case I) or from any **profession** or **vocation** (Case II). The tax treatment and computational rules for Cases I and II are practically identical and are therefore considered together.

Persons chargeable to tax under Case I would include shopkeepers, manufacturers, farmers, etc., while the charge to tax under Case II would extend to self-employed individuals carrying on professions or vocations (whether as single individuals or in partnership), such as doctors, solicitors, architects, accountants, dramatists, and jockeys. The last two are regarded as vocations rather than professions.

3.1.2   Definitions of "Profession", "Trade" and "Vocation"

Profession
The term "profession" is not defined in TCA 1997 and accordingly one must therefore look at decided tax cases to help clarify the term. The following considerations are relevant in determining whether or not a profession exists:

1.   Is the taxpayer a member of a professional body?
2.   Does the professional body:

    (a) limit admittance to membership to persons who have successfully completed examinations and/or undergone a period of specified training?

    (b) prescribe a code of ethics, breach of which may incur disciplinary measures against the member?

3.   Does the occupation require mainly intellectual skill?

4.   Is his/her relationship with clients in the nature of contracts **for** services, rather than contracts **of** service (e.g. employments)?

Examples of individuals regarded as carrying on a profession would include teachers, doctors, opticians, actors and journalists.

Vocation

In decided tax cases, the word "vocation" has been compared with a "calling". Decided tax cases have held that the following are vocations:

- a bookmaker;
- a dramatist; and
- a jockey.

Trade

Section 3 TCA 1997 defines "trade" as including "every trade, manufacture, adventure or concern in the nature of trade". The question of whether or not a trade is carried on is a **question of fact** rather than a point of law. The courts have held this definition to include profits or gains arising from trading in the normal sense of the word but also from **isolated** transactions and activities. Profits from farming and from dealing in development land are assessable under Case I.

3.1.3 *"Badges of Trade"*

Guidance as to what constitutes "trading" is available from case law and from a set of rules drawn up in 1955 by the **UK Royal Commission on the Taxation of Profits and Income**. These rules, known as the **"Badges of Trade"**, have been approved by the Irish courts. The six "Badges of Trade" listed by the Commission are as follows:

1.   **The Subject Matter of the Realisation**

    The general rule here is that property, which does not give its owner an income or personal enjoyment merely by virtue of its ownership, is more likely to have been acquired with the object of a trading transaction than property that does, e.g. the principal private residence of an individual is more likely to have been bought for the purposes of his and his family's personal enjoyment rather than for the purposes of a trading transaction.

2.   **Length of the Period of Ownership**

    As a general rule, property acquired for a trading or dealing purpose is realised within a short time after acquisition. However, there may be many exceptions to this rule.

3.   **Frequency or Number of Similar Transactions by the Same Person**

    If the individual completed a number of transactions involving the same sort of property in succession over a period of years or there have been several such realisations at about the same date, a presumption arises that there has been a dealing in respect of each, i.e. that they were trading transactions.

4.   **Supplementary Work on or in Connection with the Property Realised**

    If the property is improved or developed in any way during the ownership so as to bring it into a more marketable condition, or if any special marketing efforts are made to find or attract purchasers, such as the opening of a sales office or a large-scale advertising campaign, then this would provide some evidence of trading. Where there is an organised effort to obtain profit, there is likely to be a source of taxable income. However, if nothing at all is done, the suggestion would tend to go the other way.

5. **The Circumstances Giving Rise to the Realisation of the Property**
    There may be some explanation, such as a sudden emergency or opportunity calling for the realisation of cash, which may eliminate the suggestion that any plan of dealing prompted the original purchase, i.e. in the case of "an unsolicited offer that cannot be refused".

6. **Motive for the Transaction**
    Motive is extremely important in all cases. There are cases in which the purpose of the transaction is clearly discernible. Circumstances surrounding the particular transaction may indicate the motive of the seller and this may in fact overrule the seller's own evidence.

It is important, however, to appreciate that the 'whole picture' must be taken into account, so that the weight given to the various factors may vary according to the circumstances. Furthermore, it is important to recognise that any given factor may be present to a greater or lesser degree, and that the absence (or presence) of any single factor is unlikely to be conclusive in its own right.

There are a number of significant tax cases which consider this matter:

- The **profit motive** was considered in the UK case of *Erichsen v. Last* (1881) when the judge defined trading as "where a person habitually does and contracts to do a thing capable of producing a profit, and for the purpose of producing a profit, he carries on a trade or business".
- The matter of supplementary work was considered in the UK case of *Martin v. Lowry* (1927) where the judges referred to the "mantle of trading" which the merchant donned as a result of the elaborate selling organisation he employed to sell his aeroplane linen to the public.
- Lord Sands in the UK case of *Rutledge v. Inland Revenue* (1929) considered the subject matter of the realisation in this case which was a consignment of toilet paper that Lord Sands considered must be bought for resale and so be "an adventure in the nature of the trade" under the terms of the relevant legislation.
- The case of *Jenkinson (HMIT) v. Freedland* (1961) brought a note of sobriety to the badges as the judge reminded us, "the facts of each case must be considered not merely the motive of acquisition, and conclusion arrived at" but that "the true position is that all facts in each case must be considered".

3.1.4 Basis of Assessment – Cases I and II, Schedule D

The income assessable under Cases I and II is normally based on **the accounting period of 12 months ending during the year of assessment,** e.g. profits earned by a trader for the year end 30 June 2016 are assessed in the tax year 2016.

There are, however, special provisions when a trade or profession **commences** or **ceases** business, or changes its accounting date.

3.1.5 Commencement Years

The date on which a trade commences is a question of fact. The *Birmingham & District Cattle By-Products v. Inland Revenue* (1919) case established some tests which are still used to determine when a trade actually commences. These can be summarised as follows:

- The date when premises are acquired?   NO
- The date when staff are hired?   NO
- The date when supplier contracts are signed?   NO
- The date when raw materials/stock are received?   YES

First Year
The basis of assessment for the first tax year is the **profit from the date of commencement to the end of the tax year**. If the accounts of the individual do not coincide with this period, then the assessable profit is arrived at by **time apportionment**.

The first year of assessment is always the tax year during which the trade or profession commenced.

Example 3.1
Mr Jones commenced to trade as a builder on 1 July 2015 and prepared accounts for 18 months to 31 December 2016.

In this case, Mr Jones will be assessed under Case I as a builder for the first year of assessment, i.e. 2015, on the basis of the profits from 1 July 2015 to 31 December 2015. These will be arrived at by time-apportioning the 18 months results to 31 December 2016, i.e. the amount assessed for 2015 will be 6/18ths of the total profits for the period.

Second Year
1. If there is a 12-month accounting period ending in the second tax year and it is the only accounting period ending in that year, assess the taxable profits of that 12-month accounting period.

Example 3.2
Donna commences to trade on 1 June 2015. Accounts are prepared for the year ended 31 May 2016.
Taxable profits for year ended 31 May 2016 = €24,000.
Accounts are prepared annually to 31 May.

Tax Year		Period	Calculation	Taxable Profit
2015	(1st year)	01/06/2015–31/12/2015	€24,000 × 7/12ths	€14,000
2016	(2nd year)	01/06/2015–31/05/2016	€24,000 × 12/12ths	€24,000

---

2. If there is an accounting period **other than one of 12 months** ending in the second tax year and it is the only accounting period ending in that tax year and the trade had commenced not less than 12 months before that date, assess the taxable profits of the year ending on that date.

Example 3.3
Lisa commences to trade on 1 May 2015. Accounts are prepared for the 17 months ending 30 September 2016.
Taxable profits for the 17 months ending 30 September 2016 = €68,000.
Accounts are prepared yearly to 30 September thereafter.

Tax Year		Period	Calculation	Taxable Profit
2015	(1st year)	01/05/2015–31/12/2015	€68,000 × 8/17ths	€32,000
2016	(2nd year)	01/10/2015–30/09/2016	€68,000 × 12/17ths	€48,000

---

3. If there are **two or more accounting periods** ending in the second tax year, and the trade commenced not less than 12 months before the later date, assess the taxable profits of the year ending on the **later** date. (You may add two or more accounting periods to make up the 12 months.)

Example 3.4
Rose commences to trade on 1 July 2015. Accounts are prepared for the 10 months ending 30 April 2016.
Taxable profits for the 10 months ending 30 April 2016 = €10,000.
Accounts are prepared for the 8 months ending 31 December 2016.
Taxable profits for 8 months ending 31 December 2016 = €6,000.

Tax Year		Period	Calculation	Taxable Profit
2015	(1st year)	01/07/2015–31/12/2015	€10,000 × 6/10ths	€6,000
2016	(2nd year)	01/01/2016–31/12/2016	€10,000 × 4/10ths +	
			€6,000 × 8/8ths	€10,000

---

4.   In any other case, assess the actual profits for the tax year.

Example 3.5
David commences to trade on 1 November 2015. Accounts are prepared for the 8 months ending 30 June 2016.
Taxable profits for 8 months ending 30 June 2016 = €32,000.
Accounts are prepared for the year ending 30 June 2017.
Taxable profits for year ending 30 June 2017 = €46,000.

While there is an accounting period ending in the second tax year, 2016, David did not commence to trade at least 12 months before this date. Accordingly, for the second tax year, David is taxed on the actual profits arising in that tax year.

Tax Year		Period	Calculation	Taxable Profit
2015	(1st year)	01/11/2015–31/12/2015	€32,000 × 2/8ths	€8,000
2016	(2nd year)	01/01/2016–31/12/2016	€32,000 × 6/8ths +	
			€46,000 × 6/12ths	€47,000

Third Year
The basis of assessment for the third year of assessment is **the accounting period of 12 months ending during the tax year**, i.e. if 2016 was the third year of assessment for a sole trader and he prepared a set of accounts for the 12 months to 30 September 2016, then these accounts would form the basis for tax year 2016 (subject to the option discussed below).

Option
If the actual profits of the **second** tax year are less than the profits assessed under the rules outlined above, then the difference can be deducted from the taxable profits of the third year.

Example 3.6	*Profit*
Date of commencement 1 July 2014	
Accounts for 12 months to 30 June 2015	€52,000
Accounts for 12 months to 30 June 2016	€48,000
Accounts for 12 months to 30 June 2017	€30,000
Computation:	**Final Assessment**
First Year of Assessment 2014	
Profit period 01/07/2014 to 31/12/2014, i.e. €52,000 × 6/12ths	€26,000

continued overleaf

Second Year of Assessment 2015		
12-month accounting period ending 30 June 2015		€52,000
Third Year of Assessment 2016		
12-month accounting period (basis period) ending 30 June 2016		€48,000
Assessable profits		
Amount assessed in second year (2015)	€52,000	
Less: actual profits for the second year		
(€52,000 × 6/12ths) + (€48,000 × 6/12ths)	€50,000	
Excess		(€2,000)
Final assessment 2016: €48,000 – €2,000		€46,000

Fourth and Subsequent Years

The basis period for any particular year of assessment will normally be the accounting period of 12 months ending during the tax year. The taxpayer has no options for these years.

3.1.6 Cessation Years

The date on which a trade ceases is when all its trading stock has been sold or when it ceases to manufacture (although it continues to purchase products to resell). This is demonstrated by the case of *Gordon and Blair Ltd v. Inland Revenue* (1962), where a brewery was held to have ceased the trade of manufacturing beer and commenced the trade of selling beer.

Final Year

The final year of assessment is based on the profits from the beginning of the tax year to the date of cessation, i.e. if the taxpayer ceases on 31 August 2016, the last year of assessment will be 2016, so the 2016 assessment will be based on the actual profits from 1 January 2016 to 31 August 2016. Accounting period profits are time-apportioned where necessary.

Penultimate (second last) Year

The profits assessable for this year are those of an accounting period of 12 months ending during the year of assessment. However, the assessment for the penultimate year must be revised to the actual amount of profits for that year if this yields a higher figure.

Where an assessment has to be revised and an additional tax liability arises, the obligation is on the taxpayer to include it in the self-assessed tax return in the year in which the cessation occurred.

Example 3.7

J. Jones, who traded as a butcher for many years, retired on 30 June 2016. The results for the last few years of trading were as follows:

Year ended 30/09/2014	Profit	€36,000
Year ended 30/09/2015	Profit	€48,000
9 months to 30/06/2016	Profit	€45,000

Computation:
Final Tax Year 2016
Basis of Assessment: 01/01/2016 to 30/06/2016

€45,000 × 6/9ths	€30,000

continued overleaf

Penultimate Year 2015	
Original assessment based on profits year ended 30/09/2015	€48,000
Revise to Actual if Actual Profits > €48,000:	
Actual profits 2015:	
€48,000 × 9/12ths + €45,000 × 3/9ths	€51,000

3.1.7 Change in Accounting Date

Where there is a change to the accounting date of an **ongoing** trade or profession in a particular tax year, the basis of assessment for that tax year is a **12-month period** ending on the **new accounting date**. If there are more than one set of accounts ending in a particular tax year, the basis of assessment for that tax year is a 12-month period ending on the **later** of the accounting dates.

Revision of Previous Year

Where there is a change to the accounting date, the assessment for the previous tax year must be reviewed and if the profits of a corresponding period ending in the previous tax year are higher, the profits assessed for the previous tax year are revised upwards.

Example 3.8	
Julie Birch has been trading for a number of years to a year end of 31 May. In 2016 Julie changed her accounting year end to correspond with the financial year, i.e. 31 December. Her results are as follows.	
	Profit
Accounts for 12 months to 31 May 2015	€22,000
Accounts for 12 months to 31 May 2016	€38,000
Accounts for 7 months to 31 December 2016	€30,000
Computation:	**Final Assessment**
Year of Assessment 2016	
Profit period 01/01/2016 to 31/12/2016,	
i.e. €38,000 × 5/12ths + €30,000 × 7/7ths	€45,833
Previous Year of Assessment 2015	
12-month accounting period ending 31/05/2015	€22,000
Revise to actual for period 01/01/2015 to 31/12/2015:	
i.e. €22,000 × 5/12ths + €38,000 × 7/12ths	€31,333
Additional assessment 2015	**€9,333**
Note that the tax due on the revised 2015 assessment must be paid on or before the due date for the 2016 assessment, i.e. 31 October 2017.	

3.1.8 Short-lived Businesses

Where a trade or profession is set up and discontinued within three tax years and the profits on which the individual is assessed for the three tax years exceed the actual profits arising in the same period, the individual may elect to have the profits of the second last year of trading reduced to the actual profits arising. By electing to reduce taxable profits for the second last year to actual, the individual is taxable on actual profits for all three years. An election for this treatment must be made before the specified return date for the year of cessation.

Example 3.9

M. Ryan commenced trading on 1 July 2014 and ceased trading on 31 March 2016. The Case I profits for these years were as follows:

Year ended 30 June 2015	Profit	€65,000
9 months ended 31 March 2016	Profit	€30,000

Computation:

First Year of Assessment 2014

Profit period 01/07/2014 to 31/12/2014

   i.e. €65,000 × 6/12ths   <u>€32,500</u>

Second Year of Assessment 2015

12-month accounting period ending 30/06/2015   €65,000

Last Year 2016

Actual 01/01/2016 to 31/03/2016

   €30,000 × 3/9ths   €10,000

Second Year Excess:

Amount assessed in second year (2015)   €65,000

Less: actual profits for 2015

   (€65,000 × 6/12ths) + (€30,000 × 6/9ths)   <u>€52,500</u>

Excess   <u>(€12,500)</u>

Final assessment 2016: €10,000 – €12,500   <u>€NIL</u>

In the absence of any relief in this case, the individual would be taxed on profits of €107,500 for the three tax years, whereas actual profits arising in the three years were only €95,000. If the individual elects to be taxed on actual profits arising in the second year, i.e. 2014, he would be assessed as follows:

2014: Actual as above	€32,500
2015: Elect for actual €65,000 × 6/12ths + €30,000 × 6/9ths	€52,500
2016: Actual (with no second year excess as second year taxed on actual) €30,000 × 3/9ths	<u>€10,000</u>
Profits assessed for three years	<u>€95,000</u>

3.1.9 Post-cessation Receipts

Income received after a trade has ceased (e.g. bad debts recovered) is assessed under Schedule D Case IV (net of any post-cessation expenses). Unused capital allowances from the ceased trade may be offset against the income. The Case I/II cessation assessments are not adjusted.

3.1.10 Revenue Concession in Death Cases

A trade or a profession is treated as being **permanently discontinued** on the death of the person carrying on the trade, even if their personal representative or successors continue the trade after their death. Accordingly, the death of a person will normally trigger the **Case I and II cessation provisions** as outlined above. However, Revenue will, by concession, allow a trade to be treated as a **continuing** one where the trade is continued on by the **deceased's spouse or civil partner**. In such a case, provided the deceased's spouse or civil partner elects for such treatment, the cessation provisions are not applied to the deceased and the commencement provisions are not applied to the deceased's spouse or civil partner. If the election is made for the year in which the trader dies, Case I profits for the year of death are apportioned between them on a time basis.

Before making the election outlined above, the liabilities of the deceased and the surviving spouse or civil partner should be calculated on the basis that the trade is a continuing one and also on the basis of the cessation and commencement provisions being applied to see which basis will result in the lower tax liability.

3.1.11 Partnerships

A partnership is regarded as a single unit for the purposes of determining tax-adjusted profits.

How Partners are Assessed

For the purposes of tax assessment, each partner's share of the total profits is treated as **personal** to that partner, as if they arose from a **separate trade or profession**.

As a consequence, commencement and cessation rules apply to each partner **individually** when he or she enters/leaves the partnership. For taxation purposes, a partnership continues no matter how many partners are admitted or leave, provided there are **at least two partners at all times**, one of whom was a partner immediately prior to the admission of a new partner. A partnership **ceases** to exist when:

- the business ceases, **or**
- only one partner remains (i.e. sole trader), **or**
- a completely different set of partners takes over from the old partners.

The "**precedent partner**" arranges for the firm's tax computation to be prepared and submitted to the partnership's Inspector of Taxes. This partner is resident in the State, and

- is the first named partner in the partnership agreement, **or**
- if there is no agreement, the first named partner in the partnership name, e.g. Smith, Jones & Company.

If no partner is resident in the State, the agent or manager of the partnership who is resident in the State is deemed to be the precedent partner.

The 1890 Partnership Act defines "partnership" as "the relationship which exists between persons carrying on a business in common, with a view of profit".

Other Items

1. Interest on Capital

Interest on capital is a distribution of profit and is, accordingly, a disallowable expense in computing the partnership firm's profits or losses for a period.

Interest on capital must, however, be carefully distinguished from interest paid by the partnership in respect of a loan made to the partnership by an individual partner. Such interest, provided the funds borrowed had been used for the partnership business, would be an allowable Case II deduction.

2. Salaries

Salaries paid to a partner are treated in the same manner as drawings taken out of a business by a sole trader, i.e. they are disallowed for Case II computation purposes.

3. Rent Paid to a Partner

If a partner beneficially owns the premises from which the partnership is operated and lets the premises on an arm's length basis to the partnership, then the rent will be allowed as a deduction in computing the partnership profits and the landlord partner will be assessed personally under Case V on the rental income.

4. Sole Trader to Partnership

When an individual, who previously operated as a sole trader, commences business in partnership with one or more others, then he is deemed to have ceased their old trade (and the cessation provisions will apply) and a new trade is deemed to commence from the date of commencement of the partnership.

5. Anti-avoidance

Section 1008 TCA 1997 states that the tax-adjusted profits of a partnership **must**, for tax purposes, be apportioned **fully** between the partners each year, with these profits being taxable at the partners' **marginal tax rates**. This section was introduced by **FA 2007** to counter the practice of not apportioning tax-adjusted profits between partners (for tax purposes), as any amounts not apportioned were chargeable to tax at the standard rate only on the precedent acting partner.

3.2 Case III, Schedule D

3.2.1 Income Assessable

Income tax under Case III is assessed on the following sources of income:

- Interest, annuities and other annual payments, wherever arising, provided it is receivable **without** the **deduction of tax at source** at the standard rate, **nor** does it suffer **deposit interest retention tax (DIRT)**.
- United Kingdom dividends received by Irish resident shareholders. An individual is assessed on the **cash amount received** exclusive of any tax credit. Under the terms of the Irish/UK double tax agreement, the dividend may be taxed in the UK. There is **no entitlement** to a repayment of this tax credit.
- Income arising from foreign securities and possessions.
  Examples are:
  - dividends and interest from United Kingdom companies;
  - net rents (after deductions for allowable rental expenses) from property situated abroad;
  - interest from foreign securities; and
  - income from foreign employments or businesses.
- Interest on most Government and semi-State securities, where interest is paid **without** deduction of tax.
- Income arising to any person as a **member** of the **European Parliament** is chargeable to tax under **Case III** where the income is payable out of money provided by the budget of the **European Union**. Where the income is payable out of money provided by the Irish State, it is chargeable to tax under Schedule E (section 127A TCA 1997).
- All discounts.
- Deposit interest from EU financial institutions – late filing only.

  Interest received by an individual on a deposit account with an EU bank, building society, credit union or Post Office (or the EU equivalent of one of these institutions) will be subject to tax at the same rate as deposit interest received by individuals from lending institutions in Ireland. Such interest will be regarded as income chargeable to tax under **Case IV**.

3.2.2 Basis of Assessment

The basis of assessment for income falling within Case III is the **actual income** arising in the year of assessment.

3.2.3 Exempt Interest

The following interest is exempt from income tax:

- Interest or bonuses arising to an individual from Savings Certificates, Savings Bonds and National Instalment Savings Schemes with An Post.
- Interest on savings certificates issued by the Minister for Finance.
- Interest on overpayments of tax.
- Interest paid on certain government securities to persons who are not ordinary resident and/or domiciled in the State.

3.3 Case IV, Schedule D

This was originally a "sweeping up" case to catch any profits or gains not falling under any of the other cases of Schedule D and not charged under any other Schedule. In recent years, however, legislation has tended to use Case IV for charging certain specific items.

3.3.1 Income Assessable under Case IV, Schedule D

Republic of Ireland Bank, Building Society or Credit Union Interest
All interest paid on deposits held with Republic of Ireland banks, building societies or credit unions, irrespective of when or how often the interest is paid/credited, is subject to deposit interest retention tax (DIRT). Dividends paid/credited to **share accounts** of credit unions are also subject to DIRT. The DIRT rate is currently 41%.

While there is no further tax due on this income, it may be liable to **PRSI at 4%** if the recipient is a "chargeable person" (see **Chapter 10**). It is **not liable** to Universal Social Charge (USC). It must be included in an individual's income tax computation as it could affect reliefs that are subject to restrictions based on income (which includes deposit interest), e.g. the 5% restriction for covenants. As DIRT paid is a non-refundable tax credit, it cannot be refunded to a taxpayer whose total income is taxable at the standard rate, i.e. 20%.

Income Received under Deduction of Income Tax at the Standard Rate
Certain types of income are received under deduction of income tax at the standard rate (20%). Examples include **covenants, patent royalties, interest** paid by a company to an individual and interest payments by one individual to another individual.

The **gross** amount is assessed and a **refundable tax credit** is given for the income tax deducted at source.

Example 3.10			
Mary Jane pays €8,000 net each year to her Aunt Monica under a seven-year deed of covenant. She is 85 and in excellent health. Her only other income is her DSP Old Age Pension of €11,908. Her non-refundable tax credits are €1,895. Calculate Monica's income tax liability for 2016.			
		€	€
Case IV covenant income	€8,000/0.8	10,000	
Schedule E DSP pension		11,908	21,908
Taxed as follows:			
€21,908 @ 20%		4,382	
Less: non-refundable tax credits		(1,895)	
Less: refundable tax credits	€10,000 @ 20%	(2,000)	
Income tax due		487	

Refund of Pension Contributions

If a director or employee has made contributions to a Revenue-approved superannuation scheme and subsequently receives a refund of his contributions, the refund is assessed to tax under Case IV at the standard rate of tax (20%). The administrator of the scheme deducts this tax at source at the time of the refund. The net amount received by the employee is treated as **exempt** and is not included in his income tax computation.

Withdrawals of up to 30% from additional voluntary contributions (AVCs), under section 782A TCA 1997, are taxed at the marginal rate under PAYE Schedule E rules and do not come under Case IV Schedule D (see **Section 3.5.1**).

Retirement Lump Sum Benefits

Amounts **in excess** of the maximum lifetime retirement **tax-free lump sum** of **€200,000** in respect of pension benefits taken will be subject to tax in two stages. The portion between **€200,000 and €500,000** will be taxed **under Case IV** at the **standard rate** of income tax in force at the time of payment. Any portion above that will be taxed under Schedule E at the recipient's marginal rate of tax.

Post-cessation Receipts of a Trade or Profession

Post-cessation receipts generally arise where a person dies and money earned by him is not received until after his death. These receipts, less any expenses, which would be allowable under Case I/II rules, are assessed to tax under Case IV.

Transfer of Right to Receive Rent

Where an individual receives a capital sum, the consideration for which is:

- the transfer to another person of the right to receive rent, **or**
- the grant of a lease where another person is entitled to receive rent under the lease,

the capital sum received is taxable as income under Case IV in the year in which the person becomes entitled to the capital sum, or the year in which the capital sum is received, if earlier.

Profits from Unknown or Unlawful Activities

Profits arising from unknown or unlawful activities may be assessed as miscellaneous income under Case IV.

Other Investment Income

Special Term Accounts

All interest and dividends paid on special term (medium or long-term) deposit accounts are fully liable to DIRT at the prevailing rate of **41%**.

However, if the deposit holder is **aged 65** or over or is **permanently incapacitated**, he may include the interest in his income tax computation for the purpose of obtaining a refund of DIRT, **or** he may make a declaration seeking the interest to be paid gross (see **Section 3.3.3**).

Shares in Lieu of Dividend from Non-quoted Irish Resident Companies

The amount of cash dividend foregone is taxable as Case IV income and dividend withholding tax is ignored. This applies only to the issue of shares in a company if the person does so as the result of the exercise of a choice given to them to take shares in lieu of a dividend or other distribution.

3.3.2 Basis of Assessment

The basis of assessment for income falling within Case IV is the actual income arising in the year of assessment, i.e. if Case IV income arises in June 2016, then this income will be taxable in 2016. Generally, unless tax legislation specifically states otherwise, income is taxable only when **received**. Accordingly, Case IV income is generally taxed on a **receipts** basis.

3.3.3 Deposit Interest Retention Tax (DIRT)

If the amount of DIRT deducted is greater than the individual's income tax liability on this interest, **no refund** is due **unless**:

- the individual (or spouse, if married) is aged 65 or more; **or**
- the individual (or spouse, if married) is permanently incapacitated during the year of assessment.

The interest received must always be included in an individual's income tax computation. This is because it is income **liable** to tax. It may also be liable to PRSI. Income subjected to DIRT is not liable to USC.

Relief from Payment of DIRT
Section 267 TCA 1997 provides a relief whereby deposit interest can be paid, **without the deduction of DIRT**, to those aged over 65 whose total income does not exceed the relevant tax exemption limits or to those permanently incapacitated, upon the completion of the relevant declaration form (Forms DE1 and DE2) (see www.revenue.ie).

Individuals who qualify for a refund of DIRT paid (being aged over 65 or permanently incapacitated) may apply to Revenue, on a **Form 54**, for a refund of DIRT where their total annual income for the year exceeds, or marginally exceeds, the exemption limit, but their annual tax credits are such that they would be entitled to a full or partial refund of DIRT.

Section 266A TCA 1997 entitles a first-time buyer of a house or apartment, who purchases or self-builds a property between **14 October 2014 and 31 December 2017**, to claim a refund of DIRT paid on savings up to a maximum of 20% of the purchase price.

3.4 Case V, Schedule D

3.4.1 Income Assessable Under Case V

The following income is assessable under Case V:

- Rents in respect of any premises or lands in Ireland, i.e. offices, shops, factories, land, etc.
- Receipts in respect of an easement (right over land, e.g. a right of way). An easement includes any right in, over or derived from any premises in the State.
- Certain premiums received for the granting of a lease.

3.4.2 Basis of Assessment

Tax is charged under Case V on the income arising during the year of assessment. The rent taken into account is the amount receivable in the tax year **whether or not** it is actually received. However, if the taxpayer claims and proves that the whole or part of a rent was not received due to it being irrecoverable because of:

- the default of the person liable, **or**
- because the taxpayer waived payment of the rent without consideration and in order to avoid hardship,

then the rent not received is **excluded** from the Case V computation.

3.4.3   Commencement and Cessation

A Case V source does not commence until **rental income arises**, not when the property is acquired. A Case V source does not **cease** until the property is **disposed** of. There are no other special commencement or cessation rules for Case V income.

3.5   Schedule E

3.5.1   Income Assessable under Schedule E

The following classes of income are subject to taxation under Schedule E:

- Emoluments from all offices and employments. Examples include: directors' fees, salaries, wages, bonuses and commission paid to employees.
- Private pensions and annuities. Examples include pensions paid to former directors, employees or their dependants.
- Withdrawals from Additional Voluntary Contributions of up to 30% of the value of funded AVCs will be liable to tax under Schedule E (exempt from USC and PRSI).
- Benefits in kind and perquisites. Examples include: benefits derived from the use of a company car; the provision of rent-free accommodation to an employee; holiday vouchers and preferential loans.
- Certain lump sum payments deriving from an office or employment, either before its commencement or after its cessation. Examples include: inducement payments; non-statutory redundancy payments; round sum expense allowances; ex-gratia and compensation payments on retirement and dismissal.
- Income arising to any person as a member of the European Parliament is chargeable to tax under Schedule E where the income is payable out of money provided by the Irish State. Where the income is payable out of money provided by the budget of the European Union, it is chargeable to tax under Case III Schedule D (section 127A TCA 1997).
- Treatment of flight crews. Section 127B TCA 1997 provides that any income arising to an individual, whether resident in the State or not, from any employment exercised aboard an aircraft that is operated:
    - in international traffic, and
    - by an enterprise that has its place of effective management in the State,
  is chargeable to tax under Schedule E.
- Social welfare benefits **taxable** under Schedule E include:
    - State Pension (Contributory)*
    - State Pension (Transition)*
    - State Pension (Non-contributory)
    - Contributory Widow's, Widower's or Surviving Civil Partner's Pension*
    - Contributory Guardian's Allowance*
    - Illness Benefit
    - Invalidity Pension
    - Maternity Benefit (including Adoptive Benefit and Health and Safety Benefit)
    - One Parent Family Payment
    - Non-contributory Widow's, Widower's or Surviving Civil Partner's Pension
    - Non-contributory Guardian's Pension
    - Social Assistance Allowance for Deserted Wives
    - Social Assistance Allowance for Prisoners' Wives
    - Carers Allowance
    - Blind Person's Pension
    - Occupational Injuries Benefit

- Disablement Benefit
- Jobseeker's (formerly Unemployment) Benefit (the first €13 per week is not taxable).
- * *Including any amounts in respect of a qualifying adult dependant but **excluding** any amount in respect of a qualifying child dependant.*

Social welfare benefits **not taxable** under Schedule E include:

- Jobseeker's (formerly Unemployment) Allowance
- Child Benefit
- Disability Allowance
- Family Income Supplement
- Household Benefits
- Fuel Allowance
- Statutory Redundancy Payments
- Respite Care Grant
- Persons in receipt of Jobseeker's Benefit due to "short-time employment" (e.g. where an individual's normal working week is cut to, say, three days). The benefit received for days of unemployment is exempt
- Water Conservation Grant (currently €100) paid to persons registered with Irish Water on or before 30 June 2015.

3.5.2 Meaning of "Offices" and "Employment"

Offices

The term "offices" is not defined but has been held under tax case law to mean:

"A subsisting permanent, substantive position, which has an existence independent of the person who filled it, and which went on and was filled in succession by successive holders".

Employment

The **distinction** between an **employee** and a **self-employed** person is not set out in tax legislation. In general, case law has determined that an employee is a person who holds a post and who has a **contract of service** with an employer, which basically involves the relationship of master and servant.

A self-employed person will provide services under a **contract for services**. Whether or not a person is an employee or a self-employed person will normally be clear from the facts of the particular case. However, sometimes the distinction between an employee and a self-employed person is not entirely clear and, accordingly, the issue has been the subject of a number of cases.

The UK case of *Market Investigations Ltd v. Minister of Social Security* (1969) established a fundamental test which has been quoted in subsequent cases. It established the fundamental test: "Does the person performing the services perform them as a person in business on his own account?"

If the answer is "yes", then the contract is a contract **for** services; if "no", then there is a contract **of** services.

If an individual is found to be performing the services as a person in business on his own account, then this indicates that the individual is self-employed rather than an employee.

The Irish case of *Henry Denny and Sons Ltd T/A Kerry Foods v. Minister for Social Welfare* (1998) follows this test and established three other tests to determine control, integration and economic relations to discover which type of contract existed.

The *Denny* case involved an examination of the employment status of supermarket demonstrators/ merchandisers of food products. The court found that the demonstrators were in fact employees rather than self-employed.

The Employment Status Group devised the following tests to determine employee or self-employed status:

1. **The terms of the contract**

   If, under the terms of the contract under which the person provides his services, he is entitled to holiday pay, sick pay, pension entitlements, company car or other benefits, he is more likely to be an **employee** rather than self-employed. If the contract provides that the person is required to work fixed hours on particular days, then he is more likely to be an employee, although this is not always the case.

2. **The degree of integration of the person into the organisation to which his services are provided**

   The greater the degree of integration into the organisation, the more likely the person is to be regarded as an employee.

3. **Whether the person provides his own helpers**

   If the individual is free to hire others to do the work he has agreed to undertake and he sets the terms under which such persons are employed, this is more indicative of a self-employed person rather than an employee.

4. **Whether the person provides his own equipment**

   If a person provides significant pieces of equipment to carry out the work he has agreed to undertake, this is also indicative of a self-employed person rather than an employee.

5. **The extent of the control exercised over the individual**

   Generally, a self-employed person will have more control over the work he does than an employee in terms of how, when and where it is to be carried out.

6. **The degree of responsibility for investment and management**

   A person who is responsible for running a business, who uses his own capital and is responsible for determining the running and expansion of a business is clearly a self-employed person. This is essentially the test described above, which examines if the person is performing the service as a person in business on his own account.

7. **The degree of financial risk taken**

   An individual who risks his own money by, for example, buying assets and bearing their running costs and paying for overheads and large quantities of materials, is more likely to be self-employed. Financial risk could also take the form of quoting a fixed price for a job, with the consequent risk of bearing the additional costs if the job overruns. However, this will not mean that the worker is self-employed unless there is a real risk of financial loss.

8. **Opportunity to profit from sound management**

   A person whose profit or loss depends on his capacity to reduce overheads and organise his work effectively is likely to be self-employed.

See the *Code of Practice for Determining Employment or Self-Employment Status of Individuals* (June 2010) at **Appendix 2**.

3.5.3 Basis of Assessment: Schedule E

All income taxable under Schedule E is assessed on the **actual income** of the year of assessment, **irrespective** of the tax year in which it is actually paid and **regardless** of whether taxed under PAYE or not.

For example, a salesperson may earn and be paid a salary for the tax year 2016 and is subsequently paid a commission in February 2017 in respect of his sales during the tax year 2016. Despite the fact that the commission is not received until 2017, it is still a Schedule E emolument for 2016, i.e. the tax year in which it was **actually** earned. It should be noted that, when calculating an employee's income tax liability, the credit given for PAYE paid is the PAYE deducted from emoluments paid in the tax year, regardless of the year in which the emoluments paid are taxable. Therefore, PAYE deducted from commission paid in February 2017 in respect of sales made during the tax year 2016, will be given as a credit in calculating the salesman's tax liability for 2017 even though the commission paid is taxable in 2016.

Special Treatment of Company Directors

In practice, the basis of assessing company directors under Schedule E is by reference to the amount charged in the company's audited accounts, which end during the actual tax year. Additional salary voted to directors will generally be reflected by way of an amended P60.

3.5.4 Assessment in Respect of Benefits in kind

"Benefits in kind" are:

- living or other accommodation;
- entertainment;
- domestic or other services; and
- other benefits or facilities of whatever nature provided by an employer to an employee (or director),

and are chargeable to income tax under Schedule E.

Section 120 TCA 1997 includes as a taxable benefit in kind, any benefit provided by a public body to an office holder or employee, **whether employed directly** by that body or not. The liability to tax also applies in respect of benefits provided by an employer for an employee's or director's spouse, family, servants, dependants or guests. In addition, "perquisites", i.e. remuneration in non-money form which are convertible into money or money's worth, are also chargeable to income tax under Schedule E.

Examples of benefits in kind are the use of a company car, loans at a preferential rate of interest, free or subsidised accommodation. Examples of perquisites are medical insurance premiums, payment of club subscriptions and vouchers.

3.5.5 Commencement/Inducement Payments

Payments received in connection with the commencement of an employment are **taxable**, under Schedule E, as emoluments of the new office or employment where the payment is made under the terms of a contract of service or in consideration of future services to be rendered. However, where it can be shown that the payment is **compensation** for the loss of some right or benefit as a result of taking up the new employment, the payment may not be subject to income tax.

Inducement Payments

An employer may pay a prospective employee a lump sum to induce them to accept an office/other position or as compensation for giving up some valuable right as a result of accepting the position. The question as to whether the payment is taxable under Schedule E as an emolument of the new office/employment has to be decided based on the facts and the true nature of the agreement.

For example, in the UK case of *Glantre Engineering Ltd v. Goodhand (HMIT)* (1983) an inducement fee was paid by a company to a chartered accountant working for an international firm of accountants to enter into the company's services. In the case, it was held that the payment was made to obtain the accountant's services in the future and was therefore taxable under Schedule E.

Payments made **as compensation** for, and as an inducement to, the employee to **give up a personal advantage** before employment is taken up are not taxable under Schedule E.

For example, in *Pritchard v. Arundle* (1972) an allotment of shares was given by a company to persuade a chartered accountant in practice to work for the company. In this case, it was held that the fee was not in the nature of a reward for future services but an inducement to give up an established position and status and therefore not taxable under Schedule E.

In the case of *Jarrold v. Boustead* (1963), inducement payments to rugby union footballers for the permanent loss of their amateur status upon signing on as professional footballers for rugby league were held not to be taxable.

In *Riley v. Coglan* (1967), an amateur player received a signing-on fee upon joining a rugby league club as a professional, a proportionate part of which was refundable if he did not continue to serve the club for the period stipulated in the agreement. The payment was held to be a reward for future services and therefore liable to tax under Schedule E, distinguishing *Jarrold v. Boustead* (1963).

3.5.6 Termination Payments

Special taxation rules apply to lump sum payments made to employees after the termination of their employment. These are commonly referred to as 'golden boots' (compensation payments) or 'golden handshakes' (ex-gratia payments).

Section 123 TCA 1997 imposes a charge to tax under Schedule E on payments made after an individual has retired or been dismissed from office. The charge covers payment to holders of offices, or employments, whether made by the employer or by a third person, and includes payments to the executors or administrators of a deceased person (except as outlined in **Section 4.5.2**).

The actual date(s) of payment of the lump sum(s) is irrelevant. The legislation deems the payment to have been made **on the date of termination** of the employment. Any assessment for income tax arises in the tax year in which the employment terminated.

The charge also extends to payments made to the spouse, civil partner or any relative or dependant of a person who holds or has held an office or employment, or to any person on his behalf (except as outlined in **Section 4.5.2**).

Section 201(8) TCA 1997 introduced a life-time tax-free limit on termination payments of €200,000 in respect of any payment made on or after 1 January 2011. This €200,000 limit is reduced by any exempt payment which an employee may have previously received.

Payments **in kind** are chargeable on their market value at the time they are given, e.g. a present of a company car, say, at a valuation of €4,000 would be included with the termination payment. Any contribution from the employee towards the cost may be deducted.

Pay in lieu of notice which is payable under the terms of the employee's contract is taxable as normal remuneration. Pay in lieu of notice, which is not provided for under the terms of the employee's contract, or by employment law, is treated as a termination payment.

Holiday pay is treated as regular salary and does not form part of the termination payment.

Payments to which section 123 TCA 1997 applies come within the scope of PAYE, but relief is given under section 201 TCA 1997, with the result that tax is charged only on the **excess of the payment** over the **higher** of the following:

1. basic exemption;
2. increased exemption; or
3. standard capital superannuation benefit (SCSB).

3.5.7 Retirement Lump Sum Benefits

Under certain Revenue-approved pension schemes, taxpayers can receive a retirement lump sum tax-free. **Section 790AA TCA 1997** states that the maximum **lifetime** retirement **tax-free lump sum** will be **€200,000** in respect of benefits taken on or after **1 January 2011**. Amounts in excess of this tax-free limit will be subject to tax in two stages. The portion between **€200,000 and €500,000** will be taxed (**under Schedule D Case IV**) at the **standard rate** of income tax in force at the time of payment, currently 20%, while any portion above that will be taxed (**under Schedule E**) at the recipient's **marginal rate of tax**.

The figure of €500,000 represents 25% of the **standard fund threshold** of **€2 million**. The standard rate charge is "ring-fenced" so that no reliefs, allowances or deductions may be set or made against that portion of a lump sum subject to that charge.

Although tax-free lump sums taken after 7 December 2005 and before 1 January 2011 are unaffected by the new rules, they will count towards 'using up' the new tax-free amount. In other words, if an individual has already taken tax-free retirement lump sums of €200,000 or more since 7 December 2005, any further retirement lump sums paid to the individual on or after 1 January 2011 will be taxable. These earlier lump sums will also count towards determining how much of a lump sum paid on or after 1 January 2011 is to be charged at the standard or marginal rate as appropriate.

Exemptions

Lump sum payments in the following circumstances are **completely exempt**:

- payments to approved pension schemes;
- certain allowances to members of the Defence Forces and under Army Pension Acts;
- statutory redundancy payments; and
- lump sum payments made to employees under certain company restructuring schemes involving agreed pay restructuring.

3.5.8 Lump Sum Payments on Account of Death or Disability

Section 201 TCA 1997 extended the tax-free **lifetime limit of €200,000** in respect of termination or ex-gratia payments to cover lump sum payments made on account of the death or injury or disability of an employee or office holder. Any amount where the non-statutory element of the payment exceeds €200,000 will be taxable in full under Schedule E.

3.5.9 Share Option Schemes

Share options arise when employees or directors are granted an option to acquire shares in their employer's company or its parent company, at a fixed price, at some time in the future.

Share Option Schemes

If the employee has been granted a share option by reason of his employment, under general Schedule E principles, a taxable emolument arises. Section 128 TCA 1997 contains the income tax and capital gains tax rules that apply to share options granted to an employee or director on or after 6 April 1986.

A person who realises a gain taxable by virtue of section 128 is deemed to be a **chargeable** person for self-assessment purposes for that year, unless an Inspector of Taxes has exempted them from filing a return.

Thus, a person whose income normally consists only of Schedule E salary and who pays all his tax under the PAYE system is required to file a return in accordance with the **self-assessment** system.

Short Options – Less than Seven Years

Short options are options that must be exercised **within seven years** of being granted. Short options are charged to income tax in the year the option is **exercised** on the difference between the price paid (the option price) for the shares and the market value of the shares at the **date of exercise** (date shares acquired). Universal Social Charge (USC) and PRSI are also payable on the difference. However, employer and employee PRSI (but excluding USC) will not apply where share-based remuneration was the subject of a written agreement entered into between the employer and employee **before** 1 January 2011.

Long Options – Longer than Seven Years

Long options are options capable of being exercised **more than seven years** after being granted. Long options are taxed:

- in the year the option was granted (on the difference between the market value of the shares at the **date of grant** and the option price), **and**
- in the year the option was exercised (as above) – but the shareholder is entitled to a **credit** for tax paid on the earlier charge on grant.

Relevant Tax on Share Options (RTSO)

- Where share options are exercised, the employee or director must pay **RTSO within 30 days** of the date of exercise.
- **Form RTSO1** must be completed and forwarded **with payment** to the office of the Collector-General **within 30 days**.
- Tax is due at the **marginal** rate of income tax (currently 40%). Where a person's total income for the year is liable only at the standard rate of income tax, an application may be made to the Inspector of Taxes to pay at the lower rate. This must be done and the RTSO paid within 30 days of exercise.
- USC and PRSI are payable on the options.

Restricted Shares

If there is any restriction on the employee's ability to sell the shares acquired under an employee share option, Revenue accepts that the benefit received by the employee is less valuable. Accordingly, where there is a **genuine restriction** on the employee's ability to sell the shares, the taxable value is reduced depending on the number of years for which the restriction will apply, as follows:

Number of Years of Restriction on Sale	% Reduction in Taxable Value
1 year	10%
2 years	20%
3 years	30%
4 years	40%
5 years	50%
>5 years	60%

Approved Share Option Schemes (ASOS)

ASOS are schemes for which Revenue approval, in accordance with Schedule 12C TCA 1997, has been received.

Section 897 TCA 1997 states that an employer is obliged to return details of all benefits, non-cash emoluments and payments, and pension contributions provided to directors and certain employees that have not been subjected to PAYE. **Form P11D** must be returned by **31 May** of the year following the tax year.

Section 897B TCA 1997 makes it mandatory for employers to file returns regarding shares and other securities awarded to directors and employees before **31 March** of the year following the tax year **(Form RSS1)**. This mandatory return must be made electronically.

3.5.10 Magdalene Laundries Payments

Ex-gratia payments made on or after 1 September 2013 to beneficiaries under the scheme, administered by the Minister for Justice, Equality and Defence in respect of women who were admitted to, and worked in,

Magdalene Laundries, will not be subject to income tax or capital gains tax, nor be treated as a gift or inheritance for the purposes of capital acquisitions tax.

3.5.11 Living Donors

Section 204B TCA 1997 exempts from income tax any compensation payable to a living donor for the donation of a kidney for transplantation, under the conditions defined by the Minister for Health.

3.5.12 Reserve Members of the Garda Síochána

Section 204A TCA 1997 states the annual allowance payable to reserve members under the Garda Síochána (Reserve Members) Regulations 2006 is exempt from income tax.

3.5.13 Compensation Awards made under Employment Law

Section 192A TCA 1997 provides for an exemption from income tax for compensation awards made by a "relevant authority" to an employee or former employee as a result of the employee's rights and entitlements in law having been infringed or breached through, for example, discrimination, harassment or victimisation.

In this instance a "relevant authority" includes the Labour Court, Workplace Relations Commission, Employment Appeals Tribunal, etc., or the Circuit Court and the High Court.

Payments made in respect of remuneration, e.g. salary or holiday pay, arrears of pay, changes in functions or procedures of an employment or the termination of an employment will continue to be taxable in the normal way.

3.6 Schedule F

3.6.1 Income Assessable under Schedule F

Dividends and certain other distributions paid by **Irish resident** companies to individual shareholders are liable to tax under Schedule F. Dividends received by Irish resident individuals are received after the deduction of **dividend withholding tax (DWT)** at the standard rate of tax. The recipient can claim an off-set for DWT against his tax liability and, where DWT exceeds his tax liability, the balance will be refunded.

Shares in Lieu of Dividends
A quoted company issues a number of shares which have a value, at the date of distribution, equal to:

- the dividend foregone, **reduced by**
- an amount equal to income tax at the standard rate on the amount of cash foregone.

The amount taxable in the hands of the shareholder is the full amount of the gross dividend foregone, and credit is given for the DWT.

Where the distributing company is a **quoted** (i.e. on the Stock Exchange) company, the shareholder is taxed on this distribution under **Schedule F**. Where the distributing company is unquoted, the shareholder is taxed under **Case IV, Schedule D** (see **Section 3.3.1**).

The redemption of bonus shares and bonus debentures is also taxable as income under Schedule F.

Exempt Dividend Income
Dividends paid by Irish resident companies from **profits** arising from the occupation of **woodlands**, managed on a commercial basis with a view to the realisation of profits, are exempt from Income Tax in

the hands of the shareholder. In the case of such dividends they are ignored for income tax purposes but should be disclosed in the income tax return. Dividends are, however, subject to PRSI and USC.

3.6.2 Basis of Assessment

The amount assessable on the individual is the amount received **in the tax year plus DWT** (i.e. the **gross** amount of the distribution).

The date on which the dividend is **paid** determines the tax year, irrespective of the accounting year's profit out of which the dividend was declared.

Questions

Review Questions
(See Suggested Solutions to Review Questions at the end of this textbook.)

Question 3.1

Ms Lola commenced trading on 1 June 2015 and makes up accounts to 31 May. Her trading results are as follows:

	€
01/06/2015–31/05/2016	48,000
01/06/2016–31/05/2017	39,000
01/06/2017–31/05/2018	37,200

Requirement
Compute Ms Lola's Case I assessable profits for the first four years.

Question 3.2

Mr Charlie commenced trading on 1 May 2015 and makes up accounts to 31 October. His trading results are as follows:

	€
01/05/2015–31/10/2015	44,800
01/11/2015–31/10/2016	54,400
01/11/2016–31/10/2017	53,600

Requirement
Compute Mr Charlie's Case I assessable profits for the first three years.

Question 3.3

Jim commenced practice as a solicitor on 1 May 2015. Tax-adjusted profits for the opening years were as follows:

	€
1 May 2015 to 30 April 2016	48,000
Year ended 30 April 2017	60,000
Year ended 30 April 2018	9,600

Requirement

Compute Jim's Case II assessable profits for the first four tax years.

Question 3.4

Donna Ross resigned from her job at AIB to sell children's clothing full time on eBay. She provided you with the following information:

P45 showing gross pay from 1 January to cessation on 30 April 2016 of €20,300, with PAYE deducted of €3,902.

She tells you that she has traded on eBay part-time for a "few" years. She sold only household items or sale bargains picked up while shopping. She estimates that her sales were €5,000 in 2014 and her costs were minimal since the items sold were "lying about the house". She used the family computer and packed the product in her garage. In 2015 she spotted a market opportunity when she bought a job lot of designer children's clothes for €10,000 and sold them on eBay individually for €20,000 in just one month! This prompted her to quit her job and start trading from 1 May 2016. Her tax-adjusted profit for the year ended 30 April 2017 was €179,400.

Donna is a 32-year old single parent.

Requirement

Compute the income tax payable by Donna for 2016 and 2017 assuming personal tax credits of €4,950 for 2016 and €3,850 for 2017.

Advise Donna, with reasons, if her eBay activity for 2014 and 2015 is taxable as trading income.

Question 3.5

Ms Dora ceases trading on 31 December 2016. She made up her accounts annually to 31 May. Her trading results were as follows:

	€
Year ended 31/05/2014	64,000
Year ended 31/05/2015	72,000
Year ended 31/05/2016	9,600
Period ended 31/12/2016	12,000

Requirement

Compute Ms Dora's Case I assessable profits for the last three years.

Question 3.6

Mr Diego ceases trading on 31 May 2016. He made up his accounts annually to 31 July. His trading results were as follows:

	€
Year ended 31/07/2014	32,000
Year ended 31/07/2015	60,000
Period ended 31/07/2016	40,000

Requirement

Compute Mr Diego's Case I assessable profits for his last three tax years.

Question 3.7

Alex, a single man, traded for many years as a butcher. He retired on 30 September 2016 and he started work for Fagan Organic Lamb as a salesman. His tax-adjusted profits for the periods to the date of cessation were as follows:

	€
Year ended 30/09/2015	24,000
Year ended 30/09/2016	240,000

His P60 for 2016 showed gross pay of €15,000 and PAYE paid of €3,485.

Requirement

Compute the income tax payable by Alex for 2016, assuming tax credits were €3,300, and advise if any changes are needed in other years.

Question 3.8

J. Cog retired on 30 September 2016 from his newsagency business after trading for 40 years. His profits for the immediate years prior to cessation were:

	€
Year ended 31 October 2013	40,000
Year ended 31 October 2014	65,000
Year ended 31 October 2015	64,000
11 months to 30 September 2016	24,000

Requirement

Calculate J. Cog's assessable profits for the last four years of assessment.

Question 3.9

Alex and Bill have traded as partners sharing equally for many years. They prepare accounts each year to 30 September. On 1 October 2012 a new partner, Colin, is brought in. From that date profits are shared as follows: Alex 40%; Bill 40%; and Colin 20%.
Tax-adjusted trading profits were as follows:

	€
Year ended 30/09/2012	20,000
Year ended 30/09/2013	25,000
Year ended 30/09/2014	30,000
Year ended 30/09/2015	30,000
Year ended 30/09/2016	35,000

On 30 September 2014, Alex left the partnership and from that date Bill and Colin have shared profits and losses equally.

Requirement

Calculate the assessable profits for Alex, Bill and Colin for the years 2012–2016 inclusive.

Question 3.10

June, Mary and Karen had been carrying on a business for many years, sharing profits in the ratio 40:30:30. Karen retired on 30 June 2013 and was replaced by Jill. The profit-sharing ratio remained unchanged.

Louise was admitted to the partnership on 1 July 2015, from which date profits and losses were shared equally by all the partners. The partnership ceased to trade on 31 December 2016, when the business was transferred to a limited company.

The tax-adjusted profits of the partnership were as follows:

	€
Year ended 30 June 2012	40,000
Year ended 30 June 2013	60,000
Year ended 30 June 2014	54,000
Year ended 30 June 2015	50,000
Year ended 30 June 2016	36,000
Six months ended 31 December 2016	20,000

Requirement

Calculate the assessable profits for the years 2013–2016 for all the partners.

Question 3.11

Maeve, who is widowed, is in receipt of the following sources of Irish income (dividend income received net of DWT):

Company	Dividend
	€
Tyson Limited	17,520
Holyfield Manufacturing Limited	1,600
	19,120

Deposit interest received net	
	€
Permanent TSB Bank	6,300
Credit Union interest	1,200
Long-term account interest	720
	8,220
Social Welfare Contributory Widow's Pension	11,976

Requirement

Compute Maeve's 2016 income tax liability. Her personal tax credits are €2,190.

Computation of Taxable Income

4.1   Trade and Professional Income: Cases I and II, Schedule D

4.1.1   Introduction

A taxpayer, carrying on a trade or profession, will prepare accounts based on commercial and accounting principles to arrive at their net profit for a particular year. However, the net profit per the accounts **is not the taxable profit**, as the Income Tax Acts (now TCA 1997) have their own set of rules for determining the taxable profit of a person carrying on a trade or profession. Accordingly, the net profit per an individual's accounts will inevitably need **adjustment** to arrive at "**tax-adjusted**" profits for income tax purposes.

The sequence of steps required to arrive at taxable income (i.e. the amount of income on which tax is payable) is outlined overleaf.

Net Profit Per Accounts

ADD/DEDUCT

Adjustment for amounts not allowable for tax purposes

EQUALS

Tax-adjusted Profits

ADD

Other Income

EQUALS

Total Income

DEDUCT

Allowances/Reliefs

EQUALS

Taxable Income

4.1.2 Allowable and Disallowable Items

There are two fundamental principles in deciding whether an item is properly included in a profit and loss account when calculating a Case I or Case II adjusted profit or loss:

1. The distinction between capital and revenue. If an item is of a **capital** nature, it must be **disallowed** in computing profits for income tax purposes.
2. Even if an item is of a **revenue** nature, it **may still** be specifically disallowed by statute as a deduction in computing trading profits.

4.1.3 Capital versus Revenue Receipts

Capital receipts and expenditure (including profits and losses) are **not assessable** under income tax as they are usually assessable under **capital gains tax**.

When deciding for tax purposes whether a receipt is capital or revenue, the following general rules apply:

Capital Receipt

The proceeds from the sale of fixed assets, i.e. assets which form part of the permanent structure of a business, is a capital receipt and is not liable to income tax.

Revenue Receipt

The sale of circulating assets (i.e. assets acquired in the ordinary course of a trade and sold) is a revenue receipt. There are five basic principles:

1. Payments for the sale of the **assets** of a business are *prima facie* **capital** receipts.
2. Payments received for the destruction of the recipient's **profit-making apparatus** are receipts of a **capital** nature.
3. Payments in lieu of **trading receipts** are of a **revenue** nature.
4. Payments made in return for the imposition of substantial restrictions on the **activities** of a trader are of a **capital** nature.
5. Payments of a **recurrent** nature are **more likely** to be treated as **revenue** receipts.

Income/Gains Not Taxable Under Cases I and II, Schedule D

The following income is not taxable under Cases I and II, Schedule D:

(a) **Profits on sale of fixed assets**

Profits or gains on the disposal of fixed assets or investments are **exempt** from income tax.

(b) **Grants**

Employment grants paid by the IDA, Enterprise Ireland or SOLAS are exempt from income tax. Capital grants on fixed assets (e.g. IDA grants) are also exempt from income tax.

(c) **Investment income**

- Irish dividends – taxable under Schedule F.
- UK dividends – taxable under Case III, Schedule D.
- Deposit interest received – taxable under Case IV, Schedule D.

(d) **Interest on tax overpaid**

Interest received on tax overpaid is exempt from income tax.

(e) **Rental income**

Rental income is taxable under Case V, Schedule D.

4.1.4 Capital versus Revenue Expenditure

Capital expenditure is **not** a deductible expense when calculating net trading profits for income tax. Where capital expenditure or capital losses (e.g. loss on sale of fixed assets) have been deducted in computing accounts profits, they will be **disallowed** when computing profits for tax purposes. However, certain allowances for wasting capital assets may be deducted after tax-adjusted Case I profits have been ascertained, i.e. **capital allowances**.

Note the judicial statement of Lord Cave in the case of *British Insulated and Helsby Cables v. Atherton* (1926), which is frequently used by the courts to assist them in resolving the problem of whether expenditure is of a revenue nature, and therefore allowable, or of a capital nature, and therefore disallowed:

"When an expenditure is made, not only once and for all, but with a view to bringing into existence an asset or an advantage **for the enduring benefit of a trade** ... there is very good reason (in the absence of special circumstances leading to an opposite conclusion) for treating such an expenditure as properly attributed not to revenue but to capital."

4.1.5 Allowable and Disallowable Case I and II Deductions

Disallowable Deductions

The main statutory provision disallowing expenditure is section 81 TCA 1997. This contains specific provisions disallowing various types of expenditure, the most important of which are:

- Expenditure not **wholly and exclusively** laid out for the purposes of the trade. (This is the general deductibility test applied for Case I and Case II purposes).
- Maintenance of the parties and their families and private or domestic expenditure.
- Rent of any dwelling house **not used** for the trade.
- Any sum expended **over and above** repairs to the premises, implements, utensils or articles employed for the purposes of the trade or profession.
- Any loss not connected with the trade or profession.
- Any capital withdrawn from, or employed as, capital in the trade or profession or any capital employed in improvements to premises occupied by the trade or profession.
- Debts, other than bad debts, or a **specific** estimation of doubtful debts.
- Any annuity or other annual payment (other than interest) payable out of the profits or gains.
- Any royalty or other sum paid in respect of the use of a patent.
- Any consideration given for goods or services, or to an employee or director of a company, which consists, directly or indirectly, of shares in the company or a connected company, or a right to receive such shares.
- Any sum paid or payable under any agreement with a connected person, resident outside of the State, as compensation for an adjustment to the profits of the connected person. Transfer pricing adjustments can only be obtained under double taxation agreements or through EU Convention mechanisms.

Expenses Commonly Disallowed

1. **Expenses or losses of a capital nature:**
   - Depreciation
   - Loss on sale of fixed assets
   - Improvements to premises
   - Purchase of fixed assets.

   Note that capital allowances may be claimed on certain assets.

2. **Applications or allocations of profit:**
   - Income tax
   - Transfers to a general reserve
   - Drawings.

3. **Payments from which tax is deducted:**
   - Royalties.

4. **Expenses not wholly and exclusively laid out for the purposes of the business:**
   - Private element of certain expenses
   - Rental expenses (allowable against Case V rents)
   - Charitable and political donations and subscriptions
   - Life assurance premiums on the life of the taxpayer or his spouse
   - Fines and penalties.

5. **General provisions**

   Provisions made **in accordance with FRS 12/IAS 37,** *Provisions, Contingent Liabilities and Contingent Assets,* are allowed for tax purposes **if** the following conditions were satisfied:
   - the trader has a present obligation to incur the expenditure as a result of a past action;
   - the amount of the provision required can be determined with a reasonable degree of accuracy; **and**
   - the expenditure in respect of which the provision is made would be an allowable deduction in arriving at profits, e.g. a provision for capital expenditure would not be allowable.

6. **Other**

(a) **Bad debts:**
   - Bad debts written off – **allowable**
   - Bad debts recovered – **taxable**
   - Increase in a **specific** provision for bad debts – **allowable**
   - Decrease in a **specific** provision for bad debts – **taxable**
   - Increase in a **general** provision for bad debts – **not allowable**
   - Decrease in a **general** provision for bad debts – **not taxable**

(b) **Premiums on short leases**

   If the taxpayer carries on a trade or profession in a premises leased for a period of less than 50 years, a proportion of any premium paid on the lease is allowable in computing the profits of a trade or profession.

   The amount allowable on the premium paid is calculated by

$$\text{Premium} \times \frac{51 - \text{Duration of the lease}}{50}$$

   spread over the life of the lease.

Example 4.1

On 1 June 2016 James rents a premises from Mr White for 25 years, at a rent of €2,000 per month, subject to a premium of €20,000.

Allowable premium:

$$€20,000 \times \frac{51 - 25}{50} = €10,400$$

2016:

Allowable premium (€10,400 × 1/25th × 7/12ths)	€243
Rent paid (€2,000 × 7)	€14,000

2017:

Allowable premium (€10,400 × 1/25th)	€416
Rent paid (€2,000 × 12)	€24,000

(c) Entertainment expenses

General entertainment expenses incurred are **completely disallowed**. Expenditure on **staff** entertainment is allowable, provided its provision is not incidental to the provision of entertainment to third parties.

(d) Legal expenses regarding:
- Debt recovery – allowable
- Acquisition of assets – not allowable
- Renewal of short lease – allowable
- Product liability claims and employee actions – allowable

(e) Repairs

Replacement/redecoration repairs not involving material improvements are allowable. Expenditure on improvements/extensions, new assets, etc. is not allowable.

As a general rule, expenditure incurred on **repairs** to buildings is deductible as a normal Case I or Case II expense. The concept of repair is that it **brings an item back to its original condition**. In this connection, the following particular points are critical:

(i) The expenditure must have **actually** been incurred. For instance, provisions for work to be done in the future are not allowable, as clearly the expenditure has not been incurred (unless the conditions outlined in relation to general provisions at (5) above are satisfied).

(ii) The term "repairs" does **not include** improvements and alterations to premises. In this connection, it is not possible to claim a revenue deduction for the portion of the improvements or alterations which would represent the cost of repairs that could otherwise have been carried out.

(iii) The replacement of a capital asset or the "entirety" will not be treated as a repair. This would cover, for instance, the reconstruction of a trader's premises.

The test to be applied is really whether or not the repair entails the **renewal** of a **component part** of the entirety. If it does, it will be regarded as a repair. On the other hand, if it is regarded as the **renewal of an entirety**, it will be treated as a capital expenditure.

A separate identifiable portion of a building or structure may be regarded as an **entirety** in its own right and, accordingly, its replacement would be disallowed. A practical test is whether or not they are of **sufficient size and importance** to be regarded as an entirety. Examples of entireties from case law include the following:

- A large chimney situated apart from other factory buildings.
- A ring in an auction mart.
- A stand in a football ground.
- A barrier which protects a factory against the overflow from an adjoining canal.

It appears that it is necessary to show that the item which has been replaced is **ancillary** to the complete building. In practice, the accounting treatment adopted and the total cost involved may be important factors.

Repairs to newly acquired assets In *Odeon Associated Theatres Limited v. Jones* (1971) it was held that the expenditure on repairs to a newly acquired asset may be deductible provided at least that:

- the cost is properly charged to a revenue account in accordance with the correct principles of commercial accountancy; **and**
- the repairs are not improvements; **and**
- the expenditure is not incurred to make the asset **commercially viable** on its acquisition; **and**
- the purchase price was not **substantially** less than it would have been if it had been in a proper state of repair at the time of purchase.

(f) Leased motor vehicles

In the case of a leased vehicle, where the list price exceeds the limit prescribed, a proportion of the lease hire charges are disallowed by reference to the CO_2 emissions of the cars. The CO_2 categorisations and allowances are as follows:

Vehicle Category	CO_2 Emissions (CO_2g/km)	Leasing Charges Restriction
A/B/C	0g/km up to and including 155g/km	Lease hire charge $\times \dfrac{\text{(List Price} - \text{Relevant Limit)}}{\text{List Price}}$
D/E	156g/km up to and including 190g/km	Lease hire charge $\times \dfrac{\text{(List Price} - \text{(Relevant Limit} \times 50\%))}{\text{List Price}}$
F/G	191g/km and upwards	Lease hire charge disallowed

The relevant limit is €24,000 for the period 2007–2016.

Example 4.2

Joe, who is self-employed and prepares annual accounts to 30 September, leased a car on 20 July 2016, when its retail price was €25,000. Lease charges of €6,000 are included in Joe's accounts for year-end 30 September 2016. Joe has agreed with the Inspector of Taxes that 1/3rd of the usage is private. Joe's car falls into Category D.

Lease Charges:	€6,000
Less: Private element 1/3rd	(€2,000)
Business element	€4,000

Disallowed lease payment:

$$€4,000 \times \frac{(€25,000 - (€24,000 \times 50\%)}{€25,000} \quad = \quad €2,080$$

2016:

Lease charge disallowed (€2,000 + €2,080)   =   €4,080

(g) Interest on late payment of tax

Interest on late payment of any tax (including VAT, PAYE, etc.) is not allowed in computing tax-adjusted profits.

(h) Patent fees

Fees incurred in obtaining, for the purposes of a trade, the grant of a patent or the extension of the term of a patent are allowable.

(i) Redundancy payments

Statutory redundancy payments are specifically allowable. Amounts in excess of statutory entitlements are unlikely to be deductible where a cessation of trade has taken place but would be allowed if the trade continued.

(j) Renewal or registration of trademarks

Expenses on renewal or registration of trademarks are specifically allowable.

(k) Capital payments for 'know-how'

Payments of a capital nature to acquire technical or other information for the purpose of the trade are specifically allowable as a Case I expense. There are two exceptions to this rule as follows:

- No deduction is allowed where the know-how is acquired as part of the acquisition of the **whole or part** of another business.
- No deduction is allowed where the purchase of the know-how is from a **connected** party, unless the acquiring company exploits it in the course of a trade.

(l) Expenditure on scientific research

The full amount of any non-capital expenditure on scientific research is allowable as a deduction in computing the profits of a trade. In addition, sums paid to establishments, approved by the Minister for Finance, to carry on scientific research, and sums paid to Irish universities to enable them to carry on scientific research, are also deductible. This rule applies **whether or not** the payments are **related** to the existing trade currently being carried on.

(m) Accountancy/taxation fees

Normal accounting, auditing and taxation compliance costs are allowable. **Special costs** associated with Appeal Hearings are likely to be **disallowed** following the decision of *Allen v. Farquharson Brothers*, where the costs of employing solicitors and counsel in connection with an appeal against income tax assessments were disallowed.

(n) Pre-trading expenses

Under section 82 TCA 1997, an allowance **may** be claimed in respect of pre-trading expenses in the case of a trade or profession **provided** that the expenses:

- were incurred for the purpose of the trade or profession; **and**
- were incurred within three years of commencement; **and**
- are not otherwise allowable in computing profits.

Where an allowance is granted for pre-trading expenses, it is treated as if the expenditure were incurred **on the date** on which the trade or profession **commenced**.

Examples of qualifying pre-trading expenses include accountancy fees, market research, feasibility studies, salaries, advertising, preparing business plans and rent.

These pre-trading expenses are deductible against the income of the trade. If the expenses exceed the income and there is a loss, this loss cannot be offset against other income but can only be carried forward against future income of the same trade.

(o) Long-term unemployed

JobsPlus Incentive is a scheme administered by the Department of Social Protection to encourage and reward employers who offer employment opportunities to the long-term unemployed.

Two levels of payment are available:

1. a payment of **€7,500** paid over **two** years to an employer for each person recruited who has been unemployed for **more than 12 months** (four months for young people under 25) but less than 24 months, **and**
2. **€10,000** paid over two years to an employer for each person recruited who has been unemployed for **24 months or more**.

In order to qualify an employer must offer full-time employment of at least **30 hours per week**, spanning at least four days per week, to eligible recruits, i.e. that employee must be on the payroll and subject to PAYE, PRSI and USC. The income received by the employer under this scheme is not taxable and a deduction for gross wages paid in respect of these employees is allowed in the normal way (see www.welfare.ie).

(p) Key-man insurance

Key-man insurance is insurance taken out by an employer in his/her own favour against the death, sickness or injury of an employee (i.e. the key man) whose services are **vital** to the success of the employer's business.

In general, premiums paid under policies insuring against loss of profits consequent on certain contingencies **are deductible** for tax purposes in the period in which they are paid. Correspondingly, all **sums received** by an employer under such policies are treated as **trading receipts** in the period in which they are received. Key-man insurance policies qualify for this treatment where the following conditions are satisfied:

- the sole relationship is that of employer and employee;
- the employee does not have a substantial proprietary interest in the business;
- the insurance is intended to meet loss of profit resulting from the loss of the services of the employee, as distinct from the loss of goodwill or other capital loss; **and**
- in the case of insurance against death, the policy is a short-term insurance providing only for a sum to be paid, in the event of the death of the insured, within a specified number of years. Short term generally means five years but, in practice, if all other conditions are satisfied and the policy cannot extend beyond the employee's likely period of service with the business, i.e. not beyond his term of contract or beyond retirement age, then a longer term policy will qualify.

4.1.6 Taxation Treatment Different from Accounting Treatment

Finance Leases

Assets leased under finance leases may be included as fixed assets in accounts, and interest and depreciation for such assets included in the profit and loss account.

For tax purposes, capital allowances **may not** be claimed in respect of such assets. Instead, a deduction is given for **gross lease payments** made, i.e. interest plus capital. The adjustments to be made to the accounts profit for finance lease assets are as follows:

- add back interest and depreciation charged in respect of finance lease assets; **and**
- give a deduction for gross lease payments (interest and capital) made.

Pension Contributions

Ordinary annual contributions by an employer to a **Revenue-approved** pension scheme for the benefit of employees are **allowable** for tax purposes in the year in which they are **paid**. Thus, any **accruals** in respect of ordinary annual pension contributions due which have been included in arriving at accounts profit will have to be disallowed.

If an employer makes a **special contribution** to a Revenue-approved pension scheme and the total amount of the special contributions made in the year **does not exceed** the **total ordinary annual contributions** paid in the year, relief is given for the special contributions in the year in which they are paid. If, however, the total amount of the special contributions paid **exceeds** the total ordinary annual contributions paid, relief for the special contributions made is **spread forward** over a number of years subject to a maximum of five years. The number of years over which relief is given is calculated by dividing the total special contributions paid by the total ordinary contributions paid. If the factor produced by this calculation is between one and two, relief is given over two years; otherwise, the factor is rounded to the nearest whole number.

Example 4.3

An employer makes the following pension contributions in 2016:

Ordinary annual contribution (OAC)	€10,000
Special contribution (SC)	€27,000

As the SC made **exceeds** the OAC, relief for the SC will be **spread forward**. The **number of years** over which relief is given is calculated as follows:

$$\frac{\text{Special contribution}}{\text{Ordinary annual contribution}} = \frac{€27,000}{€10,000} = 2.7 \text{ rounded up to 3}$$

Relief for the SC will be given over **three years**. In the first two years, the amount of relief given will **equal the amount of the OAC,** with the balance of the relief given in the third year. Accordingly, relief for the SC of €27,000 made in 2016 will be given as follows:

Tax Year	Relief Given
2016	€10,000
2017	€10,000
2018	€7,000

Ordinary Annual Contribution less than €6,350

If the amount of the OAC is less than €6,350, in calculating when relief for a SC is due, the amount of the OAC may be assumed to be €6,350.

Example 4.4

An employer makes the following pension contributions in 2016:

Ordinary annual contribution (OAC)	€5,000
Special contribution (SC)	€8,000

As the OAC is less than €6,350, for the purposes of the calculation the OAC is taken to be €6,350.

$$\frac{\text{Special contribution}}{\text{Ordinary annual contribution}} = \frac{€8,000}{€6,350} = 1.26$$

As 1.26 is between one and two, relief is given over two years as follows:

Tax Year	Relief Given
2016	€6,350
2017	€1,650

4.1.7 Computation of Tax-adjusted Profits

In order to arrive at "tax-adjusted" Case I and Case II trading profits, the following procedure should be adopted.

Step 1: Start with the **net profit/loss** per the profit and loss account.

Step 2: Add this to any expenses charged in the accounts that are **not allowable deductions** for income tax purposes, e.g. depreciation.

Step 3: Add any trading **income that has not been credited** in arriving at the net profit per the accounts.

Step 4: Deduct any expenses which **have not been charged** in the accounts and which the TCA 1997 allows to be deducted.

Step 5: Deduct receipts that are of a **capital nature** and those that are chargeable under **another Schedule or Case**, e.g. deposit interest, profit on sale of motor vehicle, etc.

Example 4.5

Mr Bailey has operated a sports goods shop for 10 years. The profit and loss account for this business for the year ended 31 December 2016 is as follows:

Profit and Loss Account for the year ended 31 December 2016

	Notes	€	€
Sales			313,759
Less:			
Cost of sales			226,854
Gross profit			86,905
Add:			
Deposit interest received		1,300	
Profit on sale of equipment		580	1,880
			88,785
Less Expenses:			
Wages and PRSI	1	45,000	
Rates	2	2,200	
Insurance	3	8,100	
Light and heat	2	850	
Telephone	4	970	
Repairs	5	3,400	
Motor and travel expenses	6	5,440	
General expenses	7	4,575	
Loan interest	2	9,000	
Bank interest and charges		3,260	
Depreciation		4,450	87,245
Net profit for the year			€1,540

Notes to the accounts:

1. Included in wages are:

	€
Salary to self	20,000
Salary to wife	2,000
Own PRSI	800
Bonus to staff	2,500

2. In March 2011, Mr Bailey purchased, for €100,000, the shop premises in which the business had been carried on for the previous three years. Since 2011, the top floor, which is a self-contained flat, has been occupied free of charge by Mr Bailey's elderly father, who takes no part in the business. 20% of the rates, property insurance, light and heat relate to the flat, which represents 10% of the value of the whole property.

    The loan interest relates to interest paid on a loan taken out for the purchase of the premises.

3. Analysis of insurance charge

	€
Shopkeepers' all-in policy	1,400
Retirement annuity premiums for self	3,000
Permanent health insurance for self	2,400
Motor car insurance	800
Property insurance	500
	8,100

continued overleaf

4. Telephone/home expenses

    Telephone costs include Mr Bailey's home telephone and 25% of the total charge is for personal use. Mrs Bailey carries out most of her bookkeeping duties at home and a special deduction of €156 is to be allowed for costs incurred in carrying out these duties at home. This item has not been reflected in the Profit and Loss Account.

5. Included in the repairs charge are:

	€
Purchase of display stand	500
Repairs to shop front	600
Plumbing repairs	800

6. Analysis of motor and travel expenses

    Included in the motor and travel expenses is the cost of a trip to London to a sport goods' wholesale exhibition. Mr Bailey attended the exhibition on two days and then spent a further five days visiting friends and relatives. Details of the expenses are as follows:

	€
Air fare	140
Hotel bill (for seven days)	400
Entertaining overseas exhibitor	100
	640

    The remainder of the expenses relate to Mr Bailey's motor car, which had a market value of €25,000 when first leased on 1 March 2014. It is a Category C emissions car.

	€
Lease of car	2,880
Running expenses	1,920
	4,800

    His annual travel (in km) was made up of:

Personal	9,600
Business	19,200
Home to business	3,200
Total	32,000

7. Analysis of general expenses

	€
Covenant to church (net)	405
Donation to church building fund (includes full-page advertisement in magazine – €200)	1,000
Subscriptions to trade association	350
Accountancy fee	1,100
Branded sponsorship of 'open day' at local golf club	900
Entertainment – customers	520
Entertainment – staff Christmas party	300
	4,575

Computation of Case I Tax-adjusted Profits for the year ended 31 December 2016

	Notes	€	€
Net profit per accounts			1,540
Add Back:			
Depreciation		4,450	
Wages and PRSI	1	20,800	
Rates (20%)		440	
Insurance	2	5,500	
Light and heat (20%)		170	

continued overleaf

Loan interest (10%)		900	
Telephone (25%)		242	
Repairs	3	500	
Motor and travel expenses	4	2,949	
General expenses	5	1,725	37,676
			39,216

Deduct:

Deposit interest		1,300	
Profit on sale of equipment		580	
Mrs Bailey business telephone		156	(2,036)

Adjusted Case I Profits   **37,180**

Note 1. Wages and PRSI

	€
Salary to self	20,000
Own PRSI	800
Disallowed, as these are drawings	20,800

Note 2. Insurance

Retirement annuity premiums for self	€3,000
Permanent health insurance for self	€2,400
Property insurance (20%)	€100
Disallowed	€5,500

The restriction in respect of the motor car insurance is included in Note 4.

Note 3. Repairs

Display stand is capital expenditure – disallow

Note 4. Motor and Travel Expenses

	€
Leasing charges	2,880
Running expenses	1,920
Motor car insurance	800
Cost per accounts	5,600
Total travel (in km)	32,000
Personal mileage	(9,600)
Home to business	(3,200)
Business	19,200 km (60%)

DISALLOW:

	€
Private element car:	
€5,600 × 40% =	2,240

Lease restriction car*:	
€2,880 × 60% = €1,728 × (25,000 − 24,000)	69
25,000	

As the car is a Category C emissions car, no further restriction applies.

Air fare and hotel bill (none allowable because of duality of purpose**)	540
Business entertainment	100
Motor and travel disallowed	2,949

**The strict position is that because the expenditure was not incurred "wholly and exclusively" for the purpose of the trade, none of the expenditure is allowable. In practice, however, it would normally be acceptable to claim a deduction for a proportion of the total expenditure equal to the business element, e.g. 2/7ths.*

Note 5. General Expenses

	€
Covenant to church	405
Donation to church building fund (excluding magazine advertisement)	800
Entertainment – customers	520
	1,725

The sponsorship of the 'open day' at the local golf club is allowable as advertising.

4.1.8 Partnerships

Apportionment of Tax-adjusted Profits

The partnership firm will prepare an annual profit and loss account, which will be the basis of a tax-adjusted profits computation. Case I and Case II rules regarding allowable and disallowable expenses are applied in arriving at the firm's tax-adjusted profits figure. The only unusual feature is that partners' **salaries/drawings/wages are not allowable** as they are an **appropriation of profit** (i.e. effectively the same as the drawings of a sole trader). Similarly, **interest paid on partners' capital accounts** is not an allowable deduction in arriving at the tax-adjusted profit.

The tax-adjusted profits of the partnership are divided among the partners in accordance with:

- the specific terms of the partnership agreement regarding **guaranteed salaries and interest on capital**; and
- the **profit-sharing ratio** that existed during the accounting period.

Example 4.6

Smith and Jones are in partnership as engineers for many years, sharing profits 60/40. The profit and loss account for this business for the year ended 30 April 2016 is as follows, after allowing for salaries and interest on capital payable to the partners under the partnership agreement:

Profit and Loss Account for the year ended 30 April 2016			
	Notes	€	€
Gross Fees			200,000
Less:			
Overheads		50,000	
Salaries paid to partners	1	41,000	
Interest paid on partners' capital accounts	2	13,000	
Rent paid to Smith for partnership premises		35,000	
Entertainment expenses		15,000	154,000
Net profit for the year			46,000
Note 1: Salaries			
Smith		18,000	
Jones		23,000	
		41,000	
Note 2: Interest paid on capital accounts			
Smith		6,000	
Jones		7,000	
		13,000	

Computation of Case II Taxable Profits 2016	€	€
Net profit per accounts		46,000
Add Back:		
Salaries paid to partners	41,000	
Interest paid on partner's capital accounts	13,000	
Disallowed entertainment expenses	15,000	69,000
Assessable profit 2016		115,000

continued overleaf

Apportionment of Assessable Profit	Total €	Smith €	Jones €
Salaries	41,000	18,000	23,000
Interest paid on capital accounts	13,000	6,000	7,000
Balance (apportioned 60:40)	61,000	36,600	24,400
Case II taxable profits 2016	**115,000**	**60,600**	**54,400**

4.2   Case III, Schedule D

4.2.1   Introduction

As outlined in **Chapter 3**, income falling under Case III is the actual income arising in the year of assessment. Income which is received gross, i.e. without the deduction of tax, is taxable on the amount that **accrues** over the year of assessment.

4.2.2   Deductions Available

Allowable deductions against Case III income for tax purposes are limited to a deduction for foreign tax suffered at source where it is not available as a tax credit under a double taxation agreement, and to expenses allowable against foreign rental income (using the same eligibility criteria for expenses allowable against Case V rental income).

4.2.3   Computation of Case III Income

Interest arising outside the EU, which would be deposit interest subject to deposit interest retention tax (DIRT) if it were payable in Ireland, is taxable under Case III at the prevailing Irish DIRT rate (2016: 41%). EU deposit interest income is taxable as Case IV at the prevailing Irish DIRT rate (41%).

Example 4.7

Brian, who is single, is a self-employed architect. In 2016 he had Case II income of €100,000. During 2016 Brian also received interest of €1,800 from a Spanish deposit account. Brian pays his full tax liability for 2016 on or before 31 October 2017 (the due date for the filing of his 2016 income tax return). His tax credits are €2,200.

Income Tax Computation 2016		
Income:		
	€	€
Adjusted Case II income	100,000	
Case IV income	1,800	
Taxable Income		101,800
Tax Calculation:		
€33,800 @ 20%	6,760	
€1,800 @ 41%	738	
€66,200 @ 40%	26,480	33,978
€101,800		
Less:		
Personal tax credit		(1,650)
Earned income tax credit		(550)
Tax payable 2016		**31,778**

4.3   Case IV, Schedule D

4.3.1   Introduction

As outlined in **Chapter 3**, income falling under Case IV is the **actual** income received in the year of assessment. Income is therefore generally taxed on a **receipts** basis.

4.3.2   Special Treatment of Income Subject to DIRT

Deposit interest from Republic of Ireland banks, building societies and credit unions, where the interest is paid or credited to ordinary deposit accounts on an annual or more frequent basis or at intervals exceeding 12 months, is subject to deposit interest retention tax (DIRT) at a rate of 41% (from 1 January 2014).

How to include DIRT income in the income tax computation:

Step 1:   Gross up the net interest received by dividing by 0.59 (i.e. 1 minus the 41% rate).

Step 2:   Add a new rate band for Case IV interest income @ 41% for the amount of the gross interest.

Step 3:   Include the DIRT credit (i.e. 41% of gross interest) as a non-refundable tax credit.

Example 4.8

Joe, who is single, is employed by a local supermarket. His gross salary for the tax year 2016 was €36,000 (PAYE €4,340) and he received net interest on his AIB deposit account of €750. This was subject to DIRT at 41%. His tax credits for 2016 are the personal tax credit of €1,650 and the employee tax credit of €1,650.

Income Tax Computation 2016		
Income:	€	€
Schedule D Case IV:		
AIB (€750 × 100/59)	1,271	
Schedule E	36,000	
Total taxable income		37,271
Tax Calculation:		
€1,271 @ 41%	521	
€33,800 @ 20%	6,760	
€2,200 @ 40%	880	
€37,271		8,161
Less: Non-refundable Tax Credits:		
Basic personal tax credit	1,650	
Employee tax credit	1,650	
DIRT paid (€1,271 @ 41%)	521	(3,821)
Tax liability		4,340
Deduct: PAYE paid		(4,340)
Net tax payable		**NIL**

DIRT is not refundable, even where the taxpayer only pays income tax at the standard rate (20%).

Example 4.9

Monica works in the local hair salon and earned a salary of €21,000 gross in 2016 (PAYE deducted was €900). She received interest of €1,210 (net of DIRT at 41%) from PTSB in 2016. Monica has personal tax credits of €3,300 for 2016.

continued overleaf

Income Tax Computation 2016			
	€	€	€
Income:			
Schedule E income		21,000	
Schedule D Case IV income:			
PTSB (€1,210 × 100/59)		2,051	
Taxable income			23,051
Tax Calculation:			
€21,000 @ 20%	4,200		
€2,051 @ 41%	841		5,041
Less: Non-refundable Tax Credits:			
Personal tax credit	1,650		
Employee tax credit	1,650		
DIRT paid (€2,051 @ 41%)	841		(4,141)
Tax liability			900
Deduct: PAYE paid			(900)
Net tax payable			**NIL**

Even though Monica has surplus capacity at the 20% rate (€33,800 – €21,000 = €12,800), her Case IV income is liable to tax at 41%.

4.3.3   Deductions Available

Income tax legislation gives no guidance as to what expenses are deductible in computing Case IV profits. However, in practice, the general rule is that any expenses incurred in earning the Case IV income will be treated as allowable deductions.

4.3.4   Case IV Losses

Case IV losses may be set against Case IV profits of **the same year** of assessment or, alternatively, set against Case IV profits of **subsequent** years.

4.3.5   Computation of Case IV Profits

Example 4.10
John and Brigid Murphy had the following income for 2016:

John Murphy	€
Salary (gross)	50,000
PAYE deducted	(10,312)
Bank ordinary deposit interest (net)	2,336
Credit Union interest:	
– deposit account (net)	176
– medium-term share account (net)	295
Brigid Murphy	
Salary (gross)	32,000
PAYE deducted	(3,100)

continued overleaf

Bank interest received:		
– ordinary deposit account (net)	190	
– long-term account (net)	785	
Non-refundable tax credits:		
– married couple tax credit	3,300	
– employee tax credits – €1,650 × 2	3,300	

Income Tax Computation 2016		
Income:	€	€
Schedule D Case IV:		
– John Murphy (Note 1)	4,758	
– Brigid Murphy (Note 2)	1,653	6,411
Schedule E		
– John Murphy	50,000	
– Brigid Murphy	32,000	82,000
Total taxable income		**88,411**
Tax Calculation:		
€6,411 @ 41%	2,629	
€67,600 @ 20%	13,520	
€14,400 @ 40%	5,760	21,909
€88,411		
	€	€
Less: Non-refundable Tax Credits:		
Married couple tax credits	3,300	
Employee tax credits	3,300	
DIRT paid (€6,411 @ 41%)	2,629	(9,229)
Tax liability		12,680
Deduct: PAYE paid		
– John Murphy	10,312	
– Brigid Murphy	3,100	13,412
Tax refund due		(732)

Note 1:
John Murphy

Bank interest:		
– ordinary deposit account (net)	2,336	
Credit Union interest:		
– deposit account (net)	176	
– medium-term share account (net)	295	
Interest net	2,807	
Interest gross (€2,807 × 100/59)	**4,758**	

Note 2:
Brigid Murphy

Bank interest:		
– ordinary deposit account (net)	190	
– long-term account (net)	785	
Interest net	975	
Interest gross (€975 × 100/59)	**1,653**	

Example 4.11

Mary Byrne is a widow aged 66 who has been incapacitated for a number of years. Her son Peter has executed an annual covenant of €5,000 in her favour. Her only other source of income is her pension of €25,000 (PAYE €915). Her personal tax credits for 2016 are €2,435 and her employee tax credit is €1,650.

Mary Byrne – Income Tax Computation 2016	€	€
Income:		
Case IV, Schedule D (gross covenant income)	5,000	
Schedule E – pension	25,000	
Total/taxable income		**30,000**
Tax Calculation:		
€30,000 @ 20%	6,000	
Tax liability		6,000
Less: Non-refundable Tax Credits		
Personal tax credit	2,435	
Employee tax credit	1,650	(4,085)
Less: Refundable Tax Credits		
Tax deducted by Peter on payment of covenant	1,000	
PAYE paid	915	(1,915)
Tax refund due		**NIL**

4.4 Rental Income – Case V, Schedule D

4.4.1 Introduction

As outlined in **Chapter 3**, income taxable under Case V is Irish rental income **receivable** in the year of assessment.

4.4.2 Premiums on Short Leases

Prior to the passing of FA 1963, it was possible for a landlord to avoid being taxed on income from let property by letting the property at a large "once-off" premium in the first year and charging a nominal rent thereafter. The "once-off" premium was treated as a capital receipt and was not within the charge to income tax. FA 1963 introduced legislation so that a certain proportion of a premium on a "short lease" is taxable under Case V. The 1963 legislation is now embodied in **section 98 TCA 1997**.

Calculation of Taxable Portion of Premium

Where a landlord receives a premium on the creation of a "short lease" (i.e. the duration of the lease does not exceed 50 years), this will be treated as receiving an amount **by way of rent** (in addition to any actual rent), as computed by the following formula:

$$\text{Premium} \times \frac{51 - \text{Duration of the lease}}{50}$$

Example 4.12
On 1 June 2016, Mr White rents a premises to Mr Blake for 25 years at a rent of €2,000 per month, subject to a premium of €20,000.

Taxable portion of premium:

$$€20,000 \times \frac{51 - 25}{50} = €10,400$$

Case V assessable 2016:	€
Taxable portion of premium	10,400
Rent receivable (€2,000 × 7)	14,000
Total assessable	**24,400**
Case V assessable 2017:	
Rent receivable (€2,000 × 12)	**24,000**

4.4.3   Allowable and Disallowable Deductions

The following amounts may be deducted from the gross rents receivable (section 97 TCA 1997):

- Rent payable on the property (e.g. ground rent).
- Rates payable on the property (e.g. commercial property rates, water rates, refuse, etc.).
- The cost of goods or services which the landlord is obliged to provide and for which he receives no separate consideration (e.g. gas, electricity, waste disposal).
- Cost of repairs, excluding improvements and items treated as capital expenditure.
- Cost of insurance, maintenance and management of the property.
- Loan interest paid on money borrowed for the purchase, improvement or repair of an industrial or commercial property is allowable, but interest charges incurred prior to the first letting are not deductible.
- **75%** of the loan interest on money borrowed for the purchase, improvement or repair of a residential property are allowable but, as above, interest charges incurred prior to the first letting are not deductible.

    Where interest accrues on a loan taken out to acquire a residential premises from a spouse, or civil partner, such interest is not deductible. In this context spouse or civil partner does not include a legally separated or divorced spouse, a legally separated civil partner or where the civil partnership has been legally dissolved.

    A deduction for loan interest will **not be allowed** unless the landlord **registers all tenancies** that exist in relation to that property with the **Private Residential Tenancies Board (PRTB)**, in accordance with the **Residential Tenancies Act 2004**.
- Section 15 FA 2015 introduced a new provision whereby landlords who are registered with the PRTB and who rent to tenants in receipt of **housing benefit** (i.e. payments under the rent supplement, housing assistance or rental accommodation schemes) can claim **100%** of the loan interest against rental profits. Effective from **1 January 2016**, the property must be available to social tenants for a minimum of three years and the additional relief will be granted retrospectively to the landlord at the end of the three-year period.
- Accountancy fees incurred in drawing up rental accounts and keeping rental records.
- Mortgage protection and life assurance policy premiums paid.
- Wear and tear allowances may be claimed on the cost of fixtures and fittings for furnished lettings at a rate of **12.5%** per annum on a **straight-line basis**.

Allowable expenses are normally deducted on an **accruals basis** rather than on a paid basis. In order to be deductible, the expense must be incurred **wholly and exclusively** for the purpose of earning the rent and must be **revenue** rather than **capital** in nature.

Disallowable Deductions

Expenses not deductible against Case V income include:

- **Local property tax (LPT)** is not allowable as a deduction against Case V income.
- Expenses incurred in respect of a property **before** the first lease commences in respect of that property (other than legal and advertising expenses). In the case of interest and rent, **no deduction** is allowed for either interest or rent payable in respect of a period before the property is first **occupied** by a lessee.
- Expenses incurred **after** the termination of a lease are not deductible. However, expenses incurred **after** the termination of one lease **and before** the commencement of another lease in respect of the property are deductible provided the following three conditions are satisfied:
  1. the expenses would **otherwise** be deductible;
  2. the person who was the lessor of the property **does not occupy** the premises during the period when the property is **not let**; and
  3. the property is let by the **same lessor** at the end of the period.

4.4.4   Rent-a-Room

Where an individual rents out a room (or rooms) in a "qualifying residence" and the gross income received (including sums arising for food, laundry or similar goods and services) **does not exceed €12,000 per annum**, this income will be **exempt** from income tax. It is also not liable to PRSI or USC but it must be included in an individual's income tax return. In determining whether the limit has been exceeded for the tax year, no deductions for expenses incurred are made. Where the income **exceeds €12,000**, the **entire** amount is taxable.

A "qualifying residence" is a residential premises situated in the State which is occupied by the individual as his or her sole or main residence during the year of assessment.

Room rentals under this scheme **will not affect**:

- mortgage interest relief available to the individual who qualifies for relief; or
- principal private residence relief for CGT purposes on the disposal of the house.

Where the room or rooms are rented out by more than one individual, the €12,000 limit is divided **between** the individuals.

An individual may, if they wish, elect to have any income/losses from this source assessed under the normal rules for rental income (e.g. if there is a rental loss on the room).

Exclusions

Rent-a-Room exemption will not apply where:

1. the room is rented to a child of the individual or the civil partner of the individual renting the rooms;
2. the individual receiving the rent (or a person connected to them) is an office holder or employee of the person making the payment (or someone connected to them) (section 216A TCA 1997);
3. the income is from the provision of accommodation to occasional visitors for short periods. Use of the room as **guest accommodation** rather than for residential purposes is not permitted, including where such accommodation is provided through online accommodation booking sites (e.g. Airbnb.com).

4.4.5   Rents Paid to Non-residents

Rents paid to a non-resident person must be paid under deduction of tax at the standard rate (currently 20%), and the tax paid over to the Revenue Commissioners. Failure to deduct tax leaves the tenant liable for the tax that should have been deducted.

4.4.6 Case V Losses

Case V losses incurred in a year of assessment can be carried forward **indefinitely** and used against **future** Case V profits. Unutilised Case V losses may **not be set off** against any other type of income. A net profit or loss is computed for each property **separately** for the particular tax year. The profits/losses are then aggregated to arrive at the total profit/loss for the tax year.

Section 384 TCA 1997 provides that Case V capital allowances arising in a year are to be deducted against Case V income arising in that year **in priority** to Case V losses that are brought forward from a prior year.

If a property is let otherwise than on an arm's length basis and the rent receivable is insufficient to cover expenses, any loss arising is to be carried forward until the property is re-let on a commercial basis. Tax relief is therefore not available for those losses against rental profits from other properties.

4.4.7 Computation of Case V Income

Example 4.13

John Black has owned rental properties for several years. You are given the following information about the properties owned during the tax year 2016.

Property A	€
Rent receivable	40,000
Expenditure incurred:	
Insurance (for all of 2016)	1,200
Repairs (incurred December 2016)	400
Interest on loan to acquire the property	36,000

This property is let on a 10-year lease, which commenced on 1 April 2016. A premium of €20,000 was payable on commencement of the lease. The property was acquired on 1 January 2016 for €450,000 with a bank loan taken out on the same date. This is a commercial property.

Property B	€
Rent receivable	9,600
Expenditure incurred:	
Insurance	280
Painting exterior	740
Repairs to door and alarm following burglary	1,250
LPT	225

Property B is a residential property which was let at €800 per month on a two-year lease that commenced on 1 January 2015. The tenant left suddenly in December 2016 leaving rent owing for the month of November and December. Mr Black subsequently found out that the tenant had emigrated to Australia and has written off the rent owing as a bad debt. The property was re-let to another tenant in February 2017.

Property C	€
Rent receivable	6,000
Expenditure incurred:	
Insurance	500
Construction of conservatory (May 2016)	12,400
Interest	15,000
LPT	315

continued overleaf

Property C had been let until 30 November 2015 at €1,000 a month. It was vacant until re-let on a one-year lease from 1 September 2016 at €1,500 a month. This is a residential property. The tenancies in properties B and C are registered with the PRTB.

Property D	€
Rent receivable	30,000
Expenditure incurred:	
Interest	25,000

Mr Black acquired property D from his wife in 2010 for €450,000. Mrs Black had inherited the house from her mother in 2010. Mrs Black used funds from the sale of property D to Mr Black towards the cost of a new house purchased by Mr and Mrs Black as their principal private residence.

Case V Assessment 2016	Notes	Prop. A €	Prop. B €	Prop. C €	Prop. D €
Rent received/receivable	1	40,000	8,000	6,000	30,000
Income element of premium	2	16,400	0	0	0
Gross rent		56,400	8,000	6,000	30,000
Deduct:					
Insurance	3	900	280	500	0
LPT	5		0	0	
Repairs/painting		400	1,990	0	0
Loan interest	4	27,000	0	11,250	0
Total deductions		28,300	2,270	11,750	0
Net profit/(loss)		28,100	5,730	(5,750)	30,000
Case V Assessable 2016					
Total					**€58,080**

Note 1
Property B

	€
Rent receivable	9,600
Less amount written off as bad debt	(1,600)
Total rent	8,000

Note 2
Property A

Taxable portion of premium: $€20,000 \times \dfrac{51 - 10}{50} = €16,400$

Note 3
Property A
Expenses incurred before first letting are disallowed (3/12ths)

Insurance allowed $€1,200 \times 9/12\text{ths} = €900$

Note 4
Property A
Expenses incurred before first letting are disallowed (3/12ths)

Loan interest allowed: $€36,000 \times 9/12\text{ths} = €27,000$
Commercial — no 75% restriction

Property C
Interest incurred between lettings is allowable. However, as it is a residential property and registered with the PRTB, interest is restricted to 75% of the amount charged.

$$€15,000 \times 75\% = €11,250$$

continued overleaf

Property D
Interest incurred is not allowable, as property was acquired from wife.

Note 5
Local property tax (LPT) is not allowable.

4.5 Employment Income – Schedule E

4.5.1 Introduction

As already outlined in **Chapter 3**, income from all offices and employments, pensions and annuities, benefits in kind, perquisites and certain lump sum payments deriving from an office or employment are assessable to income tax under Schedule E in respect of the actual income in the year of assessment.

4.5.2 Treatment of Termination Payments

Payments to which this section applies come within the scope of PAYE, but relief is given under section 201 TCA 1997 where tax is charged only on the **excess of the payment** over the **higher** of the:

1. basic exemption;
2. increased exemption; **or**
3. Standard Capital Superannuation Benefit (SCSB).

Basic Exemption
Section 201 TCA 1997 provides relief in the form of a **basic exemption of €10,160 plus €765 for each complete year of service** in the computation of the taxable portion of the lump sum received.

Increased Exemption
Schedule 3 TCA 1997 provides for an **increase in the basic exemption** by an **additional €10,000** where the taxpayer claiming relief has not lodged a claim for relief from taxation in respect of a lump sum payment received on the termination of an office or employment in the previous 10 years.

If, under a Revenue-approved superannuation scheme, the taxpayer receives or is entitled to receive a tax-free pension lump sum, then the **additional exemption** is **reduced** by the amount of the pension lump sum up to a maximum of €10,000.

Standard Capital Superannuation Benefit (SCSB)
A relief, known as the Standard Capital Superannuation Benefit (SCSB), may be deducted in computing the amount chargeable to income tax if it is **greater** than the basic exemption.

It is calculated as follows:

$$\frac{\text{Last 3 Years' Remuneration}}{3} \times \frac{\text{No. of Complete Years of Service}}{15 \text{ Years}}$$

Note:
1. Last three years' remuneration is to the **date of the termination of the office** or employment, i.e. not the remuneration for the last three tax years.
2. Where the period of employment was **less than three years**, the amount of the last three years remuneration is replaced by the **full remuneration** earned by an individual throughout the period of employment, and the average figure is computed based on that lesser period.

3. The SCSB calculated under the above formula **must be reduced** by any **tax-free lump sum received or receivable** under a Revenue-approved pension scheme (excluding refunds of personal contributions by the employee to such a scheme).
4. Only **full years** of service are taken into account, e.g. if an individual was employed for 10.5 years, only 10 years is used for the purpose of the fraction.
5. The definition of a tax-free lump sum received or receivable under a Revenue-approved pension scheme includes the **actuarial value** of any **future** lump sum which may be received from the pension scheme. This applies both for the increased basic exemption and for the SCSB.

Lifetime Tax-free Limit

Section 201 TCA 1997 introduced a new **lifetime** aggregate tax-free limit of **€200,000** in respect of payments made on/after **1 January 2011**. It also provides that the €200,000 limit will be reduced by the aggregate of any **prior** tax-free payments (including basic exemption and SCSB deductions) which have been received, thus ensuring that the maximum lifetime tax-free termination payment cannot exceed €200,000.

Example 4.14

James Smith was an employee of Games Ltd for 30.5 years. He was made redundant by the company on 30 September 2016 and received €90,000 as a termination payment. Mr Smith is married and his spouse has no income. His credits include the married credit of €3,300 and the employee credit of €1,650.

His salary from 1 January 2016 to date of redundancy 30 September 2016 was €45,750 gross (PAYE paid €5,030).

Mr Smith's last three years' remuneration as an employee was:

Y/E 30/09/2016	€52,250
Y/E 30/09/2015	€48,000
Y/E 30/09/2014	€39,500

Mr Smith has never received a termination payment before and will be entitled to a tax-free lump sum of €8,000 from an approved superannuation fund.

Basic Exemption Calculation   €

Basic exemption		10,160
Years of service: 30 × €765		22,950
		33,110
Increase in basic exemption	10,000	
Less: tax-free pension lump sum	(8,000)	2,000
Total basic exemption		**35,110**

SCSB Calculation

$$\frac{€52,250 + €48,000 + €39,500}{3} \times \frac{30 \text{ Years}}{15 \text{ Years}}$$

$$€46,583 \times \frac{30}{15} = 93,167$$

Less: tax-free pension lump sum	(8,000)
Total SCSB	**85,167**

continued overleaf

The SCSB deduction is taken as it exceeds the increased basic exemption of €35,110 that would otherwise be available in this case.

James Smith – Income Tax Computation 2016	€	€
Schedule E:		
Salary		45,750
Termination payment	90,000	
Less: SCSB	(85,167)	4,833
Taxable income		**50,583**
Tax (Married couple – one income):		
€42,800 @ 20%	8,560	
€7,783 @ 40%	3,113	11,673
Less Tax Credits:		
Basic personal tax credit	3,300	
Employee tax credit	1,650	(4,950)
Net tax liability		6,723
Less:		
PAYE paid		(5,030)
Tax payable		**1,693**

Example 4.15

Paddy Jayne was an employee of BCI Ltd for 19 years. He was made redundant by the company on 1 June 2016 and received the following redundancy package:

	€
Statutory redundancy	23,400
Non-statutory redundancy	190,000
Pay in lieu of notice	2,750
Company car	15,000
Total lump sum	**231,150**

Mr Jayne is also entitled to a tax-free lump sum of €215,000 from his pension fund. Mr Jayne's average salary over the past three years was €183,000.

Calculation of Exemption due	€
Basic exemption	10,160
Years of service: 19 × €765	14,535
	24,695
Increase in basic exemption*	NIL
Total basic exemption	**24,695**

*NIL as pension lump sum is greater than €10,000.

continued overleaf

SCSB Calculation	
€183,000 × 19/15	231,800
Less: pension lump sum (restricted to €200,000)	(200,000)
Total SCSB	**31,800**
Calculation of Taxable Amount	€
Statutory redundancy**	NIL
Non-statutory redundancy	190,000
Pay in lieu of notice	2,750
Company car	15,000
Less: SCSB	(31,800)
Taxable lump sum	**175,950**
**Statutory redundancy is exempt from tax.	

4.5.3 Treatment of Retirement Lump Sum Benefits

Under certain Revenue-approved pension schemes, taxpayers can receive a retirement lump sum tax-free. Section 790A TCA 1997 states that the maximum **lifetime** retirement **tax-free lump sum** will be **€200,000** in respect of benefits taken **on or after 1 January 2011**. Amounts in excess of this tax-free limit will be subject to tax in two stages. The portion between **€200,000 and €500,000 (2013: €575,000)** will be taxed (**under Case IV, Schedule D**) at the **standard rate** of income tax in force at the time of payment, while any portion above that will be taxed (under Schedule E) at the recipient's **marginal rate of tax**.

The figure of €500,000 (2013: €575,000) represents 25% of the new lower **standard fund threshold** of **€2 million (2013: €2.3 million)**. The standard rate charge is 'ring-fenced' so that no reliefs, allowances or deductions may be set or made against that portion of a lump sum subject to that charge.

Although tax-free lump sums taken after 7 December 2005 and before 1 January 2011 are unaffected by the new rules, they will **count towards** 'using up' the new tax-free amount. In other words, if an individual has already taken tax-free retirement lump sums of €200,000 or more since 7 December 2005, any further retirement lump sums paid to the individual on or after 1 January 2011 will be taxable. These earlier lumps sums will also count towards determining how much of a lump sum paid on or after 1 January 2011 is to be charged at the standard or marginal rate as appropriate.

Example 4.16

John Bartlett retired in January 2016 and was paid a retirement lump sum from his pension of €800,000 on 31 January 2016. This is the first such lump sum he has received. He is charged to tax as follows:

- the first €200,000 is exempt;
- the next €300,000 is taxed at the standard rate for 2016; and
- the balance, i.e. €300,000, is taxed at his marginal rate for 2016.

If John receives any future retirement lump sum, it will be subject to tax at the marginal rate in the year it is paid.

Example 4.17

David Murphy is paid a retirement lump sum on 1 July 2016 of €400,000. He had previously received a retirement lump sum of €220,000 on 1 January 2009. The earlier lump sum has 'used up' David's entire tax-free limit of €200,000 so that all of the lump sum taken on 1 July is taxable. Even though the earlier lump sum is not taxable, it affects the rate of tax applying to the later lump sum. David is charged to tax on the following:

	€
Lump sum received 1 January 2009	220,000
Lump sum received 1 July 2016	400,000
Total received	620,000

The earlier lump sum has 'used up' the €200,000 tax-free limit, and €20,000 of the €300,000 is taxable at the marginal rate.

Lump sum taxable:

At the standard rate – Case IV, Schedule D	300,000
Less: amount 'used up' in earlier lump sum	(20,000)
Taxable at standard rate	**280,000**
Taxable at marginal rate – Schedule E:	
Lump sum	400,000
Less: amount taxable at standard rate	(280,000)
Taxable at the marginal rate	**120,000**

Note that the amount taxable is only the total of the lump sum received in 2016.

4.5.4 Valuation of Share Option Benefits

Share options arise when employees or directors are granted an option to acquire shares in their employer's company or its parent company, at a fixed price, at some time in the future.

Share Option Schemes

Short Options – Less than Seven Years

A "short option" scheme is where the share option must be exercised within seven years from the date the option was granted. Income tax, PRSI and USC are charged on the difference between the option price paid and the market value of the shares at the **date of exercise**.

Example 4.18

On 1 June 2010 James Doyle was granted an option, by reason of his employment, to acquire 5,000 shares in LoCo Ltd at €2 per share. The option must be exercised before 1 June 2016. No consideration was paid for the granting of the share option. James exercises his option on 1 May 2016 and acquires 5,000 shares at €2 each. The market values of the shares at the relevant dates are as follows:

	€
1 June 2010 (5,000 × €2.50)	12,500
1 May 2016 (5,000 × €3.50)	17,500

Taxable Gain 2016:	€
Market value of the shares on 1 May 2016	17,500
Less: option price paid (5,000 × €2)	(10,000)
Gain	7,500

This gain is chargeable to tax, PRSI and USC under Schedule E in 2016. No taxable gain arises in the year of grant of the option even though the option price was less than the market price of the shares at that date.

Long Options – Longer than Seven Years
Income tax is charged on the difference between the market value of the shares at the **date of grant** and the option price, *and* on the difference between the option price paid and the market value of the shares at the **date of exercise**. The shareholder is entitled to a credit for tax paid on the earlier charge on grant.

Example 4.19

On 1 June 2010, James Doyle was granted an option, by reason of his employment, to acquire 5,000 shares in LoCo Ltd. at €2 per share. James has until 1 June 2019 to exercise this option. No consideration was paid for the granting of the share option. James exercises his option on 1 May 2016 and acquires 5,000 shares at €2 each. The market values of the shares at the relevant dates are as follows:

	€
1 June 2010 (5,000 × €2.50)	12,500
1 May 2016 (5,000 × €3.50)	17,500

James paid income tax at the marginal rate in 2010 and in 2016.

Income Tax Gain 2010:	€
Market value of the shares on 1 June 2010	12,500
Less: option price	(10,000)
Gain	2,500
Taxed @ 41%	1,025

Income Tax Gain 2016:	€
Market value of the shares on 1 May 2016	17,500
Less: option price paid	(10,000)
Gain	7,500
Taxable @ 40%	3,000
Less: tax paid in 2010	(1,025)
Tax payable 2016	1,975

Income tax on each gain is payable within 30 days.

The income tax due on the exercise of a share option is known as **RTSO** (relevant tax on share options), and must be paid to the Collector–General not later than **30 days** after the date on which the share option is exercised. It is not paid through the PAYE system.

4.5.5   Valuation of Benefits in Kind

General Rule
Except where there are **specific statutory valuation rules**, the amount of the taxable benefit ("notional pay") liable to PAYE, PRSI and USC is:

A.   For **benefits in kind**, the higher of:
   1.   the cost to the employer of providing the benefit, **or**
   2.   the value realisable by the employee for the benefit in money or money's worth,
   Less: any amount made good/refunded to the employer by the employee.

B.   For **perquisites**, which are benefits readily converted into cash (e.g. vouchers), the amount assessable is the amount the employee can realise, on conversion, rather than the cost of providing the perquisite.

It is the employer's responsibility to calculate the value of the benefit and collect the PAYE, PRSI and USC due thereon through the payroll when the benefit is given.

Tax on Benefits in Kind

Benefits received from an employer by an employee whose **total remuneration** (including benefits in kind) is **€1,905** or more in a tax year are taxable. Where the employee is a **director**, the benefits are taxable **regardless** of the level of remuneration. The main points with regard to tax on benefits in kind are:

- Income tax due on benefits must be collected through the operation of PAYE on the taxable value of the benefit (see below).
- PRSI, USC and employer PRSI are also due on benefits in kind and must be collected by the employer through the PAYE system.
- The notional pay liable to PAYE, PRSI and USC in respect of benefits in kind must be the **best estimate** that can reasonably be made by the employer at the time the benefit is being provided.
- *Small Benefit Exemption.* From **22 October 2015**, a non-cash benefit in kind with a value **not exceeding €500** (previously €250) is not subject to PAYE, PRSI or USC. However, no more than one benefit given to an employee in a tax year will qualify and, where a benefit **exceeds €500**, the **full value** of the benefit is subject to PAYE, PRSI and USC.

Specific Statutory Valuation Rules

Specific statutory valuation rules must be used to determine the taxable value in relation to the following benefits:

1. the transfer of ownership of property;
2. the free use of property without transfer of ownership;
3. the provision of living or other accommodation;
4. the provision of cars, vans and bicycles; and
5. the provision of preferential loans.

1. Transfer of Ownership of Property

Where the employer gives an asset to the employee/director that the employer has previously used, the **market value of the asset at the date it is transferred** to the employee/director is taken to be the benefit in kind.

If, on the other hand, the asset is purchased by the employer and not used before being given to the employee, then the **cost to the employer** will be the BIK.

2. The Free Use of Property without Transfer of Ownership

If an asset of the employer (excluding accommodation) is available for use by the employee personally, the benefit to be assessed on the employee must include the annual value of the use of the asset in addition to any day-to-day outgoings connected with the asset. Where an employer provides an asset (other than premises, land or motor vehicles) for use by an employee, the annual value of the use of the asset is deemed to be **5% of the market value** of the asset at the date the asset was first provided by the employer. If, however, the employer pays an annual rent or hire charge in respect of the asset and the amount paid by the employer exceeds 5% of the market value of the asset, that amount is the taxable benefit.

Example 4.20

On 1 May 2016, an employer acquired an antique dining room table and chairs for €15,000 for an employee's house. The table and chairs remain in the ownership of the employer.

Tax Year	Calculation	Taxable Benefit
2016	(€15,000 @ 5%) × 8/12ths	€500
2017	€15,000 @ 5%	€750

Where an employer provides an employee with the use of an asset which has been used or depreciated since the employer acquired it, the annual value of the use of the asset is deemed to be 5% of the market value of the asset when first provided to any employee.

Example 4.21

An employer acquired a dining room table and chairs for €20,000 in 2009, which were used in the employer's premises for entertaining clients. On 1 July 2016, the table and chairs, which were then valued at €12,000, were given to an employee for use in his own home. The table and chairs remain in the ownership of the employer.

Tax Year	Calculation	Taxable Benefit
2016	(€12,000 @ 5%) × 6/12ths	€300
2017	€12,000 @ 5%	€600

---

3. Provision of Living or Other Accommodation

Where accommodation is owned and provided by the employer for use by an employee, the value of the benefit to the employee is the aggregate of:

- the annual value of the premises (including land); and
- any outgoings (excluding the cost of acquisition) incurred by the employer in connection with the provision of the accommodation.

The **annual value** is the annual rent which the employer might reasonably expect to obtain if the property were rented on an arm's length basis, and on the basis that the tenant undertook to pay the usual tenant expenses and the landlord undertook to bear the cost of repairs, insurance and other expenses necessary to maintain the premises in a state to command that rent.

Generally, Revenue will apply a rule of thumb of **8% of the market value** of the accommodation supplied as being the annual letting value. However, where a vouched lower figure is available (e.g. an auctioneer's estimate), this may be used for the annual letting value.

Example 4.22

Harry, who earns €25,000 per annum, is supplied with a company apartment by his employer. The apartment originally cost €180,000 and its current market value is €160,000.
His employer pays the following expenses in relation to the upkeep of the apartment:

	€
Insurance	600
Housekeeping supplies	1,500
Management charge	900
Heating and light	1,100
	4,100

The benefit in kind (BIK) assessable on Harry would be as follows:

	€
Annual letting value: 8% × €160,000 (market value)	12,800
Add: expenses paid by the employer on behalf of Harry	4,100
Schedule E BIK	16,900

€16,900 would be added to Harry's other Schedule E income in arriving at his total tax liability.

If Harry was obliged to contribute, say, €1,500 annually to his employer, in consideration for the accommodation being put at his disposal, this would be deducted from the benefit in kind of €16,900 in arriving at the net benefit assessable on him of €15,400.

Exemptions

A taxable benefit will **not** arise where an employee (excluding directors) is **required**, by the terms of his employment, to live in accommodation provided by the employer in part of the employer's business premises, so that the employee can properly perform his duties ("better performance" test) and either:

- the accommodation is provided in accordance with a practice which, since before 30 July 1948, has commonly prevailed in trades of the class in question as respects employees of the class in question, **or**
- it is necessary, in the case of trades of the class in question, that employees should reside on the premises.

In practice, it is accepted that the "better performance" test is met where:

- the employee is required to be on call outside normal hours; and
- the employee is in fact frequently called out; **and**
- the accommodation is provided so that the employee may have quick access to the place of employment.

Examples of such employees include: a Garda, who has to reside at the station in a country village; chaplains and governors in prisons; managers or night care staff in residential or respite centres; caretakers living on the premises.

4. Provision of Cars and Vans

(a) Company Cars

Where a car is available for the **private** use of an employee, the employee is chargeable to PAYE, PRSI and USC in respect of that use.

A "car" means any mechanically propelled road vehicle designed, constructed or adapted for the carriage of the driver, or the driver and one or more other persons and **excludes**:

- motor-cycles (i.e. a vehicle with less than four wheels) where the weight does not exceed 410kg;
- company vans; and
- vehicles of a type not commonly used as a private vehicle and unsuitable to be so used.

The value of the benefit is calculated by reference to the "**cash equivalent**" of the private use of a company car, **less** amounts made good by the employee to the employer.

To arrive at the cash equivalent, the employer must first apply a **business kilometre-related percentage** to the **original market value (OMV)** of the car supplied, as per the table below.

Annual Business Kilometres	Cash Equivalent (% of OMV)
24,000 or less	30%
24,001 to 32,000	24%
32,001 to 40,000	18%
40,001 to 48,000	12%
48,001 and over	6%

Finance Act (No. 2) 2008 introduced a revised method of calculating the cash equivalent by reference to the CO_2 emission category of the car. However this revised method, which was to be effective for

cars provided on or after 1 January 2009, is still subject to a commencement order by the Minister for Finance and is therefore ignored for the purpose of this text.

Step 1: Calculate the original market value (OMV) of the car
The OMV of the car is the price (including any customs duties, VAT, VRT), which the car might reasonably have been expected to fetch, if sold in the State immediately before the date of its first registration.

Generally, the **OMV** is taken to be the **list price** of the vehicle, **including VAT** and **VRT**, at the time of **first registration**. In cases where:

▨ an exceptionally large discount was obtained (a fleet discount), **or**
▨ the discount cannot be determined (e.g. car traded in against a new car), **or**
▨ the car in question was purchased second-hand,

claims in respect of discounts are limited to the discounts **normally available** on a single retail sale on the open market. Discounts **in excess of 10%** will not normally be accepted unless there is documentary evidence available to support such a discount in respect of a single car sale. It should be emphasised that the **valuation for second-hand cars** is still the **OMV** of the car and **not** the **second-hand cost** of the car.

Step 2: Calculate the cash equivalent using the appropriate percentage, having ascertained the business kilometres for the year
Business kilometres means kilometres incurred by the employee that they are **necessarily obliged to incur in the actual performance of the duties of their employment** (e.g. kilometres travelled incurred in driving to work and returning home are not business kilometres but personal). In order to arrive at the amount of business kilometres the total kilometres for the year should be reduced by the amount of personal kilometres where this can be established; where the amount of personal kilometres is not available, a minimum of **8,000 private kilometres** should be subtracted. The employer may accept lower levels of private kilometres, but only where the employee can provide documentary evidence in this regard.

Example 4.23
Sarah is provided with a company car from 1 January 2016. The OMV of the car is €25,000. Sarah did a total of 36,800 kilometres for 2016.

Benefit in kind:	€
Total kilometres	36,800
Less: private element	(8,000)
Business kilometres	28,800
Percentage applicable: 24% (24,000–32,000 km)	
BIK (cash equivalent): €25,000 @ 24%	€6,000

Alternative Calculation for Employees with Low Business Kilometres
Employees whose annual business kilometres do not exceed 24,000 kilometres may reduce their cash equivalent by 20% where the following conditions are satisfied:

▨ the employee works at least 20 hours per week;
▨ the employee travels at least 8,000 business kilometres per annum;
▨ the employee spends at least **70%** of his or her working time away from the employer's premises; and
▨ a logbook detailing the employee's business kilometres, business transacted, business time travelled and date of journey, is kept and certified by the employer as correct.

Example 4.24
Joe drives 16,000 business kilometres per annum. The OMV of the company car is €20,000. The car was first provided in 2014. Joe satisfies all of the conditions above.

Benefit in kind:	€
€20,000 @ 30%	6,000
Less: 20% reduction	(1,200)
BIK	4,800

Step 3: Company car not available for a full year
If the employee is provided with the car for only part of the particular tax year, the business kilometre thresholds and the cash equivalent percentages used should be adjusted by the following fraction:

$$\frac{\text{No. of days in the year the car was available to employee}}{365}$$

Example 4.25
Alison is provided with a car with an OMV of €25,000 for the first time on 1 July 2016. Her business kilometres for the period 1 July to 31 December 2016 are 16,320 kilometres.

Fraction adjustment: $\frac{184 \text{ days}}{365 \text{ days}}$ (01/07/2015 to 31/12/2016) 0.5041

Multiplying 0.5041 by the annual business kilometres and their cash equivalent (see above), the revised table becomes:

Annual Business Kilometres	Cash Equivalent (% of OMV) (Category C)
12,098 or less (24,000 × 0.5041)	15.12% (30% × 0.5041)
12,098–16,131 (32,000 × 0.5041)	**12.10%** (24% × 0.5041)
16,131–20,164 (40,000 × 0.5041)	9.07% (18% × 0.5041)
20,164–24,197 (48,000 × 0.5041)	**6.05%** (12% × 0.5041)
24,197 and over	**3.02%** (6% × 0.5041)
Benefit in kind: €25,000 @ 9.07% = €2,267	

Change of Car
This calculation will also be used in a year where there is a **change of car**, as the annual business kilometre thresholds and the cash equivalent percentages must be calculated for each car **separately**.

In practice, it is simpler to **annualise** the employee's business kilometres and use the original table to determine the correct percentage to use. In this example, kilometres of 16,320 for 184 days is equivalent to 32,374 km for 365 days (16,320/184 × 365 = 32,374). As 32,374 falls into the category 32,000–40,000 business kilometres, the appropriate percentage is 18%. The employee's taxable benefit for 2016 is therefore: €25,000 × 18% × 184/365 = €2,268.

Step 4: Amounts reimbursed by employee to employer
The cash equivalent is reduced by any amount which the employee reimburses to the employer in respect of any part of the costs of providing or running the car. In order to qualify as a deduction, the costs must be made good **directly by the employee to the employer**, i.e. if Joe pays for his own petrol, there is no deduction, but if Joe's employer pays for the petrol and Joe reimburses his employer, then Joe is entitled to a deduction for the reimbursement.

Where the employee makes a contribution to the employer towards the cost of the car, the amount of the contribution is **deducted** from the cash equivalent in the year in which the contribution is paid. If the contribution **exceeds** the cash equivalent in that year, the excess is carried forward and offset against the cash equivalent the following year.

Example 4.26

Paul's employer provides him with a car with an OMV of €30,000 on 1 July 2016. Paul reimburses his employer €500 towards the cost of the car on 1 August 2016 and agrees to reimburse his employer €500 annually thereafter. Paul travels 19,200 business kilometres annually.

Benefit in kind:		€
2016	€30,000 × 30% × 6/12ths	4,500
	Less: amount reimbursed	(500)
	BIK 2016	4,000
2017	€30,000 × 30%	9,000
	Less: amount reimbursed	(500)
	BIK 2017	8,500

(b) Company Vans

Where a van is made available to an employee for private use, the employee is taxable on the cash equivalent of the benefit of the van, reduced by any amount that the employee is required to, and actually, makes good to the employer in respect of the cost of providing or running the van. The "cash equivalent" of the benefit of a van is **5% of the OMV** of the van. The business kilometre-related percentage does not apply to vans. OMV is calculated in the same manner as for cars.

A van means a mechanically propelled road vehicle which:

- is designed or constructed solely or mainly for the carriage of goods or other burden; and
- has a roofed area or areas to the rear of the driver's seat; and
- has no side windows or seating fitted in that roofed area or areas; and
- has a gross vehicle weight not exceeding 3,500 kilograms.

If the employee is provided with the van for part only of the particular tax year, then the cash equivalent is reduced on a *pro rata* basis, i.e. if the van is provided for five months, then only 5/12ths of the cash equivalent is taken.

Exemption from Benefit in Kind

The private use of the van will be exempt from benefit in kind if:

- the van is necessary for the performance of the duties of the employee's employment;
- the employee is required, by the person who made the van available, to keep the van at his private residence, when not in use;
- apart from travel between the employee's private residence and workplace, other private use of the van is prohibited by the employer; **and**
- the employee spends **at least 80%** of his time away from the premises of the employer.

Car and Van Pool Exemption

No benefit will be assessed on an employee in respect of a car or van that is in a 'pool' available for employees generally. A car or van will be treated as belonging to a 'pool' where:

- the car or van must have been made available to, and actually used by, **more than one** employee and it is not ordinarily used by any one of the employees to the exclusion of the others; **and**

⬚ any private use of the car or van made by any of the employees is merely incidental to its business use; **and**

⬚ it is not normally kept overnight at the home of any of the employees.

5. Provision of Preferential Loans

A "preferential loan" means a loan made by an employer to an employee, a former or prospective employee or their spouses, in respect of which no interest is paid, or interest is paid at a rate lower than the "specified rate". It does not include any loan made by an employer to an employee in the course of the employer's trade, on an arm's length basis, where normal commercial rates of interest are charged.

The specified rates for tax year 2016 are:

Qualifying home loans	4% (2015: 4%)
All other loans	13.5% (2015: 13.5%)

The difference between the interest actually paid by the preferential borrower during the particular tax year and the amount of interest calculated at the specified rate, and any waiver of interest, is treated as a perquisite chargeable to PAYE, PRSI and USC under Schedule E.

Example 4.27

Christopher is employed by a bank and has been advanced the following non-mortgage loans:

1. €10,000 interest-free loan
2. €20,000 loan at the rate of 4.5% per annum
3. €30,000 loan at the rate of 14% per annum

Interest due in respect of the €20,000 loan for the year ended 31 December 2015, amounting to €900, was unpaid at 31 December 2016, and was waived by his employer during the tax year 2016.

The amounts treated as perquisites under Schedule E and included as Christopher's income for the tax year 2016 will be as follows:

		€
Loan No. 1	€10,000 × 13.5% deemed interest rate	1,350
Loan No. 2	€20,000 × (13.5% – 4.5%)	1,800
Loan No. 3	Not a preferential loan (rate not less than 13.5%)	Nil
Total		3,150
Interest waived during 2016 by bank		900
Amount assessable as a Schedule E perquisite for 2016		4,050

---

6. Other Benefits

(a) Benefits on Death or Retirement

The expense of providing any pension, lump sum, gratuity or other like benefit to be given on the death or retirement of a director or employee is **exempt**. The exemption is only given to the extent that the provision is for the benefit of the director or employee themselves or for their spouse/civil partner, children or dependants. This exemption would, for instance, cover normal pension and retirement scheme payments, and death-in-service payments, made by the employer on behalf of the employee.

(b) Medical Insurance

The benefit, which is subject to PAYE, PRSI and USC, is the gross premium, i.e. the amount paid to the insurer **plus** the tax relief at source (TRS) payable by the employer on behalf of the employee. The employee may claim a standard rate tax credit in respect of the gross premium, subject to certain limits (see **Section 6.3.2**). Medical check-ups, which an employee is **required** to undergo by his employer who pays for them, are not a taxable benefit.

(c) Expense Allowances

(i) *Round Sum Expense Allowance* In general, a round sum expense allowance advanced to an employee to be disbursed at the employee's discretion is regarded as taxable Schedule E income (i.e. a perquisite). It is then open to the employee to make a formal claim for a deduction against this income in respect of the actual expenses (including capital allowances) incurred in the performance of their duties.

(ii) *Employee Motor Expenses* Where an employee uses their **own private car** for business purposes, the employer may reimburse the employee for allowable motor expenses by way of a flat-rate kilometric allowance. If the employee bears all motoring costs and is reimbursed for the business element of motoring costs by the employer at rates which do **not exceed** the **Civil Service rates**, then such costs may be paid **tax-free** by the employer and are not taxable in the hands of the employee. The employer does not have to seek prior approval from Revenue for the tax-free payment of costs in line with Civil Service rates, provided the employer operates a satisfactory system of control over the payment and keeps adequate records.

(iii) *Employee Subsistence Allowances* Where an employee performs their duties of employment while temporarily away from their normal place of work, or while working abroad on a foreign assignment, the employer may reimburse the employee for actual expenses incurred or, alternatively, may pay the employee a flat rate subsistence allowance to cover costs incurred by the employee. Where the employee pays all subsistence expenses and is reimbursed for these expenses by a flat-rate subsistence allowance, then such an allowance may be paid **tax-free** by the employer and is not taxable in the hands of the employee, provided the allowance paid is **in line** with prevailing **Civil Service subsistence rates**.

The employer **does not** have to seek prior approval from Revenue for the payment of such tax-free subsistence allowances, provided the employer notifies Revenue that it pays subsistence allowances in accordance with Civil Service rates, and that the employer operates a satisfactory system of control over the payment and keeps adequate records.

Where the employee's job is such that travel is an integral part of the job (e.g. a sales representative), or where the employee carries out much of their duties at the premises of the employer's customers, their "normal place of work" is regarded as the **employer's** business premises.

(iv) *Removal/Relocation Expenses* An employer may make the payment or reimbursement of certain removal/relocation expenses, incurred by an employee in moving house to take up employment, free of tax. The employer must ensure that the following conditions are satisfied:

- the reimbursement to the employee, or payment directly by the employer, must be in respect of removal/relocation expenses actually incurred;
- the expenses must be reasonable in amount;
- the payment of the expenses must be properly controlled; and
- moving house must be necessary in the circumstances.

Expenses that can be reimbursed free of tax are those incurred **directly** as a result of the change of residence and include such items as:

▨ auctioneer's and solicitor's fees and stamp duty arising from moving house;
▨ removal of furniture and effects and insurance on items in transit or in storage;
▨ storage charges and cleaning costs of stored items;
▨ travelling expenses on removal;
▨ temporary subsistence allowance while looking for accommodation at the new location;
▨ rent (vouched) for temporary accommodation for up to three months.

With the exception of any temporary subsistence allowance, all payments must be matched with receipted expenditure. The amount reimbursed or borne by the employer may not exceed expenditure **actually incurred**. Any reimbursement of the **capital cost** of acquiring or building a house or any **bridging loan interest** or loans to finance such expenditure would be **subject to tax**. The concession applies to relocations within the same organisation and relocations in order to take up a new employment.

(v) *Directors' Travel and Subsistence Expenses* Travel expenses paid or reimbursed to a director (executive or non-executive) to attend meetings (including board meetings), if not chargeable to income tax as income, are taxable as perquisites under the PAYE system.

Section 6 FA 2015 introduced an exemption from income tax for vouched travel and subsistence expenses payable to **non-resident, non-executive directors** attending a "relevant meeting", which is a meeting attended by a director in their capacity as a director for the purposes of the conduct of the affairs of the company. The exemption does not apply to non-executive directors who are resident in Ireland.

(d) Meals and Meal Vouchers

(i) *Canteen Meals* Where free or subsidised meals in staff canteens are provided and **available to all employees,** a taxable benefit **does not** arise. If the facility is not available to all employees, the running costs of the canteen must be apportioned between the employees entitled to use the canteen and taxed as a benefit.

(ii) *Meal Vouchers* Where an employer provides luncheon or meal vouchers to employees, a taxable benefit **does arise** on the **face value** of the vouchers (except for the first 19c per voucher).

(e) Crèche or Childcare Facilities

(i) *Employer-provided facility* Where an employer provides free or subsidised childcare facilities for employees, a taxable benefit arises.

(ii) *Independent facility* Where an employer pays for, or subsidises, the cost to an independent crèche or childcare facility, the cost borne by the employer **is a taxable benefit**.

(f) Sports and Recreational Facilities

(i) *Facilities provided on the employer's premises* Where sports and recreational facilities are made available on the employer's premises and are **available to all employees**, a taxable benefit **does not** arise. If the facilities are not available to all employees, the running costs must be apportioned between the employees entitled to use the facilities and taxed as a benefit.

(ii) *Corporate Membership paid by the employer* Where a corporate membership to sports and recreational facilities is paid by an employer on behalf of an individual employee or specified employees, the amount paid must be apportioned equally among all the employees who are entitled to and indicate an intention to participate in the scheme, and be taxed as a benefit.

(g) Professional Subscriptions

Where an employer pays a subscription to a professional body on behalf of an employee, or reimburses the employee who has paid such a subscription, a taxable benefit arises and must be included in remuneration as a benefit in kind.

However, where the professional subscriptions can be claimed by the employee as a tax deduction under **section 114 TCA 1997** as a **"wholly, exclusively and necessarily"** incurred expense of the employee in the performance of his employment duties, Revenue will not seek to have such subscriptions taxed as a benefit in kind where:

- there is a **statutory requirement** for membership of a professional body;
- there is a requirement for a **practising certificate** or licence; **or**
- membership of the professional body is an **indispensable condition** of employment **and** the duties of the employment require the employee to exercise that profession and the employee so exercises such a profession.

For example, where a legal practice employs a solicitor to act in that capacity and the employee cannot practise as a solicitor unless the employee is a member of the Law Society of Ireland, then the annual subscription to the Law Society paid by the employer is not deemed to be a benefit in kind. However, where the solicitor is employed by the legal practice as its human resources manager and it is not an indispensable condition of that employment that the employee is a member of the Law Society (though the employer deems it desirable), payment by the employer of such a subscription is taxable as a benefit in kind (reference: Revenue *eBrief 19/11*).

(h) Course or Exam Fees

Where an employer pays, or refunds, an employee for the cost of any course or exam fee, this will not be treated as a taxable benefit if the course undertaken is **relevant to the business** of the employer, where it leads to the acquisition of skills or knowledge which are:

- **necessary** for the duties of the employment; **or**
- **directly related** to increasing the effectiveness of the employee's or director's present or prospective duties in the office or employment.

(i) Examination Awards

Where an employee is given an award for passing an exam or obtaining a qualification, no taxable benefit arises provided:

- the examination/qualification bears some relationship to the employee's duties; **and**
- the award is of an amount that can reasonably be regarded as a reimbursement of the expenses likely to have been incurred in studying for the qualification or sitting the examination.

(j) Staff Discounts

Discounts given by employers on the purchase of goods by an employee are **not** regarded as a taxable benefit if the sum paid by the employee **is equal to or greater than the cost** to the employer of acquiring or manufacturing the goods.

However, where goods are sold **below** the employer's cost, the **difference** between that cost and the price paid **is a taxable benefit**.

(k) eWorking Employees

"eWorking", according to Revenue, is a method of working, using information and communication technologies, in which the work that is carried out is **independent** of location. This includes working from home on a **full-time** or **part-time** basis. eWorking involves working, for substantial periods, outside the employer's premises, logging onto the employer's computer remotely, sending and receiving e-mail or data remotely and developing ideas, products or services remotely.

Revenue outlined the following practices with regard to eWorking employees:

- Where computers or other ancillary equipment, such as printers, fax machines, etc., are provided by the employer, **primarily for business use**, to enable the employee to work from home, **no taxable benefit** will arise in respect of **incidental** private use.

- No taxable benefit will arise in respect of the provision of a telephone line for business use.
- No taxable benefit will arise in respect of office furniture or similar equipment provided it is used primarily for business use.
- The employer may make a payment of up to **€3.20 per day tax-free** to an employee to cover additional heating and electricity costs. If actual expenditure incurred by the employee exceeds this amount, the employee may make a claim for a Schedule E tax deduction in respect of the excess.

Note that these arrangements **only apply to eWorking employees**. They do not extend to employees who, in the normal course of employment, sometimes bring work home in the evenings, etc.

(l) Provision of Computer Equipment, etc.
Where, **for business purposes**, an employer provides an employee with computer equipment, high-speed internet access, a second home telephone or a mobile phone, and the employer bears the cost of installation and use, no taxable benefit will arise where **private use is incidental** to the business use of the item.

(m) Travel Passes
Where an employer provides an employee with a monthly or annual travel pass for use on bus, train, light railway (e.g. LUAS and DART) and commuter ferries, the pass is not treated as a taxable benefit, provided the pass is issued by an "approved transport provider" as defined by section 118(5A) TCA 1997. Section 118B TCA 1997 provides that an employee may "sacrifice" salary in exchange for the travel pass benefit.

(n) Car Parking
While car-parking facilities provided by employers for employees are **not treated** as a taxable benefit, **FA (No. 2) 2008** introduced a parking levy for employer-provided parking spaces in the major urban areas of Cork, Dublin, Galway, Limerick and Waterford, which is still subject to a Commencement Order by the Minister for Finance, and is therefore ignored for the purpose of this text.

(o) Employee Security
Costs and expenses incurred by an employer, or incurred by an employee and reimbursed by an employer, in the provision of an asset or service for the improvement of the personal security of the employee, is not treated as a taxable benefit if the necessity for the provision of the security service is due to a "**credible and serious threat**" to the employee's physical security which arises **wholly or mainly** from his employment, e.g. a key-holder in a bank.

An "asset" in this context includes equipment or a structure, but does not include any mode of transport, or a dwelling or grounds attached to a dwelling.

(p) Staff Entertainment
Staff Christmas parties and special occasion inclusive events or meals are not a taxable benefit where the cost involved is **reasonable**.

(q) Long-service Awards
A taxable benefit will **not arise** in respect of long-service awards where the following conditions are satisfied:
- the award is made as a testimonial to mark long service of **not less** than 20 years;
- the award takes the form of a tangible article of reasonable cost;
- the cost does **not exceed €50** for **each year of service**; and
- no similar award has been made to the recipient within the previous five years.

This treatment **does not apply** to awards made in cash or in the form of vouchers, bonds, etc. Such awards are fully taxable.

(r) Provision of a Bicycle ("Cycle to Work" scheme)

A taxable benefit will **not arise** in respect of the first €1,000 spent on a bicycle and related safety equipment for an employee for the purpose of travelling to/from work or between jobs where the following conditions are satisfied:

- a claim is made only once every five years;
- an employee may 'sacrifice' salary in exchange for the benefit (but must repay within 12 months); and
- electrically assisted pedal cycles are not covered.

(s) Company Shares/Share Awards

The benefit accruing to an employee from the receipt of shares and other securities awarded to employees in their employer company, or its parent company, is a **taxable benefit** and must be included in remuneration as a benefit in kind. The benefit is therefore subject to PAYE, EE PRSI and USC. **Note that it is not subject to employer PRSI.** Gains or benefits on **share options** are subject to self-assessment and are not taxable under the PAYE system as a benefit in kind (see **Section 4.5.4**).

(t) Company Credit/Charge Cards

Where the card is provided by the employer **exclusively** for business usage, any stamp duty or membership fee paid by the employer is **not** a taxable benefit. Where, however, the card can be used for **private** purchases or payments, any payments **not repaid** by the employee **are** taxable benefits and subject to PAYE, PRSI and USC.

(u) Provision of Newspapers, Periodicals, etc.

Where an employee is provided with free newspapers, periodicals, etc. which are **generally related** to the employer's business, a taxable benefit does **not** arise.

(v) Exceptional Performance Awards/Staff Suggestion Schemes

Where an employer has schemes in place to reward exceptional performance or staff suggestions, any awards received under such schemes, whether cash or gifts/vouchers, **are** taxable benefits.

(w) Annual Allowance Paid to Reserve Members of An Garda Síochána

The annual allowance in respect of out-of-pocket expenses paid to Reserve Members of An Garda Síochána is exempt from income tax (section 204A TCA 1997) and shall not be included in the calculation of taxable income.

(x) Expenses Paid to State Examinations Commission Examiners

Effective from **1 January 2016**, section 7 FA 2015 exempts from income tax any travel and subsistence payments (where these do not exceed Civil Service rates) payable by the State Examinations Commission to any examiner employed by them.

4.5.6 Expenses Allowable under Schedule E

In order for an expense to be deductible from an employee's or director's Schedule E income, it must be shown that it was incurred "**wholly, exclusively and necessarily in performing the duties of the office or employment**". The test is extremely difficult to satisfy in practice as:

- the employee or director must be **necessarily** obliged to incur the expense; **and**
- the expense must be wholly, exclusively and necessarily incurred; **and**
- the expense must be incurred in the **actual performance** of the duties.

It will be noted that **all of the above tests** must be satisfied. The difficulty of satisfying the tests is obvious in considering the dicta of judges in deciding cases. For instance, Judge Vaisey said, in the case of *Lomax v. Newton* (1953), that the rules are notoriously rigid now and restricted in their operation. He observed:

"An expenditure may be necessary for the holder of an office without being necessary to him in the performance of the duties of that office. It may be necessary in the performance of those duties without being exclusively referable to those duties. It may perhaps be both necessarily and exclusively and still not be wholly so referable. The words are indeed stringent and exacting, compliance with each and every one of them is obligatory for the benefit or relief to be claimed successfully."

Restriction of Expense Deduction in Respect of Leased Cars

Where the list price of a leased vehicle exceeds the **relevant limit** (currently **€24,000**), the amount of leases charges (relating to the business use of the car) are further restricted by reference to the CO_2 emissions of the car, as per the table below:

Vehicle Category	CO_2 Emissions (CO_2 g/km)	Leasing Charges Restriction
A/B/C	0g/km up to and including 155g/km	Lease hire charge $\times$ $\dfrac{\text{(List Price 2 Relevant Limit)}}{\text{List Price}}$
D/E	156g/km up to and including 190g/km	Lease hire charge $\times$ $\dfrac{\text{(List Price 2 (Relevant Limit} \times 50\%))}{\text{List Price}}$
F/G	191g/km and upwards	Lease hire charge disallowed

Example 4.28

Joe Jones, who is a salesman, leases his own car to carry out his duties under his contract of employment. The Category D car was first leased on 1 January 2014 when its retail price, after cash discount, was €25,000. Joe incurred lease charges of €8,000 in 2016 and 80% of his mileage was related to his employment.

	€
Lease charges	8,000
Less: private element 20%	(1,600)
Business element	6,400

Disallowed lease payment:

Car Category D/E: $€6,400 \times \dfrac{(€25,000 - (€24,000 \times 50\%))}{€25,000}$	3,328

Disallowed lease payment for Joe Jones:

Private element of lease charges	1,600
Restriction: Category D car	3,328
Total lease payment restriction	4,928

4.6   Schedule F

4.6.1 Introduction

As outlined in **Chapter 3**, dividends and other distributions paid by Irish resident companies after the deduction of dividend withholding tax (DWT) are liable to tax under Schedule F.

4.6.2 Computation of Schedule F Income

The amount assessable on the individual is the amount received in the tax year plus DWT.

Example 4.29

Jane Conway, who is single, received the following Irish dividends from LXX plc in respect of their accounting year ended 31 March 2016:

Interim dividend (net) paid 30 September 2016	€2,640
Final dividend (net) paid 1 May 2017	€1,360

Jane also had Schedule E income of €33,500 for 2016 (PAYE deducted €3,500). Her personal tax credit was €1,650 and her employee tax credit was €1,650.

Jane Conway Income Tax Computation 2016	Notes	€	€
Schedule E:			
Salary			33,500
Schedule F:			
Net dividend received 2016	1	2,640	
Dividend withholding tax deducted		660	
Gross Schedule F income			3,300
Taxable Income			36,800
Tax:			
€33,800 @ 20%		6,760	
€3,000 @ 40%		1,200	
€36,800			7,960
Less Tax Credits:			
Basic personal tax credit		1,650	
Employee tax credit		1,650	(3,300)
Net Tax liability			4,660
Less:			
PAYE paid		3,500	
Dividend withholding tax		660	(4,160)
Tax payable			500

Note 1:

Net dividend received €2,640 × 100/80 = gross dividend of €3,300.

The dividend is not apportioned so the dividend paid on 30 September 2016 is taxable in full in 2016.

Note also that the accounting year's profit, out of which the dividend is paid, is irrelevant. The date of the payment of the dividend determines the tax year. Therefore the dividend paid on 1 May 2017 is assessable in 2017.

Questions

Review Questions

(See Suggested Solutions to Review Questions at the end of this textbook.)

Question 4.1

Joseph Murphy is a trader. He prepares accounts annually to 31 December. His profit and loss account for the year ended 31 December 2016 was as follows:

	Notes	€		€
Salaries	1	61,864	Gross profit	112,500
Travelling expenses	2	17,512	Discounts received	7,349
Commissions		7,236	Dividends from Irish Co.	2,813
Interest on late payment of VAT		1,121	Interest on National Loan Stock	2,250
Interest on late payment of PAYE		1,238	Deposit interest	170
Depreciation		13,793	Profit on sale of fixed assets	5,063
Bank interest		4,008		
Subscriptions	3	1,225		
Repairs	4	6,480		
Bad debts	5	2,475		
Legal fees	6	1,069		
Accountancy fees		2,250		
Net profit		9,874		
		130,145		130,145

Notes:

1. Salaries include a salary to Mr Murphy of €7,500 and a salary paid to his wife of €5,000 for her work as secretary.

2. Travelling expenses include €1,000 for a holiday trip by Mr and Mrs Murphy.

3. Subscriptions

	€
Political party	75
Local football club	50
Traders association	500
Trade papers	200
Old Folks Home	150
Sports club	250
	1,225

4.   Repairs account

	€
Opening provision for repairs	855
Expenditure during period	2,335
New extension to office	3,000
Closing provision for repairs	2,000
Profit and loss account charge	6,480

The closing repairs provision represents a general provision for expenditure not yet incurred.

5.   Bad debts account

	€
Opening provision – general	(5,100)
Bad debts recovered	(2,675)
Bad debts written off	2,275
Closing provision – general	7,975
Profit and loss account charge	2,475

6.   Legal fees

	€
Bad debts recovery	60
Sale of freehold	1,009
	1,069

Requirement

Compute Joseph Murphy's Case I taxable profits for 2016.

Question 4.2

Andy Reilly operates a consultancy business providing technical advice. He has carried on business for many years and makes up annual accounts to 31 December. His profit and loss account for the year to 31 December 2016 is set out below:

	€	€
Fees charged		178,000
Less: Direct costs:		
Technical salaries and employment expenses	64,000	
Stationery and printing	4,000	
Repairs to equipment	980	
Professional indemnity insurance	370	
Motor vehicle expenses (Note 1)	6,250	
Depreciation – equipment	2,500	
– motor vehicles	3,000	(81,100)
		96,900
Deduct overheads:		
Rent, rates and property insurance	11,000	
Repairs to premises (Note 2)	6,500	
Lighting and heating	1,100	
Office salaries	7,200	
Telephone and postage	400	
Advertising	800	

Entertaining (Note 5)	3,900	
Bad debts (Note 3)	550	
Defalcations (Note 4)	6,000	
Successful claim by client not covered by insurance	2,500	
Andy Reilly's drawings	20,000	
Depreciation – office equipment and fittings	<u>900</u>	<u>(60,850)</u>
		<u>36,050</u>

Net profit before taxation

Notes.

1. €4,000 of the total motor vehicle expenses relate to Andy Reilly's car; 40% of Andy's total travel in his car is on business. The other motor expenses relate to sales representatives' cars, all of which cost €19,000.
2. Repairs to premises include the charge for constructing two additional garages adjoining the firm's buildings for the sales representatives' cars. This amounted to €3,150.
3. The bad debts charge includes a credit for the recovery of a specific debt amounting to €350 and the creation of a general bad debt reserve amounting to €275.
4. The defalcations were traced to staff and were not covered by insurance.
5. The charge for entertainment comprises the following:

	€
Private holiday for Andy Reilly (June 2016)	1,200
Tickets for Andy Reilly and his friend to All Ireland football final	300
Staff Christmas party	1,200
Business meals with customers	<u>1,200</u>
	<u>3,900</u>

Requirement
Compute Andy Reilly's Case I tax-adjusted profit for 2016.

Question 4.3

Tony set up business as a car dealer/garage proprietor on 1 October 2015. His first accounts were made up for the 15-month period ended 31 December 2016 and subsequently to 31 December each year. The first two sets of accounts show the following results:

	15 months to 31/12/2016	Year Ended 31/12/2017
	€	€
Sales: cars	250,000	200,000
Sales: workshop	<u>100,000</u>	<u>90,000</u>
	<u>350,000</u>	<u>290,000</u>
Direct costs		
Cost of cars sold	211,500	168,300
Salesman's salary and commission	15,000	13,000
Workshop labour and parts	<u>62,500</u>	<u>66,000</u>
	<u>289,000</u>	<u>247,300</u>
Gross profit	<u>61,000</u>	<u>42,700</u>

General and administrative costs

Accountancy		1,500	1,250
Advertising		900	1,100
Bad debts	(Note 1)	2,500	400
Depreciation		3,000	2,400
Drawings		15,000	12,000
Entertaining	(Note 2)	1,500	700
Insurance		5,000	4,000
Interest	(Note 3)	18,000	14,000
Legal fees	(Note 4)	400	600
Light and heat		2,250	1,800
Office staff salaries		10,600	8,500
Postage, telephone and stationery		1,500	1,200
Sundries	(Note 5)	1,250	650
Travel expenses	(Note 6)	<u>1,950</u>	<u>1,500</u>
		65,350	50,100
Net loss		<u>(4,350)</u>	<u>(7,400)</u>

Notes:		15 months to 31/12/2016	Year Ended 31/12/2017
		€	€
1.	Bad debts		
	General provision	2,500	–
	Bad debt written off	–	2,900
	General provision no longer required	–	<u>(2,500)</u>
		<u>2,500</u>	400
2.	Entertaining		
	Hospitality for representatives of car manufacturer during negotiations for supply of cars	800	–
	Entertaining customers	<u>700</u>	<u>700</u>
		<u>1,500</u>	<u>700</u>
3.	Interest		
	Interest on loan from car manufacturer to buy stock	9,500	7,000
	Interest on bank loan to establish business	<u>8,500</u>	<u>7,000</u>
		18,000	14,000
4.	Legal fees		
	Advice on supply agreement with car manufacturer	250	200
	Recovery of outstanding debts	–	200
	Defending customer claim re: faulty car	<u>150</u>	<u>200</u>
		400	600
5.	Sundries		
	Security	500	300
	Drinks at staff Christmas party	150	150
	Subscription to trade association	200	200

Political donation	100	–
Charitable donation (eligible charity)	50	–
Interest on late payment of VAT	250	=
	1,250	650

6. Travel expenses
    These expenses contain no disallowable element.

Requirement

(a) Compute the Schedule D, Case I profit for the 15 months ended 31 December 2016 and the year ended 31 December 2017.

(b) Calculate Tony's Case I taxable profits for 2016.

Question 4.4

John Smith commenced trading on 1 May 2016. The profit and loss account from 1 May 2016 to 30 April 2017 shows the following information:

	Notes	€	€
Sales		201,230	
Less: cost of sales		140,560	
		60,670	
Interest received	1	390	
Gross profit			61,060
Expenses			
Wages	2	23,500	
Motor expenses	3	1,860	
Depreciation		1,250	
Rent and rates		12,800	
Leasing charges	4	4,300	
Repairs	5	3,900	
Telephone		800	
Bank interest and charges		3,800	
Sundry expenses	6	3,400	
Insurance	7	2,630	58,240
Net profit for the year			**2,820**

Notes:

1. Interest received

	€
Post Office Savings Certificates	390

2. Included in wages charges are:

	€
Wages to Mrs Smith (wife), as book-keeper	1,800
Wages to self	5,200
Accrued bonus for sales assistants	500
Own PRSI	200

3. Motor expenses

Motor expenses relate solely to Mr Smith's own motoring and include a €100 fine for careless driving. 60% of total travel by car is for business purposes. Motor insurance has been included under the insurance charge.

4. Analysis of leasing charges (all operating leases)

	€
Lease of till	300
Lease of shelving	1,200
Lease of Mr Smith's car	2,800
	4,300

The motor car had a market value of €25,000 when first leased on 1 May 2016. It has an emissions rating of Category D.

5. Repairs

	€
Painting outside of shop	1,000
Repairing shop front damaged in accident	1,300
Insurance claim re above accident	(900)
Extension to shop	1,500
General provision for repairs	1,000
	3,900

6. Sundry expenses

	€
Trade subscriptions	250
Interest on the late payment of income tax	120
Covenant to church (4th annual net payment)	260
Covenant to son at university (3rd annual net payment)	710
Christmas party for staff	560
Accountancy	1,500
	3,400

7. Insurance

	€
Business "all-in" policy	270
Motor car	300
Retirement annuity premiums – single	500
Retirement annuity premiums – annual	600
Life assurance	460
Key-man life assurance on salesman	500
	2,630

Requirement

Compute John Smith's adjusted trading profits for income tax purposes for the year ended 30 April 2017.

Question 4.5

Polly Styrene has been in business for many years manufacturing shoes and she makes up her accounts to 31 December each year. Her Profit and Loss account for the year ended 31 December 2016 was as follows:

	Notes	€	€
Gross profit			145,000
Less:			
Wages and salaries	1	90,000	
Light, heat and telephone	2	6,000	
Postage and stationery		500	
Repairs and renewals	3	5,000	
Legal and professional fees	4	3,000	
Bad debts	5	2,000	
Travel and entertainment	6	2,500	
Bank interest	7	3,500	
Insurance		3,000	
Freight		4,000	
Sundries	8	3,500	
			123,000
Net profit			**22,000**

Notes:

1. Wages and salaries includes €8,000 for Polly Styrene.
2. Light, heat and telephone includes €1,500 for light, heat and telephone at the residence of Polly Styrene. One-sixth is business related.
3. Repairs and renewals

Painting and decorating	1,600
Extension to shops	1,400
Provision for future repairs	2,000

4. Legal and professional fees

Debt collection	1,200
Accountancy	1,500
Surveyor's fees re: abortive purchase of premises	300

5. Bad debts

Trade debts written off	2,800
Bad debt recovered	(200)
Decrease in general reserve	(600)

6. Travel and entertainment

Car expenses*	1,500
Christmas drinks for employees	400
Entertaining customers	600

    * The car cost €32,000 and was bought in 2011. Private use is one-third.

7. Bank interest

Bank interest	1,500
Lease interest	2,000

    Polly leased plant and equipment through ABC Commercial Finance under a three-year finance lease. The total repayments (capital and interest) for the year were €18,600.

8. Sundries

Advertising	1,551
Trade protection association	100
Political party subscription	1,000
Parking fines	49
Rubbish disposal	300
Donation to St Luke's Institute of Cancer Research**	500

**St Luke's Institute of Cancer Research is a charitable organisation, which is an "approved body" for charitable donations relief purposes.

Requirement
Calculate the Schedule D, Case I taxable adjusted profit for 2016.

Question 4.6

Jack and John are in partnership as accountants for many years. The profit and loss account for the year ended 30 April 2016 was as follows:

		€	€
Gross fees			200,000
Less:	Overheads	100,000	
	Jack's salary	20,000	
	John's salary	21,000	
	Jack's interest on capital	6,000	
	John's interest on capital	7,000	154,000
	Profit for the year		**46,000**

Disallowable expenses included in general overheads amount to €26,000.

The profit-sharing ratio (after salaries and interest on capital) for the year ended 30 April 2016 was 50:50.

Requirement
Prepare the Case II computation and allocate the profits to the partners.

Question 4.7

Anthony and Sandrine Kelly are married and have four children, one of whom is incapacitated. They are both resident and domiciled in Ireland. Details of their income for the tax year 2016 is as follows:

Anthony Kelly:	€
Salary	50,000
(PAYE deducted)	(5,800)
AIB ordinary deposit interest (gross) 31/12/2016	130
Credit Union interest (gross) – deposit account	80
Credit Union interest (gross) – medium-term share account	100
Vodafone (UK) dividend received	900

Sandrine Kelly:

Salary	28,000
(PAYE deducted)	(4,000)
Dresdner Bank (Germany) deposit interest gross	2,000
Independent Newspapers plc (Irish) dividend received net	2,500

Requirement

Calculate their liability to income tax for 2016 on the assumption that a valid election for joint assessment is in force. Their personal tax credits are €9,900.

Question 4.8

David Lee, who is a single person aged 44, works for a travel agency. He lives with his daughter Judy, aged 14, whom he maintains. He had the following income and outgoings:

	Tax Year 2016
	€
Income:	
Salary (gross)	42,000
Ordinary bank interest (net)	500
Interest on government loans (gross)	1,130
Ordinary building society interest (net)	140
Dividend from Credit Union regular share account (net)	29
Outgoings:	
PAYE deducted	4,637
Post Office (Note)	1,200

Note: David buys €100 worth of Post Office Savings Certificates every month.

Requirement

Calculate David Lee's income tax liability for 2016, stating clearly the amount payable by, or refundable to, him. His personal tax credits are €4,950.

Question 4.9

Mr O'Reilly owns several properties which he lets. Details of his income from these properties and the letting terms are as follows:

Property A (residential property)   Acquired in November 2012 and let on a five-year lease expiring in November 2017 at a monthly rent of €500 payable monthly in advance. The rent due on 1 December 2016 was not received until 10 January 2017. Interest of €5,500 was incurred evenly during the year on a bank loan taken out to acquire the property. The property is registered with the PRTB.

Property B (commercial property)   Acquired on 1 April 2016 and let for the first time on 1 August 2016 on a 21-year lease at a full annual rent of €12,000 payable monthly in advance A bank loan was raised to help purchase the property and interest of €1,800 was paid on 30 June 2016 and €3,600 on 31 December 2016. A premium of €10,000 was also received under the terms of the new lease.

Property C (residential property)   Let at a full annual rent of €6,000 under a seven-year lease which expired on 30 April 2016. The property was vacant until 1 November 2016, when it was let again on a five-year lease at a full rent of €9,000 per annum. The property is registered with the PRTB.

Property D (residential property) Let to Mr O'Reilly's aunt on a 21-year lease from 1 May 2004, at an annual rent of €52 (not a full rent).

Mr O'Reilly is responsible for repairs on all properties, except for Property A, in respect of which there is a "tenants repairing" lease.

During the tax year 2016, the following additional expenses were incurred:

Property B

		€
30 April	Dry rot repairs	950
30 June	Window broken by vandals	80
31 December	Storm damage	1,400

Property C

20 May	Blocked drains	90
31 July	Painting	700
31 October	Advertising for tenant	130

Property D

28 September	Roof repairs	160

Requirement

Compute Mr O'Reilly's rental income assessable under Schedule D, Case V for the tax year 2016.

Question 4.10

Sonya, a widow, has recently brought you details of her rental income, which will be needed to prepare schedules supporting her tax return. All properties are non-residential. Relevant information is as follows:

Property 1 This property is let on a 10-year lease. The lease was granted in December 2010 at an annual rent of €16,000, payable monthly in arrears, subject to review every three years.

Property 2 This property is let at a rent of €8,000 per annum, payable monthly in advance.

Property 3 This property is let at a rent of €9,600 per annum, payable monthly in advance. The instalment of rent due on 1 December 2016 was not received until 10 January 2017. This property was first let some years ago.

Property 4 This property was first let on a 15-year lease on 30 June 2016 and a rent of €9,000 per annum, payable quarterly in arrears on 30 September, 31 December, 31 March and 30 June, subject to review every three years.

Property 5 This property is let on a 15-year lease, expiring in June 2017, at a nominal rent of €10 per month, payable annually in advance on 30 June. The tenant is Sonya's sister.

The expenses (all allowable) paid in 2016 by Sonya for each property were:

	€
Property 1	4,300
Property 2	1,200
Property 3	800
Property 4	NIL
Property 5	900

In addition, mortgage interest of €1,400 gross was paid on a loan to finance the purchase of Property 3. Her property portfolio is entirely commercial.

Requirement
(a) Prepare a schedule summarising Sonya's property income assessable in 2016.
(b) Sonya is contemplating an investment in:
  (i) The National Instalment Savings Scheme
  (ii) Government Securities

  Prepare notes briefly summarising the tax effects of each of these investments.

Question 4.11

Mr Houghton, a single person aged 60, retired from Liver Ltd on 30 June 2016 after 18 years' service. As a token of its appreciation, the board of directors of Liver Ltd voted him a lump sum of €65,000.
  Mr Houghton's remuneration for the three years prior to retirement was as follows and it **accrued evenly throughout the year**.

	€
Year to 30 June 2014	52,000
Year to 30 June 2015	55,000
Year to 30 June 2016	57,000

On 30 June 2016 Mr Houghton also commuted part of his pension to a tax-free lump sum of €3,000 and received an annual pension thereafter of €18,000. His total PAYE deducted for the tax year 2016 was €4,940.

Requirement
Calculate Mr Houghton's income tax liability for the tax year 2016. His personal tax credits are €3,300.

Question 4.12

Mr Moran, who is 57 years old, retired on 30 September 2016 after 18 years and three months of service with his employer. He received a lump sum of €30,000 from his employer and a tax-free lump sum of €19,000 from his employer's pension scheme. His remuneration for the last three years to the date of retirement was:

	€
Year ended 30/09/2016	37,250
Year ended 30/09/2015	34,500
Year ended 30/09/2014	32,625

His only other income in 2016, apart from the lump sum, was a salary of €28,500. Mr Moran is married with no dependent children. His wife has no income of her own. His total PAYE deducted for 2016 was €750.

Requirement
Calculate his tax liability for the tax year 2016. His personal tax credits are €4,950.

Question 4.13

Mr Lynch was made redundant by his employer, Tree Ltd, on 31 December 2016. He received a lump sum payment of €30,000 (excluding statutory redundancy).
  He also received a refund of his pension contributions of €5,600, from which income tax of €1,120 was deducted. He had been employed by the company for 10 complete years and had not received a termination

lump sum payment from any previous employer. Mr Lynch's remuneration for the three years prior to his redundancy was:

	€
Year to 31 December 2016	43,000
Year to 31 December 2015	35,000
Year to 31 December 2014	30,000

Total PAYE deducted from salary and lump sum payment in the tax year 2016 was €6,600.

Requirement
Calculate the balance of income tax payable (or repayable) in respect of Mr Lynch for the tax year 2016, assuming he is a widower with no dependent children and qualifies for a €3,840 tax credit.

Question 4.14

Terence Flynn, who is married, had been manager of a garage in Co. Monaghan until 30 September 2016. At that date, due to falling petrol sales and high taxes, the garage closed and Mr Flynn was made redundant. His wife has no income.
    You are given the following additional information regarding Mr Flynn:

1. He received an ex-gratia lump sum of €57,000 from his employer as compensation for loss of office. This was in addition to his statutory redundancy payments of €7,800. He also received holiday pay of €2,000 to which he was entitled. He has no entitlement to a tax-free pension lump sum payment.
2. He had worked in the garage for 15 full years. He received pay-related Jobseeker's Benefit of €188 a week for eight weeks in the period October–November 2016.
3. On 1 December 2016, he moved to Dublin to take up a new job with a multinational oil company at a salary of €2,500 per month, together with a benefit in kind projected at €2,000 per annum.

His earnings for the last four years to 30 September were:

	€
Year ended 30/09/2016	47,000
Year ended 30/09/2015	54,000
Year ended 30/09/2014	52,000
Year ended 30/09/2013	50,000

His pay accrued evenly from month to month.
    The total PAYE deducted from both employments for the tax year 2016 was €3,030.

Requirement
(a) Calculate the amount of the lump sum that is liable to tax.
(b) Calculate the tax year 2016 income tax liability with a personal tax credit of €4,950.

Question 4.15

Dermot O'Donnell, a single parent with one five-year-old son, was an employee of Super McBurgers, a fast food restaurant chain. He has been employed by the company for 15 years and 8 months. He was made redundant on 30 September 2016. You have the following information:

1. As part of the redundancy package he received:

Statutory redundancy	€8,000
Holiday pay	€1,200

Company car worth	€22,500
Ex-gratia payment	€40,500

2. In the period from 1 January 2016 to 30 September 2016, Dermot earned a salary (including benefit in kind on his company car) of €37,000. PAYE deducted was €3,500.
3. He commenced new employment in Burger Palace on 1 November 2016 and his earnings in the period to 31 December 2016 were €4,200 (PAYE deducted was €100).
4. Dermot's salary was pensionable and, as part of the termination package, Super McBurgers made a special contribution of €11,700 into his Revenue-approved pension scheme. Dermot is entitled to a tax-free lump sum payment under the terms of the pension scheme. The actuarial value of the lump sum entitlement on 1 October 2016 was €22,000.
5. His salary and benefit in kind for the prior tax years were as follows:

	€
y/e 30/09/2016 salary	46,000
BIK	2,900
y/e 30/09/2015 salary	36,000
BIK	2,000
y/e 30/09/2014 salary	39,000
BIK	3,100

Requirement
(a) Calculate the tax-free termination payment that can be made to Dermot O'Donnell.
(b) Compute Dermot's final liability to income tax for the year 2016 with tax credits of €4,950.

Question 4.16

Sid Harvey is an employee of General Services Ltd. His gross basic salary for 2015 amounted to €38,000 and for 2016 amounted to €40,000.

His employer also gives him €100 every month by way of a round sum expense allowance to meet incidental outlay. He is not obliged to provide his employer with receipts to account for this expenditure.

Sid is supplied with a company car, which was bought second-hand by General Services Ltd in July 2014 for €15,000. The car is a 2010 model and originally cost €35,000 (after 10% cash discount) when first registered. General Services Ltd pay all the outgoings in respect of the running of the car. However, Sid is required to reimburse the company for private fuel and the cost of insurance. The amount reimbursed by Sid for fuel and insurance during 2016 came to €1,300. In recognition of the fact that he has the car available to him during leisure hours, Sid is also obliged to make a monthly contribution of €100 to his employer. This is deducted from his salary. Sid's total travel by car in the tax year 2016 amounted to 40,000 km, of which 26,400 km were in the course of the performance of his duties. Sid spends approximately 50% of his working time away from the premises of General Services Ltd.

General Services Ltd also provide a free apartment to Sid. The market value of the apartment is estimated at €110,000.

General Services Ltd pay the annual management charge and light and heating costs of the apartment which, for 2016, amounted to €890. The apartment was purchased for €55,000 in 1998.

Sid receives free meals in the staff canteen on the days in which he is located at his head office. The cost of providing these meals to his employer amounted to approximately €300. The staff canteen is available to all staff and all meals are provided free.

On 1 November 2012, General Services Ltd provided Sid with a €1,000 interest-free loan to enable him to go on his annual holidays. On 1 February 2016, the board of directors of General Services Ltd decided to waive repayment of the loan, together with 2016 interest outstanding at that date.

Sid is not married and paid €13,900 PAYE in the tax year 2016.

Requirement

(a) Calculate the amount of benefit in kind to be included with Sid's gross pay for PAYE purposes for 2016.

(b) Compute Sid's income tax liability for the tax year 2016, clearly showing all workings. His personal tax credits for 2016 are €3,300.

Question 4.17

Terry is reviewing an offer from a new employer, Rich Bank plc, to start on 1 January 2016. In addition to an attractive salary of €70,000, Rich Bank plc have offered to take over his mortgage loan of €125,000, which he used to purchase his first main residence in January 2008. The rate of interest payable on the loan is 2%.

His employer will also provide an interest-free loan of €10,000 to pay Terry's affiliation fees at the Posh Golf and Country Club. The bank will pay annual membership of €3,500 on his behalf.

He will also be provided with a new VW Passat car in CO_2 emissions Category C, which has an original market value of €30,000. The bank will pay all expenses. Terry estimates that he will drive 46,400 km in the tax year 2016, of which 10,400 km will be private, which he must reimburse to the bank at a rate of 15c per km.

Terry is married and will earn €75,000 with no benefits if he stays in his current job in 2016. He pays 5% on his mortgage and estimates that his car costs €10,500 per annum. He is not a member of any golf club and has no business mileage in his current job. His wife cares for their two children and does not work outside the home.

Requirement

(a) Calculate the taxable benefits assessable for 2016 from his new employer. Assume he has tax credits of €5,950.

(b) Prepare income tax computations for both jobs and advise which leaves him better off.

You may ignore tax relief on the mortgage loan for the purposes of this question.

Question 4.18

Philip Stodge is employed as a commercial representative by his employer. Details of his income are as follows:

	2016	2015
	€	€
Gross salary	41,600	28,200
Sales commission	6,000	9,000

The following additional information is available:

1. PAYE deducted amounted to €4,900 for 2016 and €2,500 for 2015.

2. The sales commission of €6,000 earned during 2016 was paid to him on 1 June 2017 and the commission earned for 2015 was paid in July 2016.

3. He receives a monthly lump sum expense allowance of €100 to meet routine incidental expenses, such as telephone calls, tips, etc. In addition, his employer pays his hotel accommodation costs directly. He is obliged to provide his own car, pay all operating expenses and non-hotel meal costs personally.

4. Philip runs an Audi A4 car, which he first leased on 6 April 2013 for €27,000 on taking up his present employment. His car operating costs were as follows:

	2016	2015
	€	€
Lease charges	5,700	5,700
Car tax	500	480
Car insurance	850	750
Petrol	3,200	2,800
Tyres	–	150
Maintenance	400	230
Crash repairs	1,500	0
	6,450	4,410

He maintains receipts for all his motor expenses and 90% of his total mileage is undertaken in the performance of the duties of his employment. The emissions rating of his car is Category B.

5. In addition to car expenses, Philip has made the following expense claims (vouched with receipts) in his tax returns in respect of expenses not reimbursed by his employer:

	2016	2015
	€	€
Work-related telephone charges	180	120
Cost of new suit	450	340
Cost of advanced commercial correspondence course	150	–
Taxi/train fares while on business	130	100
	910	560

6.   Philip is married and his wife earned €5,500 (PAYE €230) in 2016.

Requirement

Compute Philip Stodge's tax liability for the tax year 2016, claiming the maximum reliefs available. His personal tax credits are €6,600.

Question 4.19

Frank, a sales representative who is single (tax credits €3,300), received a salary of €50,000 and sales commission of €8,000 from his employer during 2016. To visit his customers, Frank used a car costing €51,000, which he had leased new on 1 July 2014 (emissions rating Category F). Lease charges paid in the tax year 2016 were €6,600. During the tax year 2016, he incurred the following motor expenses:

	€
Petrol	4,300
Insurance	1,500
Motor tax	1,480
Repairs and service	1,400

Frank travelled 44,800 km in 2016, of which 8,960 km were for private purposes.

   Frank's employer has suggested that they enter into a new arrangement whereby the employer would provide Frank with a Category C motor car costing €31,000 and pay all the expenses. In return, Frank would receive his normal salary and two-thirds of his usual commission.

Requirement

(a) Calculate Frank's gross income tax liability (before credit for PAYE deducted) for the tax year 2016.

(b) Recalculate Frank's income tax liability for the tax year 2016, assuming that the new arrangement had been in force during the entire year and that the car was first provided in 2016. Advise Frank which arrangement is financially more advantageous.

Capital Allowances and Loss Relief

Learning Objectives

In this chapter you will learn:

- how the accounting depreciation rules are disregarded in favour of a separate system of capital allowances to reflect expenditure on buildings, plant and machinery;
- the distinction between 'plant and machinery' and 'industrial buildings' and the characteristics of each;
- what constitutes allowable expenditure for capital allowances purposes;
- how capital allowances are granted in reducing taxable income;
- the tax consequences of purchases and disposals of plant, machinery and industrial buildings;
- the different treatments available for lessors and lessees;
- how losses incurred in a trade are treated for income tax purposes; and
- the use of losses against other types of income.

5.1 Capital Allowances: Plant and Machinery

5.1.1 Introduction

In arriving at the tax-adjusted trading profits of a business, depreciation for accounting purposes is specifically disallowed. The computation of adjusted profits **does not** include any capital allowances either. Capital allowances are a **separate calculation** and are included in the income tax computation as a **deduction** from taxable Case I and Case II profits, or Schedule E income, by reference to the **tax year,** i.e. capital allowances for the 2016 tax year are deducted from the tax-adjusted trading profits for 2016.

The basic objective of the system of tax capital allowances is to allow the business a **deduction** against assessable business profits for the **net cost of certain capital assets employed** for the purpose of the business.

5.1.2 Meaning of "Plant"

The basic test applied is to determine whether the specific capital asset in question is **functional** to the operation of the business, as distinct from representing the **setting** in which the business is carried out.

There is no statutory definition of plant and machinery for the purposes of capital allowances. Accordingly, one must have recourse to case law to determine various tests which must be satisfied if an item of expenditure is to qualify as "plant" for the purposes of capital allowances. The question of whether an item is plant is a **matter of fact**, which will be decided according to the circumstances of each particular case. The question of whether an item is **machinery** can, in certain circumstances, be an easier test to satisfy as it is usually an **either/or** test. However, where there is any doubt, as for plant, the question is a **matter of fact** that will be decided by the circumstances of **each** case.

The most quoted definition of the word "plant" arose under a case, *Yarmouth v. France* (1887), in connection with the Employer's Liability Act 1880, in which Lord Justice Lynley said:

> "There is no definition of plant in the Act, but in its ordinary sense, it includes whatever apparatus is used by a businessman for carrying on his business – not his stock-in-trade, which he buys or makes for sale but all goods and chattels, fixed or moveable, live or dead, which he keeps for permanent employment in the business."

To determine whether an item would qualify as plant, relevant case law has indicated that the following tests are applied:

- Is the item functional or merely a setting in which the business is carried on?
- Is the expenditure incurred directly on the provision of plant and not, for instance, on the provision of finance which is used to acquire plant?
- Does the expenditure replace an item previously regarded as plant?
- Is the expenditure related to an entire unit or is it merely expenditure on part of a larger, non-functional unit?

As the practice in relation to plant has resulted mainly from a study of case law, brief details of some of the more important cases on the subject are outlined below:

Jarrold v. Good (1962)

In this case, reference was made to the case of *J. Lyons & Co. v. Attorney General* (1944) in which it was stated as a principle that "the term (plant) does not include stock-in-trade, nor does it include the place where the business is carried on". It was held in this case that purpose-built partitioning, although forming part of the setting of the business, was an essential part of the equipment necessary for the operation of the business and should, therefore, be regarded as plant. The partitions in this case were moveable and it was contended that they were specifically designed to enable employees to carry out their duties according to the state of the company's business and were and could be moved as required by the volume of the company's activities.

CIR v. Barclay, Curle & Co Ltd (1969) 45TC22

This case, concerning expenditure on a dry dock, was heard by the House of Lords in 1969. The main facts of the case were as follows.

Shipbuilders constructed a dry dock that involved the excavation of some 200,000 tons of earth and rock, which was then lined throughout with 100,000 tons of concrete. The installations included a dock gate, pump and valves, piping, electrical machinery, etc. The dock acted like a hydraulic chamber in which a volume of water, variable at will, could be used to lower a ship so that it could be exposed for inspection and repair, and to raise it again to high tide level. The taxpayer contended that the dock was a single and indivisible entity, performing the function of a large hydraulic lift cum vice, and that the expenditure on both the excavation and concrete work was incurred on the provision of machinery and plant.

The House of Lords found in favour of the taxpayer and the following quote from Lord Reid is important in considering the tests to be applied:

> "It seems to me that every part of the dry dock plays an essential part in getting vessels into a position where work on the outside hull can begin and that it is wrong to regard either the concrete or any part of

the dock as a mere setting or part of the premises in which the operation takes place. The whole dock is, I think, the means by which, or plant with which, the operation is performed."

This decision stressed the functional test as opposed to the setting test.

Schofield (HMIT) v. R & H Hall (1974)

In this case, the company claimed capital allowances on expenditure it incurred on the construction of two silos which were used to take grain from ships and to dispense it to customers. The silos consisted of large concrete structures into which were built concrete bins, a small structure, the workhouse containing machinery and plant, and machinery consisting of gantries, conveyor belts, mobile chutes, etc. The taxpayer claimed that all of the expenditure qualified for capital allowances as plant and machinery. It was held that, considering the function of the silos in relation to the company's trade, they seemed an essential part of the overall trade activity. Their function was to hold grain in a position from which it could be conveniently discharged in varying amounts. Accordingly, they found that the silos were plant, qualifying for wear and tear allowances.

An important aspect of the case was the **detailed description of the plant** given by the company by way of documentation and evidence.

S. O'Culachain (Inspector of Taxes) v. McMullan Brothers (1995)

In this case, it was claimed that forecourt canopies at petrol filling stations constituted plant for capital allowances purposes on the grounds that the canopies were essential to provide advertising, brand image and attractive surroundings, and therefore created an ambience and had a function in carrying on the business.

The Revenue Commissioners argued that the canopies provided no more than shelter from the rain and wind and played no part in the trade of selling petrol.

It was held that the canopies performed a function in the actual **carrying out** of the trade and therefore qualified for capital allowances as an item of plant.

Hampton (HMIT) v. Fortes Autogrill Ltd (1979)

It was held that a false ceiling is not plant on the basis that it simply provided a covering which was not functional to the actual carrying on of the catering business by the taxpayer.

5.1.3   Wear and Tear Allowance

Plant and Machinery
This is an annual allowance for the wear and tear of plant and machinery (new or second-hand) in use for the purpose of a trade, profession or employment at the end of an accounting period.

The qualifying asset must be **owned** by the taxpayer and **in use**, wholly and exclusively for the purposes of the taxpayer's trade, profession or employment, **at the end** of the relevant basis period for the year of assessment. (The basis period is the accounts year from which the tax year is calculated.)

The allowance is calculated on the **cost price** of the plant **less** any grants received. The **wear and tear rate is 12.5%** on expenditure incurred from 4 December 2002 on a straight-line basis.

The wear and tear allowance is an **annual** allowance. The only circumstance in which a full 12.5% will not be granted is where the **basis period** for the particular tax year, for which the allowance is being claimed, **is less than 12 months**.

This would only occur in the **year of commencement** of trade. (The year of cessation of trade may also be less than 12 months but no annual allowance would be due for that year as the asset would not be in use at the end of the basis period.)

It is important to emphasise that it is the **length of the basis period** that determines whether or not a full annual allowance is available and **not the period from the date of purchase** of an asset to the end of the particular basis period.

In the year of acquisition, a full year's wear and tear allowance is granted (provided the basis period is at least 12 months long).

In the year of disposal or cessation of use, no wear and tear allowance is granted, as the asset is not in use at the end of the basis period.

Example 5.1	Plant & Machinery @ 12.5%	Vehicles @ 12.5%	Total
	€	€	€
Opening qualifying cost of assets purchased on 1 Jan 2012	50,000	0	50,000
Add:			
Additions at qualifying cost	25,000	20,000	45,000
Deduct:			
Disposals at qualifying cost	(7,000)	0	(7,000)
Cost of assets qualifying for wear and tear allowance (A)	**68,000**	**20,000**	**88,000**
Opening tax written down value (TWDV) at 1 Jan 2016	**25,000**	0	25,000
Add:			
Additions at qualifying cost during the basis period, i.e. y/e 30/09/2016	25,000	20,000	45,000
Deduct:			
TWDV of assets sold during the basis period, i.e. y/e 30/09/2016	(3,500)	0	(3,500)
	46,500	20,000	66,500
Wear and tear for 2016 (Line A × qualifying rate)	(8,500)	(2,500)	(11,000)
TWDV @ 31/12/2016	**38,000**	**17,500**	**55,500**

Motor Vehicles

The wear and tear rate for motor vehicles, other than that used in a taxi or car hire business, is 12.5%, straight-line, on expenditure incurred from 4 December 2002.

For income tax basis periods ending on or after 1 January 2007, the allowable cost of new and second-hand cars (for wear and tear allowance purposes) is restricted to a **maximum limit of €24,000** (specified limit).

Section 380L TCA 1997 introduced certain additional restrictions on capital allowances available on cars which are based on CO_2 emissions levels for vehicles bought on or after 1 July 2008.

There are three categories:

1. Category A/B/C Vehicles   121–155g/km
2. Category D/E Vehicles   156–190g/km
3. Category F/G Vehicles   191g/km and upwards

Vehicle Category	Capital Allowances Available
A, B and C	Use the specified amount regardless of cost.
D and E	Two steps to calculate limit: 1. Take the lower of the specified limit or cost. 2. Limit is 50% of the above amount.
F and G	No allowance available.

No restrictions apply to:

- Commercial vehicles, e.g. lorries, vans, etc.
- Cars used for the purposes of a taxi business.
- Cars used for the purpose of a car hire business.

The wear and tear allowance for cars used in a **taxi or car hire** business is **40%** on a **reducing balance** basis. The "specified amount" reduction, i.e. the maximum cost limit of €24,000, does not apply to such cars.

Where a business asset is partly used for private purposes, the wear and tear allowance is calculated as normal and is then reduced by the private element. However, the full annual allowance is deducted when arriving at the tax written down value at the end of each tax year.

Example 5.2

Joe, who is self-employed **and** prepares annual accounts to 31 December, purchased a new car on 1 August 2016 which cost €35,000 (emissions Category D). His annual travel is 32,000 kilometres, of which 8,000 are private. Joe's sales director, Sarah, also has a company car, which was purchased on 30 September 2013 (emissions Category C) for €25,000. Sarah's travel is 56,000 kilometres, of which 44,800 are business related.

Wear and Tear Calculation **Motor Vehicles @ 12.5%**	Notes	Sarah's Car €	Joe's Car €
Tax Written Down Value (TWDV) 01/01/2013		–	
Additions y/e 31/12/2013	1	24,000	
Wear and tear allowance 2013		(3,000)	
TWDV 31/12/2013		21,000	
Wear and tear allowance 2014		(3,000)	
TWDV 31/12/2014		18,000	
Wear and tear allowance 2015		(3,000)	
TWDV 31/12/2015		15,000	
Additions 2016	2		12,000
Wear and tear allowance 2016		(3,000)	*(1,500)
TWDV 31/12/2016		12,000	10,500

Notes:
1. Sarah's car cost is restricted to €24,000 for 2013. As Sarah is an employee, there is no private motoring restriction.
2. Joe's car is restricted to 50% of €24,000 for 2016 as a Category D car.

*The wear and tear allowance on Joe's car will be further restricted to the business use only, i.e.

$$1,500 \times \frac{(32,000-8,000)}{32,000} = 1,125$$

5.1.4 Balancing Allowances and Charges

Profits and losses on the disposal of fixed assets are **not included** in the tax-adjusted profits of a business. In order to adequately capture these profits and losses, the capital allowances systems use balancing charges and balancing allowances to reflect any profit or loss on the disposal of an asset.

A balancing allowance arises when the sales proceeds of an asset are less than its tax written down value (loss on disposal).

A balancing charge arises when the sales proceeds of an asset are greater than its tax written down value (profit on disposal).

Note that the "tax" profit or loss will not be the same as the profit or loss on disposal in the accounts, due to the differing rates and rules between depreciation and tax capital allowances.

Balancing allowances and charges may arise when one of the following occurs:

- The trade or profession ceases, therefore the assets are no longer "in use".
- An asset, on which wear and tear allowances were claimed, is sold/scrapped.
- An asset permanently ceases to be used for the purposes of the trade, profession or employment.

In computing the balancing allowance/charge, market value is imposed where the sales proceeds are **not** at arm's length or there are no sale proceeds (e.g. takeover/gift of a business asset for personal use).

Limitation of Balancing Charges

A balancing charge is limited as follows:

- it **cannot exceed** the aggregate of the wear and tear allowances **already claimed** on the asset; and
- in respect of plant and machinery, it will not arise where the **disposal proceeds are less than €2,000**. However, this restriction does not apply if the disposal is to a connected person.

Example 5.3

Damien Jones is self-employed and prepares annual accounts to 30 June. Damien disposed of the following assets:

	Counting Machine	Binding Machine	Printer
Date of disposal	23/01/2016	10/06/2016	28/04/2016
Proceeds	€6,250	€220	€1,750
Original cost	€5,000	€900	€4,000
TWDV 01/01/2016	€4,000	€425	€1,250

Balancing Allowance/Charge Calculation

	€	€	€
TWDV 01/01/2016	4,000	425	1,250
Less:			
Sale proceeds	(6,250)	(220)	(1,750)
Balancing allowance/(charge)	(2,250)	205	(500)
Restricted to:			
Balancing allowance/(charge)	*(1,000)	205	**NIL

*The balancing charge on the counting machine is restricted to the amount of wear and tear allowances already claimed (cost €5,000, less WDV €4,000 = €1,000).
**No balancing charge will apply in respect of the printer as the sales proceeds are less than €2,000.

Year end 30 June 2015 formed the last basis period (i.e. 2015) for which wear and tear allowances were claimed. The assets were disposed in y/e 30 June 2016, which is the basis period for 2016. No wear and tear allowance is claimable in the year of disposal.

Replacement Option

If plant and machinery (including motor vehicles) is replaced with **similar** equipment, any balancing charge arising on the old equipment may be **deferred**. If such a claim is made, the cost of the new equipment is **reduced by the balancing charge** deferred. This claim is referred to as the "replacement option". This option may only be claimed to avoid a balancing charge if a similar item replaces the item of plant sold.

Example 5.4

Damien Jones sold printing equipment and a balancing charge of €1,000 arose. He bought replacement equipment on 10 January 2016 for €6,000. This equipment was in turn sold on 29 March 2017 for €6,050.

	Printing Equipment €
Balancing Allowance/Charge Calculation	
2016:	
Cost of new printing equipment	6,000
Less:	
Balancing charge on original asset	(1,000)
Qualifying cost of replacement asset for capital allowances	5,000
Wear and tear allowance 2016 @ 12.5%	(625)
TWDV 31/12/2016	4,375
2017:	
TWDV 01/01/2017	4,375
Less:	
Sales proceeds	(6,050)
Balancing charge	(1,675)
Restricted to:	
Actual allowances granted (including deferred balancing charge): €625 + €1,000	(1,625)

Motor Cars

As the qualifying cost of a motor car for wear and tear allowance is capped at **€24,000**, any balancing allowance/charge on disposal must too be restricted in the same proportion as the **original restriction** to the actual cost of the vehicle. The deemed sales proceeds are calculated as follows:

$$\text{Total sales proceeds} \times \frac{\text{Restricted value of car}}{\text{Original cost of car}}$$

Where there is private use, any balancing allowance/charge is further restricted to the proportion of business use.

Example 5.5

Damien Jones purchased a new car on 15 January 2014 for €25,000 (emissions Category A). He sold the car on 15 April 2016 for €15,500. Business usage was agreed at 75%. Damien prepares accounts to 30 June each year.

	Motor Vehicle 12.5% €	Allowable 75% €
Wear and Tear Allowance		
TWDV 01/01/2014	–	

continued overleaf

Additions y/e 30/6/2014 (restricted to €24,000)	24,000	
Wear and tear allowance 2014	(3,000)	(2,250)
TWDV 31/12/2014	21,000	
Wear and tear allowance 2015	(3,000)	(2,250)
TWDV 31/12/2015	18,000	
Disposal:		
WDV 01/01/2016	18,000	
Deemed proceeds: €15,500 × 24,000/25,000	(14,880)	
Balancing allowance	(3,120)	
Restricted to business use of 75%		(2,340)

5.1.5   Treatment of Capital Grants, Hire Purchase, Lessors, Lessees and VAT

Capital Grants

For capital grants expenditure incurred since 29 January 1986, the qualifying cost is the **net cost**, i.e. total cost minus the grant receivable. For expenditure incurred prior to that date, the qualifying cost is the total cost before Government grants.

Hire Purchase

For hire purchase situations, a full wear and tear allowance is allowed in respect of the first tax year in the basis period for which the asset is put into use and every year thereafter, subject to the qualifying conditions continuing to be met.

For the purposes of computing the wear and tear allowance, the qualifying cost is limited to the cost of the asset **exclusive** of the hire purchase charges, i.e. interest. The interest charge is allowable against taxable profits.

The timing of the actual hire purchase instalments is not relevant provided the agreement is executed during the relevant basis period.

Treatment of Lessors

A person who **leases** plant or equipment to other individuals carrying on qualifying trades or professions will be entitled to a wear and tear allowance in respect of the cost of the plant and equipment leased, provided it can be shown that the **lessor** bears the burden of wear and tear.

Treatment of Lessees

Section 299 TCA 1997 states that, where plant and machinery is leased to a person (lessee) who is carrying on a trade and the **lessee** bears the burden of wear and tear, then the lessee is **deemed** to have incurred the capital expenditure on the assets and is therefore entitled to claim capital allowances on the assets. The lessee was also able to claim a deduction for the full lease payments payable to the lessor which, in some cases, allowed a double deduction for the cost of the asset.

Section 299 TCA 1997 also ensures that an entitlement to capital allowances only exists where:

1.   a joint election is made by both lessor and lessee, **and**
2.   the lessor has made a claim under section 80A TCA 1997 to be taxed on the income of the lease in accordance with its accounts, **and**

3. the amount of the lease payments deducted by the lessee does not exceed the amount included by the lessor as income in his accounts, **and**
4. in computing his profits, the lessee is not entitled to deduct an amount equivalent to the cost of the asset to the lessor.

The lessee is not entitled to a deduction for both the "capital" element of the lease payments **and** capital allowances on the equipment, but will get a deduction against taxable profits for the interest.

Qualifying Cost and VAT

The qualifying cost of plant and equipment for wear and tear purposes is the **actual expenditure incurred** on the plant or equipment **exclusive** of VAT, which is recoverable. If, however, an **unregistered** business is involved, then the VAT element of the purchase price obviously represents a cost and the **total cost, including VAT**, would be allowable.

5.1.6   Unutilised Capital Allowances

Where the capital allowance claim for a particular year of assessment exceeds the assessable profits from the trade or profession concerned, the excess may be used in the following two ways:

- the excess capital allowances may be **carried forward** indefinitely against assessable profits in future years from the **same** trade or profession until such time as they have been utilised; or
- the capital allowances may be used to **create** or **augment** a **loss claim** that can be used to reduce the individual's total income liable to income tax in that year.

It should be noted that there is **no right** to carry forward unutilised capital allowances in the case of an **employment**. This is probably not important in practice, as it is difficult to envisage a situation where Schedule E income of an employee would be insufficient to offset any capital allowance claim made.

5.2   Capital Allowances: Industrial Buildings

5.2.1   Introduction

Capital allowances are available in respect of expenditure incurred on **certain types** of building. Such buildings are referred to as "industrial buildings". **If a building is not an industrial building, then no capital allowances are available**.

5.2.2   Meaning of "Industrial Buildings"

Unlike the term "plant", TCA 1997 contains a clear definition of what is meant by an "industrial building". It is defined as a **building or structure in use**:

- For the purposes of a trade carried on in a mill, factory, or other similar premises.
- For the purpose of a dock undertaking.
- For the purposes of growing fruit, vegetables or other produce in the course of a trade of market gardening.
- For the intensive production of cattle, sheep, pigs, poultry or eggs in the course of a trade other than farming.

- For the purpose of a trade of **hotel-keeping**, which includes:
    - holiday camps registered with Fáilte Ireland;
    - a guest house or holiday hostel registered in the register of guest houses/holiday hostels kept under the Tourist Traffic Acts; **or**
    - buildings as part of a caravan/camping site registered under the Tourist Traffic Acts. These include laundry rooms, toilets and showers, café/canteen, etc.
- As a laboratory used wholly or mainly for mineral analysis in connection with the exploration for, or the extraction of, oil, gas and minerals.
- For the purposes of a trade which consists of the operation or management of an airport and which is an airport runway or an airport apron used solely or mainly by aircraft carrying passengers or cargo for hire or reward.
- For the purpose of operating or managing a private nursing home. (The nursing home must be registered with the HSE under the Health (Nursing Homes) Act 1990.)
- For the purpose of the recreation of employees by an employer who carries on any of the above trades.
- For the purpose of operating a convalescent facility (approved by the HSE and subject to the Health (Nursing Homes) Act 1990).
- For the purpose of operating a private hospital.
- For the purpose of operating a qualifying mental health centre.
- For the purpose of operating a qualifying specialist palliative care unit.
- For the purpose of the operation or management of a qualifying sports injuries clinic.
- For the purposes of maintaining, repairing, overhauling or dismantling aircraft used to carry passengers or cargo for hire or reward.

The following types of building or structure are specifically **excluded** from the definitions of "industrial buildings". Buildings or structures used:

- as a dwelling house;
- as a retail shop;
- as a showroom or office; or
- for a purpose ancillary to any of the foregoing.

The **site cost** is specifically disallowed for the purposes of industrial buildings allowances. However, expenditure incurred on the **development** of such a site would be allowable. This would include the cost of preparing, cutting, tunnelling, levelling land and the installation of services on the site.

In relation to the items excluded above, TCA 1997 provides an **exception** if the following conditions can be satisfied:

1. the retail shop, showroom, etc. must be physically **part of a larger structure** which qualifies, **and**
2. the cost of expenditure on such retail shops, showrooms, etc. must **not exceed 10%** of the total expenditure on the building or structure, inclusive of any grant-aided expenditure, but **exclusive** of the site cost.

It should be noted that the exclusion for offices refers to **administrative offices**, and would **not include**, for instance, **a drawing office**, as under case law it is held to be an industrial building, as it is used for **purposes ancillary to the industrial operations** carried out in the rest of the factory.

Example 5.6	€
Site cost	5,000
Cost of factory portion of building	55,000
Cost of administrative offices portion of building and factory shop	5,000

The €55,000 expenditure on the factory portion of the building qualifies for a 20% government capital grant.

The appropriate fraction to work out the 10% test is as follows:

$$\frac{\text{Cost of administrative offices}}{\text{Total cost of factory and offices exclusive of site cost}} = \frac{5,000}{60,000} = 8.33\%$$

In this case, therefore, the administrative offices and shop will qualify in full for capital allowances. If, however, the computation worked out at, say, 12%, no part of the expenditure on the offices and shop would qualify.

5.2.3 Industrial Buildings Annual Allowance

To qualify for industrial buildings annual allowance, the building or structure must be **in use** on the **last day of the chargeable period** (basis period in the case of income tax) for the purpose of a **qualifying trade**.

Industrial buildings annual allowance rate is normally **4% per year**. This is on a **straight-line** rate and is calculated as a **percentage of the qualifying cost** of the industrial building (exclusive of grants).

Annual allowance is also known as **writing down allowance**.

5.2.4 "Tax Life" of Industrial Buildings

The "tax life" of an industrial building is an important and unusual feature of industrial buildings allowances. Generally, the **length of the tax life** is determined by the **rate of annual allowance applicable** to the industrial building in question. The following table summarises the annual allowance rates.

Type of Expenditure	Date Incurred	Writing Down Allowance Rate	Time Limit on Balancing Charge "Tax Life"
Factories, mills and docks		4%	25 years
Buildings for growing fruit and vegetables by market gardener		10%	10 years
Production of cattle, sheep, pigs, poultry and eggs by non-farmer		10%	10 years
Hotels	04/12/2002 to date	4%	25 years
Guest houses and holiday hostels	04/12/2002 to date	4%	25 years
Nursing home (Note 1)	03/12/1997 to 31/12/2009	6.67%/5%	15/20 years
Convalescent facility (Note 1)	02/12/1998 to 31/12/2009	6.67%/5%	15/20 years
Childcare facilities	02/12/1998 to 30/09/2010	10%/6.67%	10/15 years
Private hospital (Note 1)	15/05/2002 to 31/12/2009	10%/6.67%	10/15 years
Sports injury clinic	15/05/2002 to 31/12/2006	10%/6.67%	10/15 years

Note 1: Nursing Homes: For buildings first used **after** 1 February 2007, the tax life is **15 years**. For capital expenditure incurred under contracts or agreements that were entered into on or after **1 May 2007** and before **31 December 2009**, the tax life **is 20 years**. **Finance Act 2007** capped the qualifying expenditure on the latter at **50%** for individuals and **75%** for companies.

Finance Act 2009 provided for the **termination** of capital allowance schemes for registered nursing homes, convalescent facilities, private hospitals and mental health facilities (but not palliative care centres) on qualifying expenditure incurred **after 31 December 2009**.

Treatment of Property-based Capital Allowances

Section 409 TCA 1997 states that passive investors will not be able to claim accelerated capital allowances beyond the original tax life of the scheme where the tax life ends after 1 January 2015. If the tax life ended before 1 January 2015, the passive investor cannot carry forward any unused allowances.

A **5% property relief surcharge** also applies to investors (both passive and active) with gross income greater than €100,000. The surcharge is collected as an additional Universal Social Charge (USC) of 5% on the amount of income sheltered by property reliefs in a given year. (See **Section 8.11** for more detail on the USC.)

5.2.5 Balancing Allowances and Charges

If the building is sold, and the "**tax life**" of the relevant qualifying expenditure has **elapsed**, then the vendor **does not** suffer a **balancing charge** and the purchaser is **not entitled** to capital allowances in respect of that expenditure (see exception below).

If, on the other hand, any industrial building is sold **before** its tax life has elapsed, the vendor must compute a balancing allowance/charge in the normal way, and the purchaser is **entitled to annual allowances** in respect of all or part of the cost of the building or structure. The allowances available to the purchaser of a second-hand industrial building are only available provided it is **used** as an industrial building. If this condition is satisfied, the annual allowance, based on the **lower** of the price paid for the second-hand building and the original cost of the building, is granted. The annual allowance available is spread **equally** (i.e. on a straight-line basis) over the **balance of the tax life** of the building.

No balancing allowance arises on the sale of an industrial building where the vendor and the purchaser are connected to each other.

Exception

However, with the following property-based tax schemes, the tax life is seven years, but a balancing charge can be triggered if the building is sold **within 10 years** of its first use prior to 1 February 2007. The schemes in question are:

- private hospitals;
- nursing homes, nursing home residential units and convalescent facilities;
- childcare facilities; and
- sports injury clinics.

If a building is sold **after** its tax life has expired but **before** the 10-year period, then the balancing charge due may be reduced by the unused capital allowances that would, but for the introduction of the curtailment from the 2015 tax year, have been carried forward. Note that these allowances will not be allowable against any other income or gain, merely the balancing charge on the building in question.

5.2.6 Qualifying Cost, Foreign Properties and Lessors

Qualifying Cost

The qualifying cost for the purposes of industrial buildings allowance depends on whether or not the **vendor is a builder**.

If the **vendor is a builder**, the qualifying cost for allowance purposes is equal to:

$$\text{Total Purchase Price} \times \frac{\text{Construction Expenditure}}{\text{Site Cost + Construction Expenditure}}$$

If the vendor is a **non-builder**, the qualifying cost is deemed to be the **lower of**:

- the actual construction expenditure, or
- the net price paid (calculated using the above formula).

The purpose of these rules is to prevent allowances being claimed on any element of the profit or gain made by an investor on the sale.

Foreign Properties

Expenditure incurred on or after 23 April 1996 on industrial buildings situated outside the State does not qualify for any allowances.

Lessors

The landlord will qualify for industrial buildings allowance where the lessee is carrying on a qualifying trade in the building.

The allowance can also be claimed if the building is leased to the Industrial Development Authority (IDA Ireland), the Shannon Free Airport Development Company (SFADCo) or Údarás na Gaeltachta, who in turn sub-lease the building to a tenant who carries on a qualifying trade.

5.2.7 Unutilised Industrial Buildings Allowance

Where an industrial building is used for the purpose of a qualifying trade, industrial buildings annual allowance (IBAA) is available as a deduction against the tax-adjusted profits of the trade. Any excess can be carried forward.

Lessors

Lessors of industrial buildings can set their IBAA against all rental income in the year. Where capital allowances exceed the rental income, the excess can be offset against other income, subject to a **maximum offset of €31,750**. The further excess can be carried forward against future rental profits in priority to Case V losses brought forward. Allowances carried forward from an earlier year are first deducted against Case V income, before allowances for the current year are deducted.

Industrial buildings annual allowance on hotels in excess of rental income **cannot** be offset against non-rental income, **except** where the expenditure was incurred **prior** to 3 December 1997.

Acquisition from a Company

Where an individual acquires an industrial building from a company, the excess of the capital allowances over the rental income of that building may only be carried forward against future rental income of **that** building, i.e. the excess may **not be offset** against rental income from **other** properties or against any other income.

Example 5.7

Jack Brown acquired a second-hand industrial building on 1 December 2013. He is entitled to annual capital allowances of €70,000 in respect of the new property and in 2016 he received rental income of €20,000 for that property. Jack had other rental income of €10,000 and non-rental income of €50,000 for 2016.

Tax Computation 2016	€	€
A. Property acquired from an individual		
Case V income	30,000	
Less: capital allowances	(70,000)	
Excess capital allowances	(40,000)	
Restricted to: maximum offset		(31,750)
Non-rental income		50,000
Taxable income 2016		**18,250**
Capital allowances carried forward against rental income		
Excess allowances	40,000	
Less: utilised against non-trading income	(31,750)	
Allowances carried forward	8,250	
B. Property is a hotel and acquired from an individual		
Case V income	30,000	
Less: capital allowances	(70,000)	
Restricted to: total Case V income		(30,000)
Net Case V income		–
Non-rental income		50,000
Taxable income 2016		**50,000**
Capital allowances carried forward against all rental income		
Capital allowances	70,000	
Less: utilised 2016	(30,000)	
Allowances carried forward	40,000	
C. Property acquired from a company		
Case V income	30,000	
Less: capital allowances	(70,000)	
Restricted to: amount of rent from new building		(20,000)
Net Case V income		10,000
Non-rental income		50,000
Taxable income 2016		**60,000**
Capital allowances carried forward against rental income from new building only		
Capital allowances	70,000	
Less: utilised 2016	(20,000)	
Allowances carried forward	50,000	

5.3 Loss Relief

5.3.1 Introduction

Section 381 TCA 1997 provides relief for a loss sustained, in a trade, profession, employment or farming, by way of deduction from **any other income** chargeable to tax in that year. The loss is deducted from **gross income** before deduction of charges on income or personal allowances/reliefs.

Any loss not relieved under section 381 can be **carried forward** and set-off against the profits of the **same** trade or profession in subsequent years (section 382 relief). The loss must be set-off against the **first** subsequent year's trading profits, and so on. Losses may be carried forward indefinitely provided the trade that incurred the loss **continues** to be carried on.

Terminal loss relief can be claimed in respect of a loss incurred in the **final** year of a trade or profession. This loss can be **carried back** against profits from the same trade or profession for the last **three years** of assessment preceding that year in which the cessation occurs.

5.3.2 "Legal Basis" and "Conventional Basis"

The strict legal interpretation of section 381 relief indicates that it is the **actual** loss for a particular tax year that may be relieved ("legal basis"). In practice, however, relief will be granted against the total income of the taxpayer for the **year of assessment** in which the accounting period ends ("conventional basis"), e.g. a section 381 claim for a €10,000 loss for the accounts year ended 30 September 2016 is available for 2016. Note, however, the following **exceptions** where the **legal basis** is applied:

- In the first, second and third year of a **commencing** business.
- For any year of assessment immediately **following** a year of assessment where section 381 relief was allowed on the legal basis.
- Where the claimant formally **claims** the legal basis.
- In the year of **cessation** of a business, any relief under section 381 is allowed in respect of the loss applicable to the period from the beginning of the tax year to the date of cessation, e.g. cessation on 30 June 2016, so loss period is 1 January 2016 to 30 June 2016, therefore section 381 claim for 2016.

5.3.3 Effect of Capital Allowances

Capital allowances for a year of assessment may be used to create or augment a loss, provided that such allowances are **first** set-off against any **balancing charge** arising in the year of assessment to which they relate, which are not covered by capital allowances forward.

Example 5.8

Mary White has been in business for many years and prepares annual accounts to 30 June. Her details are as follows:

	€
Tax-adjusted profit for the y/e 30 June 2016	9,000
Capital allowances 2016:	
– Wear and tear allowance	7,000
– Balancing allowances	500
– Balancing charge	3,000
Unutilised capital allowances forward from 2015	9,600
Section 381 Claim 2016	**€**
Tax-adjusted Case I profit y/e 30/06/2016	9,000
Deduct: capital allowances forward (€9,600; limited to actual profit)	(9,000)
Net Case I	**Nil**
Balancing charge 2016	3,000
Deduct: balance of capital allowances forward (€9,600 − €9,000)	(600)
Net balancing charge	2,400
Deduct: wear and tear allowance 2016	(7,000)
Balancing allowances 2016	(500)
Section 381 loss (available to reduce total income for 2016)	**(5,100)**

5.3.4 Order of Relief

A section 381 loss is deemed to first reduce the earned income of the individual, then the unearned income, next the earned income of the spouse/civil partner and finally the unearned income of the spouse/civil partner. This is relevant in calculating the allowance for retirement annuities.

5.3.5 Amount of Relief Taken

A section 381 loss must be used up to the **full amount** of the loss available, or the amount of the **gross income** for the year of assessment, whichever is less. A section 381 loss **cannot** be **partially** used so as to leave sufficient income to cover charges and use up tax credits, or to allow the taxpayer to avoid being taxed only at higher rates. (See **Section 5.3.7** for restrictions on relief.)

5.3.6 Section 381 Relief Claim

Any claim for relief under section 381 must be made, in writing, to the Inspector of Taxes not later than two years after the end of the year of assessment in which the loss is incurred. In practice, the claim is normally made as part of filing the income tax return.

Section 381 relief is not compulsory and is only applied if a claim is made.

5.3.7 Restriction of Section 381 Relief for Non-active Individuals

Section 381B TCA 1997 limits, but does not prevent, the claiming of loss relief by individuals not engaged in a trade in an "active capacity". This section limits the amount of loss relief that can be claimed by an individual under section 381 to **€31,750** (annualised) and is effective from 1 January 2015.

"Active capacity" is stipulated, by section 381C TCA 1997, to be more than **10 hours a week** by an individual personally engaged in the day-to-day management or conduct of the activities of the trade or profession. In addition, the activities of the trade or profession must be carried out on a commercial basis (and not as a loss-making exercise). The restriction does not apply to losses arising from:

- farming;
- marketing gardening;
- a trade consisting of a Lloyd's underwriting business;
- qualifying expenditure for relief for significant buildings and gardens (section 482); or
- capital allowances arising from specified reliefs (including writing down or balancing allowances).

Where an individual carries on two or more trades, the €31,750 limit is an **aggregate** limit between all trades. Any loss not allowable by reference to the new limit will be available to carry forward as a section 382 loss.

Example 5.9

Jack and Jill share profits and losses equally in their catering business. John also works as a hotel manager and devotes approximately eight hours a week to the catering business in which Jill works full time. Their results for the year ended 2016 were as follows:

Trading loss year ended 31 December 2016 €82,500

	Jack	Jill
Trading loss (apportioned 50:50)	€41,250	€41,250
Average hours per week engaged in business	8	40
Loss relief available under section 381	€31,750	€41,250
Loss carry forward (section 382)	€9,500	€Nil

5.3.8 Section 382 Loss Relief

Method of Relief

Section 382 loss relief is available where a person incurs a loss in any trade or profession and it entitles him to carry it **forward** for set-off against the assessable profits (after deduction of capital allowances) of **the same trade or profession**.

The loss must be used, as far as possible, against the first subsequent year's trading profits, and so on.

Loss relief under section 382 is only available where it has not already been effectively relieved under section 381 or by time apportionment in commencement and change of accounting date situations. Losses may be carried forward indefinitely provided the trade which incurred the loss continues to be carried on.

Limitation on Section 382 Loss Relief

A loss can only be carried forward under section 382 provided it has not already been effectively relieved by any one or more of the following:

- section 381 relief; and
- relief by way of apportionment or aggregation of profits and losses (as in a "commencement" situation).

Example 5.10

A trader commenced business on 1 February 2016 and makes up accounts to 30 September each year. His results were as follows:

	Profit/(Loss)
	€
7 months to 30 September 2016	(7,000)
Year to 30 September 2017	7,200
Year to 30 September 2018	6,000

His assessable profits for first three years of assessment are calculated as follows:

Year of Assessment	Basis Period	Assessment
2016	01/02/2016 to 31/12/2016	
	(7,000) + (3/12 × 7,200) = (5,200)	Nil
2017	Year ended 30/09/2017 = 7,200	
	Less: loss forward = (5,200) (Note)	2,000
2018	Year ended 30/09/2018:	
	Profits:	6,000

Note: loss 30/09/2016 (7,000)

Less: utilised
2016 (1,800)
2017 (5,200) (7,000)
(Nil)

5.3.9 Section 382 Relief Arising due to the Third Year Adjustment

As you are aware, the profits assessable in the third year of assessment are based on the basis period of 12 months ending during the year of assessment, but this figure can be reduced by:

Profits assessable in the second tax year
Less: actual profits of the second year of assessment.

Where this deduction is greater than the amount of the original profits assessable for the third year, then the excess is treated as if it were a loss forward under section 382.

The claim for this deduction must be in writing and must be included in the self-assessment tax return for the third year of assessment.

Loss relief in respect of the excess **cannot be claimed under section 381**.

Example 5.11
Derek commenced to trade as a furniture manufacturer on 1 July 2016. His results were as follows:

	Profit
	€
Period 1 July 2016 to 30 June 2017	28,000
Year ended 30 June 2018	7,000
Year ended 30 June 2019	60,000

Computation of Assessable Profits

Year of assessment	Basis period	Amount assessable
		€
2016	01/07/2016 to 31/12/2016	14,000
	(€28,000 × 6/12)	
2017	y/e 30/06/2017	28,000
2018	y/e 30/06/2018 (Note)	Nil

Note:

Amount assessable for second year, i.e. 2017:	28,000
Less: actual profits for 2017:	
(€28,000 × 6/12) + (€7,000 × 6/12) = €14,000 + €3,500	17,500
Excess	10,500
Final 2018 assessment: €7,000 − €10,500	(3,500) i.e nil

The excess of €3,500 is carried forward under section 382 against future trading profits for 2019 onwards.

Questions

Review Questions
(See Suggested Solutions to Review Questions at the end of this textbook.)

Question 5.1

Regina Briers, a sole trader in business for many years, makes up accounts to 30 April each year. During the year ended 30 April 2016, she bought the following second-hand assets:

		€
10/05/2015	Office equipment	€1,000
20/04/2016	Printer	€3,500

The tax written down value of her other assets at 1 January 2016 was as follows:

Motor vehicle (Cat. D) (purchased 01/12/2015 for €35,000)   €10,500

Plant and machinery (purchased 10/06/2014 for €2,500)   €1,875

Requirement
Prepare the capital allowances schedule for 2016.

Question 5.2

Lillian Hanney has practised as a self-employed dentist for many years and makes up accounts to 30 June each year. During the year ended 30 June 2016, she purchased the following assets:

		€
10/07/2015	Chairs for waiting room	1,000
22/02/2016	X-ray machine	4,100

The details of her other assets are as follows:

		Cost	TWDV at 01/01/2016
Year of Acquisition	**Tax Year**	**€**	**€**
Bought y/e 30/06/2013	2013	15,000 (12.5%)	9,375
Bought y/e 30/06/2014	2014	9,000 (12.5%)	6,750

Requirement
Prepare the capital allowances schedule for 2016.

Question 5.3

Barney Connor is a self-employed accountant who has been in business for many years and prepares accounts to 30 September each year. During the year ended 30 September 2016, he purchased the following assets:

		€
29/12/2015	Computers	8,000
01/03/2016	Desktop calculator	120
08/06/2016	Desks	1,800
05/08/2016	Printer ink cartridges	750
20/09/2016	Filing cabinets	2,300
		12,970

The filing cabinets were not delivered until 15 October 2016.
Plant and machinery bought during the y/e 30 September 2012 for €10,000 had a TWDV at 1 January 2016 of €5,000.

Requirement
Prepare the capital allowances schedule for 2016.

Question 5.4

A business commenced on 1 October 2016 and its first accounts were prepared to 30 September 2017. Office equipment was purchased on 12 December 2016 at a cost of €1,000 and immediately put into use.

Requirement

Prepare the capital allowances schedule for the tax years for which the first accounts to 30 September 2017 relate.

Question 5.5

Sean's business commenced trading on 1 June 2016 and the first accounts were prepared to 31 May 2017. Machinery was purchased on 8 December 2016 for €10,000 and immediately put into use.

Requirement

Prepare the capital allowances schedule for the tax years for which the first accounts to 31 May 2017 relate.

Question 5.6

Joan O'Reilly is a bookbinder who commenced business as a sole trader on 1 May 2016. In the year ended 30 April 2017, she purchased the following second-hand assets:

		€
21/05/2016	Bookbinding machine	9,000
10/04/2017	Computer	1,700

Requirement

Prepare the capital allowances schedule for the tax years for which the first accounts to 30 April 2017 relate.

Question 5.7

Cormac Molloy is a self-employed farmer who has been in business for many years and prepares accounts to 31 December each year. Here are his motor vehicle details:

Motor car cost 01/08/2016	€21,000	Emissions Category D
Total estimated annual km	20,000 km	
Total estimated private km	5,000 km	(i.e. 75% of total kms is business)

Requirement

Calculate the capital allowances schedule for the car for 2016.

Question 5.8

Joseph Ryan is a shopkeeper who is in business many years and prepares accounts to 30 June each year. On 10 November 2015 he bought a second-hand car for €27,000 (emissions Category C). The private use is one-third.

Requirement

Calculate the capital allowances schedule and tax written down value of the car for 2016.

Question 5.9

Dan Bell is a doctor who prepares his accounts up to 31 December each year. In the year ended 31 December 2016 he purchased a second-hand car for €25,000 on 20 May 2016 and new office equipment for €1,000 on 1 February 2016. (Assume 70% business use for motor car and emissions Category A.)

Dan Bell also sold equipment on 28 January 2016 for €3,500. The tax written down value of the equipment at 1 January 2016 was €7,500 (cost €15,000). Dan has been in practice for many years.

Requirement

Calculate the capital allowances schedule and the tax written down value of the assets for 2016.

Question 5.10

Joe Bracken is a butcher who prepares annual accounts to 30 September. He has traded for many years. His car is used 70% for business purposes. The cost of his second-hand car (purchased in October 2014) was €27,000. He sold his car in January 2016 for €20,000.

Requirement

Calculate the balancing charge or allowance due on the car.

Question 5.11

Fitzroy carries on a manufacturing business in Dublin. He has been in business for many years and prepares annual accounts to 30 April. During the year ended 30 April 2016 the following transactions took place:

1. Second-hand plant costing €17,000 on 1 May 2006 was sold in February 2016 for €2,200. (Tax written down value at 1 January 2016 was nil.)
2. Plant that was acquired new for €25,000 in November 2008 was sold for €1,500 in January 2016. (Tax written down value at 1 January 2016 was nil.) New plant was acquired for €50,000 on 15 April 2016.
3. On 20 December 2014 he purchased second-hand plant costing €10,000. (Tax written down value at 1 January 2016 was €8,750.)
4. Fitzroy has two lorries. One cost €20,000 on 5 January 2016 and the other €26,000 on 1 December 2008. (Tax written down value at 1 January 2016 was nil.)
5. Fitzroy owns a car that he bought on 16 July 2012 for €25,000 (emissions Category C). One-third of his travel relates to business use.

Fitzroy has no other assets in respect of which capital allowances were claimed.

Requirement

Compute maximum capital allowances for 2016 and 2017, assuming no further additions or disposals are made.

Question 5.12

Sarah commenced to trade as a hairdresser on 1 June 2013. She made the following tax-adjusted profits:

12 months ended 31 May 2014	–	€59,000
12 months to 31 May 2015	–	€46,000
12 months to 31 May 2016	–	€120,000
12 months to 31 May 2017	–	€160,000

During the above periods she bought and put the following assets into use:

1 June 2013	–	General equipment €26,000 (second-hand)
1 September 2013	–	Additional hairdryers €800 (second-hand)
10 April 2014	–	Chairs €1,400 (second-hand)
23 April 2014	–	Car (60% business use) €14,000 (second-hand)

Requirement
Compute assessable profits and associated capital allowances for first four years of assessment.

Question 5.13

Joe Bloggs has operated a newsagent/tobacconist/confectionery shop for many years. He has previously dealt with his own income tax affairs and supplies the following details relating to his business for the year ended 31 December 2016:

	€	€
Gross profit	26,880	
Sale proceeds of old equipment	1,500	
Building society interest received (gross)	<u>210</u>	28,590
Less: Overhead Costs		
Wages to self	5,200	
Motor expenses	1,750	
Light and heat	1,200	
Wages to wife as book-keeper and assistant	1,500	
Wages to other employees	7,600	
Advertising	270	
Christmas gifts to customers (bottles of whiskey)	300	
Depreciation:		
Motor car	500	
Fixtures and equipment	400	
Rates	800	
Covenant to church (net) paid on 31 December 2016	105	
Repairs to yard wall	200	
Painting of shop	450	
New cash register (purchased 1 February 2016)	380	
Deposit on new shelving (paid 10 February 2016)	1,000	
New display freezer (purchased 1 March 2016)	600	
Insurance	375	
Insurance on contents of flat	100	
Hire-purchase instalments on new shelving 8 @ €240	1,920	
Payment to self in lieu of rent	2,000	
Sundry expenses	<u>2,250</u>	
		<u>(28,900)</u>
Loss for year		<u>(310)</u>

Mr Bloggs owns the property which consists of the shop and the flat above the shop where he and his wife live. He estimates that 25% of the heat and light relate to the living accommodation.

The motor car cost €14,000 on 1 January 2011. Mr Bloggs has advised you that business travel accounts for 75% of his annual motoring.

The new shelving costing €5,633, excluding VAT, was purchased under a hire-purchase agreement and you have calculated that interest charges of €376 have arisen before 31 December 2016.

At 1 January 2016, the following were the tax written down values of the equipment and shelving, and the motor car:

	€
Equipment and shelving (cost €2,500 in January 2012 and sold for €1,500 in 2016)	1,250
Motor car	5,250

Requirement

Compute:

(a) Joe Bloggs taxable Case I income for 2016; and
(b) his capital allowances schedule for 2016.

Question 5.14

Mr Goa, a long-established manufacturer, acquired a new industrial building on 30 April 2012 for €160,000 (including land costing €20,000). On 1 May 2013 he sold the building for €190,000 (land being valued at €25,000) to Mrs Statham, who immediately commenced trading from it at that date, also as a manufacturer. Mr Goa's accounts are made up to 30 June each year. Mrs Statham made up her first set of accounts to 30 April 2014 and thereafter on a yearly basis.

Requirement

Calculate the industrial buildings annual allowances for Mr Goa and Mrs Statham for the years of assessment 2012–2016.

Question 5.15

James built and occupied a factory for the purpose of his trade during the year ended 30 June 2016.

His costs were as follows:	€
Site purchase cost	10,000
Site development costs	5,000
Construction of factory	95,000
Construction of adjoining administrative office	10,000
Construction of adjoining showroom	15,000
Total cost	135,000

Requirement

Compute James's industrial buildings annual allowance for 2016.

Question 5.16

Mr Plant carries on a manufacturing trade in Ireland. He prepares his annual accounts to 31 December. During the year ended 31 December 2016, he incurred the following capital expenditure:

1. He purchased new office furniture and equipment on 30 March 2016 for €10,000. The items involved were brought into use immediately.
2. He purchased a new truck on 30 September 2016 for €25,000 for the purposes of the trade.
3. On 30 November 2016, he placed deposits on two items of machinery:
   (a) €5,000 on a used milling machine for delivery on 31 January 2017; and
   (b) €4,000 on a new pump for delivery on 15 February 2017.
4. He purchased a new car on 1 April 2016 for €26,000, which is emissions Category D. The agreed portion of business usage is 75%. He sold his existing car on the same date for €7,500 in a straight cash deal. The car originally cost €26,000 in December 2011. The allowable cost for wear and tear purposes had been restricted to €24,000.
5. On 15 April 2016 he purchased new machinery for €24,000, which was brought into use immediately. He received a grant of €4,000 on the purchase of the machinery.
6. On 31 July 2016 he purchased a second-hand factory premises for €120,000. The original qualifying cost of the factory premises for capital allowances purposes was €75,000, and the building has a remaining tax life of 15 years. The factory premises were brought into use within three months of the date of purchase.
7. In October 2016 he commenced building an extension to his original factory premises. The expenditure incurred to 31 December 2016 was €60,000 on actual building work and €8,000 on architect's fees. The extension is due to be completed in March 2017. A grant of €10,000 had been received on the expenditure incurred to 31 December 2016.

The situation regarding assets acquired prior to 1 January 2016 is as follows:

	Date of Purchase	Cost €	Tax Written Down Value at 01/01/2016 €
Fixtures and fittings 12.5%	2013	12,000	7,500
Plant and machinery 12.5%	2013	13,500	8,437
Motor car 12.5%	10/12/2011	24,000	9,000
Trucks 12.5%	June 2014	18,750	14,062

Requirement
Compute Mr Plant's capital allowances schedule for 2016.

Question 5.17

Janet has been in business for many years as a manufacturer. She prepares accounts to 31 May each year. During the year ended 31 May 2016, she engaged in an expansion programme. She incurred capital expenditure and received capital sums as follows:

2 June 2015	Sold machinery for €14,000. This machinery had cost €35,000 when purchased. The written down value at the date of sale was nil.
15 June 2015	Purchased new replacement machinery costing €49,000 on which rollover relief was claimed. This machinery qualified for a grant of €10,000.
30 June 2015	Purchased a second-hand industrial building for €220,000. The building had cost the original owner €120,000 to construct in June 2004.
1 August 2015	She sold her office building, which had been located some distance away from the industrial buildings. The office building had cost €20,000 in May 1995. Proceeds received from the sale amounted to €60,000.
31 October 2015	Completed an extension to the industrial building purchased on 30 June.

Details of the expenditure are as follows:

	€
Levelling of site	2,000
Architect's fees	3,000
Offices	6,000
Factory	<u>59,000</u>
	<u>70,000</u>

1 November 2015	Purchased two new cars for sales representatives at a cost of €26,000 each, which are emissions Category C. She partly funded the purchases by trading in a car used by one of the sales representatives for €12,500. That car had cost €24,000 when purchased in June 2011 and had a tax written down value of €12,000 at the date of disposal.
30 May 2016	Purchased a second-hand photocopier at a cost of €2,000. The copier was not put into use until June 2016.

The situation regarding assets bought prior to 1 June 2015 is as follows:

	Date of Purchase	Cost €	Tax Written Down Value at 01/01/2016 €
Plant and machinery (12.5%)	July 2011	10,000	5,000
Delivery truck (12.5%)	November 2008	17,000	2,125
Motor vehicles (12.5%)	June 2011	24,000	12,000

Requirement

Compute the capital allowances due for the tax year 2016.

Question 5.18

Linda works part time as a marketing manager for a soft-furnishings company. She also owns and runs, on a commercial basis, a children's clothing business in which she works at least 15 hours a week. Linda's income is as follows:

	€
Trading loss for year ended 30 September 2016	(60,000)
Salary for 2016	80,000

Requirement
Compute Linda's assessable income for 2016.

Question 5.19

Earl Jones works full time as a programmer with a local software company. He also runs a small mail-order business in his spare time and devotes approximately seven hours a week to the business. His income for the tax year 2016 is as follows:

	€
Trading profit/(loss) y/e 30 June 2016	(40,000)
Salary	55,000
Interest on Government Securities	25,000

Requirement
Compute Mr Jones' assessable income for 2016.

Question 5.20

Mr Fool, who has traded for many years, has the following profits and capital allowances:

Profit y/e 31/12/2016	€20,000
Capital allowances 2016	(€37,000)

He also had a balancing charge of €10,000 for 2016.

Requirement
What is Mr Fool's taxable income for 2016?

Question 5.21

John has been in business for many years and prepares annual accounts to 30 September. He has a tax-adjusted profit for year ended 30 September 2016 of €9,000. The capital allowances position for 2016 is:

	€
Wear and tear allowance	7,000
Balancing allowances	500
Balancing charge	(3,000)

Unutilised capital allowances forward from 2015 amount to €9,600.

Requirement
Calculate the capital allowances available to John in 2016.

Question 5.22

Jim's only source of income is his travel agency business, which he has carried on for many years. He prepares annual accounts to 30 June. Recent tax-adjusted results are as follows:

	€
Y/e 30/06/2014 tax-adjusted loss	(18,000)
Y/e 30/06/2015 tax-adjusted profit	17,000
Y/e 30/06/2016 tax-adjusted profit	50,000

Jim is single.

Requirement

Calculate Jim's assessments for all years, claiming relief in the earliest possible year.

Question 5.23

Basil Bond has the following income:

	Tax Year		
	2014	**2015**	**2016**
	€	€	€
Rents	20,000	30,000	25,000
Irish taxed interest (gross)	1,000	1,200	1,200
Trading profit/(loss) for y/e 30 September in tax year	80,000	(37,000)	45,000

The above sources of income have existed for many years.

Requirement

Calculate the assessable income for 2014 to 2016 inclusive, claiming optimum relief for losses.

Tax Credits and Reliefs and Charges on Income

Learning Objectives

In this chapter you will learn:

- the main income tax credits available to individual taxpayers;
- the manner of granting tax relief at the standard rate and at the marginal rate;
- expenditures which attract tax relief – mortgage interest payments, fees to third-level institutions, etc.;
- the operation of tax relief at source;
- the concept of charges on income and the granting of tax relief for the payment of charges; and
- special tax incentive-based reliefs.

6.1 Introduction

Prior to 6 April 1999, an individual was entitled to personal allowances, which were deductions allowable against **income** when calculating taxable income. FA 1999 commenced the process of giving these allowances as **credits** against **income tax liabilities** instead of **deductions** against **income**. A full tax credit system was introduced with effect from 6 April 2001, where every €1,000 of a personal tax allowance is now equivalent to a **tax credit** of €200, i.e. the tax allowance at the standard rate of 20%.

However, it must be noted that some reliefs are still given as a **deduction from income** and, therefore, obtain tax relief at the marginal rate, i.e. 40% for 2016 (2014: 41%).

There are three methods of granting tax relief for reliefs relating to personal status, expenses incurred or source of income:

1. Non-refundable tax credit – related to personal circumstances, e.g. married tax credit **or** related to expenses incurred, e.g. rent paid.
2. Refundable tax credit, e.g. Dividend Withholding Tax.
3. Deduction from income source (e.g. pension) **or** deduction from total income (e.g. employment of carer for an incapacitated person).

As a general rule, the taxpayer must be **tax resident** in Ireland before tax credits are given. **Non-refundable** tax credits **cannot** reduce the tax due **below zero**, **nor** can they **reduce** the tax payable on **charges on income** (e.g. covenants).

Refundable/Non-refundable Tax Credits

Generally, credits for tax withheld from income are refundable (e.g. PAYE, DWT), whereas all other tax credits (e.g. basic personal tax credits, incapacitated child, home-carer, etc.) are not refundable. However, DIRT is only repayable in certain circumstances: where the individual is not liable, or is not fully liable, to income tax **and** is aged 65 years or over in the tax year **or** became permanently unable to maintain himself by reason of mental or physical infirmity.

6.2 Personal Tax Credits

6.2.1 Introduction

Personal tax credits are credits to which an individual is entitled depending on their personal circumstances, e.g. married, civil partner, single, widowed, employed, etc. The amount of the qualifying credit is the same for each individual.

6.2.2 Chart of Personal Tax Credits

Description	Tax Year 2015 €	Tax Year 2016 €
Single Person	1,650	1,650
Married Couple/Civil Partners	3,300	3,300
Widowed Person/Surviving Civil Partner – in the year of bereavement	3,300	3,300
Widowed Person/Surviving Civil Partner in the years following the year of bereavement: – without dependent children – with dependent children*	2,190 1,650	2,190 1,650
Single Person Child Carer Credit (additional)	1,650	1,650
Widowed Person/Surviving Civil Partner – Parent (additional) — First year after bereavement — Second year after bereavement — Third year after bereavement — Fourth year after bereavement — Fifth year after bereavement	3,600 3,150 2,700 2,250 1,800	3,600 3,150 2,700 2,250 1,800
Employee (PAYE) Tax Credit	1,650	1,650
Earned Income Tax Credit	0	550
Blind Person Both Spouses/Civil Partners Blind Guide Dog Allowance**	1,650 3,300 825	1,650 3,300 825
Age Credit (65 years and over) – Single/Widowed Person/Surviving Civil Partner – Married/Civil Partners	245 490	245 490
Incapacitated Child	3,300	3,300
Dependent Relative – Income limit	70 13,904	70 14,060
Home Carer – Income limit lower – Income limit upper	810 5,080 6,700	1,000 7,200 9,200

* Also entitled to Single Person Child Carer Credit.
** Standard rate @ 20%.

6.2.3 Basic Personal Tax Credits

The basic personal tax credits are determined by the marital or civil partnership status of the taxpayer.

Single Tax Credit
This credit is available to individuals, other than married/civil partners or widowed.

Married/Civil Partners' Tax Credit
This is available for a year of assessment where:

- a married couple (including married same-sex couples) or civil partners are jointly assessed; or
- where the couple are living apart and one party, in the year of assessment, is wholly or mainly maintained by the other, and that person is not entitled to deduct any legally enforceable maintenance payments to the other when computing his or her total income for the year of assessment.

Widowed/Surviving Civil Partner Tax Credit
This is available to a widowed person or a surviving civil partner and varies depending on whether there are dependent children and the year of the bereavement.

1. Widowed Person/Surviving Civil Partner Without Dependent Children
A widowed person/surviving civil partner without a dependent child will get the Widowed Person/Surviving Civil Partner Tax Credit in the year of bereavement **(2016: €3,300)**.
    For subsequent years the person will receive the Widowed Person/Surviving Civil Partner (without dependent children) Tax Credit **(2016: €2,190)**.

2. Widowed Person/Surviving Civil Partner With Dependent Children
A widowed person/surviving civil partner with a dependent child will get the Widowed Person/Surviving Civil Partner Tax Credit in the year of bereavement **(2016: €3,300)**.
    For subsequent years, as long as the person has dependent children, the person will get the Widowed Person/Surviving Civil Partner (with dependent children) Tax Credit **(2016: €1,650) and** the Single Person Child Carer Credit **(2016: €1,650)**.
    In addition, there is a Widowed Person/Surviving Civil Partner – **Parent** Tax Credit available for the **first five years** after the year of death as follows:

- €3,600 in the first year after bereavement
- €3,150 in the second year after bereavement
- €2,700 in the third year after bereavement
- €2,250 in the fourth year after bereavement
- €1,800 in the fifth year after bereavement.

A widowed person/surviving civil partner with a dependent child who is cohabiting with a partner is **not entitled** to the allowances available for persons with a dependent child, but will qualify for the Widowed/Surviving Civil Partner (without dependent children) Tax Credit **(2016: €2,190)**.

A "qualifying child" for the purpose of this allowance is a child who:

- is born in the year of assessment; **or**
- is a child of the claimant, or a child in the custody of the claimant, who is maintained by the claimant at the claimant's own expense for the whole or part of the year of assessment; **or**
- is **under 18 years** at the start of the year of assessment; **or**
- if **over 18 years** at the start of the year of assessment:

- is receiving full-time education at an educational establishment or is in full-time training with an employer for a trade or profession, **or**
- is permanently incapacitated by reason of mental or physical infirmity and, if he or she has reached 21 years of age, was so incapacitated before reaching that age.

"Child" includes a stepchild, a child whose parents have not married, and an adopted child.

Single Person Child Carer Credit

The Single Person Child Carer Credit (SPCCC) replaced the **One-Parent Family Credit** on **1 January 2014**. This is a tax credit for single people who are caring for a "qualifying child" (see above) on their own. The credit is available to the **primary claimant**, i.e. the individual with whom the qualifying child resides for the whole, or greater part, of the year. It is possible for a qualifying primary claimant to **surrender** his or her entitlement to the credit in favour of another qualifying individual, i.e. a **secondary claimant.**

The credit cannot be claimed where any claimant (either primary or secondary) is:

- jointly assessed for tax, i.e. as a married person or civil partner;
- married or in a civil partnership (unless separated);
- cohabiting, **or**
- a widow/widower/surviving civil partner in the year of bereavement;
- in the case of a secondary claimant, the qualifying child must live with the claimant for **at least 100 days** in the year (not required to be consecutive).

Unlike the previous One-Parent Family Credit only **one** Single Person Child Carer Credit is available to **either** the primary claimant **or** the secondary claimant, irrespective of the number of children and the time spent with each parent. The person in receipt of the SPCCC is also entitled to the increased single standard rate tax band of €37,800.

Example 6.1

Jenny is divorced from Colin and is the primary carer of their three children, Sarah, James and Ben. The children spend weekends and some holidays with Colin (more than 100 days in a year). Both Jenny and Colin are single and are not cohabiting. Their non-refundable tax credits for 2016 are as follows:

	Jenny	Colin
Single Tax Credit	€1,650	€1,650
Single Person Child Carer Credit	€1,650	NIL
Standard rate tax band	€37,800	€33,800

Jenny agrees to surrender her entitlement to SPCCC to Colin. Their non-refundable tax credits for 2016 are:

	Jenny	Colin
Single Tax Credit	€1,650	€1,650
Single Person Child Carer Credit	NIL	€1,650
Standard rate tax band	€33,800	€37,800

Where a primary claimant surrenders his or her entitlement to the tax credit, **two or more** secondary claimants can claim the credit provided they satisfy the requirements above.

Example 6.2

Susan, who is single, has two children, Jack and Patrick, and is a qualifying primary claimant. Jack resides with his father, Seán, for more than 100 days in the year; Patrick resides with his father, Stephen, for more than 100 days in a year. If Susan surrenders her entitlement to SPCCC, both Seán and Stephen can each claim SPCCC provided they satisfy all the other criteria.

continued overleaf

	Susan	Seán	Patrick
Single Tax Credit	€1,650	€1,650	€1,650
Single Person Child Carer Tax Credit	NIL	€1,650	€1,650
Standard rate tax band	€33,800	€37,800	€37,800

If Susan does not surrender her entitlement to SPCCC, their credits for 2016 are as follows:

	Susan	Seán	Patrick
Single Tax Credit	€1,650	€1,650	€1,650
Single Person Child Carer Tax Credit	€1,650	NIL	NIL
Standard rate tax band	€37,800	€33,800	€33,800

Note that a primary claimant is only entitled to **one credit** regardless of the number of qualifying children residing with him or her and cannot surrender the credit in respect of one child and retain the credit in respect of other children. Where, however, there is more than one child between the claimants, both parents can make a claim as the primary claimant in respect of one child each, provided the child is not the subject of a claim by any other person.

Example 6.3

Sharon and David are separated and have two children: Lucy, who lives full time with her mother, and Eoin who lives full time with David.

Sharon is the primary claimant for Lucy and is entitled to SPCCC and the increased single standard rate tax band, while David is the primary claimant for Eoin so he too is entitled to SPCCC and the increased tax band.

Example 6.4

Mary is a widow since 2011 with one dependent child. She has not remarried and lives alone with her child. What are her non-refundable tax credits (NRTC) for 2016?

	€
Widowed person – with dependent children	1,650
Single Person Child Carer Credit	1,650
Widowed parent 5th year	1,800
Total NRTC 2016	5,100

The credit must be claimed in writing by submitting to Revenue either claim form SPCC1 (primary claimant) or SPCC2 (secondary claimant).

6.2.4 Employee (PAYE) Tax Credit

An individual who is in **receipt of emoluments** chargeable under Schedule E and subject to the PAYE system is entitled to this tax credit. In the case of joint assessment and where **each** spouse/civil partner is in employment, the credit is available to each spouse/civil partner.

The employee tax credit **cannot exceed** the individual's Schedule E income at the standard rate of tax, i.e. if the individual's salary for 2016 is €1,000, the employee tax credit would be limited to €200 (€1,000 @ 20%).

An individual may also receive the employee tax credit where they receive income from an employment held **outside the State** and where the income has been subject to a tax deduction system similar to the Irish PAYE system, e.g. an Irish individual, living in Dundalk and working in Newry for a UK employer, receives his salary after deduction of UK PAYE. The individual will be entitled to the employee tax credit.

The employee tax credit is **not applicable** to emoluments paid:

- by a company to **proprietary directors**, their spouses/civil partners or children (see below). A "proprietary director" means a director of a company who is the beneficial owner of, or able to control, either directly or indirectly, more than 15% of the ordinary share capital of a company;
- by a person to their spouse, civil partner or child;
- by a partnership to the spouse, civil partner or child of one of the partners.

Children of proprietary directors who are employees in the business will only get the employee tax credit where:

- the child is required to devote, throughout the tax year, substantially the whole of their time to the duties of the employment; **and**
- the child's gross salary from the employment is at least €4,572; **and**
- the child is in insurable employment for PRSI; **and**
- PAYE is operated on the child's salary.

Note that proprietary directors and/or their spouses/civil partners or children may be entitled to the earned income tax credit available from 1 January 2016.

6.2.5 Earned Income Tax Credit

Section 3 FA 2015 introduced the earned income tax credit applicable from **1 January 2016**. The credit is available to those with earned income who are not entitled to the PAYE tax credit of €1,650, or can only claim a portion of the PAYE tax credit. "Earned income" can generally be taken to mean income charged under Cases I and II of Schedule D (i.e. trading or professional income) and income earned under Schedule E that does not attract the PAYE tax credit (e.g. emoluments of proprietary directors).

The credit for 2016 is the **lower** of either:

- 20% of the earned income; or
- €550.

If the individual is also entitled to a portion of the PAYE tax credit, the aggregate PAYE tax credit and earned income tax credit cannot exceed €1,650. Where joint assessment applies, a separate tax credit may be due in respect of each spouse's individual income.

Example 6.5

Joe is a proprietary director of GS Games Ltd and earned €85,000 in 2016. His wife Susan, who took early retirement, has a PAYE pension of €6,200 and Schedule D Case I income of €12,000. They are jointly assessed. Calculate their tax liability for 2016.

Income		€	€
Joe: Schedule E salary			85,000
Susan: Schedule E pension			6,200
Case I Schedule D			12,000
Taxable income			103,200
Tax Calculation			
€61,000 (€42,800 + €18,200)	@ 20% =	12,200	
€42,200 Balance	@ 40% =	16,880	29,080
€103,200			
Less: non-refundable tax credits:		4,080	12,640
Basic personal tax credit (married)		3,300	
Employee tax credit – Susan (€6,200 @ 20%)		1,240	
Earned income tax credit – Joe (maximum)		550	
Earned income tax credit – Susan (€1,650 – €1,240)		410	(5,500)
Tax liability			**23,580**

6.2.6 Blind Person's Tax Credit

A blind person is entitled to a "blind person's tax credit". If a married couple or civil partners are both blind, they are entitled to double the tax credit.

An individual does not have to be completely blind to obtain the credit. A medical certificate showing the degree of blindness is required before the credit will be granted.

An additional allowance (deductible from total income) is available if an individual or the individual's spouse/civil partner has a guide dog and is a registered owner with the Irish Guide Dog Association. The amount of the additional credit is €825 at the standard rate.

6.2.7 Age Tax Credit

In addition to a basic personal tax credit, an individual may claim the "age tax credit" where he, or his spouse/civil partner, is at least 65 years of age during the year of assessment. The married couple's/civil partners' age tax credit may be claimed where only one of the couple is aged 65 or more.

6.2.8 Incapacitated Child Tax Credit

Where an individual has a "qualifying child" living with him at any time during the year, he is entitled to an "incapacitated child tax credit".

In this context, a "qualifying child" is one who:

- is **under** the age of 18 and is permanently incapacitated by reason of mental or physical infirmity; **or**
- **if over** the age of 18, is permanently incapacitated by reason of mental or physical infirmity from maintaining himself, and was so before he reached 21 years of age, **or** was in full-time education/training with an employer when he became so incapacitated; **and**
- is a child of the claimant or, if not such a child, is in the custody of the claimant, and is maintained by the claimant at the claimant's own expense for the whole or part of the year in question.

"Child" includes a stepchild, an adopted child, a child whose parents have not been married or an informally adopted child or any child of whom a person has custody. The credit is available for **each qualifying** child.

Where two or more persons are entitled to relief in respect of the same child, i.e. where both parents maintain the child jointly, the tax credit is **allocated among** those persons by reference to the amount which each spends in maintaining the child.

Qualifying Incapacities

The incapacity of the child must be such that it permanently prevents the child from being able, in the long term (i.e. when over 18 years of age), to maintain himself/herself independently. If the incapacity can be corrected or relieved by the use of any treatment, device, medication or therapy (e.g. coeliac disease, diabetes, hearing impairment which can be corrected by a hearing aid, etc.), the child will not be regarded as permanently incapacitated for the purposes of this relief.

The following are examples of disabilities which are regarded as permanently incapacitating:
cystic fibrosis, spina bifida, blindness, deafness, Down's syndrome, spastic paralysis, certain forms of schizophrenia, acute autism (this list is not exhaustive).

Note that a person who is entitled to an incapacitated child tax credit is not entitled to a dependent relative tax credit (see below) in respect of the same child.

6.2.9 *Dependent Relative Tax Credit*

An individual who proves that they maintains at their own expense a "dependent relative" is entitled to a "dependent relative tax credit". A "dependent relative" is defined as:

- a relative of the claimant or of their spouse/civil partner who is incapacitated by old age or infirmity from maintaining themselves; **or**
- the widowed father or widowed mother of the claimant or the claimant's spouse/civil partner, whether incapacitated or not; **or**
- the son or daughter of the claimant who lives with the claimant and upon whom they are dependent, by reason of old age or infirmity.

If the income of the dependent relative exceeds the specified limit (2016: €14,060), the dependent relative tax credit is not available.

Where two or more persons jointly maintain a dependent relative, the tax credit is allocated between them in proportion to the amount which each spends in maintaining the relative.

6.2.10 *Home Carer Tax Credit*

This is claimable by a married couple or civil partners who are jointly assessed where one spouse/civil partner (i.e. the home carer) works in the home caring for one or more dependent persons. The tax credit will be granted where:

- the couple are married or civil partners and are **jointly assessed**;
- one or more qualifying persons normally **reside** with the claimant and his/her spouse/civil partner (or, in the case of an aged or incapacitated person, resides nearby within 2 km); and
- the home carer's **income** is not in **excess of €7,200** (2015: €5,080). A reduced tax credit applies where the income is between **€7,200 and €9,200**. In calculating total income, no account is taken of the carer's allowance payable by the Department of Social Protection, but such allowance is a taxable source of income.

A "dependent" person is defined as:

- a child for whom Department of Social Protection Child Benefit is payable, i.e. children under 16 and children up to age 18 in full-time education, **or**
- a person aged 65 years or more in the year, **or**
- an individual who is permanently incapacitated by reason of mental or physical infirmity.

Note: a spouse/civil partner cannot be a "dependent" person.

Only **one** tax credit is given **regardless** of the number of dependent persons being cared for.

For **2016**, if the home carer has total income of **€7,200** (2015: €5,080) or less, the full tax credit is given. If the income of the home carer is in excess of **€7,200**, the tax credit is reduced by **one-half of the excess over the limit**. For example, if the home carer has income of €8,000, a tax credit of €600, i.e. (€1,000 − (€8,000 − €7,200) × ½), may be claimed. If, however, a home carer has income of €9,200, i.e. (€1,000 − (€9,200 − €7,200) × ½), no tax credit is due.

Where the income of the home carer exceeds the permitted limit, the credit **will be granted** for that year if the home carer qualified for the credit in the **immediately preceding** tax year. However, in these circumstances the tax credit granted is **restricted to the tax credit** granted in the previous tax year.

Note that married couples/civil partners **cannot claim** both the home carer's tax credit and the increased standard rate band for dual-income couples, but they can claim whichever of the two is more beneficial.

Example 6.6

Jim and Katie Bloom are jointly assessed and they have two children under the age of 16 years. Jim has a salary of €47,000 and Katie has investment income of €7,800.

Option One: Claim Increased Standard Rate Tax Band 2016	€	€
Taxable Income:		
Jim	47,000	
Katie	<u>7,800</u>	<u>54,800</u>
Taxation:		
€50,600 @ 20% (Jim max. €42,800 + Katie €7,800)	10,120	
<u>€4,200</u> @ 40%	<u>1,680</u>	11,800
€54,800		
Tax Credits		
Married credit	3,300	
Employee credit (Jim)	<u>1,650</u>	<u>(4,950)</u>
Tax liability		**6,850**

Option Two: Claim Home Carer Tax Credit 2016	€	€
Taxable Income:		
Jim	47,000	
Katie	<u>7,800</u>	<u>54,800</u>
Taxation:		
€42,800 @ 20% (Jim max. €42,800 only)	8,560	
<u>€12,000</u> @ 40%	<u>4,800</u>	13,360
€54,800		
Tax Credits		
Married credit	3,300	
Home carer €1,000 – ((€7,800 – €7,200) × 50%)	700	
Employee credit (Jim)	<u>1,650</u>	<u>(5,650)</u>
Tax liability		**7,710**

As their tax liability is lower if the increased standard rate tax band is claimed, Jim and Katie should claim this instead of the home carer tax credit.

A married couple or civil partners, **where both persons have income**, are entitled to a standard rate tax band of up to €67,600. A married couple or civil partners cannot claim **both** the increased standard rate tax band **and** the home carer tax credit. However, they can claim whichever of the two gives them a lower tax liability.

In practice, when calculating tax credits and standard rate cut-off point applicable, Revenue will grant whichever option is more beneficial.

6.2.11 Home Renovation Incentive Scheme

Section 477B TCA 1997 provides for the Home Renovation Incentive (HRI) scheme whereby homeowners can claim a **tax credit of 13.5%** of "qualifying expenditure" on the renovation, repair or improvement of a "qualifying home" by "qualifying contractors" between **25 October 2013 and 31 December 2016**. Finance Act 2015 extended the relief to certain rented residential premises, but only for expenditure carried out between 15 October 2014 to 31 December 2016. Relief may also be available where planning permission is granted up to 31 December 2016 but the work is not completed until 31 March 2017.

Qualifying Expenditure

Expenditure that qualifies for HRI includes payments for the following "works" paid to a qualifying contractor:

- painting and decorating
- rewiring
- plastering
- plumbing
- tiling
- window replacement
- attic conversions
- fitted kitchens
- extensions and garages
- driveways, landscaping and septic tank repair or replacement.

The **VAT** rate on the works must be **13.5%**.

Tax relief can be claimed on expenditure **over €4,405** (excluding VAT) up to a **maximum of €30,000** (excluding VAT). The amount claimed can be based on one total sum or a combination of payments to different qualifying contractors. The qualifying expenditure is reduced by any insurance claim received, or by a multiple of **three times** of any grant received.

Example 6.7

Mary Byrne paid DC Insulating €20,000 (excl. VAT) for external wall insulation in September 2016. She applied for and received a Better Energy Home Scheme grant of €2,700 in November 2016.

Her qualifying expenditure for HRI is:

	€
Paid to DC Insulating	20,000
Less: grant received (€2,700 × 3)	(8,100)
Qualifying expenditure	11,900
Tax credit @ 13.5%	1,606

Qualifying Residence

A "qualifying residence" is a residential premises situated in the State, which the taxpayer must own and live in as their main residence, or a residential premises which the taxpayer has bought and will use as a main home when the works have been completed.

The HRI scheme was extended to certain rental properties owned by individual landlords, but only in relation to expenditure carried out in the period 15 October 2014 to 31 December 2016. The property must be occupied, or will be occupied within six months of completion of the qualifying work, under a tenancy which has been registered with the **Private Residential Tenancies Board** (PRTB). If, as the result of the qualifying work, the residential unit is converted into more than one unit, **each** rental unit will be a qualifying residence and the maximum credit of €4,050 will be available for each unit.

Relief under HRI is **not available** on newly built homes, holiday homes or a complete reconstruction of an uninhabitable house.

Qualifying Contractor

A "qualifying contractor" is one who is registered for VAT and is tax compliant. The contractor must provide, to the homeowner or landlord, evidence of his business name and VAT number (e.g. an invoice or quotation) and either:

- a relevant contracts tax (RCT) rate notification, which should be dated no more than 30 days before the start of the work and show an RCT rate of either zero or 20%; *or*
- a current tax clearance certificate.

Before commencing qualifying work the contractor must enter the following details on the HRI online system:

- contractors name, tax reference number and VAT registration number;
- property ID number (as per the local property tax (LPT) return);
- name of the homeowner making the claim;
- the address of the qualifying property;
- the estimated cost of the work, including the estimate for VAT;
- the estimated duration of the work including the estimated start and end dates;
- if the property is a rental property, and if applicable, the number of units into which the rental property is being converted.

Tax Credit

The tax credit is calculated at **13.5%** on all qualifying expenditure between **€4,405 and €30,000 (excluding VAT)**. The minimum credit available is **€595** and the maximum credit available is **€4,050**. The tax credit is given over the two years following the year in which the work is carried out. For example, a credit of €1,500 for works carried out in 2016 is available in 2017 (€750) and in 2018 (€750).

Example 6.8

John Swan decided to do some renovations to his home and hired a number of contractors to carry out the work.

1. In December 2015 he hired KC Builders to carry out a complete renovation of his kitchen. He paid KC Builders €11,350 (including VAT at 13.5%) in June 2016 when the work was completed. KC Builders is a qualifying contractor who supplied John with a detailed quotation and invoice together with a valid tax clearance certificate.
2. John hired Pat Grout to paint the downstairs rooms and paid him €1,702.50 (including VAT) in September 2016. Pat Grout supplied John with evidence of his business name and VAT number but failed to produce a RCT notification or a tax clearance certificate.

John can claim the following tax credit in January 2017:

	€
KC Builders: €10,000 @ 13.5%	1,350
Pat Grout (*Note*)	NIL
Total tax credit	1,350
Split:	
2017	675
2018	675

Note: as Pat Grout failed to produce a RCT notification or a valid tax clearance certificate, he is not considered a qualifying contractor for the purposes of the HRI scheme.

Procedure to Claim Tax Credit

The qualifying contractor(s) must enter the details of the qualifying works carried out on behalf of the taxpayer on the **electronic HRI system within 28 days** of the completion of the works. The taxpayer cannot claim the HRI tax credit if the works and payments details are not on the electronic HRI system. The qualifying contractor will require details of the **Property ID** (from local property tax correspondence) in order to enter the HRI details. The taxpayer can check the HRI system to ensure that the contractor has entered all the details of the works carried out.

For **homeowners** the claim for the tax credit is made **electronically** by the taxpayer and will be included in the taxpayer's tax credits over the next two years. Where a taxpayer cannot use all of the HRI tax credit in one year, it can be **carried forward** as a tax credit to the following years.

For **landlords** qualifying under the scheme, the claim is also made electronically from **January 2016**. Expenditure on rented accommodation for the period 15 October 2014 to December 2014 is deemed to be carried out in 2015, consequently any resultant tax credit **cannot** be claimed until 2016. Unlike homeowners, if the landlord does not have a tax liability in the year of assessment, the HRI tax credit cannot be carried forward as a tax credit to subsequent years.

6.3 Tax Reliefs at the Standard Rate

6.3.1 Introduction

These reliefs are available in the same manner as the personal tax credits at **Section 6.2**, but the amounts of the relief **vary** depending on the expenditure involved. These reliefs are granted at the standard rate of tax and are given as a credit against the income tax liability.

6.3.2 Medical Insurance

Relief is available for premiums, paid to an authorised insurer or society, in respect of insurance to provide for the payment of actual medical expenses of the individual, his/her spouse/civil partner and dependants.

Relief is also available in respect of premiums paid on **dental insurance** policies for non-routine dental treatment provided by those insurers who only provide dental insurance.

The relief is granted **"at source"**, i.e. the amount of the gross premium is **reduced** by the **tax credit** available (20%). The medical insurance company **reclaims the 20% tax** from Revenue and the taxpayer **does not** need to make a separate claim for relief.

Section 470 TCA 1997 introduced a limit to the amount of relief that can be claimed. The relief is limited to:

- 20% of the premium paid up to a maximum of **€1,000** per adult, per policy;
- 20% of the premium paid up to a maximum of **€500** per child, per policy.

The definition of a "child" for the purposes of this relief has been amended to include an individual, **under the age of 21**, who is entitled to a health insurance contract at a reduced child rate. The maximum credit of €1,000 at the 20% rate is available for all adults aged 21 years and over, regardless of whether they are in full-time education or whether or not they are paying a child-reduced rate of premium.

Where an employer pays medical insurance premiums for an employee, the employee is treated as if they had received additional salary equal to the gross medical insurance premium payable. In these circumstances, the employer pays the premium to the medical insurer net of the tax credit allowable, and pays the tax deducted (tax relief at source (TRS)) to Revenue. The employee must then claim a tax credit for this tax deducted.

Example 6.9

Monica, aged 25, is an employee of Scalp Ltd and earned €50,000 (PAYE paid €9,900) in 2016. Scalp Ltd also paid her medical insurance of €1,200 net to VHI.

Income:		€	€
Schedule E salary			50,000
Benefit in kind:			
Medical insurance (net paid to VHI)		1,200	
Tax credit (TRS paid to Revenue)		200	
Medical insurance (gross)			1,400
Taxable income			51,400

Tax Calculation:	€		
€33,800 @ 20%	6,760		
€17,600 @ 40%	7,040	13,800	
€51,400			
Less: Non-refundable Tax Credits:			
Basic personal tax credit		1,650	
Employee tax credit		1,650	
Medical insurance: €1,000 @ 20%		200	(3,500)
Tax liability			10,300
Deduct: PAYE paid			(9,900)
Net tax payable			**400**

6.3.3 Rent Paid by Certain Tenants

Tax relief may be claimed by tenants for rent paid in respect of rented residential accommodation, which is their sole or main residence, except where the tenant is a child of the landlord. However, section 14 FA 2011 provided for the phasing out of this relief, over the period **2011 to 2017**, for individuals who were renting a property at **7 December 2010**; and the **abolition** of relief to new claimants or those claimants who were not tenants at 7 December 2010.

The tax credit is equal to the **lower** of the **actual rent paid** at the standard rate of tax **or** the **specified limit** at the standard rate of tax.

The "specified limits" for **2016** are as follows:

	Rent Limit 2016	Max. Tax Credit 2016
	€	€
Person **under** 55 years:		
Married/Widowed/Civil Partners	800	160
Single	400	80
Person **over** 55 years:		
Married/Widowed/Civil Partners	1,600	240
Single	400	120

For years **2017 to 2018** the "specified limits" will be as follows:

Year	Married/Widowed/Civil Partners under 55 years	Single under 55 years	Married/Widowed/Civil Partners over 55 years	Single over 55 years
	€	€	€	€
2017	400	200	800	400
2018	Nil	Nil	Nil	Nil

Any claim to relief for rent paid must be supported by the following:

1. A Revenue form (**Form Rent 1**) completed by the tenant which sets out:
   (a) tenant's name, address and income tax reference number;
   (b) the name, address and tax reference number of the landlord;
   (c) the address of the rented premises; and
   (d) full details of the tenancy concerned; **and**

2. A receipt from the landlord showing:
   (a) the tenant's name and address;
   (b) the name, address and tax reference number of the landlord;
   (c) the amount of rent paid in the year of assessment;
   (d) the period in respect of which the rent was paid; and
   (e) the amount of rent payable each month.

"**Rent**" which qualifies for the relief is limited to the amount paid in return for the **use** of the premises and adjoining garden or grounds. It **does not** include the following:

- amounts paid for repairs or maintenance;
- amounts paid for the provision of goods and services, e.g. furniture in a furnished accommodation letting; or
- any payment made which has a right of reimbursement, e.g. a deposit.

6.3.4 Fees Paid for Third-level Education and Training Courses

Third-level Education
Relief is available, under **section 473A TCA 1997**, for "qualifying fees" paid in the tax year in respect of an "approved course" to an "approved college" on behalf of the individual or any other person. (There does not need to be a defined relationship between the taxpayer and the subject of the tax relief claim.)

"Qualifying fees" are fees in respect of tuition (including the Student Contribution) of an "approved course", net of any grant or scholarship.

"Approved college" means a college/university in the State or in the EU or in a non-EU Member State which is maintained/assisted by public funds of that country. (See Revenue website www.revenue.ie for a full list of colleges.)

An "approved course" is:

- a full-time or part-time undergraduate course which is of at least two academic years' duration; or
- a postgraduate course of at least one year's duration, but not exceeding four years. This course must lead to a postgraduate award based on exam and/or thesis.

Relief is available on qualifying fees per course, per academic year, e.g. if an individual pays qualifying fees for two students attending college in an academic year, he is entitled to relief up to the maximum limit for **each** of these students.

The maximum level of qualifying fees (including the Student Contribution) per academic year is **€7,000** per course, per student. Where fees, in respect of which relief has been claimed, are fully or partly refunded, the taxpayer must notify Revenue within **21 days**.

Relief is **not** available in respect of:

- Any part of the qualifying fees that are, or will be, met directly or indirectly by grants, scholarships, an employer or otherwise.
- Administration, registration or examination fees.
- For **2015 and subsequent years**, the **first €3,000** (2014: €2,750) of all fees where **any one** of the students is a **full-time** student.
- For **2015 and subsequent years**, the **first €1,500** (2014: €1,375) of all fees where **all** of the students are **part-time**.

Example 6.9

Mary Weary has three children in third-level education in 2016. Details of fees paid for 2016 are as follows:

Student	Student Contribution	Tuition Fees	Total
April (Full-time)	€3,000	Nil	€3,000
Seán (Full-time)	€3,000	€6,000	€9,000
Kate (Part-time)	€1,500	€3,000	€4,500

Tax Relief Available:

April	€3,000
Seán (max.)	€7,000
Kate	€4,500
Less: disallowed	(€3,000)
Allowable	€11,500
Relief @ 20%	€2,300

Training Courses

Relief is given for tuition fees paid for certain approved training courses, of less than two years' duration, in the areas of **information technology** and **foreign languages**. For 2016, relief applies to fees ranging from €315 to €1,270. The relief is given as an additional tax credit equal to the fees paid, subject to the €1,270 maximum, at the standard rate of tax.

The course must result in the awarding of a certificate of competence, not just a certificate of attendance.

6.3.5 Home Loan Interest Payments

Since 1 January 2002, tax relief for home mortgage interest is granted **at source** by the mortgage lender **(tax relief at source (TRS))**. Prior to this, the relief was only given through the tax credit system. Tax credits are **still available** for qualifying loans from **non-TRS** sources. Under TRS, the mortgage lender gives the relief either in the form of a reduced monthly mortgage payment or a credit to the borrower's funding account.

All individuals who have a "qualifying mortgage" on their main residence are entitled to apply to Revenue to have the relief on the **interest paid** on their qualifying mortgage **applied at source** by the lender.

Interest Paid/Credited

Prior to **1 January 2014**, many lenders calculated TRS based on the amount of interest charged to a mortgage account irrespective of whether or not that interest was paid by the borrower. From **1 January 2014** lenders are obliged to grant the TRS based on the amount of interest **actually paid** by the borrower in the year. Borrowers who pay the correct mortgage amount (be it capital and interest or interest only) are not affected, but where borrowers are in default or do not pay the full amount of the mortgage repayment, the TRS is reduced to reflect the actual amount paid.

Qualifying Mortgage

A "qualifying mortgage" is a secured loan, used to purchase, repair, develop or improve an individual's **sole or main** residence, which must be situated in the State or an EEA State. An individual can also claim relief in respect of a mortgage paid in respect of a separated/divorced spouse/civil partner and/or a dependent relative for whom a dependent relative tax credit is claimed. Mortgage interest relief **cannot** be claimed in respect of an investment property.

Mortgage Interest Relief Ceilings

- Mortgages taken out **prior to 1 January 2004** are no longer eligible for mortgage interest relief. However, top-up loans/equity release loans taken out since 1 January 2004 on these pre-2004 loans may be eligible for mortgage interest relief, provided they adhere to the "qualifying mortgage" criteria above.
- Mortgages taken out **from 1 January 2004 to 31 December 2012**, subject to qualifying mortgage criteria, are eligible for mortgage interest relief until **31 December 2017**.
- Mortgages taken out **after 31 December 2012** will **not qualify** for mortgage interest relief.

For mortgage interest relief, a distinction is made between **first-time buyers** and **non-first-time buyers**. It is also important to note that the upper limits relief applies for the tax year in which the mortgage was taken out (not when the taxpayer first claimed the relief), plus six subsequent qualifying tax years. Note also that after year seven, the rates are those that apply to non-first-time buyers.

Table 1: Interest Ceilings or Upper Limits for First-time Buyers							
Status	Ceiling	Rate of Relief Years 1 & 2	Max. relief available	Rate of Relief Years 3, 4 & 5	Max. relief available	Rate of Relief Years 6 & 7	Max. relief available
Single	€10,000	@ 25%	€2,500	@ 22.5%	€2,250	@ 20%	€2,000
Married/Widowed/ Civil Partnership	€20,000	@ 25%	€5,000	@ 22.5%	€4,500	@ 20%	€4,000

Table 2: Interest Ceilings or Upper Limits for Non-first-time Buyers			
Status	Ceiling	Rate of Relief	Max. relief available
Single	€3,000	@ 15%	€450
Married/Widowed/Civil Partnership	€6,000	@ 15%	€900

Notwithstanding the rates of tax relief mentioned above, for individuals who purchased their first principal private residence on or **after 1 January 2004 and on or before 31 December 2008**, the rate of tax relief will be **30%** of the interest paid for the tax years **2016 to 2017**.

Table 3: Interest Ceilings for First-time Buyers for Tax Years 2016–2017

Year loan taken out	2016 Ceiling @ Rate	2017 Ceiling @ Rate
2012	S: €10K @ 22.5% M/W/CP: €20K @ 22.5%	S: €10K @ 20% M/W/CP: €20K @ 20%
2011	S: €10K @ 20% M/W/CP: €20K @ 20%	S: €10K @ 20% M/W/CP: €20K @ 20%
2010	S: €10K @ 20% M/W/CP: €20K @ 20%	S: €3K @ 15% M/W/CP: €6K @ 15%
2009	S: €3K @ 15% M/W/CP: €6K @ 15%	S: €3K @ 15% M/W/CP: €6K @ 15%
2008	S: €3K @ 30% M/W/CP: €6K @ 30%	S: €3K @ 30% M/W/CP: €6K @ 30%
2007	S: €3K @ 30% M/W/CP: €6K @ 30%	S: €3K @ 30% M/W/CP: €6K @ 30%
2006	S: €3K @ 30% M/W/CP: €6K @ 30%	S: €3K @ 30% M/W/CP: €6K @ 30%
2005	S: €3K @ 30% M/W/CP: €6K @ 30%	S: €3K @ 30% M/W/CP: €6K @ 30%
2004	S: €3K @ 30% M/W/CP: €6K @ 30%	S: €3K @ 30% M/W/CP: €6K @ 30%

Table 4: Interest Ceilings for Non-first-time Buyers for Tax Years 2016–2017

Year loan taken out	2016 Ceiling @ Rate	2017 Ceiling @ Rate
2012	S: €3K @ 15% M/W/CP: €6K @ 15%	S: €3K @ 15% M/W/CP: €6K @ 15%
2011	S: €3K @ 15% M/W/CP: €6K @ 15%	S: €3K @ 15% M/W/CP: €6K @ 15%
2010	S: €3K @ 15% M/W/CP: €6K @ 15%	S: €3K @ 15% M/W/CP: €6K @ 15%
2009	S: €3K @ 15% M/W/CP: €6K @ 15%	S: €3K @ 15% M/W/CP: €6K @ 15%
2008	S: €3K @ 15% M/W/CP: €6K @ 15%	S: €3K @ 15% M/W/CP: €6K @ 15%
2007	S: €3K @ 15% M/W/CP: €6K @ 15%	S: €3K @ 15% M/W/CP: €6K @ 15%
2006	S: €3K @ 15% M/W/CP: €6K @ 15%	S: €3K @ 15% M/W/CP: €6K @ 15%
2005	S: €3K @ 15% M/W/CP: €6K @ 15%	S: €3K @ 15% M/W/CP: €6K @ 15%
2004	S: €3K @ 15% M/W/CP: €6K @ 15%	S: €3K @ 15% M/W/CP: €6K @ 15%

Although TRS is **not available** for the following loans, a non-refundable tax credit is available on the interest payable at the standard tax rate (subject to the same interest limits as TRS):

- loans to acquire a residence that qualifies for mortgage interest relief in an EEA State;
- non-mortgage loans, e.g. term loans for home improvements; and
- loans from non-TRS lenders, e.g. employers or foreign banks.

Example 6.11

Sean Smith, a single man, received a loan from his employer (not a bank) to assist with the purchase in 2012 of his first residence. He paid interest of €10,500 in 2016.

His non-refundable tax credit for 2016 is limited to the **lower** of the actual interest paid @ 22.5% (year 5) **or** the €10,000 limit for a first-time buyer.

Interest paid: €10,500

Mortgage allowance restricted to:　　　　€2,250 (€10,000 × 22.5%)

6.3.6   Medical Expenses

Section 469 TCA 1997 provides for relief by way of tax credit at the standard rate (with the exception of nursing home expenses, which may be claimed at the marginal rate – see **Section 6.4.3**), in respect of **un-reimbursed** medical expenses incurred by the individual on their **own behalf**, or **on behalf of others**.

There is no requirement for a defined relationship between the taxpayer and the subject of the tax relief claim.

"Medical expenses" include expenses incurred on:

- Cost of doctors' and consultants' fees.
- Items/treatments prescribed by a doctor/consultant (see below).
- Maintenance or treatment in a hospital or other location (whether in Ireland or not) where such expenses were **necessarily** incurred for the services of a medical practitioner or diagnostic procedures carried out on the advice of a medical practitioner.
- Physiotherapy or orthoptic treatments prescribed by a practitioner.
- Costs of speech and language therapy carried out by a speech and language therapist for a qualifying child.
- Transport by ambulance.
- Costs of educational psychological assessments carried out by an educational psychologist for a qualifying child.
- Certain items of expenditure in respect of a child suffering from a serious life-threatening illness (including relief for mileage to/from hospital at €0.17 per km, relief for some telephone costs, overnight accommodation costs for parents, hygiene products and special clothing).
- Kidney patients' expenses (including relief for mileage to/from hospital at €0.17 per km, and, depending on whether the patient uses hospital dialysis, home dialysis or CAPD, relief for electricity, telephone and laundry costs up to a maximum amount).
- Specialised dental treatment – (see below).
- Routine maternity care.
- In-vitro fertilisation.

Section 469 TCA 1997 specifically excludes **cosmetic surgery**, unless such surgery is necessary to ameliorate a physical deformity arising from or directly related to:

- congenital abnormality;
- personal injury; or
- disfiguring disease.

The emphasis on medical expenses relief appears to be relief for **unavoidable** health costs as opposed to those that are **discretionary**.

The following, where **prescribed by a doctor**, qualify for medical expenses relief:

- Drugs and medicines.
- Diagnostic procedures.
- Orthoptic or similar treatment.
- Hearing aids.
- Orthopaedic bed/chair.
- Wheelchair/wheelchair lift (no relief is due for alteration to the building to facilitate a lift).
- Glucometer machine for a diabetic.
- Engaging a qualified nurse in the case of a serious illness.
- Physiotherapy or similar treatment.
- Cost of a computer where it is necessary to alleviate communication problems of a severely handicapped person.
- Cost of gluten-free food for coeliacs. As this condition is generally ongoing, a letter (instead of prescriptions) from a doctor stating that the individual is a coeliac sufferer is acceptable. Receipts from supermarkets in addition to receipts from chemists are acceptable.

Where qualifying health care is only available outside Ireland, reasonable travelling and accommodation expenses can also be claimed. In such cases the expenses of one person accompanying the patient may also be allowed where the condition of the patient requires it.

The following **dental treatments** qualify for relief, provided the **dentist** supplies a Form MED2:

- Bridgework.
- Crowns (including post and core buildups made from materials other than gold).
- Tip replacing.
- Veneers/Rembrandt-type etched fillings.
- Endodontics – root canal treatment.
- Orthodontic treatment (including provision of braces).
- Periodontal treatment.
- Surgical extraction of impacted wisdom teeth.

Tax relief is not available for routine dental care, i.e. the cost of scaling, extraction and filling of teeth, and the provision and repair of artificial teeth and dentures.

Tax relief is also **not available** for **routine ophthalmic care**, i.e. the cost of sight testing, provision and maintenance of spectacles and contact lenses.

Relief may be claimed, electronically, at the end of the year of assessment by using Revenue's myAccount, if an employee, or when submitting Form 11 through ROS under self-assessment. In certain circumstances Revenue may request submission of Form MED1 detailing medical expenses paid or incurred.

Receipts do not have to be submitted to claim relief, but only receipted expenditure can be claimed. Receipts must be retained for a period of six years. A claim for tax relief must be made within four years after the end of the tax year to which the claim relates. To claim relief for the year 2016, for example, you must submit your claim before the end of the year 2020.

6.4 Tax Reliefs at the Marginal Rate

6.4.1 Introduction

Tax reliefs at the marginal rate are given as a deduction against taxable income.

6.4.2 Employment of Carer for Incapacitated Person

Where an individual employs a person to take care of a **family member** who is totally incapacitated by reason of old age or physical or mental infirmity, the individual is entitled to a deduction from his **total income** in calculating his taxable income. For 2016, this deduction is the lesser of the amount actually borne by the individual in employing the carer and **€75,000**.

Where two or more persons employ the carer, the allowance will be apportioned between them in proportion to the amount borne by each. A separate carer's allowance is available for each totally incapacitated person for whom the individual incurs expense. Carers may be employed on an individual basis or through an agency.

The **incapacitated child tax credit** (see **Section 6.2.7**) and/or the **dependent relative tax credit** (see **Section 6.2.8**) **cannot** be claimed where this carer's allowance is being claimed in respect of the same incapacitated relative.

The deduction for the first year of claim will be limited to the lower of the actual cost incurred or the maximum deduction of €75,000 **apportioned** by reference to the number of months during the year in which the individual was permanently incapacitated.

6.4.3 Nursing Home Expenses

Relief is available for expenses paid to a nursing home for health care, maintenance or treatment. Section 469 TCA 1997 states that the expenses will only qualify if the nursing home provides **24-hour nursing care on-site**. Section 469 also states that, even if the individual has received State support under the **Fair Deal** scheme (NHSSA 2009), any contribution to nursing home fees by the individual over and above the Fair Deal scheme will be allowable at the marginal rate.

6.4.4 Permanent Health Benefit Schemes

Relief is given for premiums payable under Revenue-approved permanent health benefit schemes, which provide for periodic payments to an individual in the event of loss of income in consequence of ill health.

Relief is given by way of **deduction** from the individual's total income.

Allowable premiums are **restricted** to a **maximum of 10% of total income**. (Total income is income from all sources before deducting reliefs allowable as deductions in calculating taxable income, e.g. allowance for employed person taking care of incapacitated person, etc.)

Any **benefits** payable under such schemes are **chargeable to tax** under PAYE.

6.4.5 Relief for the Long-term Unemployed

Section 472A TCA 1997 provides that where an individual, who has been unemployed for at least 12 months and has been in receipt of **Jobseeker's Benefit or Jobseeker's Assistance**, takes up employment of at least **30 hours**' duration per week which is capable of lasting **at least 12 months**, he will be entitled to a **deduction** from his emoluments from that employment in calculating taxable income as follows:

	Deduction for Self	Deduction for each Qualifying Child
Year 1	€3,810	€1,270
Year 2	€2,540	€850
Year 3	€1,270	€425

"Qualifying child" has the same definition as **Section 6.2.3** above.

Participation in activities such as the SOLAS-administered **Community Employment Scheme** or **Jobs Initiative** is treated as being periods of unemployment for the purposes of qualifying under this section, provided the individual was in receipt of Jobseeker's Benefit or Jobseeker's Assistance immediately before commencing the activity.

This allowance is also available to those who have been in receipt of either disability allowance or blind person's pension for 12 months or more.

This scheme is no longer available for employments commencing on or after 1 July 2013. Tax relief is available for employments that commenced on or before 30 June 2013 and will therefore cease in 2016.

Section 472AA TCA 1997 provides relief for long-term unemployed individuals who start a **new business**. The scheme provides an exemption from income tax for individuals who set up a qualifying business and who have been unemployed for a period of at least 12 months prior to starting the business. The exemption is up to a maximum of €40,000 per annum for a period of two years. The scheme runs to 31 December 2016.

To qualify for relief the business must:

- be set up between 25 October 2013 and 31 December 2016 by a qualified person (i.e. one who was long-term unemployed);
- be a new business, not one that was bought, inherited or otherwise acquired; and
- not be registered as a company.

The relief is claimed by completing the relevant section of the Form 11 income tax return each year.

6.4.6 Charitable Donations and Gifts

The tax relief for **relevant donations** made to **approved bodies** is payable directly to the approved body at a 'grossed up' **blended rate of 31%**.

The donor is required to provide the charity with a certificate stating:

- the donor's PPS number;
- a declaration that the donation is eligible for relief; and
- a declaration that the donor has paid or will pay an amount of income tax in the year of assessment at least equal to the relief due to the approved body.

The certificate may be in the form of an "annual certificate" (CHY4 Cert) or an "enduring certificate" (CHY3 Cert), the latter being valid for up to five years for recurring donations.

Where an individual makes a donation **in excess of 10%** of their **total income** to an approved body with which he or she is "associated", only an **amount equal to 10%** of the total income will qualify for tax relief. An individual is regarded as associated with an approved body if he or she is an employee or member of the approved body, or of a body associated with the approved body.

Example 6.12

George Burns made a donation of €1,000 to his local homeless shelter, which is an "approved body". Mr Burns is self-employed and pays tax at the marginal rate (40%).

Mr Burns:

Donation paid	€1,000

No further action is necessary

Homeless shelter:

Donation received from Mr Burns	€1,000
Tax refund claimable from the State:	
€1,000 ÷ (100% − 31%) − €1,000	€449
Total donation received	€1,449

Relevant Donation

In order for a "relevant donation" to qualify for relief in the hand of the approved body it must satisfy the following conditions:

- The donation must be a **minimum** amount of at least **€250** in 2016 to any one charity, approved body, educational institution or sporting body.
- The donation must be in the form of money.
- It must not be repayable.
- It must not confer any benefit on the donor or any person connected with the donor; **and**
- It must not be conditional on, or associated with, any arrangement involving the acquisition of property by the recipient from the donor or a person connected with the donor.
- The donor must be resident in the State.
- The **aggregate** of all relevant donations made by an individual to all approved bodies in a year of assessment **cannot exceed €1,000,000 (section 848A TCA 1997)**.

Approved Body

An "approved body" can be any of the following:

- An **eligible charity**, which is a charity established in the State that has been approved as an eligible charity by the Revenue Commissioners.
- A **body approved for education in the arts**. This means a body or institution approved by the Minister for Finance, which teaches approved subjects, i.e. architecture, art and design, music, film arts or other similar subjects.
- **Educational institutions** that qualify for relief include primary, secondary and third-level educational institutions (provided their programmes are approved by the Minister for Education and Science or validated by the Higher Education Training and Awards Council), bodies that promote the Universal Declaration of Human Rights and certain bodies approved for research.
- An **approved sports body** is a body which is in possession of a certificate from the Minister for Tourism, Sport and Recreation confirming that its income is exempt from tax because it is a body which was established for and exists for the sole purpose of promoting athletic or amateur games or sports and whose income is applied solely for those purposes. The sporting body must have a tax clearance certificate.

In order to qualify for relief, donations to certain sporting bodies must **additionally** satisfy the following conditions:

- The donation is made to the approved sporting body for the sole purpose of funding an approved project.
- The sporting body applies it for that purpose.
- Neither the donor nor any person connected with him obtains membership of the sports body or a right to use its facilities as a result of making the donation.

Revenue publish a list on its website of eligible charities and approved sports bodies

6.4.7 Pension Contributions

There are three categories of persons making pension contributions:
1. employees in company schemes;
2. self-employed or employees with no company pension scheme; and
3. public service employees paying the pension-related deduction (PRD).

1. Employees in Company Pension Schemes

Contributions paid by an employee to a superannuation scheme approved by the Revenue Commissioners (i.e. employees in a company pension scheme) are allowed as a deduction against gross assessable Schedule E income from the employment. The maximum allowable deduction varies depending on the age of the employee. For tax years commencing on/after 1 January 2006, the maximum allowable deductions for pension contributions are as follows:

Age	% of Remuneration
Under 30	15%
30 – 39	20%
40 – 49	25%
50 – 54	30%
55 – 59	35%
60 years	40%

The **age** of the person is taken at any time during the tax year, e.g. if a person is age 30 at any time in the tax year, he will qualify for the 20% rate.

Remuneration for this purpose includes fees, bonuses and benefits in kind.

The pension contribution paid is deducted directly from Schedule E income to arrive at the assessable Schedule E income, e.g:

	€
Gross salary of employee aged 45	35,000
Deduct: Superannuation paid (<25% of €35,000)	(2,000)
Assessable Schedule E income	33,000

There is an **earnings cap of €115,000** on remuneration. Remuneration **in excess** of this amount will not be taken into account when calculating the allowable contribution.

Where the full amount of the premium paid does not qualify for relief due to an insufficiency of remuneration, the amount not qualifying **is carried forward** and treated as a premium paid in the **next** year. Where an employee pays a retirement contribution before 31 October which is not an ordinary annual contribution, he may elect that the premium should be treated as a premium paid in the **previous tax year**. For example, an individual makes a non-ordinary annual contribution to his company pension scheme on 1 July 2016. The individual may elect to treat the contribution **as if it had been paid** in 2015 and claim relief for the contribution against his 2015 remuneration.

Section 790A TCA 1997 stipulates that, effective from 1 January 2011, the **earnings cap of €115,000** applies to **all contributions** paid in the year of assessment, **irrespective** of the fact that the contribution relates to the previous year.

Note also that the exemption from PRSI and USC on employee pension contributions has been abolished effective from 1 January 2011.

2. **Contributions to a Retirement Annuity Contract (RAC), i.e. Self-employed or Employees with no Company Pension Scheme**

Contributions paid to a retirement annuity contract (RAC) are also entitled to tax relief. The maximum amounts on which relief may be claimed in respect of qualifying premiums, for the tax years 2006, *et seq.* are as follows:

Age	% of Net Relevant Earnings
Under 30	15%
30–39	20%
40–49	25%
50–54	30%*
55–59	35%
60 and over	40%

*The **30% limit** also applies to individuals who are engaged in specified occupations and professions, **primarily sports professionals**, irrespective of age.

"**Relevant earnings**" is defined to mean the following types of income:

- non-pensionable salaries, wages, fees, benefits, etc. taxable under Schedule E; and
- Case I and Case II profits from trades or professions (including profits arising to a partner).

"**Net relevant earnings**" is defined to mean the "relevant earnings" assessable for a particular year of assessment **as reduced** by:

- Loss relief available for the particular year of assessment in respect of losses, which, if they had been profits, would constitute "relevant" income.
- Relief for capital allowances claimed in respect of the "relevant" source of income for the particular year of assessment.
- Charges paid (see **Section 6.5**) during the particular year of assessment to the extent that they cannot be set against other non-relevant income (i.e. income under Cases III, IV or V or Schedule F) of the taxpayer. Broadly, this means any earned income that is not already subject to a pension scheme.

Non-relevant income represents any income of the taxpayer for the particular year of assessment **other than** relevant income. For example, a self-employed solicitor would be assessed under Case II, Schedule D on his practice profits and this would be regarded as relevant earnings. However, the solicitor may have other sources of income assessed on him, e.g. bank deposit interest, dividend income, rents, etc. and these would **not** be taken into account in computing net relevant earnings, except and to the extent that they are used to offset charges paid during the particular year of assessment.

It is specifically provided that **remuneration from an investment company** is **not included** in computing net relevant earnings.

Example 6.13

Joe Green is a chartered accountant, aged 50, who has been in practice for many years. His Case II tax-adjusted profits assessable for 2016 are €37,000. He is entitled to Case II capital allowances of €14,000 for 2016 and he has an allowable Case II loss forward from 2015 of €10,000. His only other income is €1,500 interest from Government Securities received annually. He pays an allowable covenant to his widowed mother of €2,000 (gross) per annum and he pays €4,000 per annum under a Revenue-approved retirement annuity contract.

Net Relevant Earnings	€	€
Case II (relevant earnings)		37,000
Less:		
Loss relief	(10,000)	
Capital allowances	(14,000)	(24,000)
Charges paid in 2016 to extent not covered		
by non-relevant income:		
Gross covenant	2,000	
Less: non-relevant income (Government Securities)	(1,500)	(500)
Net relevant earnings (NRE)		**12,500**
Amount of retirement premium paid		4,000
Relief restricted to max. 30% of NRE: €12,500 @ 30%		(3,750)
Unrelieved portion of premium		250

In cases where the full amount of the premium paid does not qualify for relief in a particular year of assessment (as in **Example 6.13**), any **unrelieved portion** of the premium may be **carried forward** to the following and subsequent years and treated as a **premium paid** in those years until such time as relief has been granted. For instance, in the above example Joe did not receive relief in respect of €250 of the total €4,000 premium paid during 2016. He would, therefore, be entitled to treat the €250 unrelieved payment as a premium paid in 2017. It would be added to his annual premium of €4,000 to give a total premium paid of €4,250. Provided this amount was less than 30% of his net relevant earnings for 2017, he would be entitled to a full deduction for the €4,250 in that year.

The relief for qualifying contracts is **normally** based on the amount of the premium paid **in the actual tax year**, i.e. a premium paid on 1 December 2016 would qualify for relief in the taxpayer's computation for 2016.

To enable taxpayers to fully benefit from the relief available, a provision exists which effectively enables relief for retirement annuity premiums to be **backdated**. If a taxpayer pays a qualifying premium after the end of the tax year but **before** the due date for the **filing of his tax return** for that tax year, he may elect for the premium to be deducted in the **earlier** tax year. For example, currently an individual subject to self-assessment must file his 2015 tax return electronically **before 10 November 2016**. Such an individual may elect that a qualifying retirement annuity premium paid in the period 1 January 2016 to 10 November 2016 may be deducted from his relevant income for 2015.

This provision clearly enables the taxpayer to know with certainty what his net relevant earnings are for a particular year, thereby permitting him to effectively top-up the premiums paid to ensure that they are equal to the net relevant earnings' limits. Where the marginal rate of tax decreases between one year and the next (as between 2015 and 2014), the top-up premium can be relieved at the higher rate of tax, i.e. in 2014 @ 41%.

There is also an **earnings cap of €115,000** on net relevant earnings. Earnings **in excess** of this amount will **not** be taken into account when calculating the allowable contribution.

3.   Public Service Employees Paying the Pension-related Deduction (PRD)

Public and civil servants are required to make a pension contribution (PRD) at rates between 10% and 10.5% annually, dependent on their salary levels. From 2016 public servants with remuneration below €24,750 (January 2016) or €28,750 (from September 2016) will not be liable to PRD. The PRD is an allowable deduction against Schedule E income for tax purposes, but it is not allowable as a deduction against income liable to PRSI or USC.

6.4.8   Relief for Investment in Corporate Trades: Employment and Investment Incentive (EII)

The Employment and Investment Incentive (EII) is a tax relief incentive scheme that provides tax relief for investment in certain corporate trades. There have been many changes and amendments to the scheme but these are the rules **effective from 13 October 2015**.

The scheme allows an investor to obtain income tax relief on investments up to a maximum of **€150,000 per annum** in each tax year up to **31 December 2020**. Relief is initially available to the individual at **30%**, with **a further 10% tax relief** available where it has been **proven** that **employment levels** and **total wages** have **increased** at the company at the end of the **holding period** of **four years**, or where evidence is provided that the company used the capital raised for increased expenditure on **research and development**.

The **maximum investment** which will qualify for relief in any one tax year is **€150,000**. This limit applies to **individuals**. A married couple/civil partnership can **each** obtain individual relief on an investment of €150,000, **provided** each spouse/civil partner has sufficient taxable income to absorb the amount of his/her investment.

Where relief cannot be obtained, either because the investment exceeds the maximum of €150,000 or due to an insufficiency of income, the unrelieved amount can be carried forward and claimed as a deduction in future years **up to** and including **2020**, subject to the overall annual limit of €150,000. There is **no limit** to the **number of companies** an investor can invest in, but tax relief is subject to the **overall investment limit** of **€150,000** per annum.

Claims for EII will not be allowed unless the company qualifies for a **tax clearance certificate** at the time of the claim.

Qualifying Criteria for EII Relief

In order for the investment to qualify for relief, there are three main "qualifying" headings:

1.   qualifying individual/investor
2.   qualifying company and its trade
3.   qualifying shares.

1.   Qualifying Individual/Investor

A qualifying investor is an individual who is:

- resident in the Republic of Ireland for the tax year in respect of which he/she makes the claim;
- subscribes on his/her own behalf for eligible shares in a qualifying company; and
- is not, for the relevant period, connected with the company (as defined), where the amounts subscribed for the issued share capital exceed €500,000.

An employee or director of an investee company may invest in the company under the EII scheme, but must only have received reasonable remuneration and expenses (i.e. arm's length payments) from the company for a defined period of **four years**.

2. *Qualifying Company and its Trade*
A qualifying company is one that:

- is a **micro-, small or medium-sized enterprise** within the European Commission definition in force for the relevant period, as follows:
  - A **micro**-enterprise has **less** than **10 employees** and has an annual turnover and/or annual balance sheet total not exceeding **€2 million**.
  - A **small** enterprise has **less** than **50 employees** and has an annual turnover and/or annual balance sheet total not exceeding **€10 million**.
  - A **medium-sized** enterprise has **less** than **250 employees** and has an annual turnover not exceeding **€50 million** or an annual balance sheet total not exceeding €43 million.
- is incorporated in the State or the EEA (EU, Norway, Liechtenstein and Iceland);
- is resident in the State or is resident in another EEA Member State and carries on business in the State through a branch or agency;
- is not regarded as a firm in difficulty for the purposes of the EU's *Guidelines on State Aid for Rescuing and Restructuring Firms in Difficulty;*
- throughout the four-year holding period:
  - carries on relevant trading activities from a **fixed place of business** in the State, *or*
  - is a company whose business consists wholly of:
    - the holding of shares or securities of, or the making of loans to, one or more qualifying subsidiaries of the company, **or**
    - both the holding of such shares or securities, or the making of such loans and the carrying on of relevant trading activities, where relevant trading is carried on from **a fixed place of business in the State**;
- is an unquoted company (except in the case of companies listed on the Irish Enterprise Securities Market) and, effective for shares issued from **13 October 2015**, the company must fulfil at least **one** of the following conditions:
  - the company has not been operating in any market; **or**
  - the company is not trading for greater than **seven years; or**
  - where the company is trading for greater than seven years and is looking to raise EII for the first time, the company must be entering a new market (either product or geographical) and the amount the company wishes to raise under EII must be greater than **50%** of the company's average annual turnover in the preceding **five years**;
- has its issued share capital fully paid up; **and**
- is not intending to wind up within three years of receiving EII investment (unless for bona fide commercial reasons).

The Trade
EII is available to the majority of small and medium-sized trading companies. However, the following trading activities are **not eligible** for the scheme:

- adventures or concerns in the nature of trade;
- dealing in commodities or futures in shares, securities or other financial assets (excluding internationally traded financial services – see below);

- financing activities;
- professional service companies;
- dealing in or developing land;
- forestry;
- operating or managing hotels, guest houses, self-catering accommodation or comparable establishments or managing property used as a hotel, guest house, self-catering accommodation or comparable establishment **except** where such establishment is a "tourist traffic undertaking" and has **prior approval** from Fáilte Ireland;
- operations carried on in the coal industry or in the steel and shipbuilding sectors; and
- the production of a film (within the meaning of section 481 TCA 1997).

A company whose relevant trading activities include **international trading services** will not be a qualifying company unless it is certified by Enterprise Ireland.

3.   *Qualifying Shares*
The qualifying investor must subscribe on his/her own behalf for shares which must:

- be new ordinary share capital in a qualifying company; *and*
- carry no preferential rights as to dividends or redemption.

The whole of the company's issued share capital must be fully paid up.
The **minimum investment** in any one company is **€250**, and the maximum investment in any one company or its associated companies is **€15 million** subject to a maximum of **€5 million** in any one 12-month period.

Holding Period for Share Capital
Shares must be held by the investor for a period of **four years** after the shares have been issued.

Note: EII relief is a "specified relief" and may be restricted in the case of certain high-income individuals (see **Section 6.7**). However, F(No.2)A 2013 temporarily removed EII from the high-earners restriction for investments made in the period **16 October 2013 to 31 December 2016**.

6.4.9   Relief for Investment in Films

Since 1 January 2015, income tax relief is no longer available on individual investments in film production. A film relief scheme effective from 1 January 2015 provides for **corporation tax relief** towards the cost of production of certain films at a rate of **32%** (subject to certain limits and conditions). No individual income tax relief is available.

6.5   Relief for Charges on Income

Charges on income are payments made which are **deductible** from the **gross income** of the taxpayer, to arrive at total income or net statutory income. In order for relief to be claimed, the amount must be **actually paid** during the tax year in question and not simply incurred.

6.5.1   Payments Made Under a Deed of Covenant

A deed of covenant is a legally binding written agreement, made by an individual, to pay an agreed amount to another individual without receiving **any** benefit in return. To be legally effective, it must be properly drawn up, signed, witnessed, sealed and delivered to the individual receiving the payments. Any amount can be paid under a deed of convenant but only covenants in favour of **certain individuals** qualify for tax relief.

The person who makes the payment is called a **covenantor**. The person who receives the payment is called a **covenantee** or beneficiary.

To qualify for tax relief, a deed must be capable of **exceeding** a period of **six years**. Therefore, the period provided should be for a minimum of **seven years**.

Covenants Allowable for Tax Relief

Unrestricted tax relief is available for covenants payable to the following:

- a permanently incapacitated minor child (i.e. under 18 years) where the covenant is paid by a person **other** than the parent; and
- a permanently incapacitated person.

Tax relief is **restricted** to **5%** of the covenantor's **total income** (gross income minus all other charges) on covenants payable to persons aged 65 years or older.

Example 6.14

Marie Murphy is single and earned €42,000 from her job in 2016. She paid the following covenants during 2016:

- her permanently incapacitated sister Mary received €3,200 (net);
- her 66-year-old widowed mother received €2,400 (net).

Marie's allowable charges for 2016 were:

Incapacitated sister €3,200 (net) × 100/80	=	€4,000 gross (no restriction)
Widowed mother: restricted to the **lower** of gross amount paid		
or 5% of gross income less charges:		
Amount paid €2,400 (net) × 100/80	=	€3,000 gross
Gross income less charges:		
€42,000 – €4,000 = €38,000 @ 5%	=	€1,900
Total allowable covenants: €4,000 + €1,900	=	**€5,900**

The covenantor must deduct tax at the **standard rate** from the gross payment and **account** for it to Revenue. The covenantor must also give a **Form R185**, detailing the payment and the tax deducted, to the covenantee **each time** a payment is made.

To **claim the tax relief** in the first year, the covenantor must send the original deed of covenant together with a copy of Form R185 to Revenue. For subsequent years, only a copy of Form R185 needs to be included with the claim for tax relief.

Relief is allowed in the covenantor's income tax computation for the **gross amount paid** and he must pay over to the Revenue Commissioners the income tax which he has deducted. In practice, this liability is simply added to the covenantor's tax liability in respect of his income in the tax computation. **Tax credits**, other than credits for tax paid, **cannot reduce the tax due** on the charges. The individual always remains liable to pay the full amount of income tax on any charges.

Example 6.15

Peter Byrne is a single individual and is employed as a marketing manager. He has a salary of €43,000 for the tax year 2016 and paid PAYE of €7,100 in respect of this salary. Peter has executed an **annual** covenant of €5,000 in favour of his widowed mother, aged 66 and incapacitated, for seven years. His mother's only other source of income is €6,000 per annum.

Peter Byrne – Income Tax Computation 2016

	€	€
Schedule E salary	43,000	
Less: gross amount of covenant paid*	(5,000)	
Total/taxable income		**38,000**
Tax Calculation:		
€33,800 @ 20%	6,760	
€4,200 @ 40%	1,680	8,440
Less:		
Single person tax credit	1,650	
Employee tax credit	1,650	(3,300)
Plus:		5,140
Tax deducted on payment of covenant which must be returned to Revenue (€5,000 @ 20%)		1,000
Net tax liability		6,140
Deduct: PAYE paid		(7,100)
Tax refund due		**(960)**

*If Peter's mother was not incapacitated, the allowable covenant would be restricted to 5% of Peter's income, i.e. €43,000 @ 5% = €2,150. However, the tax deducted and due on payment of the covenant would be based on the actual payment made, not on the amount that qualifies for tax relief.

Mrs Byrne – Income Tax Computation 2016

	€	€
Income:		
Case IV, Schedule D (gross covenant income)	5,000	
Other income	6,000	
Total/taxable income		**11,000**
Covered by exemption limit – no tax liability		
Tax Calculation:		
Tax liability		NIL
Less: tax deducted by Peter on payment of covenant		(1,000)
Tax refund due		**(1,000)**

6.5.2 Interest on Loans to Invest in Partnerships

Section 253 TCA 1997 provides for interest relief to an individual in respect of a loan taken out to:

- purchase a share in a partnership; **or**
- lend money to a partnership, **provided** the money is used wholly and exclusively for the purposes of the trade or profession carried on by the partnership.

The individual must have personally acted as a partner in the conduct of the trade or profession carried out by the partnership and must not have "recovered" any capital from the partnership unless such capital is first used to repay the loan in question. An individual is treated as "recovering capital" from a partnership if:

- they sell their partnership interest;
- the partnership returns any capital or repays any loan to the partner; **or**
- the partner receives any money for the assignment of a debt due from the partnership.

F(No.2)A 2013 abolished all relief in respect of loans taken out **after 15 October 2013**, and introduced a phasing-out of interest relief on loans taken out before this date as follows:

Year	Restricted to
2016	25% of interest paid
2017 *et seq.*	No relief available

This restriction does not apply to a farming partnership as defined by section 598A TCA 1997.

Note: this relief is a "specified relief" and may be restricted in the case of certain high-income individuals (see **Section 6.7**).

6.5.3 Patent Royalties

Where an individual pays patent royalties, a deduction is not allowed for the royalties under any of the Schedules. Instead the **royalties** paid in the particular tax year are allowed as a **charge**.

6.6 Other Reliefs

6.6.1 Relief on the Retirement of Certain Sportspersons

Section 480A TCA 1997 introduced a specific relief for the tax years 2002, *et seq.*, for certain **retiring** sportspersons who are **resident** in the State. The sportspersons to whom the relief applies include the following (Schedule 23A TCA 1997):

- Athletes
- Badminton players
- Boxers
- Cyclists
- Footballers
- Golfers
- Jockeys
- Motor racing drivers
- Rugby players
- Squash players
- Swimmers
- Tennis players
- Cricketers.

The features of this relief are as follows:

1. The relief is granted by way of a repayment of tax, calculated by allowing a **deduction of 40%** against gross earnings (before deducting expenses) for **any 10 years** of assessment, chosen by the taxpayer, from the period comprising the year of retirement and the preceding 14 years of assessment.
2. The earnings to which the relief applies are those received from **actual participation** in the sport concerned, including match and performance fees, prize money and appearance fees, but **does not include** sponsorship fees, advertising income or endorsement fees, income from newspaper or magazine articles and interviews.
3. The relief **cannot** create or augment a **Case I or Case II loss**.
4. The relief will be given by way of a **tax repayment** (which will not carry interest) and is to be claimed in the year in which the sportsperson **permanently ceases** to be engaged in that sport.
5. Where the sportsperson recommences to be engaged in that sport, the relief will be **clawed back** and taxable under **Case IV**. However, this does not prevent a subsequent claim for relief if and when the sportsperson finally does retire.
6. The sportsperson must be resident in the State or, effective from **1 January 2014**, resident in an EEA or EFTA country at the **time of retirement**.
7. This relief will not affect the calculation of net **relevant earnings** for the purpose of relief for pension contributions.
8. A claim for relief must be made within four years from the end of the year of assessment in which the sportsperson retires.

6.6.2 Age Exemption

Exemptions from income tax are available to individuals aged 65 years and over, and with low incomes.

Age Exemption
Where total income does not exceed the following amounts, there is a **total exemption** from income tax for 2016 for an individual aged **65 years and over**.

Marital Status	Income Limit 2016
Single/Widowed/Surviving Civil Partner	€18,000
Married Couple/Civil Partners	€36,000

Increase in Exemption Limits for Qualifying Children
The age exemption limits are **increased** where a claimant proves that a qualifying child (children) has lived with them at any time during the tax year. The income limits are increased for **each** qualifying child as follows:

	Increase for each child
First and second child	€575
Third and subsequent children	€830

Example 6.16

Peter Blake, aged 66, is a self-employed carpenter and is married with four children. His wife, Sheila, aged 42, works full-time in the home and does not have any income. Peter had a total income of €38,000 for 2016.

Calculation of Specified Income Limit	€	€
Income limit – married couple over 65		36,000
Plus: Increase for qualifying children:		
1st and 2nd child (€575 × 2)	1,150	
3rd and 4th child (€830 × 2)	1,660	2,810
Specified income limit		38,810
Actual income		38,000
Income tax liability		**NIL**

Marginal Relief

Marginal relief may be available to a couple in a marriage or civil partnership whose total income from all sources is slightly over the exemption limit. Marginal relief will only be granted if it is more beneficial to the claimant than their tax credits. A certificate can issue during the tax year granting the relevant exemption limit and any income earned over the exemption figure is taxed at 40%.

6.6.3 Provision of Childcare Services

Section 216C TCA 1997 provides for tax relief for income received from the provision of childcare services in the individual's **own home**. The exemption applies where the income in a tax year does **not exceed €15,000** and no more than **three children** (excluding any children who normally reside in the individual's home) at any time are cared for in the individual's own home. No deductions are allowable when calculating the income limit for this relief and notification of the service being provided must be given to the HSE. Where the income exceeds €15,000, the **entire amount** becomes taxable under self-assessment. Where more than one person is providing the service in the same residential premises, the €15,000 limit is split between them.

An individual in receipt of exempt childcare income must make an annual Return of Income (Form 11) regardless of any other source of income in the year. The exempt income is not liable to USC but is **subject to PRSI**.

Example 6.17

Karen takes care of three pre-school children in her home every morning and is registered with the HSE. Her income and expenses are as follows:

Childcare receipts	€17,000
Less: provision of food/nappies, etc.	(€3,500)
Net childcare income	€13,500

As Karen's gross income from the childcare service is greater than €15,000 she is liable to tax on the full amount of her net income of €13,500.

6.6.4 Rent-a-Room Relief

Where an individual rents out a room (or rooms) in a "qualifying residence" and the gross income received (including sums arising for food, laundry or similar goods and services) **does not exceed €12,000** this income will be exempt from income tax (section 216A TCA 1997). It is also not liable to PRSI or USC, but it must be **included** in an individual's income tax return. In determining whether the limit has been exceeded for the tax year, no deductions for expenses incurred are made.

Where income exceeds €12,000 limit, the entire amount is taxable.

A "qualifying residence" is a residential premises situated in the State which is occupied by the individual as his or her sole or main residence during the year of assessment.

Room rentals under this scheme will not affect:

- mortgage interest relief available to the individual who qualifies for relief; or
- principal private residence (PPR) relief for CGT purposes on the disposal of the house.

Where the room or rooms are rented out by more than one individual, the €12,000 limit is divided between the individuals.

Exclusions

Rent-a-Room relief will not apply where:

1. the room is rented to a child or the civil partner of the individual renting the rooms; **or**
2. the individual receiving the rent (or a person connected to them) is an office holder or employee of the person making the payment (or someone connected to them) (section 216A TCA 1997); **or**
3. the income is from the provision of accommodation to occasional visitors for short periods. Use of the room as **guest accommodation** rather than for residential purposes is not permitted, including where such accommodation is provided through online accommodation booking sites (e.g. Airbnb.com).

6.6.5 Artists' Exemption

This exemption is available to individuals who are deemed by the Revenue Commissioners to have produced an original and creative "work" that is generally recognised as having cultural or artistic merit (section 195 TCA 1997).

The first **€50,000 per annum** of profits or gains earned by writers, composers, visual artists and sculptors from the sale of their work is **exempt from income tax** in Ireland in certain circumstances. Income in excess of €50,000 is subject to income tax at the individual's marginal rate.

A "work" must be original and creative, and fall into one of the following categories:

- a book or other writing
- a play
- a musical composition
- a painting or other like picture
- a sculpture.

Claimants must be individuals and resident, or ordinarily resident and domiciled, in any one or more EU Member States or another EEA State. The artists' exemption only provides an exemption from **income tax**. All exempt income is subject to USC and PRSI at the appropriate annual rates.

Note: this relief is a "specified relief" and may be restricted in the case of certain high-income individuals (see **Section 6.7**).

6.6.6 Heritage Items and Property

Sections 1003 and 1003A TCA 1997 provides that taxpayers who donate heritage items and property to the State can credit the value of those items against their liabilities for certain taxes. The taxes covered by the relief are income tax, corporation tax, capital gains tax, gift tax and inheritance tax. In order to obtain the tax credit, the heritage items or property must be donated for no consideration other than the tax credit itself.

The credit is applied first against outstanding tax, interest and penalties, then against any current liabilities to tax, with any balance remaining being available for set-off against future liabilities to tax.

The tax credit granted is non-refundable and will not give rise to any repayment of tax. No interest is payable on any over-payment which arises as a result of the tax credit.

Heritage Items

Heritage items are defined as any kind of cultural item, including:

- any archaeological item, archive, book, estate record, manuscript and painting; and
- a collection of cultural items and any collection of such items in their setting provided that the collection has been in existence for at least 30 years.

In addition, the open market value of the item or collection of items must be at least **€150,000** and, in the case of a collection, at least one item in the collection must have a minimum value of €50,000. Relief is available at **80% of the market value** of the heritage items donated.

Heritage Property

A heritage property is a building or garden and accompanying outbuildings, yards or lands (e.g. for car parks) which, following a written application by its owner, is determined by the Minister for Public Expenditure and Reform or the Commissioners of Public Works to be a building or a garden, which is:

- an outstanding example of its type;
- pre-eminent in its class;
- intrinsically of significant scientific, historical, horticultural, national, architectural or aesthetic interest; or
- suitable for acquisition by the Irish Heritage Trust or the Commissioners of Public Works.

Relief is available at **50% of the market value** of the heritage property donated.

There is a **ceiling of €6 million** on the aggregate value of heritage properties that may be approved in any one year.

Note: the relief for heritage items is a "specified relief" and may be restricted in the case of certain high-income individuals (see **Section 6.7**).

6.6.7 Foreign Earnings Deduction

Section 823A TCA 1997 provides for a special tax deduction for employees who carry out part of their employment duties in certain foreign countries, i.e. "relevant states". The table below lists the relevant states and the tax years the relief was introduced.

"Relevant State"	Year 2012	Years 2013–2014	Years 2015–2017
Brazil	■	■	■
Russia	■	■	■
India	■	■	■
China	■	■	■
South Africa	■	■	■
Egypt		■	■
Algeria		■	■
Senegal		■	■
Tanzania		■	■
Kenya		■	■
Nigeria		■	■
Ghana		■	■
Democratic Republic of the Congo		■	■
Japan			■
Singapore			■
South Korea			■
Saudi Arabia			■
UAE			■
Qatar			■
Bahrain			■
Indonesia			■
Vietnam			■
Thailand			■
Chile			■
Oman			■
Kuwait			■
Mexico			■
Malaysia			■

Qualifying Conditions

The employee must have worked in one or more of the relevant states for a minimum period of 40 "qualifying days" within a period of 12 months. A "qualifying day" is one of at least **three consecutive days** devoted substantially to carrying out the duties of employment where, throughout the whole of each such day, the employee is present in a "relevant state".

Saturdays, Sundays and public holidays, where the employee is present for the whole day in a "relevant state" and which form an unavoidable part of a business trip to that state, may be counted as "qualifying days".

Days spent travelling **directly** from the State to a "relevant state" are treated as a qualifying day but only if the travel is direct i.e. travelling via London would not qualify.

Foreign Earnings Deduction

The deduction available is the lesser of:

- **€35,000**, or
- the "**specified amount**", calculated as:

$$\frac{D \times E}{F}$$

where:

D is the number of "qualifying days" worked in a "relevant state" in the tax year;

E is all the income from the employment in the tax year **excluding** tax deductible expenses payments, benefits in kind, termination payments and payments payable under restrictive covenants **but including** any taxable share-based remuneration or share-option profits;

F is the total number of days that the relevant employment is held in the tax year (365 days in a full tax year).

The deduction is given by way of end-of-year review and must be claimed by the employee. The claim should be supported by a statement from the employer indicating the dates of departure and return to the State of the employee and the location at which the duties of the office or employment were performed while abroad.

Example 6.18

William Bryson is an Irish resident employee of Baby Gloop Ltd, and spent 97 qualifying days in India in 2016 developing new contacts with potential Indian customers. Mr Bryson was paid the following amounts in 2016:

	€
Salary 2016	120,000
Taxable share option profits	22,000
Benefit in kind	14,000
FED Relief: Specified amount: €142,000 × $\frac{97}{365}$	37,737
Restricted to	35,000

Mr Bryson will be able to claim a reduction of €14,000 (€35,000 @ 40%) in his tax liability for 2016.

Exclusions

The foreign earnings deduction does not apply to **public servants**, nor does it apply to income to which the following reliefs apply:

- Special Assignee Relief Programme (SARP)
- The remittance basis of taxation
- Key employee R&D relief
- "Split year" residence relief
- Cross-border worker relief.

6.6.8 Stock Relief

Section 666 TCA 1997 allows for a deduction, against the **farming profits** of an individual, of **25%** of the value of any **increase** in trading stock values in a chargeable period. Where the individual is a "Young Trained Farmer" as defined by S667B TCA 1997, the deduction is available at a rate of **100%** of any increase in stock values for **three** consecutive years.

Conditions

- The relief cannot create or increase a loss.
- Any excess capital allowances or losses forward from a period before stock relief was claimed cannot be carried forward once stock relief is claimed.
- The relief must be claimed in writing on or before the return filing date for the chargeable period (i.e. 31 October 2017 for chargeable period 2016).
- The relief applies up to and including the 2018 tax year.
- There is no provision for a claw-back of the relief if the value of the stock reduces in subsequent years.

Example 6.19

John Merryweather is a beef farmer from Co. Meath. His trading profits for 2016 were €60,000 and his stock values were as follows:

	€
Opening stock	20,000
Closing stock	45,000

Stock Relief:	
Case I profits	60,000
Stock relief ((€45,000 − €20,000) @ 25%)	(6,250)
Case I taxable profits	53,750

If Mr Merryweather's Case I profits were €5,000 for 2016, the stock relief would be restricted to that amount with no loss available to carry forward.

Stock Relief:	€
Case I profits	5,000
Stock relief (€25,000 @ 25%) – restricted to	(5,000)
Case I taxable profits	Nil

Example 6.20

As above, but Mr Merryweather has the following losses and capital allowances forward:

	€
Excess capital allowances forward	3,000
Unused losses forward	5,000

In this instance, Mr Merryweather would not claim stock relief as he would lose his entitlement to the excess capital allowances and unused losses forward of €8,000 in total.

6.6.9   *Living City Initiative*

The Living City Initiative (section 372AAA TCA 1997) is a scheme aimed at the regeneration of certain buildings in Dublin, Cork, Limerick, Waterford, Galway and Kilkenny. There are two types of relief under the Living City Initiative: residential relief and commercial relief.

Residential Relief
The main features of the residential relief are:

- Tax relief of **10%** of the qualifying expenditure incurred in the "qualifying period" may be claimed against total income for each of **10 consecutive years**. The "qualifying period" is a period of **five years from May 2015**.
- Relief is available at the individual's marginal income tax rate. There is no effect on PRSI or USC. There is no limit on the relief available.
- The relief applies to refurbishment and conversion work carried out, during the qualifying period, by owner/occupiers (not landlords) on a property originally built for **use as a dwelling prior to 1915**. Conversion of, for example, an old stable or a church does not qualify. The expenditure must relate to refurbishment/conversion only (not to any "new build" costs) and must be at least **10% of the value of the property** immediately before the work commenced.
- The floor area of the property must be between **38m² and 210m²**. If the property is situated within a larger building, e.g. an apartment, it is the floor area of the property and not the entire building that is relevant.
- The property must be occupied by the taxpayer as his or her **main residence** once the work has been completed. If the property is let or put to some other use before the taxpayer moves in, the tax relief is lost.
- A "letter of certification" must be obtained from the local authority before any claim for tax relief can be made.
- In the case of a refurbished/converted property acquired from a builder, the taxpayer must be the **first person** to occupy the property after its refurbishment in order to claim the relief. In this instance, the builder must specify what **percentage** of the total cost refers to the refurbishment and this percentage is the basis on which the tax relief is claimed. The builder will also have to confirm that the cost of the refurbishment was at least 10% of the value of the property pre-refurbishment.

Commercial Relief
The main features of the commercial relief are:

- Relief is given in the form of **accelerated capital allowances** on qualifying expenditure for the refurbishment or conversion of premises within the special regeneration areas for a period of **seven years**. The rate of relief is 15% per annum for the first six years and 10% in the final year.
- There is no requirement for premises to be originally built pre-1915.
- Unused capital allowances can be **carried forward** and set against the future income of the business beyond the tax life of the building (seven years), **except** in the case of passive investors.
- The expenditure must relate to refurbishment/conversion only (not to "new build" costs) and must be at least **10% of the value of the property** immediately before the work commenced.
- After refurbishment the premises must be used for retail purposes or for the provision of services within the State.

- Qualifying expenditure is limited to **€400,000 per property** for an individual investor and to **€1.6 million per property** where the investor is a company. A taxpayer can invest in more than one project simultaneously and receive relief in respect of each project. The value of the tax relief cannot exceed **€200,000** per property.
- The relief is not available to property developers or "connected persons".
- Relief will **not apply** where any of the cost of the refurbishment or conversion is met directly or indirectly by the State or any State body.

6.7 High-income Individuals Restrictions

Sections 485C–G TCA 1997 provided for limitations in the use of certain tax reliefs and exemptions (known as "specified reliefs") by high-income individuals effective. The objective is to ensure that individuals who are fully subject to the restriction pay an effective rate of income tax of approximately 30%.

The restriction applies to an individual where **all** of the following apply:

1. the "adjusted income" of an individual for the tax year is equal to or greater than an "income threshold amount" of **€125,000 or less** if the individual had 'ring-fenced' income (e.g. deposit interest); **and**
2. the **sum** of specified reliefs that are used by the individual for the tax year is equal to or greater than a relief threshold amount, which is set at **€80,000**; **and**
3. the aggregate of specified reliefs used by an individual for the tax year is greater than **20%** of the individual's adjusted income.

Adjusted Income

Adjusted income is defined as:

$$(T + S) - R$$

where:

T = the individual's taxable income (as calculated before any restriction);
S = the aggregate amount of specified reliefs used in the year; and
R = the amount of the individual's ring-fenced income for the year.

Income Threshold Amount

The income threshold amount is **€125,000 except** where the individual has ring-fenced income. Ring-fenced income is income that is normally liable to tax at a specific rate regardless of the amount received or the marginal rate of tax of the individual (e.g. deposit interest liable to DIRT at 41%). In that scenario, the income threshold amount is calculated by using the formula:

$$€125,000 \times \frac{A}{B}$$

where:

A = the individual's adjusted income for the year, and
B = the sum of T + S (same meaning as in adjusted income above).

Example 6.21

Ms Moneypenny has the following income/reliefs for 2016:

Case I income	€120,000
Less: specified reliefs	(€100,000) **(S)**
Plus: deposit interest (ring-fenced income)	€70,000 **(R)**
Taxable income (after reliefs)	€90,000 **(T)**

Ms Moneypenny's adjusted income = (T + S) − R = €120,000

Income threshold amount = €125,000 × $\dfrac{€120,000}{€190,000}$ = €78,947

The high-income individuals restriction applies to Ms Moneypenny as her adjusted income (€120,000) is > than her Income Threshold Amount (€78,947) and her specified reliefs (€100,000) are > than the relief threshold amount (€80,000).

Restriction of Relief

The specified reliefs (S) are restricted by recalculating the individual's taxable income using the formula below and taxing the recalculated amount under the normal rules.

$$\textbf{T + (S − Y)}$$

where:

Y = greater of:

- the relief threshold (€80,000), **or**
- 20% of the individual's adjusted income for the year.

Example 6.22

Using Example 6.20 above, Ms Moneypenny's recalculated taxable amount for 2016 is:

Taxable income (after reliefs)			€90,000 (T)
Specified reliefs			€100,000 (S)
Less: greater of:			
Relief threshold	€80,000	or	
20% Adjusted income (€120,000 @ 20%)	€24,000	=	(€80,000) (Y)
Recalculated taxable amount 2016			**€110,000**

Ms Moneypenny's taxable income is increased by €20,000 for 2016. This additional amount is carried forward as "excess relief" to 2017 and will be a "specified relief" in 2017 et seq.

Questions

Review Questions
(See Suggested Solutions to Review Questions at the end of this textbook.)

Question 6.1

The Joyces are a married couple, jointly assessed, with two children under 16. Mr Joyce is in receipt of employment income, of €46,000, for 2016. Mrs Joyce is a full-time home carer and has no income in 2016.

Requirement

(a) Calculate their income tax liability for 2016.

(b) What would the liability be if the home carer had income of €9,500 in 2017 (the following tax year)?

Question 6.2

The Roches are a married couple, jointly assessed, with two children under 16. One spouse has a salary of €46,000 and the other has investment income, i.e. Schedule F, of €8,000 (gross).

Requirement

Calculate their income tax liability for 2016.

Question 6.3

Mr Murray is married with two children, Michael and David. Michael was formally adopted in 2006. He is 12 years old and in receipt of €2,500 per annum from a trust set up by his aunt.

David is 14 years of age and is not in receipt of any income.

During 2016 the following medical expenses were paid:

	€
Mr Murray	80
Michael Murray	200
David Murray	210
Sean Ryan	650

Sean Ryan, his friend, was involved in a motor accident and Mr Murray paid €650 for medical treatment for him.

He also pays €100 per month towards nursing home care for his elderly mother. The nursing home provides 24-hour nursing care on-site.

Requirement

Compute Mr Murphy's allowable medical expenses for 2016 and advise how tax relief may be obtained.

Question 6.4

Rachel, aged 45, is an active partner in a firm of solicitors. Her tax-adjusted profits assessable for 2016 are €320,000. Capital allowances for 2016 are €10,000. She pays €75,000 per annum under a Revenue-approved retirement annuity contract.

On 1 June 2013 Rachel took out a loan of €100,000, which she lent to the partnership. On 1 July 2016 the partnership repaid €20,000 of the loan to Rachel. Rachel used the €20,000 repaid to buy a new car. Interest paid by Rachel during 2016 in respect of the €100,000 loan amounted to €10,000. Assume interest accrued evenly throughout the year.

Requirement

Calculate:

(a) Rachel's entitlement to interest relief for 2016.

(b) Rachel's net relevant earnings for 2016.

Question 6.5

Mr Frost is an employee of ABC Ltd. ABC Ltd paid €960 (net) to the VHI for Mr Frost in November 2016. Mr Frost is single and had a salary of €46,000 for 2016.

Requirement
Calculate Mr Frost's income tax liability for 2016.

Question 6.6

John, a separated man with no children, had a salary of €75,000 for 2016, from which PAYE of €19,950 was deducted. During 2016 John paid mortgage interest of €11,000 in respect of a house in Belfast occupied by his wife as her main residence. The mortgage in respect of this house was taken out in June 2009. John is assessed as a single person and is not a first-time buyer.

Requirement
Calculate John's income tax liability for 2016.

Question 6.7

June is a widow aged 56 whose husband died in March 2013. For 2016, she had a salary of €43,000 (PAYE deducted €5,000) and a Department of Social Protection widow's pension of €10,062. June's employment is non-pensionable. During 2016, June paid a retirement annuity premium of €2,000. June has three children whose circumstances are as follows:

(a) John is 21 years of age. He works part-time and is taking an evening degree course in computer science in UCD. During 2016 he earned €8,000 from his part-time work. Total fees payable in respect of his degree course came to €4,800, of which €3,000 was paid by June and €1,800 by John. June spent €350 on an eye test and new spectacles for John during 2016.
(b) Mary, who has been incapacitated since birth, receives a covenant net of tax at the standard rate of €3,200 per annum from her elderly aunt.
(c) David, who is 19 years of age, studies part time at Bolton Street College. He has assessable income of €500 gross per annum. David is also incapacitated since birth. June paid €500 in respect of doctors' fees and prescription medicines for David during 2016.

June and her family live in rented accommodation. June paid rent of €12,600 and a net premium to the VHI of €1,400 during 2016 for herself and Mary.

Requirement
Calculate June's income tax liability for 2016.

Question 6.8

John Fitzpatrick became 65 years of age on 1 May 2016. He is widowed for many years with no dependent children and lives alone. He is retired and his only source of income is his pension of €29,400 gross per annum.

During 2016, €1,900 of PAYE was deducted from his gross pension. He paid VHI €750 during 2016. The amount paid in respect of VHI was net of tax at the standard rate tax. John contributed €300 to an eligible charity during 2016.

John has no other source of income or allowances.

Requirement
Compute John Fitzpatrick's income tax liability for 2016 claiming all reliefs due to him.

Question 6.9

Jason and Damien are aged 61 and 66 respectively and are in a civil partnership. Their only income for 2016 was a pension of €35,000 from Jason's previous employer, from which PAYE of €2,000 was deducted. (They are not entitled to a home carer tax credit.)

Requirement
Calculate Jason and Damien's income tax liability for 2016.

Question 6.10

Bob, aged 55 in 2016, pays retirement annuity premiums to Irish Life annually to provide for a pension on his retirement as his employer does not operate a superannuation scheme.
   The amounts of the premiums paid were as follows:

	€
	€
2015	6,000
2016	4,000

Bob's salary for 2015 was €20,980 and for 2016 was €24,480.
   He is married and paid allowable charges of €3,000 in 2015 and in 2016. His only other source of income is deposit interest of €1,160 gross for 2015 and €1,195 gross for 2016.

Requirement
Calculate his retirement annuity relief for the tax year 2015 and 2016.

Question 6.11

Maria's salary for the tax year 2016 is €35,000 (PAYE deducted €4,400). She has no other income and is single.
   She made a seven-year covenant in 2011 to her incapacitated widowed father (aged 60). The total covenant payments made in the tax year 2016 were €4,000 net. Her father's only other income is rental income of €8,000 per annum.

Requirement
Calculate the 2016 income tax liability of Maria and her father.

Question 6.12

Robert O'Sullivan, a 36-year-old single man, is employed as an electrician by Midland Electrical Services Ltd. His P60 for 2016 showed gross pay of €84,000 and tax deducted of €13,780.
   He made pension contributions of €22,800 in that year directly into his PRSA and he made a covenant payment of €4,500 (gross) to his father Jack, who is 69 and in good health. He also made a covenant payment of €3,200 (net) to his permanently incapacitated brother, Anthony. He receives bank interest of €1,600 (net after DIRT) annually on 31 December each year.
   He owns an apartment, which is let. In 2016, rents received were €1,200 per month and he paid mortgage interest on the property of €3,200 and also paid €2,250 for new furniture, a management fee of €3,100 and allowable expenses of €2,600. He had a tax rental loss forward from the previous year of €3,000.
   He also invested €20,000 to buy shares in a qualifying Employment and Investment Incentive (EII) company.
   John received a cheque from Independent Newspapers plc of €5,200 (net) in respect of dividends on shares which he owns in this quoted Irish company. He also owns shares in Chemcorp, an unquoted Irish

resident pharmaceutical company. He is offered the option of receiving one share for every €5 due in cash. John would be entitled to €800 gross cash dividend from Chemcorp. He takes up the offer and received 160 shares during the tax year 2016.

He also paid €45 for a doctor's visit, non-routine dental fees of €800 for his brother Dermot (who lives with him full-time) and €125 for a new pair of reading glasses.

Requirement
Calculate Robert's income tax liability for 2016.

Question 6.13

Jenny McFee is a widow, aged 51, whose husband James died in January 2015. Jenny has three children attending college as follows:

1. Maria is 22 years old and is studying for a Masters in Biochemistry on a full-time basis. Total fees payable by Jenny were €8,500.
2. Maria's twin brother John is studying for a degree in hotel management on a part-time basis and he also works by night in a busy city centre restaurant. Total fees payable by Jenny were €1,740.
3. The youngest child Colm (18 years) commenced a training course of two years duration to study computer technology and coding. At the successful completion of the course Colm will be awarded a Certificate in Information Systems. Fees payable by Jenny were €1,300.

Jenny works part-time at JZ Ltd, a music distribution company, as company accountant. Jenny earned €55,000 in 2016 (PAYE paid €5,200) and JZ Ltd paid her VHI premium of €1,540 (net) for 2016. Jenny is in receipt of a small widow's pension of €12,150 (PAYE deducted €2,550) from James' pension plan.

Jenny also cares for James' elderly mother Rose (aged 85) who has Alzheimer's and lives with them. She employs a carer to take care of Rose while she is at work at a cost of €12,500 per annum.

Jenny has two students staying in her spare room and they paid her €7,800 for accommodation and meals. She also earned €1,200 deposit interest (net) from KBC Bank in 2016.

Requirement
Calculate Jenny's income tax liability for 2016.

Computation of Income Tax

Learning Objectives

In this chapter you will learn:

- how income tax is calculated once taxable income, under all tax heads, has been established;
- how single individuals, married couples and civil partners are assessed using single, joint and separate assessments;
- who is accountable in the case of married couples/civil partners;
- the special rules which apply in the year of marriage/civil partnership and the year of death of a spouse/civil partner; and
- the tax consequences of divorce, separation or dissolution of a civil partnership.

7.1 Introduction

Income tax is calculated on taxable income, and the tax due is then reduced by personal tax credits and refundable tax credits, resulting in net tax due or net tax refundable.

- **Gross income** is income from all sources net of relevant deductions (e.g. Schedules D, E and F).
- **Total income** or **net statutory income** is gross income reduced by charges on income (e.g. covenant payments, qualifying interest, etc.).
- **Taxable income** is total income/net statutory income reduced by personal reliefs at the marginal rate.
- **Income tax liability** is the tax calculated on the taxable income (by reference to the marital status of the taxpayer); the tax so calculated is then reduced by non-refundable tax credits, i.e. personal tax credits such as single personal tax credit, employee tax credit, etc., and other credits allowed at the standard rate such as medical expenses.
- **Tax due/repayable** is the income tax liability reduced by refundable tax credits, i.e. tax already paid, e.g. PAYE/DWT and increased by income tax deducted from payments made (e.g. covenants).

Gross Income under Schedules D, E and F

LESS

Relief for Charges Paid

EQUALS

TOTAL INCOME/NET STATUTORY INCOME

LESS

Personal Reliefs @ Marginal Rate

EQUALS

TAXABLE INCOME

Tax Payable on Taxable Income

LESS

Tax Credits @ Standard Rate

EQUALS

Tax Liability

LESS

Refundable Tax Credits (PAYE/DWT)

ADD

Tax Deducted from Payments Made

EQUALS

TAX DUE/REPAYABLE

7.2 Pro Forma Income Tax Computation

7.2.1 Employment Income Only

Joe Taxpayer Income Tax Computation for 2016				
Income:			€	€
Schedule E:	Income from employments/offices:			
	– Salary/wages/director's fee/pensions		X	
	– Bonus/commissions		X	
	– Benefits in kind		X	
	– Taxable lump sum		X	
	– Share options		<u>X</u>	<u>X</u>
	Less: Allowable expenses		(X)	
	Employee's contribution to a Revenue-approved superannuation fund		<u>(X)</u>	<u>(X)</u>

continued overleaf

Gross Income				X
Deduct:	Relief for charges paid during the tax year:			
	– Qualifying covenants paid		(X)	
	– Qualifying interest paid		(X)	(X)
Total Income/Net Statutory Income				X
Deduct:	**Personal reliefs** (i.e. reliefs @ marginal rate)			(X)
TAXABLE INCOME				X
Tax Payable:	€33,800 @ 20%		X	
	Balance @ 40%		X	X
	(Single Person)			
Deduct:	**Non-refundable tax credits**			
	(i.e. reliefs @ standard rate)			(X)
INCOME TAX LIABILITY				X
Deduct:	**Refundable tax credits:**			
	– PAYE paid in tax year		(X)	
	– Dividend withholding tax		(X)	(X)
Add:	**Income tax deducted from payments made:**			
	Tax deducted from covenant payments			X
NET TAX DUE/REFUNDABLE				X

7.2.2 Income from All Sources

Joe Taxpayer Income Tax Computation for 2016			
Income:		€	€
Schedule D:	**Case I** (self-employed traders):		
	Adjusted Case I profit in basis period	X	
	Less: Trading loss carried forward S382	(X)	
	Less: Case I capital allowances	(X)	
	Less: Allowable retirement annuity premium	(X)	X
	Case II (self-employed professionals):		
	Adjusted Case II profit in basis period	X	
	Less: Loss in profession carried forward	(X)	
	Less: Case II capital allowances	(X)	
	Less: Allowable retirement annuity premium	(X)	X
	Case III (interest and income from abroad received without deduction of income tax)		X
	Case IV (interest and income received under deduction of tax; miscellaneous income)		X
			continued overleaf

	Case V (rental income from property in the State after deduction of allowable expenses)	X	
	Less: Case V loss carried forward	(X)	
	Less: Case V capital allowances	(X)	X
Schedule E:	Income from employments/offices:		
	– Salary/wages/director's fee/pensions	X	
	– Bonus/commissions	X	
	– Benefits in kind	X	
	– Taxable lump sum	X	
	– Share options	X	
		X	
	Less: Allowable expenses	(X)	
	Less: Employee's contribution to a Revenue-approved superannuation fund	(X)	X
Schedule F:	Distributions/dividends from Irish resident companies		X
Gross Income			X
Deduct:	Relief for EII paid during the tax year	(X)	
Deduct:	Relief for charges paid during the tax year:		
	– Qualifying covenants paid	(X)	
	– Qualifying interest paid	(X)	
	– Patent royalties paid	(X)	(X)
Total Income/Net Statutory Income			X
Deduct:	**Personal reliefs** (i.e. reliefs @ marginal rate)		(X)
TAXABLE INCOME			X
Tax Payable:	€33,800 @ 20%	X	
(Single Person)	Balance @ 40%	X	X
Deduct:	**Non-refundable tax credits**		
	(i.e. reliefs @ standard rate)		(X)
INCOME TAX LIABILITY			X
Deduct:	**Refundable tax credits:**		
	– PAYE paid in tax year	(X)	
	– Dividend withholding tax	(X)	(X)
Add:	**Income tax deducted from payments made:**		
	– Tax deducted from covenants' payments	X	
	– Tax deducted from patent royalties	X	X
NET TAX DUE/REFUNDABLE			X

7.3   Tax Treatment of Married Couples or Civil Partners

7.3.1   General

A married couple means any couple, **same-sex or heterosexual**, who marry in accordance with the provisions of the Marriage Acts. Section 70 FA 2015 provides that any references in the **Tax Acts** to a man, married man or husband can be construed as including a reference to a woman, married woman or wife.

The Civil Partnership and Certain Rights and Obligations of Cohabitants Act 2010 was enacted on 19 July 2010. The Act established a civil partnership registration scheme for **same-sex** couples, which confers a range of rights, obligations and protections **consequent on registration**. It also set out the manner in which civil partnerships may be dissolved and with what conditions. Additionally, it set out a redress scheme for long-term opposite sex and same-sex cohabiting couples who are not married or registered in a civil partnership.

Legislative changes required to give effect to the taxation changes arising from the Act were included in the Finance (No. 3) Act 2011. In short, on the registration of a civil partnership, civil partners are treated **in the same way** as spouses under tax law. This does not give opposite-sex cohabiting couples or same-sex cohabiting couples the same tax treatment as married couples or civil partners. **Cohabiting couples are treated as single persons under tax law.**

7.3.2   Assessment to Tax of Married Couples and Civil Partners

Married couples and civil partners can be assessed for tax in three different ways, as follows:

- **Joint Assessment**, where all income is taxed as if it were the income of one of the spouses/civil partners, but with higher tax bands at the standard rate of tax.
- **Single Assessment**, where each spouse/civil partner is assessed to tax as if they were not married or in a civil partnership, with no transferability of unutilised credits or tax bands.
- **Separate Assessment**, where a married couple/civil partners, who are assessable on a joint assessment basis, can claim for separate assessment of their joint tax liability.

7.3.3   Joint Assessment

Under joint assessment the income of **each** spouse/civil partner is taxed as if it were the income of the assessable spouse or nominated civil partner. The couple themselves elect which one of them is to be the **assessable spouse** or **nominated civil partner** and the nomination can be done in writing or verbally to Revenue. In the absence of such a nomination, the spouse/civil partner with the highest income becomes the assessable spouse or nominated civil partner.

Joint assessment is automatic, i.e. it is provided in the legislation that a married couple or civil partners will be deemed to have elected for joint assessment **unless**, before the end of the year of assessment, **either** spouse/civil partner writes to Revenue indicating that they would prefer to be assessed as **single** individuals.

Under joint assessment, the tax credits and standard rate tax band can be allocated between spouses or civil partners in a way that suits their circumstances. For example, where one spouse/civil partner has no taxable income, all transferable tax credits and the standard rate tax band will be given to the other spouse/civil partner. The PAYE tax credit, employment expenses and the basic standard rate band of €24,800 are non-transferable.

The **income bands** chargeable at the standard rate of tax are increased, depending on whether the married couple/civil partners have one or two incomes.

Tax Year 2016	Tax Rate	Joint Assessment (One Income)	Joint Assessment (Two Incomes)
Taxable Income	20%	€42,800	€67,600*
	40%	Balance	Balance

Transferable between spouses/civil partners up to a maximum of €42,800 for any one spouse/civil partner. The balance of €24,800 is available to the lower earning spouse only.

7.3.4 Single Assessment

If a married couple/civil partners wish to be assessed on the single assessment basis, then either spouse/civil partner must give notice to this effect to Revenue before the end of the year of assessment for which they wish to be assessed as single persons. If such a notice is given for any year of assessment, it will then apply for that year and all future years **unless** withdrawn by the spouse/civil partner who gave the notice of election.

If an election for single assessment is made, then each spouse/civil partner will be assessed to income tax as if they were not married or in a civil partnership, i.e. they are effectively treated as single persons, and tax credits and reliefs are granted accordingly. In such cases, if either spouse/civil partner has tax credits or reliefs in excess of his or her assessable income, there is **no right to transfer** unutilised credits to the other spouse/civil partner. From a tax point of view, in most cases, it will probably be undesirable for married couples/civil partners to elect for single assessment unless each spouse/civil partner is fully utilising their standard rate band and income tax credits and reliefs.

7.3.5 Separate Assessment

A married couple/civil partners that are assessable on a joint basis may claim for separate assessment of their joint income tax liability. Either spouse/civil partner can make an election for separate assessment not later than 1 April in the year of assessment.

Such an application applies for the year of claim and all subsequent years and may only be withdrawn by the spouse/civil partner who made the application. An election for separate assessment will result in the **same total income tax liability** as if the spouses/civil partners were jointly assessed, with each spouse paying their portion of the total tax liability.

The amount of income tax payable by each spouse/civil partner is calculated by reference to their total income and the proportions of tax credits or reliefs to which they are entitled. Separate assessment **does not diminish** or **increase** the total liability that would have arisen under normal joint assessment.

A couple might opt for separate assessment so that they could each deal with their own tax affairs while not losing out financially.

Calculation of Separate Liabilities

1. Ascertain the gross income assessable for each spouse/civil partner and the overall reliefs and allowances due for the year.
2. Any deductions from total income, e.g. permanent health insurance, are deducted from the income of the person who incurred the expenditure.
3. Each spouse/civil partner is given a standard rate tax band equal to that applicable to a single person, i.e. €33,800. However, to the extent that one spouse/civil partner does not fully utilise the standard rate band, i.e. their income is less than €33,800, the part of the tax band not utilised may be transferred to the other spouse/civil partner, subject to the proviso that the spouse/civil partner with the higher income may not have a standard rate tax band in excess of €42,800.
4. Apportion tax credits as follows:

Basic personal tax credit	} Half each
Blind person's tax credit	} Half each
Age tax credit	} Half each
Incapacitated child tax credit	} Half each

Employee tax credit } Granted to each spouse/civil partner to the extent that each has Schedule E income to utilise the allowance

Earned income tax credit } Granted to each spouse/civil partner to the extent that each has earned income (excluding PAYE income)

Medical insurance relief, long-term care policies, college fees, employment of a carer, dependent relative, health insurance, etc. } Allowed to the person who bears the expenditure

5.   If any tax credits or reliefs are not fully utilised in calculating the tax liability of one of the spouses, then the unutilised balance is available in calculating the other spouse's/civil partner's tax liability.

Comparison of Treatment under Joint, Single and Separate Assessment

---

Example 7.1

James Cotter is married to Claire and they have one child who is incapacitated. Their income for 2016 is as follows:

	James	Claire
Salary	€52,000	€25,500
PAYE paid	€9,500	€1,300

Income Tax Calculation for 2016	Notes	€	€
– Joint Assessment			
Income:			
Schedule E			
– James		52,000	
– Claire		25,500	77,500
Tax Calculation:			
(€42,800 + €24,800) = €67,600 @ 20%	1	13,520	
(€77,500 – €67,600) = €9,900 @ 40%		3,960	17,480
Deduct:			
Basic personal tax credit (married)		3,300	
Employee tax credit	2	3,300	
Incapacitated child credit		3,300	(9,900)
Income tax liability			7,580
Deduct:			
PAYE paid			(10,800)
Tax refund due			(3,220)

Note 1:

The standard rate band is increased by €24,800, being the lower of the income of the lower income spouse (Claire €25,500) or €24,800, i.e. to an overall maximum of €67,600 at the standard rate.

Note 2:

As both are employed, both spouses are entitled to the employee tax credit.

Income Tax Calculation for 2016 – Single Assessment	€	€	€	€
		James		Claire
Income:				
Schedule E		52,000		25,500
Tax Calculation:				
€33,800 @ 20%	33,800	6,760	25,500	5,100
Balance @ 40%	18,200	7,280	0	0
		14,040		5,100
Deduct:				
Basic personal tax credit	1,650		1,650	
Employee tax credit	1,650		1,650	
Incapacitated child credit	1,650	(4,950)	1,650	(4,950)
Income tax liability		9,090		150
Deduct:				
PAYE paid		(9,500)		(1,300)
Tax refund due		**(410)**		**(1,150)**

Income Tax Calculation for 2016 – Separate Assessment	€	€	€	€
		James		Claire
Income:				
Schedule E		52,000		25,500
Tax Calculation:				
@ 20% (€67,600 – €25,500)	42,100	8,420	25,500	5,100
@ 40% (€52,000 – €42,100)	9,900	3,960	0	0
		12,380		5,100
Deduct:				
Basic personal tax credit	1,650		1,650	
Employee tax credit	1,650		1,650	
Incapacitated child credit	1,650	(4,950)	1,650	(4,950)
Income tax liability		7,430		150
Deduct:				
PAYE paid		(9,500)		(1,300)
Tax refund due		**(2,070)**		**(1,150)**

Comparison of Liability under Each Type of Assessment			
	James	Claire	Total
	€	€	€
Tax refundable 2016:			
Joint			**3,220**
Single	410	1,150	**1,560**
Separate	2,070	1,150	**3,220**

The total amount refundable is the same under joint and separate assessment. Single assessment would result in an extra amount of tax payable of €1,660.

7.3.6 Individualisation

Minister Charlie McCreevy introduced tax individualisation in Budget 2000 that was designed to move away from the system at the time, whereby the single person's tax band was doubled for married couples, to one that would involve **each** person having their **own** standard rate tax band. This process has yet to be completed, with the difference of €9,000 between the single person's tax band and the married couple/civil partners (one income) tax band remaining static since 2002.

7.3.7 Tax Treatment in Year of Marriage/Civil Partnership

Each party to the marriage/civil partnership is initially taxed as a **single** person for the complete year.

The legislation permits them to elect, after the end of the year of assessment, to have their tax liability computed on a joint assessment basis as if they had been married/were civil partners for the **whole** of the tax year in which the marriage/civil partnership took place. If this election is made, the tax saving, if any, *vis-à-vis* the amount of their combined liabilities on a single assessment basis, is scaled down in the proportion that the period of marriage/civil partnership during the tax year bears to the full tax year, i.e.:

$$\text{Tax saving} \quad \times \quad \frac{\text{number of income tax months from date of marriage/civil partnership to the end of the tax year}^*}{12 \text{ months}}$$

*An income tax month is a calendar month, with part of a month being treated as a full month in the formula.

Example 7.2
John married Mary on 15 July 2016. John earned a gross salary of €44,000 in 2016 and paid PAYE on it of €7,500. Mary earned a salary of €23,000 in 2016, on which she paid PAYE of €1,300.

continued overleaf

Assessment of John and Mary as Single Individuals for 2016

	John		Mary	
	€	€	€	€
Income:				
Schedule E		44,000		23,000
Tax Calculation:				
€33,800 @ 20%	33,800	6,760	23,000	4,600
Balance @ 40%	10,200	4,080	0	0
		10,840		4,600
Deduct:				
Basic personal tax credit	1,650		1,650	
Employee tax credit	1,650	(3,300)	1,650	(3,300)
Initial income tax liability		**7,540**		**1,300**
Deduct:				
Year of marriage relief (Note)		(768)		(132)
PAYE paid		(7,500)		(1,300)
Tax refund due		(728)		(132)

Note: Notional Liability under Joint Assessment for 2016	€	€
Income:		
Schedule E		67,000
Tax Calculation:		
€65,800 @ 20% (€42,800 + €23,000)	65,800	13,160
Balance @ 40%	1,200	480
		13,640
Deduct:		
Basic personal tax credit	3,300	
Employee tax credit	3,300	(6,600)
Total liability under joint assessment		7,040
Total combined liability under single assessment		8,840
Saving under joint assessment		1,800

Saving restricted to:

$$\frac{\text{6 months (period of marriage in tax year)}}{\text{12 months}} \times €1,800 \qquad €900$$

Split: John

$$\frac{€7,540}{€7,540 + €1,300} \times €900 \qquad €768$$

Split: Mary

$$\frac{€1,300}{€7,540 + €1,300} \times €900 \qquad €132$$

$$€900$$

7.3.8 Tax Treatment in Year of Death

The tax treatment of the surviving spouse/civil partner in the year of bereavement depends on how the surviving spouse/civil partner and the deceased were taxed **before** the bereavement.

7.3.9 Joint Assessment and Death of Assessable Spouse/Nominated Civil Partner

If the couple were assessed under joint assessment and if the **deceased** was the "assessable spouse" or "nominated civil partner", i.e. the person responsible for making a joint tax return, the **surviving spouse/civil partner** will be taxable in their **own right from the date of death** of the deceased. The surviving spouse/civil partner is entitled to the widowed person/surviving civil partner in the year of bereavement tax credit and the widowed person's/surviving civil partner's (without dependent children) tax band for this period. Any income (of the surviving spouse/civil partner and the deceased) **prior** to the death of the deceased is treated as the **income of the deceased** to the date of death.

Example 7.3

Mr Andrews, who was the assessable spouse under joint assessment, died on 1 November 2016. His salary from 1 January 2016 to the date of death was €46,000, from which PAYE of €5,900 was deducted.

Mrs Andrews was employed by a local wholesale company and earned €16,000 from 1 January to 1 November 2016 (PAYE deducted €2,200) and €3,500 from 2 November to 31 December 2016 (PAYE deducted €480).

Mr Andrews Deceased – Income Tax Liability Period 01/01/2016 to 01/11/2016		€	€
Schedule E salary self			46,000
Schedule E salary spouse			16,000
Gross income			62,000
Tax payable:			
€58,800 @ 20%	(€42,800 + €16,000)	11,760	
€3,200 @ 40%		1,280	
€62,000			
			13,040
Less: Basic personal tax credit – married		3,300	
Employee tax credits: €1,650 × 2		3,300	(6,600)
Tax liability			6,440
Less: PAYE – self		5,900	
PAYE – spouse		2,200	(8,100)
Refund due			(1,660)

Mrs Andrews – Income Tax Liability Period 02/11/2016 to 31/12/2016	€	€
Schedule E salary		3,500
Tax payable: €3,500 @ 20%		700
Less: Basic personal tax credit (year of bereavement)	(3,300)	
Tax credits limited to the amount which reduces tax liability to nil		(700)

continued overleaf

Tax liability	Nil
Less: PAYE paid	(480)
Refund due	(480)

7.3.10   Joint Assessment and Death of the Non-assessable Spouse or Non-nominated Civil Partner

If the couple were assessed under joint assessment and if the surviving spouse/civil partner was the "assessable spouse" or "nominated civil partner", i.e. the person responsible for making a joint tax return, the surviving spouse/civil partner will continue to receive the married person's/civil partner's tax credits and income tax bands for the remainder of the tax year. The surviving spouse/civil partner will be taxable on their own income for the full year of bereavement plus the deceased's income from the start of the tax year to the date of death.

Example 7.4

Jane Murphy died on 1 September 2016. Her salary from 1 January 2016 to the date of death was €36,000, from which PAYE of €5,900 was deducted.

Her civil partner, Ann Ward, is employed by a local company and earned €46,000 from 1 January to 1 September 2016 (PAYE deducted €9,200) and €13,500 from 2 September to 31 December 2016 (PAYE deducted €4,900). Ann is the nominated civil partner under joint assessment.

Ann Ward – Income Tax Calculation 2016	€	€	€
Income:			
Schedule E			
– Ann Ward (total 2016)		59,500	
– Jane Murphy (to 01/09/2016)		36,000	95,500
Tax Calculation:			
(€42,800 + €24,800) @ 20%	67,600	13,520	
Balance @ 40%	27,900	11,160	24,680
	95,500		
Deduct:			
Basic personal tax credit		3,300	
Employee tax credit (x 2)		3,300	(6,600)
Income tax liability			**18,080**
Deduct:			
PAYE paid:			
– Ann Ward (€9,200 + €4,900)		14,100	
– Jane Murphy		5,900	(20,000)
Tax refund due			**(1,920)**

7.3.11   Single Assessment and Death of a Spouse/Civil Partner

If the couple have been assessed as single persons, the deceased is taxed as a single person up to the date of death. The surviving spouse/civil partner is also taxed as a single person but is **entitled** to the widowed person/surviving civil partner in the year of bereavement tax credit (€3,300) instead of the single person's basic personal tax credit.

As can be seen from the above examples, where a couple have been jointly assessed and the **assessable spouse/nominated civil partner dies, extra tax credits** are given in the year of bereavement (i.e. widowed person/surviving civil partner in the year of bereavement personal tax credit to the surviving spouse/civil partner, the married/civil partner's personal tax credit and the couple, in effect, get an additional standard rate tax band.

Accordingly, a couple who have been assessed as single persons should consider electing for joint assessment in the year of death. An **election** can be made by the surviving spouse and the personal representative of the deceased and must be made **before the end** of the tax year in which the death occurs.

Tax Treatment of Surviving Spouse/Civil Partner for Subsequent Years

In the years following the year of bereavement, the surviving spouse/civil partner is entitled to the widowed person's/surviving civil partner's tax credit. If the surviving spouse/civil partner has dependent children, he/she will also be entitled to the Single Person Child Carer Credit and the widowed/surviving civil partner parent tax credit (for five years after the date of bereavement). The widowed person's/surviving civil partner's (without dependent children) income tax band or the one-parent family (with dependent children) tax band will also apply, depending on whether the surviving spouse/civil partner has dependent children.

Surviving Spouse/Civil Partner	With Dependent Children	Without Dependent Children
	€	€
Year of Bereavement:		
Married Person/Civil Partner Tax Credit	3,300	3,300
Maximum Standard Rate Tax Band:		
Joint/Separate Assessment	67,600	67,600
Single Assessment	37,800	33,800
Subsequent Years:		
Widowed Person/Surviving Civil Partner Tax Credit	1,650	2,190
Single Person Child Carer Credit	1,650	Nil
Maximum Standard Rate Tax Band	37,800	33,800
ADDITIONAL (for years after year of bereavement)		
Year 1:	3,600	Nil
Widowed Parent/Surviving Civil Partner Tax Credit		
Year 2:		
Widowed Parent/Surviving Civil Partner Tax Credit	3,150	Nil
Year 3:		
Widowed Parent/Surviving Civil Partner Tax Credit	2,700	Nil
Year 4:		
Widowed Parent/Surviving Civil Partner Tax Credit	2,250	Nil
Year 5:		
Widowed Parent/Surviving Civil Partner Tax Credit	1,800	Nil

7.3.12   Tax Treatment of Separated Spouses/Civil Partners

The general rule is that separated spouses/civil partners are assessed to income tax as **single individuals**. The following rules apply:

- **Legally enforceable** maintenance payments are **deductible as a charge** in arriving at the tax liability of the payer and are chargeable to income tax under Case IV of Schedule D in the hands of the receiving spouse/civil partner. **Voluntary** payments (i.e. payments which are not legally enforceable) are **not** taken into account when calculating either spouse's/civil partner's tax.

- Income tax is **not deducted** at source from legally enforceable maintenance payment arrangements by one party to the other party.

- **Legally enforceable** maintenance payments made for the use or **benefit of a child are disregarded** for tax purposes, i.e. the payer does not get a tax deduction for the payment and the child is not assessed on the payment. Only the parent in receipt of the **Single Person Child Carer Credit** (2016: €1,650) can avail of the **one-parent family** tax band (2016: €37,800), even if the child resides with each parent for part of the tax year.

Example 7.5

Mr and Mrs Pearce are separated. Under a legal deed drawn up in 2011, Mr Pearce pays Mrs Pearce €900 per month, of which €500 is specifically for their only child, Stuart, aged 8. Mr Pearce is employed by an insurance company and Mrs Pearce is employed by a local wholesale company. His salary for the tax year 2016 was €59,000 (PAYE deducted €11,000) and her salary for the tax year 2016 was €30,000 (PAYE deducted €570).

The child resides with Mrs Pearce (who is the primary claimant) during the week and with Mr Pearce at weekends and some holidays.

Mr Pearce – Income Tax Liability 2016		€
	Schedule E	59,000
Less charges:	Maintenance payments (€400 × 12)	(4,800)
	Net income	54,200
Tax payable (single person):	€33,800 @ 20%	6,760
	€20,400 @ 40%	8,160
		14,920
Less:	Basic personal tax credit	(1,650)
	Employee tax credit	(1,650)
Tax liability		11,620
Less:	PAYE deducted	(11,000)
	Tax payable	620

Mrs Pearce – Income Tax Liability 2016		€
Case IV	Schedule D	4,800
	Schedule E	30,000
		34,800
Tax payable (single person child carer):	€34,800 @ 20%	6,960
Less:	Basic personal tax credit	(1,650)
	Employee tax credit	(1,650)
	Single person child carer credit	(1,650)
Tax liability		2,010
Less:	PAYE deducted	(570)
	Tax payable	1,440
Total tax liability: Mr and Mrs Pearce		**13,630**

Example 7.6
Taking Example 7.5 above, if Mrs Pearce surrenders her entitlement to the single person child carer credit to Mr Pearce, and Stuart resides with him for more than 100 days, the potential tax saving is as follows:

Mr Pearce – Income Tax Liability 2016	€	€
Income:		
Schedule E	59,000	
Less: Maintenance payments (€400 × 12)	(4,800)	
Taxable income		54,200
Tax Calculation (single person child carer):		
€37,800 @ 20%	7,560	
€16,400 @ 40%	6,560	14,120
€54,200		
Less: Non-refundable Tax Credits:		
Basic personal tax credit	1,650	
Employee tax credit	1,650	
Single person child carer credit	1,650	(4,950)
Tax liability		9,170
Deduct: PAYE paid		(11,000)
Net tax refund due		**(1,830)**

Mrs Pearce – Income Tax Liability 2016	€	€
Income:		
Case IV, Schedule D	4,800	
Schedule E	30,000	
Taxable income		34,800
Tax Calculation (single person):		
€33,800 @ 20%	6,760	
€1,000 @ 40%	400	7,160
€34,800		
Less: Non-refundable Tax Credits:		
Basic personal tax credit	1,650	
Employee tax credit	1,650	(3,300)
Tax liability		3,860
Deduct: PAYE paid		(570)
Net tax payable		3,290
Total tax liability Mr and Mrs Pearce		**13,030**

There is a potential overall saving of €600 if Mrs Pearce surrenders the SPCCC to Mr Pearce. The saving will only apply if the parent in receipt of the SPCCC is unable to fully utilise the one-parent family tax band, currently €37,800

7.3.13 Option for Joint Assessment on Separation, Divorce or Dissolution of Civil Partnership

A separated couple can elect to be treated as a married couple for income tax purposes if:

- maintenance payments by one to the other are legally enforceable; and
- they are both resident in the State.

If the marriage/civil partnership has not been **dissolved or annulled**, and the couple obtain an Irish divorce/civil partner dissolution, then the same rules apply for income tax purposes as apply to separated spouses/civil partners, i.e.:

- they are treated as **single individuals**;
- **legally enforceable maintenance payments** are deducted as a **charge** in arriving at the income tax liability of the payer, and are chargeable to income tax under Schedule D, Case IV for the receiving spouse/civil partner;
- each spouse/civil partner will be entitled to the **single person tax credits** and **rate bands**; and
- only the parent in receipt of the **Single Person Child Carer Credit** (2016: €1,650) can avail of the **one-parent family** tax band (2016: €37,800), even if the child resides with each parent for part of the tax year.

In the case of separation, divorce or dissolution of civil partnership, the couple may elect for **joint assessment** only if:

- both individuals are **resident in Ireland** for tax purposes for the year of assessment;
- **legally enforceable maintenance payments** are made by one spouse/civil partner to the other; and
- **neither has remarried or registered a new civil partnership.**

If this election is made under section 1026 TCA 1997, the following rules apply:

- the payer **cannot deduct maintenance payments** made to the separated or divorced spouse/civil partner in arriving at their total income and the separated or **divorced spouse/civil partner is not assessed** on the maintenance payments;
- the **married person's/civil partner's tax credits** and rate bands are granted; and
- if the separated or divorced spouse/civil partner has income in their own right, apart from maintenance payments received by them, the income tax liability applicable to each spouse's/civil partner's separate income is calculated using the separate assessment procedures.

Example 7.7
Same circumstances as Example 7.5, with joint assessment option.

Mrs Pearce – Income Tax Calculation 2016

	€	€
Income:		
Schedule E		<u>30,000</u>
Tax Calculation:		
€30,000 @ 20%	6,000	
€ – @ 40%	<u>0</u>	6,000
€30,000		
Less: Non-refundable Tax Credits:		
Basic personal tax credit	1,650	
Employee tax credit	<u>1,650</u>	(3,300)

continued overleaf

Tax liability		2,700
Deduct: PAYE paid		(570)
Net tax due		**2,130**

Mr Pearce – Income Tax Calculation 2016

Income:	€	€
Schedule E		59,000
Tax Calculation:		
€33,800 @ 20%	6,760	
€3,800 @ 20% (Note)	760	
€21,400 @ 40%	8,560	16,080
€59,000		
Less: Non-refundable Tax Credits:		
Basic personal tax credit	1,650	
Employee tax credit	1,650	(3,300)
Tax liability		12,780
Deduct: PAYE paid		(11,000)
Net tax due		**1,780**
Total tax liability: Mr and Mrs Pearce		**15,480**

Note: part of standard rate tax band not used by Mrs Pearce = €3,800 (€33,800 − €30,000) can increase the standard rate tax band of Mr Pearce.

In this case, it is more beneficial for Mr and Mrs Pearce not to opt for joint assessment as not only will they lose their single person child carer credit but their combined income taxed at 20% is reduced by €4,000.

7.3.14   Tax Treatment in Year of Separation, Divorce or Dissolution

In the year of separation, divorce or dissolution where **joint assessment** had been elected for under section 1026 TCA 1997, the tax treatment of the couple is similar to the tax treatment that applies in the year of death of the assessable spouse/nominated civil partner.

Treatment of Assessable Spouse/Nominated Civil Partner

1. He or she is assessable on their entire personal income for the year of separation and their spouse's/ civil partner's income (applying appropriate basis of apportionment) for the proportion of the year up to the date of separation.
2. He or she is entitled to a **married person's/civil partner's basic personal tax credit**, €3,300 for the tax year 2016, and the benefit of the **married person's/civil partner's tax bands**.

Treatment of Non-assessable Spouse/Nominated Civil Partner

1. He or she is assessable as a single person on their own sources of income for the period of the year after the date of separation.
2. He or she is entitled only to a single person's basic personal tax credit and to the benefit of the rate bands applicable to a single person. If there are dependent children, they are entitled to a **single person child carer credit** and **one-parent family tax band**, assuming they satisfy the conditions as set out in **Section 6.2.3**.
3. Other allowances/reliefs, etc. available to them are given by reference to single person limitations.

Example 7.8

Mr and Mrs Doyle had been married for 10 years when they separated on 30 September 2016. Under the terms of the deed of separation drawn up on that day, Mr Doyle pays Mrs Doyle €300 per month, from 1 October 2016, which specifically includes €100 for the maintenance of their only child, Ruth, who lives with her mother. Mr Doyle is the assessable spouse.

Mr Doyle earned €49,000 in 2016, from which PAYE of €5,600 was deducted. Mrs Doyle earned €22,000 in 2016, from which PAYE of €3,900 was deducted. Mrs Doyle earned €16,500 (PAYE paid €2,900) for the period 1 January 2016 to 30 September 2016.

Mr Doyle – Income Tax Computation 2016

	€	€
Income:		
Schedule E – self	49,000	
Schedule E – wife 01/01/2016 to 30/09/2016	16,500	65,500
Less: Charges		
Maintenance payments (€300 – €100 × 3)		(600)
Total income		**64,900**
Tax Calculation:		
€42,800 @ 20%	8,560	
€16,500 @ 20%	3,300	
€5,600 @ 40%	2,240	
€64,900		14,100
Less: Non-refundable Tax Credits:		
Basic personal tax credit (married)	3,300	
Employee tax credit (× 2)	3,300	(6,600)
Tax liability		**7,500**
Deduct:		
PAYE paid – self	5,600	
PAYE paid – wife 01/01/2016 to 30/09/2016	2,900	(8,500)
Net tax refundable		(1,000)

Mrs Doyle – Income Tax Computation 2016

	€	€
Income:		
Schedule D, Case IV	600	
Schedule E (01/10/2016 to 31/12/2016)	5,500	6,100
Tax Calculation:		
€6,100 @ 20%		1,220
Less: Non-refundable Tax Credits:		
Basic personal tax credit	1,650	
Single person child carer credit	1,650	
Employee tax credit	1,650	
	4,950	
Restrict to amount which gives a nil tax liability		(1,220)
Tax liability		**NIL**
Deduct:		
PAYE paid (01/10/2016 to 31/12/2016)		(1,000)
Net tax refundable		**(1,000)**

Questions

Review Questions
(See Suggested Solutions to Review Questions at the end of this textbook.)

Question 7.1

Patrick and Helen have been married for a number of years. They have the following income and outgoings for the tax year 2016.

	Patrick	Helen
	€	€
Income		
Salary	10,500	50,000
Benefit in kind	–	2,100
Outgoings		
Mortgage Interest – loan taken out in 2003	4,200	–
Permanent Health Insurance	–	950
PAYE paid	830	8,000

Requirement
Compute the income tax liability on the basis that the following options had been claimed for 2016:
(a) joint assessment
(b) separate assessment
(c) single assessment.

Question 7.2

Peter and Paul entered into a civil partnership on 20 June 2016. The couple elected for joint assessment, with Peter as the nominated civil partner.
 Peter is employed by a firm of auctioneers. His gross salary for 2016 was €50,000 (PAYE deducted €10,300).
 Paul is employed by a firm of stockbrokers. He earned €26,000 gross (PAYE deducted €2,050) during 2016

Requirement
Compute Peter and Paul's tax liability for 2016 on the basis that they wish to minimise their total liability.

Question 7.3

Mr and Mrs Thorne separated in 1993. Under the terms of the deed of separation which was drawn up at that time, Mr Thorne pays Mrs Thorne €800 per month, of which €600 is specifically for their two children. The children reside with Mrs Thorne from Monday to Saturday, and with Mr Thorne on Sundays. Joint assessment does not apply.
 Mr Thorne's projected salary for the tax year 2016 is €50,000 and Mrs Thorne's projected salary is €35,000.
 The terms of the deed are being reviewed at present and Mr Thorne has suggested increasing the maintenance payments to €1,000 per month, on condition that only €100 per month is specifically for their two children, and that the deed is reviewed every year.

Mrs Thorne, who has little knowledge of income tax, has contacted you confirming that she seems satisfied with this, as long as there are no tax disadvantages arising.

Requirement
(a) Calculate Mrs Thorne's income tax liability for the tax year 2016, if:
    (i) the deed is not reviewed;
    (ii) the deed is reviewed with effect from 1 January 2016.
(b) Indicate under which situation she is better off financially and by how much.

Question 7.4

Mr and Mrs Lynch separated on 30 June 2016. Under the terms of the deed of separation drawn up on that date, Mr Lynch pays Mrs Lynch €700 per month, of which €100 is specifically for their only child, Mary, who resides with her mother. The first monthly payment is made on 1 July 2016. He also pays the mortgage on the family home, where Mrs Lynch continues to reside.

Mr Lynch's salary for 2016 was €48,000 and Mrs Lynch's salary was €15,000. Mrs Lynch's payslip for the month ended 30 June 2016 showed cumulative gross salary of €7,000 for the period 1 January 2016 to 30 June 2016. Mr Lynch had the following outgoings:

	Tax Year	
	2015	**2016**
	€	€
Gross mortgage interest		
Payable to Bank of Ireland – loan taken out in 2003	3,900	4,100
VHI payments (net of tax @ 20%)	850	895

Mr and Mrs Lynch had been jointly assessed for all years up to the year of their separation.

Requirement
Calculate Mr and Mrs Lynch's tax liability for 2016 on the basis that:
(a) Joint assessment was claimed for the year of assessment in accordance with section 1026 TCA 1997.
(b) No election was made under section 1026 TCA 1997.

If Mr and Mrs Lynch had separated during 2015, calculate their tax liability for 2016 assuming that:
(c) An election was made for joint assessment under section 1026 TCA 1997.
(d) The election under section 1026 TCA 1997 was not made.

Question 7.5

Jane DuBlanc's husband Matthew died suddenly on 30 May 2016. They have three children all aged under 18. Matthew was the assessable spouse and earned €60,000 until the date of his death (PAYE paid €19,250). Jane works as a design consultant and earned €72,000 in total for 2016 (PAYE paid €18,750). Her earnings to 30 May 2016 were €30,000 (PAYE €7,800).

Requirement
Calculate the couple's income tax liability for 2016 where:
(a) Matthew is the assessable spouse; and
(b) Jane is the assessable spouse at the date of death.

The PAYE System

8

Learning Objectives

In this chapter you will learn:

- the division of responsibilities between the employer and the taxpayer in collecting tax on employment income;
- the administration and operation of the Pay As You Earn (PAYE) system;
- the special rules for commencement and cessation of employments and for unpaid remuneration;
- the operation of employee tax credits and standard rate cut-off point (SRCOP) under the PAYE system;
- the tax treatment of Social Welfare Benefits;
- the calculation of liability to Pay Related Social Insurance (PRSI); and
- the rules relating to and the calculation of liability to the Universal Social Charge (USC) for employees and the self-employed.

8.1   Introduction

The PAYE (Pay As You Earn) system is the method used by the Revenue Commissioners to collect income tax on most **Schedule E** income.

Broadly speaking, it obliges an employer to deduct income tax from wages, salaries and other income assessable to tax under Schedule E **when the remuneration is actually paid**. The primary objective of the system is to collect the income tax due in respect of the relevant Schedule E payments so as to avoid a deferral of liability by the employees concerned.

The PAYE system is a good example of the principle of deduction of **tax at source** in operation, whereby the **payer** rather than the **recipient** of the income is liable to account for the income tax to Revenue. Under this system, it is the **employer** who is **obliged** to deduct the tax on making payments of emoluments to his employees and to account for the tax so deducted to the Collector-General. Payments made under Schedule E are **deemed** to have been paid **net of tax**. Where refunds of tax are due to the employee, the system provides, in certain circumstances, that these are made by the employer.

Under this system, much of the administration cost involved in collecting income tax due by people assessable under Schedule E is effectively put on to the employer.

8.2   Scope of Application of the PAYE System

The PAYE system applies to all income from offices or employments (including directorships and occupational pensions). The system therefore applies to:

- Salaries, wages, directors' fees, back pay, pensions, bonuses, overtime, sales commissions, holiday pay, tea money, etc.
- **Round sum expenses** must be paid under the PAYE system. Such round sum expenses would include, for example, a fixed sum (whether paid weekly, monthly or yearly) to cover expenses to be met by the employee, or an amount put at the disposal of the employee for which he or she does not have to account to the employer with receipts, vouchers, etc.
  Reimbursements of expenses actually incurred by employees in the performance of their duties of employment are not treated as "pay" for PAYE purposes.
- Travel expenses paid or reimbursed to a director, but excluding **non-resident**, non-executive directors, to attend meetings (including board meetings), are taxable as perquisites under the PAYE system.
- Commencement/inducement payments and termination payments.
- Benefits in kind (BIK) and perquisites ('perks') must be paid under the PAYE system. Examples of BIK are the private use of a company car, loans at a preferential rate of interest and free or subsidised accommodation. Examples of perks are medical insurance premiums, payment of club subscriptions and vouchers. The calculation of the taxable value of BIK and perks is included in **Chapter 4**.
- Payments by employees to employer superannuation schemes may be deducted from their gross pay for PAYE purposes. However, employee contributions to pension schemes are liable to employee PRSI and Universal Social Charge (USC) and are not deductible from gross pay for PRSI and USC purposes.
- From 1 January 2011, share-based remuneration is included as notional pay for the calculation of PAYE/PRSI and USC at the time the shares are given to the employee.

8.3   Employer's Responsibilities

8.3.1   Registration

An employer is obliged **by law** to register for PAYE purposes any employee whose earnings, if employed full time, exceed €8 per week (or €36 per month) **or**, if employed part-time, exceed €2 per week (or €9 per month). A company **must register** as an employer and operate PAYE, PRSI and USC on the pay of directors even if there are no other employees. However, a "qualifying domestic employer" does not have to register and operate PAYE on emoluments paid to a domestic employee. A qualifying domestic employer is an individual who has only one domestic employee who is paid **less than €40** a week. A domestic employee is an individual employed to carry out domestic duties, including child minding, in the private residence of the employer.

Registration for PAYE is done **online** using the Revenue On-Line Service (ROS) or through the eRegistration service if:

- the employer is currently registered for myAccount;
- the employer is registered for ROS; or
- the employer is represented by an agent.

If access to the eRegistration service is **unavailable** to the following applicants, they must submit paper applications to their local Revenue office:

- individuals who are not registered for ROS or PAYE Anytime service;
- non-assessable spouses;
- where a non-resident director exists;
- unincorporated bodies/non-profit organisations (e.g. schools, Boards of Management, charities);
- liquidators, receivers and executors;

- collection agents; and
- VAT/RCT re-registrations.

To register, one of the following forms must be completed:

- Form **TR1** – employer is an individual *or* partnership.
- Form **TR2** – employer is trading as a company.
- Form **PREM Reg** – employer who is **already registered** for income tax (either as an employee or self-employed) or for corporation tax.

Obligation to Keep a Register of Employees

Under the Income Tax (Employments) Regulations 2012, which came into force on **18 July 2012**, all employers are required to keep a "Register of Employees" (in paper or electronic format) showing the name, address, PPS number, date of commencement and, where relevant, the date of cessation of employment of all employees.

8.3.2 Deduction of Local Property Tax from Salary/Pensions

Employers (including pension providers) are required to make phased payment options available to those employees who wish to pay their local property tax (LPT) (see **Chapter 9**) as a **deduction at source** from their net salary. Where this payment option is chosen by the employee, Revenue will notify the employer on the Employer Tax Credit Certificate (P2C) of the amount of LPT to be deducted **evenly** over the pay periods between **1 January and 31 December**. The employer is required to account for and remit the LPT along with the PAYE/PRSI/USC.

LPT can only be deducted where the employer has received a P2C showing the amount of LPT to be deducted and the employer can only cease deduction of LPT from net salary when advised to do so by Revenue, i.e. the employee cannot direct the employer to commence or cancel collection of LPT. Similarly, any queries, questions or disputes regarding LPT amounts or property valuations are a matter between the employee and Revenue.

The following is an extract from an employer tax credit certificate (P2C) showing USC rates and LPT deduction:

Universal Social Charge (USC)				

Rates of USC		Exemption Case N		
			Yearly COP	**Monthly COP**	**Weekly COP**
USC Rate 1	1%				
USC Rate 2	3%	**USC Rate 1 Cut-Off Point**	12,012.00	1,001.00	231.00
USC Rate 3	5.5%	**USC Rate 2 Cut-Off Point**	18,668.00	1,555.67	359.00
USC Rate 4	8%	**USC Rate 3 Cut-Off Point**	70,044.00	5,837.00	1,347.00

The following details of gross pay for USC purposes and USC deducted, from 1 January 2016, to date of commencement of your employment, should be taken into account when calculating current USC deductions.

Total Gross Pay for USC purposes: 0.00   **Total USC deducted:** 0.00

Local Property Tax (LPT)	

Total LPT to be deducted: 520.00

LPT deductions are from an employee's net salary (i.e. **after** deducting PAYE/PRSI/USC and allowable pension contributions), but take **priority** over non-statutory deductions and any deductions under a Court Order where the Court Order was made **after 30 June 2013**.

8.3.3 Commencement of Tax Year

Before the beginning of a new tax year, the employer should ensure that they have notification of the tax credits and standard rate cut-off point (P2C) for **every** employee for the new tax year. Revenue should be notified immediately of the name and address and PPS number of any employee for which the notification has not been received.

If, on the first pay day of the new tax year, the employer has not received a tax credit certificate for the new tax year for an employee, the following options apply:

- Where the **cumulative basis** of tax deduction is in operation, the employer should use the previous year's certificate, **provided** it has the **employer's name** on it.
- Where the **non-cumulative basis** (week 1/month 1 basis) is in operation, the employer should use the tax credits and standard rate cut-off point, as advised in the **previous year's** non-cumulative tax credit certificate.
- Where the **temporary basis** of tax deduction is in operation, the employer can continue to use, on a temporary basis, the tax credits and standard rate cut-off point as advised on the **P45**, provided the P45 relates to the **current year or previous year**. Otherwise, the **emergency basis** of tax deduction will apply from 1 January until a notification is received.
- Where the **emergency basis** of tax deduction is in operation, the employer should continue to use the emergency basis on a cumulative basis.

Note: an employer is legally obliged to deduct tax and pay it over to the Collector-General whether or not a tax credit certificate has been received.

8.3.4 Cessation of Employment

Where an employee leaves the employment, takes a career break or dies while in employment, the employer should complete a **Form P45**. This is a form certifying the employee's pay, tax, PRSI and USC contributions from the **start of the tax year** to the **date of cessation** (including any LPT deductions).

Form P45 is a four-part form – Part 1 should be sent to Revenue and Parts 2, 3 and 4 given to the employee on his cessation date or with his final wages payment. It is an important form, **which cannot be duplicated**, and is required by the employee for the following:

- **to give to their next employer** – Parts 2 and 3 should be given by an employee to his new employer; who would retain Part 2 and send Part 3 to Revenue, as a request for a tax credit certificate for the employee in question;
- **any claim for a refund of tax during unemployment; and**
- **claiming Social Welfare Benefits** (Part 4).

Revenue's On-Line Service (ROS) provides a facility for the submission of Form P45 (Part 1) online and the printing of Parts 2, 3 and 4 onto computer stationery.

In the case of a deceased employee, Parts 1 to 4 together with the employee's tax credit certificate should be sent to Revenue.

To prevent fraud, an employer is **prohibited**, in any circumstances, from supplying **duplicates** of forms P45 to an employee who has left the employment and claims to have lost the original.

8.3.5 Commencement of Employment

Procedure where employer receives Parts 2 and 3 of Form P45
The new employer should follow the instructions given on Part 2 and should immediately send Part 3 to Revenue. Part 3 is effectively a request by the new employer for a tax credit certificate in respect of the employee. Until such a tax credit certificate is received, the employer should operate PAYE on the temporary basis (week 1/month 1 basis) or on the emergency basis if the letter "E" appears on the P45.

If the temporary basis is used, the weekly or monthly tax credits and SRCOP on Form P45 should be applied on a **non-cumulative** basis.

A refund of tax should not be made to an employee on the week 1/month 1 basis.

If the P45 is for a **previous** tax year, the employer is obliged to operate the **emergency basis** pending receipt of a current tax credit certificate from Revenue as a result of the submission of the Form P45.

Procedure where employer does not receive a Form P45
Form P46 should be completed and forwarded to the new employee's local Revenue office who will issue a P2C. Where a pay date occurs before receipt of a valid P2C, the employer is obliged to operate PAYE and USC on the **emergency basis**.

Procedure where new employer is given a certificate of tax credits and standard rate cut-off point
An employer who has been given a certificate of tax credits and SRCOP showing the name and registered number of **another employer** should notify Revenue on **Form P46**. If the certificate is for the current tax year, PAYE should be operated on the **temporary basis** by reference to the tax credits and SRCOP printed on the notice. If the certificate does not cover the current tax year, the employer is obliged to operate the **emergency basis** pending receipt of a current tax credit certificate and SRCOP from Revenue, as a result of the submission of a Form P46.

New employee taking up employment for the first time
If the new employee does not have a **PPS** number, they must contact and register with the **Department of Social Protection**. Once a valid PPS number is obtained, the new employee should obtain a tax credit certificate and SRCOP. The employee can secure such a certificate by completing income tax Form 12A and submitting it to Revenue. Until the employer receives a PPS number for the new employee, tax at the **marginal** rate (with no credits or SRCOP) must be deducted from all payments.

8.3.6 Duties at the End of the Tax Year

At the end of each tax year the employer must complete Revenue's **"end of year return"** Form P35 and prepare and distribute a **Form P60** for every employee in their employment at the **end** of the tax year.

Once proper records have been maintained during the year, completion of the end of year returns is relatively straightforward. It essentially involves transferring details from the employee records to the Form P35 and Form(s) P60. Form P35 must be returned electronically through ROS **before 23 February** to avoid penalties.

In summary, the employer must:

- Total and complete the bottom of each payroll record for each employee. The final figures of pay, tax, PRSI, USC and LPT entered in the coded boxes at the bottom of the payroll records should be the totals for that employee for all periods of employment with the employer during that tax year.
- Complete forms P35, P35L, P35L/T and P35LF (see below). All entries for PAYE, PRSI, USC and LPT deducted on the P35L and P35L/T should be added together and the totals transferred to the P35 Declaration.
- Calculate any PAYE, PRSI, USC or local property tax (LPT) outstanding and send the payment with the completed P35 form to the Collector-General.

■ Give a Form P60 to each employee who is employed at the end of the tax year (i.e. on 31 December). The employer will already have given a Form P45 to those employees who left employment during the year.

Form P35 is a declaration that the details being returned are correct. It is issued to all employers on record irrespective of the type of payroll system they use. This is the form on which the employer declares the overall amount of PAYE, PRSI, USC and LPT deducted from his/her employees during the tax year.

Form P35L is pre-printed with the name and PPS number of each employee. The details from the employee records are transferred to the corresponding boxes on this form. If any employee's name and PPS number are omitted from the list provided, they should be added to the list.

Form P35L/T must be completed for any employee for whom the PPS number is not known. The employee's private address, date of birth and mother's birth surname must be shown on this form. This is to ensure that the correct PPS number is traced by Revenue.

Form P35 on diskette/USB: most computer payroll systems can now produce the P35 details in soft copy for upload into Revenue's On-Line System (ROS).

Every person who was employed at any time during the tax year, even if no tax was deducted, must be returned on the P35. All documents relating to pay, tax, PRSI, USC and LPT must be retained by an employer for six years after the end of a tax year.

Form P60 is a form issued by an employer to an employee certifying details of the employee's pay, tax, PRSI, USC contributions for the tax year, along with details of local property tax (LPT) deducted in this period. Form P60 must be given to each employee who is in employment at 31 December, before 15 February in the following year. The figures on the Form P60 should be copied from the employee records. Blank P60s, either manual or computer format, are issued by Revenue to the employers each year.

8.3.7 Payment of PAYE, PRSI, Universal Social Charge and Local Property Tax

PAYE deducted, USC deductions and total PRSI contributions (the amount deducted from pay plus the amount payable by the employer) together with LPT deductions must be **remitted to the Collector-General electronically via Revenue On-Line Service (ROS) by the 23rd of the calendar month** following the month in which the deductions were made.

Each month a **Form P30** bank giro/payslip is issued by the Collector-General on which the employer's name, address, registration number and the relevant month are computer printed and taxpayer specific. Only forms **showing the correct details** should be used as otherwise payments made may not be correctly credited. The figures for total PAYE, total PRSI and total USC contributions together with total LPT deductions should be entered on the form and totalled, which will equal the amount of the payment. Where there is no PAYE, PRSI, USC or LPT liability for a particular month, the Form P30 must be returned marked "Nil".

The completed Form P30 together with any payment must be filed electronically via ROS.

Where an employer pays PAYE, PRSI, USC or LPT by monthly **direct debit**, he is only required to file an annual P35 – the monthly P30 need not be filed.

In certain circumstances, PAYE, PRSI, USC and LPT can be returned and paid on an annual or quarterly basis. Authorisation to do so is at the discretion of the Collector-General and this authorisation may be terminated at any time. Employers making total annual PAYE, PRSI and USC payments of up to **€28,800 per annum** are eligible to make payments every **three** months.

Late payments of PAYE, PRSI, USC or LPT are charged at a rate of **0.0274% for each day or part thereof (10% per annum)** for which the payment is overdue.

8.3.8   Unpaid Remuneration

Where remuneration, which is deductible as an expense in calculating Case I or Case II profits for a particular tax year, is **unpaid** at the end of the accounting period and is not paid **within six months** of that date, such remuneration is deemed to have been paid on the **last day of the accounting period** for PAYE purposes. For example, a trader's accounts for the year ended 31 December 2016 include an accrual of €10,000 for bonuses due to employees. Normally, PAYE is only due in respect of the bonuses when they are actually paid. If, however, the bonuses remain unpaid at 1 July 2017, for PAYE purposes the bonuses are deemed to have been paid on 31 December 2016, and the PAYE deductible therefrom is due for payment on 23 January 2017.

8.3.9   Credit for PAYE Paid by Certain Employees

With effect from 1 January 2006, employees who have a "material" interest in a company **will not** be entitled to a **credit** against their income tax liability for PAYE deducted from emoluments paid to them by the company **unless** there is documentary evidence to show that the PAYE **has been paid** to the Collector-General.

An employee is deemed to have a material interest in a company if they (either on their own or with one or more connected persons) or a person with whom they are connected is the beneficial owner of, or is able to control directly or indirectly, more than **15%** of the ordinary share capital of the company.

Any PAYE remitted to the Collector-General is treated as being paid first in respect of other employees of the company.

Section 997A TCA 1997 provides that PAYE remitted on behalf of proprietary directors is treated as paid in respect of each proprietary director in the **same proportion** as the emoluments paid bears to the total directors' emoluments, **provided** that the tax split does not result in a **credit exceeding** the amount of the tax actually deducted from the individual director.

8.4   Employee's Responsibilities

It is an employee's responsibility to inform Revenue about any change in circumstances that may affect their entitlement to tax credits and the amount of tax payable. In order for an employee to meet the compliance obligations they should:

- Check their tax credit certificate (TCC) to ensure they are entitled to the tax credits allocated and that they are claiming all credits to which they are entitled. If an employee is unsure as to their entitlement to any tax credit, they should contact Revenue.
- Inform Revenue of any **change** in their basic details, including life events such as marriage, civil partnership, bereavement, change of address, etc.
- Inform Revenue of any other **non-PAYE income** from whatever source (including Government sources, e.g. DSP widow's/widower's pension).
- If requested by Revenue, complete an income tax return as quickly as possible and return it no later than **31 October** in the year following that to which it relates.
- Keep all relevant documentation in support of claims for tax credits, reliefs, allowances, etc. for a period of **six years** from the end of the year to which the claim related (e.g. medical receipts supporting a medical expenses claim in 2016 must be kept until the end of the year 2022).

Revenue's *Compliance Code for PAYE Taxpayers* sets out Revenue's approach to PAYE compliance interventions and what PAYE taxpayers should do to ensure that they are fully tax-compliant. The *Code* does not apply to Revenue audits and investigations, which are covered by the *Code of Practice for Revenue Audit and other Compliance Interventions* (see **Section 10.6**).

8.5   Employee Tax Credits and Standard Rate Cut-off Point

8.5.1   Introduction

Before the beginning of the new tax year, every employee is sent a **tax credit certificate (TCC)** giving details of their tax credits and standard rate cut-off point (SRCOP) for the new tax year. This notice gives a detailed breakdown of how the total tax credits due have been calculated. At the same time, the employer is sent an employer's tax credit certificate **and SRCOP** (P2C), which gives the same information but also details the amount of local property tax (LPT) to be deducted at source from the employee's net salary. The employer is not given details of how the employee's total tax credit or SRCOP has been determined so as to preserve the confidentiality of the personal circumstances of the employee.

The employer is **obliged** to use the **latest** official tax credit certificate (P2C) that is held, even if the employee is disputing the amount of the tax credits or SRCOP that have been granted.

Under the tax credit-based PAYE system, tax is calculated at the 20% and/or 40% rates, as appropriate, on **gross pay**. Tax thus calculated is "gross tax", which is reduced by tax credits to arrive at net tax payable.

8.5.2   Tax Credits

As outlined in **Chapter 6**, an individual is entitled to certain tax credits depending on their personal circumstances, e.g. basic personal tax credit for a single person, married/civil partners, widowed person/ surviving civil partner, employee tax credit, single person child carer credit, etc. In addition, certain reliefs are given as a tax credit at the standard rate of tax, e.g. relief for college fees, etc.

8.5.3   Standard Rate Cut-off Point (SRCOP)

The SRCOP is the amount of the individual's **standard rate tax band** for the year. Tax is paid at the standard rate, currently 20%, up to the SRCOP. Any income in excess of the SRCOP is taxed at the higher rate, currently 40%.

Example 8.1

Liam Cotter is married with two children and his wife works full time in the home. Liam's salary for 2016 is €48,000.

Tax credits due for 2016:	€
Basic personal tax credit (married)	3,300
Home carer tax credit	1,000
Employee tax credit	1,650
Total	5,950

The notice of determination of tax credits and SRCOP sent to Liam will show total tax credits due to him of €5,950 for 2016. These will be expressed as a monthly tax credit amount of €495.83 (€5,950/12) and a weekly tax credit amount of €114.42 (€5,950/52).

The notice of determination of tax credits and SRCOP sent to Liam will also show a SRCOP of €42,800 (married, one income) for 2016. This will also be expressed as a monthly cut-off amount of €3,566.67 (€42,800/12) and a weekly cut-off amount of €823.07 (€42,800/52).

8.5.4 Non-PAYE Income

If an individual has small amounts of non-PAYE income, the total tax credits due may be reduced by the non-PAYE income at the standard rate of tax and the SRCOP is reduced by the amount of the non-PAYE income. This will avoid any underpayment of tax on the non-PAYE income.

Example 8.2
If, in the previous example, Liam Cotter has UK dividend income of €1,000 for 2016, his total tax credits due to him for 2016 will be reduced by €1,000 @ 20% (i.e. €200) to €5,750. His SRCOP will also be reduced by €1,000 to €41,800. This ensures that the 40% income tax due on the dividend is collected.

Tax due by Liam Cotter for 2016	€	€
Income:		
Salary	48,000	
Dividend received	1,000	
Taxable income		49,000
Tax Calculation:		
€42,800 @ 20%	8,560	
€6,200 @ 40%	2,480	
€49,000		11,040
Less: Non-refundable Tax Credits:		
Basic personal tax credit	3,300	
Home carer tax credit	1,000	
Employee tax credit	1,650	(5,950)
Tax liability		**5,090**
Tax collected under the PAYE system:		
Salary		48,000
Tax Calculation:		
SRCOP (reduced)		
€41,800 @ 20%	8,360	
€ 6,200 @ 40%	2,480	
€48,000		10,840
Less:		
Tax credits due (reduced)		(5,750)
PAYE deducted		**5,090**

Note: the onus is on the individual to inform Revenue of any non-PAYE income that is taxable.

8.5.5 Reliefs Given as a Deduction from Gross Income

Certain reliefs are given as a deduction from income rather than as a tax credit, for example, pension contributions. Where an employee is entitled to such a relief, the total tax credits due are **increased** by the amount of the relief at the standard rate of tax and the SRCOP is **increased** by the amount of the relief.

Example 8.3
If, in the previous example, Liam Cotter is entitled to deduct Schedule E expenses relating to his employment of €1,230 for 2016, his tax credits will be increased by €246 and his SRCOP will be increased by €1,230.

Tax Payable by Liam Cotter for 2016

Income:	€	€
Schedule E: Salary	48,000	
Less: deductible Schedule E expenses	(1,230)	
Taxable income		**46,770**

Tax Calculation:

€42,800 @ 20%	8,560	
€3,970 @ 40%	1,588	
€46,770		10,148

Less: Non-refundable Tax Credits:

Basic personal tax credit	3,300	
Home carer tax credit	1,000	
Employee tax credit	1,650	
		(5,950)
Tax liability		**4,198**

Tax collected under PAYE for 2016:

Schedule E: Salary		48,000

Tax Calculation:
SRCOP (increased)

€44,030 @ 20%	(€42,800 + €1,230)	8,806	
€3,970 @ 40%		1,588	
€48,000			10,394

Less: Non-refundable Tax Credits:

Basic personal tax credit		3,300	
Home carer tax credit		1,000	
Schedule E expenses	(€1,230 @ 20%)	246	
Employee tax credit		1,650	
			(6,196)
PAYE deducted			**4,198**

8.6 Computation of Liability under the PAYE System

The PAYE system obliges the employer to calculate and deduct the income tax due (if any) from the pay of every employee. This tax is then paid over monthly to the Collector-General.

8.6.1 Tax Deduction Card

An electronic tax deduction card (TDC), USC payroll card and LPT payroll card are available at www.revenue.ie to assist employers who wish to record payroll information. The electronic cards allow employers to:

▧   complete the employee's record on screen;

▧   save the record electronically on the employer's computer;

▧   print the record; or

▧   print blank deduction cards and complete them by hand.

Alternative System to Electronic TDC

For administrative purposes, an employer may wish to use a different system from the electronic TDC as follows:

▧   a PAYE/PRSI record system of the employer's own design;

▧   a computerised system; **or**

▧   a computer bureau system.

If an employer wishes to use any of these alternative tax deduction methods, he must advise his local Inspector of Taxes.

Basis of Calculation of PAYE to be Deducted from Employees

The purpose of the PAYE system is to ensure that an employee's tax liability is spread out **evenly** over the year, thus allowing the correct tax liability to be paid in full without causing hardship to the employee.

PAYE tax deductions are calculated using one of the following methods:

1. Cumulative basis
2. Non-cumulative basis (week 1/month 1 basis)
3. Temporary basis
4. Emergency basis with PPS number
5. Emergency basis where PPS number is not available.

8.6.2 Cumulative Basis

The cumulative basis is used **only** when Revenue provides a tax credit certificate and SRCOP (P2C) effective from 1 January in the tax year, in the name of the current employer.

To ensure that an employee's tax liability is spread out **evenly** over the year, PAYE is normally calculated on a **cumulative basis**. This means that, when employers calculate the tax liability of an employee, they actually calculate the **total tax due** from **1 January** to the date on which the payment is being made. The tax deducted in a particular week is the cumulative tax due from 1 January to that date, **reduced** by the amount of tax previously deducted. Any tax credits and/or SRCOP which are not used in a pay period can be carried forward to the next pay period within the tax year.

The cumulative basis also ensures that refunds can be made to an employee where the employee's tax credits and SRCOP have been increased.

If the employee is paid weekly, tax credits and SCROP are divided into weekly amounts; if monthly, the figures are divided into monthly amounts.

These are printed on the card on a cumulative basis as in the following example:

Example 8.4

Joe Long's tax credits for 2016 are €3,300 (€63.46 per week) and his SRCOP is €33,800 (€650.00 per week). He is paid weekly. Joe was paid €620 for weeks 1 to 3 and was paid €850 for week 4. His TDC (for the first 8 weeks) will show the following:

Week No.	Gross Pay	Cum. Gross Pay	Cum. Standard Rate Cut-off Point	Cum. Tax due at Standard Rate	Cum. Tax due at Higher Rate	Cum. Gross Tax	Cum. Tax Credit	Cum. Tax	Tax deducted this period	Tax refund this period
1	620.00	620.00	650.00	124.00	0.00	124.00	63.46	60.54	60.54	
2	620.00	1,240.00	1,300.00	248.00	0.00	248.00	126.92	121.08	60.54	
3	620.00	1,860.00	1,950.00	372.00	0.00	372.00	190.38	181.62	60.54	
4	850.00	2,710.00	2,600.00	*520.00	*44.00	564.00	253.84	310.16	128.54	
5			3,250.00				317.30			
6			3,900.00				380.76			
7			4,550.00				444.22			
8			5,200.00				507.68			

* Week 4 cumulative tax: SRCOP week 4 @ 20% = €2,600 @ 20% = €520.00.

Cum. Gross Pay less SRCOP week 4 @ 40% = (€2,710.00 − €2,600) @ 40% = €44.00.

8.6.3 Non-cumulative Basis (Week 1/Month 1 Basis)

In certain circumstances Revenue may **direct an employer** to deduct tax on a **week 1 or month 1 basis**. This instruction will be printed on the employer's copy of the tax credit certificate and SRCOP (P2C).

Under the week 1/month 1 basis, **neither** the pay, the tax credits **nor** the SRCOP are **accumulated**. The pay for each income tax week or month is dealt with **separately**. The tax credits and SRCOP for week 1, or month 1, are used in the calculation of tax due each week, or each month. In such cases, the employer **may not make any refunds of tax**.

8.6.4 Temporary Tax Deduction System

The temporary tax deduction form (P13/P14) must be used in the following **commencement of employment** circumstances:

1. when the employer has been given Parts 2 and 3 of a **Form P45** stating:
   (a) the employee's PPS number, **and**
   (b) the employee was not on the emergency basis, **and**
   (c) the employer has sent Part 3 of the Form P45 to Revenue and is awaiting the issue by Revenue of a tax credit certificate and SRCOP; **or**
2. when the employee has given the employer a tax credit certificate and SRCOP in the name of **another employer** and the employer has sent Form P46 to Revenue.

The entries on the temporary TDC are made on a **non-cumulative** basis and the calculation of tax due each week or month is done on the same basis as in the **week 1/month 1** procedure. This temporary procedure continues until Revenue issues the ordinary cumulative tax credit certificate to the employer.

Example 8.5
Joe Long's tax credits for 2016 are €3,300 (€63.46 per week) and his SRCOP is €33,800 (€650.00 per week). He is paid weekly. Joe was paid €620 for weeks 1 to 3 and was paid €850 for week 4. His TDC (for the first 8 weeks) will show the following:

Week 1 Basis

Week No.	Gross Pay	Standard Rate Cut-off Point	Tax due at Standard Rate	Tax due at Higher Rate	Gross Tax	Tax Credit	Tax deducted this period	Tax refund this period
1	620.00	650.00	124.00	0.00	124.00	63.46	60.54	
2	620.00	650.00	124.00	0.00	124.00	63.46	60.54	
3	620.00	650.00	124.00	0.00	124.00	63.46	60.54	
4	850.00	650.00	130.00	80.00	210.00	63.46	146.54	
5		650.00				63.46		
6		650.00				63.46		
7		650.00				63.46		
8		650.00				63.46		

Joe pays €18 more in tax on the week 1 basis than he does on the cumulative basis.

8.6.5 Emergency Basis

Revenue provides a single form for use either as an emergency TDC or as a temporary TDC (P13/P14). The emergency TDC must be used in one of the following circumstances:

1. If the employer **has not** received a tax credit certificate and SRCOP or a Form P45 for the current tax year;
2. If the employer has not received a tax credit certificate for a **previous year** which states that the certificate is valid for **subsequent or following years**;
3. The employee gives the employer a P45 with the letter "**E**" in the Tax Table box indicating that the emergency basis applies; **or**
4. The employee has given the employer a completed P45 **without** a PPS number and not indicating that the emergency basis applies.

In such cases the employee's tax is calculated as follows:

- if the **employee does not provide a PPS number** – tax is deducted at **40%** from gross pay (less pension contributions and permanent health contributions where relevant). No tax credit is due.
- if the **employee provides a PPS number** – tax is applied to gross pay (less pension contributions and permanent health contributions where relevant) as follows:
  - **Weeks 1–4 or month 1 if paid monthly** – gross tax is calculated on taxable pay, at the **standard rate** of tax (20%), up to an amount equal to **1/52nd** of the SRCOP for a single individual (2016: €33,800) if weekly paid, or **1/12th** if monthly paid. Any **balance** is taxed at the **higher rate** (40%). The gross tax, as calculated, is **reduced** by a **tax credit**, which is equivalent to **1/52nd** of the personal tax credit for a single person (2016: €1,650) if weekly paid, or **1/12th** if monthly paid.

- **Weeks 5–8 or month 2 if paid monthly** – gross tax is calculated on the taxable pay as above. However, **no tax credit** is due.
- **Each subsequent week or month if paid monthly** – gross tax is calculated on the taxable pay at the **higher rate of tax** (40%) and **no tax credit** is due.

Example 8.6

Alice Casey commenced work with a new employer in January 2016. She provides her new employer with a valid PPS number, but she has not received a P45 from her previous employer. Alice is paid €2,650 monthly with overtime of €250 in month 2 and €400 in month 3.

Emergency Basis

Month No.	Gross Pay	Standard Rate Cut-off Point	Tax due at Standard Rate	Tax due at Higher Rate	Gross Tax	Tax Credit	Tax deducted this period	Tax refund this period
1	2,650.00	2,816.66	530.00	0.00	530.00	137.50	392.50	
2	2,900.00	2,816.66	563.33	33.33	596.66	0.00	596.66	
3	3,050.00	0.00	0.00	1,220.00	1,220.00	0.00	1,220.00	
4		0.00				0.00		
5		0.00				0.00		

Where an employee has two separate periods of employment with one employer in 2016 and the emergency basis applies in **each** period of employment, the employment is deemed to be **continuous** from the start of the first period of employment to the end of the last period of employment or to 31 December 2016, whichever is earlier.

It will be readily appreciated from the foregoing that the operation of the emergency basis on any employee is extremely onerous. However, the **employer is legally obliged** to operate the emergency basis and the onus is on the employee to remove himself from the emergency basis by securing a tax credit certificate and SRCOP. Generally, completing and submitting either tax return **Form 12** or **12A** or **Form P46** can achieve this.

If an employer who is obliged by circumstances to operate the emergency system **fails** to do so, then the employer is **legally liable** for the tax that **should** have been deducted from the employee's wages and Revenue will seek to collect it from the employer.

8.7 Refunds of Tax under the PAYE System

8.7.1 Employee Taxed on Cumulative Basis

For an employee taxed on the cumulative basis, the most likely situation where they would receive a refund is where Revenue issues a **revised** tax credit certificate and SRCOP showing increased tax credits and, if applicable, increased SRCOP. In such cases, the tax paid to date may **exceed** the cumulative tax due to date and a refund may need to be made. However, tax credits are non-refundable and if tax credits to date **exceed** **cumulative gross tax**, the excess may not be refunded.

8.7.2 Employee Taxed under Week 1/Month 1/Emergency/Temporary Basis

Example 8.7
Alice Casey has been on the emergency tax basis for months 1–3 (as in **Example 8.6**). In month 4, a tax credit certificate on a cumulative basis is issued to her employer. This certificate shows cumulative tax credits of €3,300 and cumulative SRCOP of €33,800 for 2016. Alice is paid €2,650 monthly with no overtime payment for month 4.

Emergency Basis

Month No.	Gross Pay	Standard Rate Cut-off Point	Tax due at Standard Rate	Tax due at Higher Rate	Gross Tax	Tax Credit	Tax deducted this period	Tax refund this period
1	2,650.00	2,816.66	530.00	0.00	530.00	137.50	392.50	
2	2,900.00	2,816.66	563.33	33.33	596.66	0.00	596.66	
3	3,050.00	0.00	0.00	1,220.00	1,220.00	0.00	1,220.00	
Total	8,600.00	0.00				0.00	2,209.16	
5		0.00				0.00		

New "Cumulative" TDC

Month No.	Gross Pay	Cum. Gross Pay	Cum. Standard Rate Cut-off Point	Cum. Tax due at Standard Rate	Cum. Tax due at Higher Rate	Cum. Gross Tax	Cum. Tax Credit	Cum. Tax	Tax deducted this period	Tax refund this period
1	0.00	0.00	2,816.66	0.00	0.00	0.00	275.00	0.00	0.00	
2	0.00	0.00	5,633.32	0.00	0.00	0.00	550.00	0.00	0.00	
3	0.00	*8,600.00	8,450.00	0.00	0.00	0.00	825.00	*2,209.16	0.00	
4	2,650.00	11,250.00	11,266.66	2,250.00	0.00	2,250.00	1,100.00	1,150.00	0.00	1,059.16
5			14,083.32				1,375.00			
6			16,900.00				1,650.00			
7			19,716.66				1,925.00			

Transferred from emergency TDC.

8.8 Taxation of Social Welfare Benefits

8.8.1 Illness Benefit and Occupational Injury Benefit

Employees in receipt of Illness Benefit or Occupational Injury Benefit from the Department of Social Protection are **taxed** on these benefits through the PAYE system from the first day of payment. However, these benefits are **not subject to PRSI or USC**. Child dependant additions (i.e. additional payments made to claimants in respect of qualifying children) are **exempt** for tax purposes.

The Department of Social Protection **notifies all employers** of the amount of taxable Illness Benefit and Occupational Injury Benefit which an employee is entitled to receive while out sick, and also the date the payment commenced. Where the employer is not aware of the amount of an employee's Illness Benefit, the basic personal rate of payment (available from www.welfare.ie) should be assumed until advised otherwise by the Department of Social Protection. The taxable benefit notification issued to employers will state the weekly taxable amount and the date the payment commenced. The following should be noted:

▩ No payment is made for the first six days of illness.
▩ No payment is made for any Sunday during the illness period.
▩ A week's Illness Benefit represents six days.

The following are the procedures for employers where one of their employees is in receipt of Illness or Occupational Injury Benefit.

1. **If the employee is paid a top-up amount while out sick and keeps the Illness or Occupational Injury Benefit.**
   The employer should include the taxable benefits with the amount of the employee's pay and calculate the tax due accordingly. The combined amount of pay and benefits are charged to PAYE, but only the actual pay from the employer is subject to PRSI and USC.

2. **If the employer pays the employee while out sick and recoups the Illness or Occupational Injury Benefit from them.**
   In this instance the employer includes the taxable benefits with the employee's earnings, and taxes the employee's earnings under the normal PAYE procedures, but PRSI and USC are only calculated on the difference between the gross wages paid and the amount of benefit received.

3. **If the employer does not pay the employee while out sick.**
   The Department of Social Protection notifies the employer of the amount of taxable benefit the employee receives while out sick. The employer includes this amount with the employee's earnings on their return to work. In this way the taxable benefit is "caught" under the cumulative system of PAYE.

Taxable Illness Benefit should be included in the "total earnings" figures in forms P45, P60, P35L and P35L/T and shown separately in the dedicated "taxable Illness Benefit" field on each form.

Example 8.8

Sarah Underwood works for VJ Ltd and earns €1,100 per week. She pays €125 a week into her pension. Sarah was out sick for two weeks and received €188 Illness Benefit each week. VJ Ltd's illness policy is that they will top-up any Department of Social Protection (DSP) benefit to the gross amount per week that Sarah normally earns. VJ Ltd will apply PAYE/PRSI and USC as follows:

Taxable Pay	€	€
DSP Illness Benefit	188	
VJ Ltd Salary (€1,100 – €188)	912	
Less: pension contribution	(125)	
Taxable pay		**975**
Gross Pay for USC and PRSI		
DSP Illness Benefit	0	
VJ Ltd Salary (€1,100 – €188)	912	
Less: pension contribution	(0)	
		912

Illness Benefit is not subject to PRSI and USC but the pension contribution is not allowable as a deduction against salary for PRSI and USC calculations.

8.8.2   Maternity and Adoptive Benefits

Maternity, Adoptive and Health and Safety Benefits are subject to tax (as per Illness and Occupational Injury Benefits). However, the employer does not have to calculate or include these benefits with taxable income, but rather, the Department of Social Protection informs Revenue of the amount of benefit payable and the employee's annual tax credits and SRCOP are **reduced by the benefit receivable**. Revenue then issue a revised P2C to the employer showing the reductions.

As the benefits are being taxed by reducing the employee's tax credits and SRCOP, employers **do not** include figures for Maternity, Adoptive and Health and Safety Benefits on forms P45, P60 or P35L.

8.8.3   Jobseekers' Benefit

Jobseekers' Benefit (including any amount for an adult dependant) is a taxable source of income. However, the child dependant element and the **first €13** per week of benefit are exempt from tax. When an employee resumes employment having claimed Jobseekers' Benefit, Revenue will notify the new employer of the employee's earnings and net tax deducted up to the date of the resumption of employment. The employee's tax credits and SRCOP will be reduced by the amount of the taxable Jobseekers' Benefit.

8.9   Computation of Liability under Pay Related Social Insurance (PRSI)

In addition to PAYE, employers are obliged to calculate and deduct employee PRSI and USC from the pay of every employee. They are also obliged to calculate employer PRSI. The PRSI and USC are then paid over monthly to the Collector-General.

8.9.1   PRSI Contributions

Pay Related Social Insurance (PRSI) contributions are payable in respect of full-time employees and part-time employees. PRSI is deducted at source by the employer and remitted to the Collector-General.

PRSI is payable on most sources of income, including:

- salaries and pensions;
- tax-adjusted profits of a trade or profession (less capital allowances);
- dividends received;
- rental income;
- investment income, including ordinary bank deposit interest but not interest on special savings accounts or special savings incentive accounts;
- benefits in kind (e.g. company cars, vans, etc.) and perquisites (e.g. preferential loans) provided by an employer to an employee; and
- any benefits arising out of employee share schemes (e.g. approved share-option schemes, approved profit-sharing schemes, approved SAYE share option schemes).

Employee contributions to occupational pension schemes and other pension arrangements are not deductible from income which is subject to PRSI and USC. Employer contributions on behalf of the employee are also not deductible for the purpose of calculating the employer PRSI.

The pension-related deduction ("pension levy"), which is charged to earnings in the **public service** is not deductible from income that is subject to PRSI and USC.

PRSI is **not** charged on:

- social welfare payments (e.g. Illness or Maternity Benefits);
- redundancy payments (although USC is payable on the **taxable** element of a redundancy lump sum payment).

A separated person may claim a refund of PRSI on **enforceable maintenance payments** made to the person's spouse. The pay or income for PRSI purposes is reduced by the amount of the maintenance payment and the PRSI recalculated. Any overpayment of PRSI can be claimed, after the year end, from the PRSI Refunds Section of the Department of Social Protection.

8.9.2 PRSI Contribution Classes

In general, PRSI contribution classes are decided by the **nature** of the employment and the **amount** of the employee's gross reckonable earnings in any week. Most workers pay PRSI contributions at **Class A** and are covered for all social welfare benefits and pensions. However, people who earn less than €38 per week (from all employments) are covered for occupational injuries benefits only – **Class J**. Some workers in the public sector do not have cover for all benefits and pensions and they pay a modified PRSI contribution – **Classes B, C, D or H**.

Others, such as people who are retired but receiving pensions from their former job, are recorded under different classes of PRSI – **Classes K or M**. These classes do not give cover for social welfare benefits and pensions.

Self-employed individuals and company directors pay **Class S** contributions and are covered for certain pensions such as widow's, widower's or surviving civil partner's (contributory) pension, State pension (contributory) or Maternity and Adoptive Benefits.

The PRSI contribution classes are further divided into **subclasses, 0 and 1**. A8 is a subclass of **A9**, which is used for community employment participants only. These subclasses represent different bands of weekly earnings and categories of people within each earnings band, as outlined below.

Deciding the Correct PRSI Class
If there is any doubt as to whether PRSI should be paid or which class of PRSI should apply, the Department of Social Protection Scope Section may be asked to decide the issue. Before a decision is made, the employment details are investigated thoroughly by a social welfare inspector.

8.9.3 Rates of Contribution

Employee contributions and employer contributions are calculated separately and then added together to get "**Total PRSI**".

An extract of SW14 *PRSI Contribution Rates & User Guide 2016* is reproduced below. The full leaflet is available on www.welfare.ie

PRIVATE AND PUBLIC SECTOR EMPLOYMENTS
Rates of contribution from 1 January 2016

Class A: covers employees, under the age of 66, in industrial, commercial and service-type employment who have reckonable pay of €38 or more per week from all employments; and public servants recruited since 6 April 1995.

Weekly pay is the **employee's monetary pay plus notional pay** (if applicable).

Subclass	Weekly Pay Band	How much of Weekly Pay	All Income EE	All Income ER
AO	€38 – €352 inclusive	ALL	Nil	8.5%
AX	€352.01* – €376 inclusive	ALL	4%	8.5%
AL	€375.01* – €424 inclusive	ALL	4%	10.75%
A1	More than €424	ALL	4%	10.75%
* EE PRSI credit applies to earnings up to €424.				

Employee PRSI Credit

Effective from **1 January 2016**, a new employee PRSI credit of a maximum of €12 per week is available to Class A employees with gross earnings between €352 and €424 per week. The credit is reduced by one-sixth of gross earnings in excess of €352 per week. The reduced credit is then deducted from the employee PRSI liability calculated at 4% of gross weekly earnings.

Example 8.9
Julie works in a restaurant and was paid the following amounts for the first three weeks of 2016. Calculate her and her employer's liability to PRSI.

Week 1: Gross wages   €350
Week 2: Gross wages   €370
Week 3: Gross wages   €420

Week 1:

Gross wages	€350.00 Class A0
EE PRSI – 0%	NIL
ER PRSI – 8.5%	€29.75
Total PRSI	€29.75

Week 2:

Gross wages	€370.00 Class AX
EE PRSI – 4%	€14.80

PRSI Credit calculation:

Maximum credit	€12.00	
Less: 1/6th × (€370 – €352.01)	(€3.00)	
Deduct PRSI credit		(€9.00)
EE PRSI		€5.80
ER PRSI – 8.5%		€31.45
Total PRSI		€37.25

Week 3:

Gross wages	€420.00 Class AL
EE PRSI – 4%	€16.80

PRSI Credit calculation:

Maximum credit	€12.00	
Less: 1/6th × (€420 – €352.01)	(€11.33)	
Deduct PRSI credit		(€0.67)
EE PRSI		€16.13
ER PRSI – 10.75%		€45.15
Total PRSI		€61.28

SELF-EMPLOYED
Rates of contribution from 1 January 2016

Class S: covers self-employed people, including certain company directors and those with income from investments and rents.

Subclass	Weekly Pay Bands	How much of Weekly Pay	All Income EE
S0	Up to €500	ALL	4%
S1	More than €500	ALL	4%

Self-employed contributors, with annual self-employed income of over **€5,000** per annum, are liable to PRSI at Class S 4% subject to a minimum PRSI contribution of **€500 per annum**.

8.10 Universal Social Charge

The Universal Social Charge (USC) is a charge payable on **gross income**, including notional pay, **after** any relief for certain trading losses and capital allowances, but **before** pension contributions.

All individuals are liable to pay USC if their gross income is greater than **€13,000 per annum** (2015: €12,012).

Note that once the total income exceeds the relevant limit, all the income is subject to USC and not just the excess over the limit.

Persons who are **not domiciled** in Ireland are liable for USC on Irish source income in the same way as they are liable to pay income tax on it.

Directors' fees paid by an Irish company to a non-resident director are also subject to USC.

Income Exempt from USC
The following income is exempt from USC:

- Where an individual's total income for the year does not exceed **€13,000** (2015: €12,012).
- All Department of Social Protection payments, including social welfare payments received from abroad.
- Payments that are made in lieu of Department of Social Protection payments, such as Community Employment Schemes paid by the Department of Jobs, Enterprise and Innovation or Back to Education allowance paid by the Department of Education and Skills.
- Income subjected to DIRT.
- Termination payments – USC is only charged on the taxable portion of the payment, for example:
  - statutory redundancy payments – i.e. two weeks' pay per year plus a bonus week, subject to a maximum payment of €600 per week are exempt;
  - ex-gratia redundancy payments in excess of the statutory redundancy amount and after claiming one of the reliefs; basic exemption, increased exemption, or SCSB – see **Section 4.5.2**.

Special Treatment for Medical Card Holders and Individuals over 70 years
Medical card holders (aged under 70) and individuals over 70 years whose aggregate income for the year is **€60,000 or less** will only pay USC at a maximum rate of 3% on income over €12,012 per annum. Note that "aggregate income" excludes payments from Department of Social Protection. A "GP only" card is not considered a full medical card for USC purposes.

Surcharge on Self-employment Income and Bank Bonuses
There is a **surcharge of 3%** on individuals who have income from **self-employment** that **exceeds €100,000** in a year, regardless of age.

A special USC rate of **45%** applies to certain **bank bonuses** paid to employees of **financial institutions** that have received financial support from the State. Performance-related bonus payments paid to employees of Bank of Ireland, AIB, Anglo Irish Bank, EBS and Irish Nationwide Building Society are chargeable to USC at 45% where the cumulative amount of any bonus payments **exceeds €20,000** in a single tax year. Where this threshold is exceeded, the full amount is charged to USC at 45% and not just the excess over €20,000.

8.10.1 Rates and Income Thresholds 2016 – Employees

PERSONS UNDER 70 AND NOT IN RECEIPT OF A MEDICAL CARD			
THRESHOLDS			RATE OF USC
Per Year	Per Month	Per Week	Rate %
Up to €12,012	Up to €1,001	Up to €231	1.0%
From €12,012 to €18,668	From €1,001 to €1,556	From €231 to €359	3.0%
From €18,668 to €70,044	From €1,556 to €5,837	From €359 to €1,347	5.5%
In excess of €70,044	In excess of €5,837	In excess of €1,347	8.0%

PERSONS IN RECEIPT OF A MEDICAL CARD OR OVER 70 YEARS WHERE AGGREGATE INCOME IS €60,000 OR LESS			
THRESHOLDS			RATE OF USC
Per Year	Per Month	Per Week	Rate %
Up to €12,012	Up to €1,001	Up to €231	1.0%
In excess of €12,012	In excess of €1,001	In excess of €231	3.0%

PERSONS IN RECEIPT OF A MEDICAL CARD OR OVER 70 YEARS WHERE AGGREGATE INCOME IS GREATER THAN €60,000			
THRESHOLDS			RATE OF USC
Per Year	Per Month	Per Week	Rate %
Up to €12,012	Up to €1,001	Up to €231	1.0%
From €12,012 to €18,668	From €1,001 to €1,556	From €231 to €359	3.0%
From €18,668 to €70,044	From €1,556 to €5,837	From €359 to €1,347	5.5%
In excess of €70,044	In excess of €5,837	In excess of €1,347	8.0%

Employers must pay USC to the Collector-General at the same time and in the same manner as the deductions under the PAYE system.

Employers are to operate USC on a cumulative basis. Employer tax credit certificates (P2C) also feature USC rates and cut-off points.

Cumulative, Temporary and Emergency Basis for USC

- Where an employee is on the cumulative basis for PAYE, they will be on the cumulative basis for USC, and vice versa.
- Where an employee is on a week 1 basis for PAYE, they will also be on a week 1 basis for USC, and vice versa.
- Where an employee is on the emergency basis for PAYE, they will also be on the emergency basis for USC, and vice versa.

USC under the emergency basis is calculated at 8% with no cut-off point.

8.10.2 USC: Rates and Income Thresholds 2016 – Self-employed

SELF-ASSESSED PERSONS UNDER 70 AND NOT IN RECEIPT OF A MEDICAL CARD	
THRESHOLD	RATE OF USC
The first €12,012	1.0%
The next €6,656	3.0%
The next €51,376	5.5%
The next €29,956	8.0%
The remainder (> €100,000)	11.0%

SELF-ASSESSED PERSONS IN RECEIPT OF A MEDICAL CARD OR OVER 70 YEARS WHERE AGGREGATE INCOME IS €60,000 OR LESS	
THRESHOLD	RATE OF USC
The first €12,012	1.0%
The next €47,988	3.0%

SELF-ASSESSED PERSONS IN RECEIPT OF A MEDICAL CARD OR OVER 70 YEARS WHERE AGGREGATE INCOME IS GREATER THAN €60,000	
THRESHOLD	RATE OF USC
The first €12,012	1.0%
The next €6,656	3.0%
The next €51,376	5.5%
The next €29,956	8.0%
The remainder (> €100,000)	11.0%

Self-employed individuals will make a payment of USC along with their preliminary tax payment by 31 October, with any balance payable by 31 October in the following year. **The surcharge of 3% only applies to non-PAYE income that exceeds €100,000 in a year, even if the total income (PAYE and non-PAYE) exceeds €100,000.**

Example 8.10
Jim Cameron is 71 years old and is in receipt of Schedule E income, from his role as managing director of TeeHee Ltd, of €58,000 for 2016. He also has trading income of €107,000 for 2016 from his film distribution business.

USC calculation for 2016:

Gross income for USC:	€	€
Schedule E salary		58,000
Case I Schedule D		107,000
Total income		**165,000**

USC Calculation:

€12,012 @ 1.0%	120.12
€6,656 @ 3.0%	199.68
€51,376 @ 5.5%	2,825.68
€87,956 @ 8.0%	7,036.48
€7,000 @ 11.0%	770.00
€165,000	10,951.96

If Jim's income was reversed, i.e. his trading income was €58,000 and his employment income was €107,000 his USC liability would be as follows:

USC calculation for 2016:

Gross income for USC:	€	€
Schedule E salary		107,000
Case I Schedule D		58,000
Total income		**165,000**

USC Calculation:

€12,012 @ 1.0%	120.12
€6,656 @ 3.0%	199.68
€51,376 @ 5.5%	2,825.68
€94,956 @ 8.0% (balance)	7,596.48
€165,000	10,741.96

8.10.3 USC: Surcharge on Use of Property Incentives

Section 531AAE TCA 1997 provides for a **property relief surcharge** on investors (both passive and active) with **gross income** greater than **€100,000**. The surcharge will be collected as **additional** USC of **5%** on the **amount of income sheltered** by the use of certain property- and area-based capital allowances as well as section 23-type reliefs in a given year. The surcharge does not apply to income sheltered by non-property tax reliefs, such as EII or investment in film relief.

Where specified reliefs are restricted under the **high earners restriction** in any year, that relief can be carried forward to be used in subsequent years, subject to the high earners restriction applying in that year. Any income in that **subsequent year** which is sheltered by relief of this kind **will not** be subject to the surcharge, on the grounds that it already has been surcharged in an earlier year.

Example 8.11

Joe Long's income and allowances/reliefs for 2016 are as follows:

	€	€
Gross income		210,000
Less: Property reliefs	80,000	
EII relief	7,000	
		(87,000)
Taxable income		123,000
USC surcharge: Property relief €80,000 @ 5%		**4,000**

Example 8.12

Sheila Short's income and allowances/reliefs for 2016 are as follows:

	€	€
Employment income	90,000	
Rental income (gross)	12,000	102,000
Less: Case V rental expenses	2,500	
Section 23 relief	10,000	(12,500)
Taxable income		89,500

USC surcharge calculation:

	€
Rental income (gross)	12,000
Less: Case V expenses	(2,500)
Net Case V income	9,500
Less: Section 23 relief (€500 c/fwd)	(9,500)
USC surcharge – €9,500 @ 5%	**€475**

Note: where the additional 5% USC applies to a taxpayer in 2016, their preliminary tax for 2016 must be calculated as if this additional surcharge applied in 2015.

8.11   Calculation of PRSI and USC for Employees

8.11.1   PRSI

The entries on the tax deduction card are made on a **non-cumulative** basis, and the calculation of PRSI due each week or month is done on the same basis as in the **week 1/month 1** procedure.

The calculation of PRSI is demonstrated in **Example 8.12** (overleaf).

Example 8.13

Joe Long is a private sector worker. Using his TDC, calculate the PRSI payable for weeks 1–4 of 2016, assuming that Joe pays PRSI at Class A.

Week No.	Gross Pay PRSI Purposes	Social Insurance Weekly Record		PRSI Employee's Share	Total PRSI
	€	Insurable Employment	PRSI Class	€	€
1	650.00	✓	A1	26.00	95.88
2	650.00	✓	A1	26.00	95.88
3	650.00	✓	A1	26.00	95.88
4	875.00	✓	A1	35.00	129.06
5					

				€
Employee PRSI: Weeks 1 to 3	Pay €650 > €424 A1 rate applies			
		€650 @ 4%		26.00
		Total EE PRSI		26.00
Employer:		€650 @ 10.75%		69.88
		Total PRSI		95.88

				€
Employee PRSI: Week 4	Pay €875 > €424 A1 rate applies			
		€875 @ 4%		35.00
		Total EE PRSI		35.00
Employer:		€875 @ 10.75%		94.06
		Total PRSI		129.06

8.11.2 Universal Social Charge

USC is charged on a cumulative basis and, as with PAYE tax credits and rate bands, Revenue will notify employers (on employers' tax credit certificates) of the USC rates and thresholds to be applied for each employee. USC information will be shown in the section below the PAYE section. USC rates and cut-off points, along with previous USC paid or, where applicable, deducted will be shown.

The following is an extract from a tax credit certificate showing USC rates and cut-off points:

Universal Social Charge (USC)			

Rates of USC			Exemption Case N		
USC Rate 1	1%		**Yearly COP**	**Monthly COP**	**Weekly COP**
USC Rate 2	3%	**USC Rate 1 Cut-Off Point**	12,012.00	1,001.00	231.00
USC Rate 3	5.5%	**USC Rate 2 Cut-Off Point**	18,668.00	1,555.67	359.00
USC Rate 4	8%	**USC Rate 3 Cut-Off Point**	70,044.00	5,837.00	1,347.00

The following details of gross pay for USC purposes and USC deducted, from 1 January 2016, to date of commencement of your employment, should be taken into account when calculating current USC deductions.

Total Gross Pay for USC purposes: 0.00   **Total USC deducted:**   0.00

Example 8.14

Using the information from Example 8.12, calculate the USC payable for weeks 1–4 of 2016, assuming that Joe is not exempt from USC.

Date of payment	Week No	Gross Pay for USC this period	Cum. Gross Pay for USC to date	Cum. USC Cut-Off Point 1	Cum. USC due at USC Rate 1	Cum. USC Cut-Off Point 2	Cum. USC due at USC Rate 2	Cum. USC Cut-Off Point 3	Cum. USC due at USC Rate 3	Cum. USC due at USC Rate 4	Cum. USC	USC deducted this period	USC refunded this period
		€	€	€	€	€		€	€	€	€	€	€
	1	650	650	231	2.31	128	3.84	988	16.00	0.00	22.15	22.15	0.00
	2	650	1,300	462	4.62	256	7.68	1976	32.01	0.00	44.31	22.16	0.00
	3	650	1,950	693	6.93	384	11.52	2964	48.01	0.00	66.46	22.15	0.00
	4	875	2,825	924	9.24	512	15.36	3952	76.39	0.00	100.99	34.53	0.00
	5			1155		640		4940					

		€
USC: Week 1	First €231 @ 1%	2.31
	Next €128 @ 3%	3.84
	Balance: €650 – (€231 + €128) @ 5.5%	<u>16.00</u>
	Total USC (week 1)	22.15

continued overleaf

		€
USC: Week 2	First €462 @ 1%	4.62
	Next €256 @ 3%	7.68
	Balance: €1,300 – (€462 + €256) @ 5.5%	32.01
	Cumulative USC	44.31
	Less: Cumulative USC from previous week 1	(22.15)
	Total USC (week 2)	22.16
		€
USC: Week 3	First €693 @ 1%	6.93
	Next €384 @ 3%	11.52
	Balance: €1,950 – (€693 + €384) @ 5.5%	48.01
	Cumulative USC	66.46
	Less: Cumulative USC from previous week 2	(44.31)
	Total USC (week 3)	22.15
		€
USC: Week 4	First €924 @ 1%	9.24
	Next €512 @ 3%	15.36
	Balance: €2,825 – (€924 + €512) @ 5.5%	76.39
	Cumulative USC	100.99
	Less: Cumulative USC from previous week 3	(66.46)
	Total USC (week 4)	34.53

8.12 Calculation of PRSI and USC for the Self-employed

8.12.1 PRSI

PRSI is generally charged on the gross income of the taxpayer before pension contributions. Capital allowances and trading losses forward may be deducted.

A taxpayer with annual self-employed income over €5,000 will pay Class S PRSI at the rate of 4% for 2016 on all self-employed income, subject to a minimum payment of €500.

8.12.2 Universal Social Charge

USC is charged on **all income** (except deposit interest subject to DIRT) **before** pension contributions are deducted, but **after** deducting certain trade related capital allowances. Only standard rate capital allowances are allowable and must be actually used in a tax year to be deductible. Capital allowances due to persons who do not actively carry on a trade are not deductible (e.g. lessors and passive investors). USC applies to all persons whose income **exceeds €13,000 per annum** and the rates are listed in **Section 8.11** above.

Example 8.15

John Healy is a married man who owns and operates an equestrian centre in Cork. His accounts for the year ended 31 October 2016 show a tax-adjusted profit of €48,000. He has capital allowances due for 2016 of €7,000. He received gross interest of €420 on his Credit Union share account. His wife Mary is employed by the local doctor and her gross salary for 2016 was €32,000 (PAYE deducted €3,100). She received net bank deposit interest of €590 in 2016. The Healys are jointly assessed.

Calculate the income tax, PRSI and USC payable by John Healy in 2016.

Mr Healy Income Tax Computation 2016	€	€
Income:		
Schedule D, Case I	48,000	
Less: capital allowances	(7,000)	41,000
Schedule D, Case IV – John		420
Schedule D, Case IV – Mary (gross)		1,000
Schedule E – Mary		32,000
Taxable income		74,420
Tax Calculation:		
€67,600 @ 20%	13,520	
€5,400 @ 40%	2,160	
€1,420 @ 41%	582	
€74,420		16,262
Less: Non-refundable tax credits:		
Basic personal tax credit (married)	3,300	
Earned income tax credit (John)	550	
Employee tax credit (Mary)	1,650	5,500
Tax liability		**10,762**
Less: Tax paid		
PAYE deducted (Mary)	3,100	
DIRT (Mary and John)	582	(3,682)
Net tax liability		**7,080**
Universal Social Charge:		
John:		
€12,012 @ 1%	120	
€6,656 @ 3%	200	
€22,332 @ 5.5%	1,228	
€41,000		1,548
PRSI:		
Mary: (deposit interest)		
€1,000 @ 4%		40
John:		
€41,420 @ 4%		1,657
Total liability		**10,325**
Both PRSI and USC were collected from Mary's salary through the PAYE system.		

Questions

Review Questions

(See Suggested Solutions to Review Questions at the end of this textbook.)

Question 8.1

1. An employee, Mary, commenced work in 1 August 2016 under a contract with normal terms and conditions. The agreed monthly salary was €2,200. Mary's Form P45 from her previous employment showed the following amounts for the period 1 January 2016 to 31 July 2016:

Gross Salary	€16,310
Tax deducted	€1,208
Monthly tax credit	€275
Monthly SRCOP	€2,817
Month Number	7
Gross salary for USC purposes	€16,310
Total USC deducted	€484.67
Monthly USC cut-off point 1	€1,001.00
Monthly USC cut-off point 2	€554.67
Monthly USC cut-off point 3	€5,837.00

Requirement

Calculate the net pay receivable by Mary for August 2016, after deduction of PAYE, PRSI and USC, assuming that Revenue has issued a certificate of tax credits and SRCOP.

2. An employee, Andrew, who is paid €4,167 gross monthly, is provided with a company car by his employer for the first time from 1 June 2016. The original market value of the car is €28,000 (after allowing a 10% cash discount). Andrew's total annual travel is estimated at 51,200 km, of which 8,000 km are personal.

Andrew is required to pay €1,500 per annum to his employer for the private use of the car. This will be deducted monthly from Andrew's salary.

Requirement

Calculate Andrew's total gross taxable pay for June 2016.

Question 8.2

Sean, a married man, is employed by NEW Ltd from 1 July 2016. He is allowed unrestricted private use of a company van in respect of which he will incur business travel of 26,000 km per annum. NEW pays all the costs of running the van except diesel, which Sean pays for himself. Sean contributes €10 per month to NEW Ltd towards the running costs of the van. NEW bought the van second-hand for €10,000 on 30 June 2016. The van had a market value of €17,500 when first registered on 30 April 2011.

Requirement

(a) Calculate Sean's taxable benefit for 2015 in respect of his use of the company van.
(b) Sean's gross weekly wages are €500 inclusive of the benefit in kind on the van. Assuming the emergency basis of tax applies, calculate the PAYE/PRSI and USC to be deducted from Sean's first week's wages:

(i) if NEW Ltd is provided with Sean's PPS No;
(ii) if NEW Ltd is not provided with Sean's PPS No.

Question 8.3

Paul commenced work on 12 October 2016 under a contract with normal terms and conditions, at a rate of €21 per hour, with overtime accruing at time-and-a-half after 39 hours.

Paul's P45 from his previous employment showed the following details for the period 1 January 2016 to 10 October 2016:

Gross salary to date	€43,540.00	Gross salary for USC	€43,540.00
Tax deducted to date	€5,724.82	Total USC deducted	€1,782.92
Weekly Tax Credit	€95.19	USC cut-off point 1	€231.00
Week Number	45	USC cut-off point 2	€128.00
Weekly SRCOP	€823.07	USC cut-off point 3	€988.00

Paul's hours for his first week, ending 17 October 2016, were 39 plus 11 hours overtime.

Requirement

Calculate the net pay receivable by Paul for his first week after deducting PAYE/PRSI/USC using each of the following scenarios:

(a) Revenue has **not** issued a notice of determination of tax credits and SRCOP.
(b) Revenue **has** issued a notice of determination of tax credits and SRCOP in accordance with the P45.

Question 8.4

Charlotte is employed by Jolly Giants Ltd and receives a gross weekly wage of €1,050. Charlotte has a liability to LPT of €520 for 2016 and she has opted to pay for this through payroll. She informed Revenue and her employer of her payment option choice and Revenue issued a revised P2C to Jolly Giants Ltd on 9 July 2016.

Charlotte's salary details to 30 June 2016 are as follows:

Gross wages	€27,300.00
Tax deducted	€5,890.04
Weekly tax credit	€63.46
Weekly SRCOP	€650.00
Week Number 26	
Gross wages for USC purposes	€27,300.00
Total USC deducted	€1,148.03
Weekly USC Cut-off point 1	€231.00
Weekly USC Cut-off point 2	€128.00
Weekly USC Cut-off point 3	€988.00
Total LPT deducted	€260.00

Requirement

Calculate the net pay receivable by Charlotte for week 27 and week 28 in July 2016.

Question 8.5

Gillian is employed by Jingo Ltd and receives a gross monthly salary of €6,500 per month. Gillian is married to Dave and they are assessed separately. Gillian pays 10% of her gross salary into a pension fund every month. Gillian had her tonsils removed and was absent from work for two weeks in September 2016. Jingo Ltd paid her full salary, less the amount of Illness Benefit (€188 × 2 weeks) which Gillian retained.

Gillian went on maternity leave on 1 November 2016 and was in receipt of Maternity Benefit of €230 per week from that date. Jingo Ltd's maternity policy is to pay an employee 100% of her salary less the Maternity Benefit payable by the Department of Social Protection.

Gillian's gross pay to the end of August was €46,800 (cumulative tax deducted €12,013). Her monthly SRCOP is €2,816.67 and her monthly tax credit is €275.

Requirement

Calculate Gillian's net salary for September, October and November 2016.

Question 8.6

John has been employed by Care-for-Cars Ltd for a number of years and receives a gross weekly wage of €16 per hour for a 40-hour week, i.e. €640. John has asked his employer if he can work part-time for a six-week period to help out at home as his wife, Carol, has just given birth to twin boys. Care-for-Cars agree to continue paying John €16 per hour for the hours he works. John works the following hours for weeks 32 to 34:

Week 32 – 20 hours

Week 33 – 25 hours

Week 34 – 23 hours

John's details are as follows:

	€
Gross wages to week 31	**19,840.00**
PAYE deducted	1,017.11
USC deducted	669.76
Weekly tax credit	95.19
Weekly SRCOP	823.07
Weekly USC cut-off-point 1	231.00
Weekly USC cut-off-point 2	128.00
Weekly USC cut-off-point 3	988.00

Requirement

Calculate John's net wages for week 32 to week 34.

Local Property Tax

9.1   Introduction

The **Finance (Local Property Tax) Act 2012** (FLPTA 2012), provides for an annual tax called local property tax (LPT) payable by a "liable person" in respect of certain "residential" properties. It also provides for the establishment and maintenance, by the Revenue Commissioners, of a register of residential properties in the State. The Finance (Local Property Tax) Amendment Act 2013 (FLPTAA 2013) provides for the exemption from LPT of certain residential properties.

In short, the **"liable person"** in respect of a **"residential property"** at the **"liability date"** is required to pay property tax, based on the value of the residential property as of the **"valuation date"**, at a rate of **0.18%** per annum on the portion of the property value **up to** €1,000,000 and at a rate of **0.25%** per annum on the portion of the property value **exceeding** €1,000,000. The value of the residential property at the valuation date is determined by the liable person under **self-assessment**.

9.2   Definitions

9.2.1   Liable Person

The "liable person" is responsible for the submission of the LPT return and the payment of the tax due. The liable person in most cases will be the owner of the property, but the definition of liable person is quite broad and includes the following:

- Owners of Irish residential property (irrespective of whether they live in Ireland or not).
- Holders of a life-interest in a residential property.

- Persons with a long-term right of residence (for life or for 20 years or more) that entitles them to exclude any other person from the property.
- Lessees who hold long-term leases of residential property (for 20 years or more).
- Landlords where the property is rented under a short-term lease (for less than 20 years).
- Personal representatives of a deceased owner (e.g. executor/administrator of an estate).
- Trustees, where a property is held in a trust.
- Local authorities or social housing organisations that own and provide social housing.
- Where none of the above categories of liable person applies, the person who occupies the property on a rent-free basis and without challenge to that occupation.

Where co-ownership of a property arises, all owners will be held **jointly and severally liable** to the LPT, but only **one return** will be required, which will be submitted by the designated liable person.

There are no exemptions from LPT available to a liable person. However, **LPT may be deferred if the liable person satisfies certain conditions**, as outlined in **Section 9.4.3**.

9.2.2 Residential Property

For LPT purposes, residential property means any building or structure (or part of a building) which is **used as**, or is **suitable for use as**, a dwelling and includes any shed, outhouse, garage or other building or structure and grounds of up to one acre. Vacant properties are not exempt from LPT as they are "suitable for use" as a dwelling. It **excludes** a structure that is not permanently attached to the ground (e.g. caravan or mobile home).

Properties Exempt from LPT
The following type of properties are exempt from LPT:

- Any **new and previously unused** property purchased from a builder/developer between 1 January 2013 and 31 October 2019 is exempt until the end of 2019.
- Any property purchased between 1 January 2013 and 31 December 2013 will be exempt until the end of 2019. The property must be the person's **sole or main residence** and, if the property is subsequently sold or ceases to be the person's main residence between 2013 and 2019, the exemption no longer applies.
- Properties constructed and owned by a builder or developer that remain unsold and have not yet been used as a residence.
- Properties in unfinished housing estates (commonly called "ghost estates"), specified by the Minister for the Environment.
- Residential properties owned by a charity or a public body and used to provide accommodation and support for people with **special needs**, enabling them to live in the community (e.g. sheltered accommodation for the elderly or the disabled).
- Properties used by charitable bodies as residential accommodation in connection with recreational activities that are an integral part of the body's charitable purpose, e.g. guiding and scouting activities.
- Registered Nursing Homes.
- A property previously occupied by a person as their sole or main residence that has been **vacated** by the person for **12 months** or more due to long-term mental or physical infirmity. An exemption may also be obtained where the period is less than 12 months, if a doctor is satisfied that the person is unlikely, at any stage, to return to the property. In both cases, the exemption only applies where the property is not occupied by any other person. (**Note:** where a property is owned by more than one person, the owners are jointly and severally liable for the payment of the tax and this exemption will not apply if the property in question is jointly owned with others.)
- Mobile homes, vehicles or vessels.

▓ Properties **fully** subject to commercial rates. Where **part** of the property is used for commercial purposes (e.g. living accommodation over a shop), LPT is only due on the residential portion of the property. Note that even if all of a residential premises is used for commercial purposes (e.g. a guesthouse, B&B, etc.), LPT is only due where commercial rates are not paid.

▓ Diplomatic properties.

▓ Residential properties that have been certified as having significant **pyritic** damage will be exempt for a temporary period of approximately six years, commencing on 1 November immediately following the date on which the property qualifies for the exemption.

▓ A residential property purchased, built or adapted to make it suitable for occupation by a permanently and **totally incapacitated** individual as their sole or main residence. In the case of adaptations to a property, the exemption will only apply where the cost of the adaptations **exceeds 25%** of the market value of the property before it is adapted. The exemption ends if the property is sold and the incapacitated individual no longer occupies it as his or her sole or main residence.

9.2.3   Liability Date

The liability date is defined as:

▓ **1 May 2013**, in respect of the year 2013, and

▓ in respect of any other year, **1 November** in the preceding year (i.e. for 2016, the liability date is 1 November 2015).

A person who is a liable person of a residential property on 1 November 2015 is liable for LPT for 2016. If the liable person sells the residential property **after** 1 November 2015 but **before** 1 November 2016, they are still liable to LPT for 2016 but not for 2017. If the liable person sells the residential property after 1 November 2015 but before 31 December 2015, they are also liable to LPT for 2016 even though they do not own the property in 2016.

9.2.4   Valuation Date

The valuation date is the date at which the **chargeable value** of the residential property is established. Section 13 FLPTA 2012 (as amended by the Finance (Local Property Tax) (Amendment) Act 2015) states that this date is:

▓ **1 May 2013** for the tax years 2013 to 2019, **and**

▓ for each consecutive three-year period after 2019, **1 November** in the preceding year (i.e. for 2020, the valuation date is 1 November 2019).

9.3   Calculation of LPT

9.3.1   Calculation of LPT Using the Basic LPT Rate

The basic LPT percentage rates are as follows:

Property Value	Rate
Up to €1,000,000	0.18% per annum
Amounts over €1,000,000	0.25% per annum

The amount of LPT payable is the LPT percentage rate of the **market value** of the residential property at the valuation date, i.e. 1 May 2013 for years 2013 to 2019. The market value is decided by the liable person taking into account the specific characteristics of the property under self-assessment.

For the purposes of calculating LPT, property values are organised in market value bands as follows:

Valuation Band Number	Valuation Band €	Mid-point of Valuation Band €	LPT in 2014–2019 Standard Rate €
01	0 to 100,000	50,000	90
02	100,001 to 150,000	125,000	225
03	150,001 to 200,000	175,000	315
04	200,001 to 250,000	225,000	405
05	250,001 to 300,000	275,000	495
06	300,001 to 350,000	325,000	585
07	350,001 to 400,000	375,000	675
08	400,001 to 450,000	425,000	765
09	450,001 to 500,000	475,000	855
10	500,001 to 550,000	525,000	945
11	550,001 to 600,000	575,000	1,035
12	600,001 to 650,000	625,000	1,125
13	650,001 to 700,000	675,000	1,215
14	700,001 to 750,000	725,000	1,305
15	750,001 to 800,000	775,000	1,395
16	800,001 to 850,000	825,000	1,485
17	850,001 to 900,000	875,000	1,575
18	900,001 to 950,000	925,000	1,665
19	950,001 to 1,000,000*	975,000	1,755

*Residential properties valued **over €1m** will be assessed at the actual value at **0.18%** on the first €1m in value and **0.25%** on the portion of the value above €1m (no banding will apply).*

Example 9.1

John Corr's residential property has a market value of €330,000 as of 1 May 2013. His liability to LPT for 2016 is as follows:

Market value	€330,000
Valuation band number	06
Valuation band	€300,000 to €350,000
Mid-point of valuation band	**€325,000**

LPT:

€325,000 @ 0.18%	€585
LPT 2016	€585

9.3.2 Reduction of LPT Payable from 2015 Onwards

From 2015 onwards, local authorities can vary the basic LPT percentage rate on properties situated within their area. This adjustment, known as the **local adjustment factor (LAF)**, can increase or decrease the basic LPT rate by up to 15%. Since 2015 the following adjustments to the basic LPT rate have been made:

Local Authority	LPT Rate Adjustment 2015	LPT Rate Adjustment 2016
Clare County Council	15% decrease	15% decrease
Cork County Council	10% decrease	5% decrease
Cork City Council	10% decrease	10% decrease
Dublin City Council	15% decrease	15% decrease
Dun Laoghaire/Rathdown County Council	15% decrease	15% decrease
Fingal County Council	15% decrease	15% decrease
Kildare County Council	7.5% decrease	7.5% decrease
Limerick City and County Council	3% decrease	No adjustment
Longford County Council	3% decrease	3% decrease
Louth County Council	1.5% decrease	1.5% decrease
Mayo County Council	3% decrease	No adjustment
Monaghan County Council	No adjustment	7.5% decrease
South Dublin County Council	15% decrease	15% decrease
Westmeath County Council	3% decrease	No adjustment
Wicklow County Council	15% decrease	No adjustment

Note that the adjustments are **not** cumulative, e.g. in 2015 Mayo County Council reduced the LPT rate by 3% but did not reduce it in 2016.

Notification of any change is made by the relevant councils directly to Revenue who will revise the amount of LPT payable.

Example 9.2
If John Corr's residential property in **Example 9.1** is situated in the area covered by Wicklow County Council, his liability to LPT for 2016 is as follows:

Market value	€330,000
Valuation band number	06
Mid-point of valuation band	**€325,000**

LPT for 2016 only

€325,000 @ 0.18%	€585

John's 2015 and 2016 LPT record will include the following information:

LPT charge for 2015 (basic rate)	€585
Local authority reduction @ 15%	€(88)
Total LPT charge 2015	€497

LPT for 2016:

€325,000 @ 0.18% (no LPT rate adjustment)	€585

9.4 LPT Returns and Payment of LPT

9.4.1 LPT Returns

LPT returns (**LPT1**) were issued by Revenue to residential property owners in early 2013, with estimates of the amount of LPT due for each property. The liable person in respect of the residential property, or properties, was responsible for completing the return and paying LPT. The liable person could authorise another person (e.g. a relative) to complete and submit the return on their behalf.

Revenue's estimate of LPT was only a **guideline** and the **onus remains** with the liable person to **self-assess** their liability to LPT, i.e. the liable person must determine the market value of the residential property and calculate and pay the LPT accordingly.

An LPT return submitted in 2013 is valid for the years 2013 to 2019.

Liable persons obliged to file and pay online are:

- owners of **more than one** residential property;
- owners already required to submit tax returns and pay online (e.g. those who pay income tax under self-assessment); and
- any **company** that owns residential properties will have to pay and file for LPT online.

Some points to note regarding returns:

- Where a liable person **does not receive** an LPT return (LPT1) and an estimate from Revenue under self-assessment, they are **obliged** to contact Revenue to make an LPT return.
- If a person receives an LPT return and they are **not the liable person**, they must contact Revenue and state who the liable person is (if known).
- Where an **exemption** is being claimed, the return must be completed and filed by the relevant deadlines and the owner must state in the return which exemption condition the property satisfies (e.g. first-time buyer, ghost estate, etc.).
- Where a **deferral** (full or partial) is being claimed, the return must be completed and filed by the relevant deadlines and the owner must state in the return which deferral exemption is being claimed (see **Section 9.4.3**).

If the liable person did not previously qualify for an LPT exemption but now does, the exemption can be claimed by writing to Revenue and providing details of the exemption being claimed.

In most cases a residential property that was exempt from LPT on 1 May 2013 continues to be exempt until the end of the current valuation period (31 October 2019), even where the property is sold or ownership is transferred by way of gift or inheritance.

9.4.2 Payment of LPT

LPT liabilities can be paid in one single payment or phased out into equal instalments. Monthly direct debit payments for 2016 commenced on 15 January 2016 and continue on the same date each month thereafter. The payment method selected for 2015 will automatically apply for 2016 and subsequent years unless Revenue is otherwise advised.

LPT can be paid **in full** by:

- single debit authority – for 2016 payment will be deducted from the bank account no earlier than 21 March 2016;
- cheque or by debit/credit card (payable on date of instruction); or

- cash payments (including debit/credit card) through approved Payment Service Providers (An Post, Omnivend, Payzone or PayPoint).

LPT can be paid on a **phased basis from 1 January 2016** by:

- deduction at source from salary or occupational pension;
- deduction at source from certain payments received from the Department of Social Protection but the deduction cannot reduce the DSP personal rate payment to less than €186 per week;
- deduction at source from scheme payments received from the Department of Agriculture, Food and the Marine;
- direct debit; or
- cash payments (including debit/credit card) in equal instalments through approved Payment Service Providers.

Where the deduction at source option is chosen by the liable person, Revenue will advise the employer, pension provider or the relevant Government department of the amount to be deducted. Interest does not apply to phased payments.

9.4.3   Deferral of LPT

There are no **exemptions** from the payment of LPT, but **deferral arrangements** are provided whereby a person may opt to defer, or partially defer, payment of the tax if certain conditions are met. Interest will be charged on LPT amounts deferred at a rate of **4%** per annum. The deferred amount, including interest, will attach to the property and will have to be paid before the property is sold or transferred.

There are four separate categories of deferral of LPT available:

1. Income Threshold
2. Personal Representative of a Deceased Person
3. Personal Insolvency
4. Hardship.

1.   Income Threshold

The income threshold that determines whether a deferral may be claimed for a particular year is based on a person's **gross income** for the year. At the liability date for a year, i.e. 1 November 2015 for 2016 (and each 1 November after that), a claimant must estimate what their likely gross income will be for that year, i.e. the year in which the liability date falls and not the year the LPT payment is due. Gross income is all income before any deductions, allowances or reliefs that are allowed to be deducted when calculating a person's taxable income for income tax purposes. It **includes** income that is exempt from income tax and income received from the Department of Social Protection, but **excludes** child benefit.

The standard income thresholds may be **increased** where a claimant pays **mortgage interest**. The increase is limited to **80% of the gross interest** (i.e. before tax relief at source is given) that is actually paid or that is likely to be paid in a particular year. As with gross income, a claimant must estimate at the liability date the amount of mortgage interest that is likely to be paid by the end of the year.

A property for which deferral is claimed must be the **sole or main residence** of the claimant and deferral based on income thresholds is not available for landlords or second homes.

INCOME THRESHOLD CRITERIA

	Deferral Condition Number	Condition
Full Deferral	1	Gross income for the year unlikely to exceed **€15,000** (single or widow) and **€25,000** (couple*).
Full Deferral	2	Gross income for the year unlikely to exceed the **adjusted income** limit. This adjusted income limit is calculated by increasing the €15,000 (single or widow) and €25,000 (couple) thresholds by **80%** of the expected gross mortgage interest payments.
Partial Deferral (50%)	3	Gross income for the year unlikely to exceed **€25,000** (single or widow) and **€35,000** (couple).
Partial Deferral (50%)	4	Gross income for the year unlikely to exceed the **adjusted income** limit. This adjusted income limit is calculated by increasing the €25,000 (single or widow) and €35,000 (couple*) thresholds by **80%** of the expected gross mortgage interest payments.

*A couple includes a married couple, civil partners and certain cohabitants. Cohabitant is defined in section 172 of the Civil Partnership and Certain Rights and Obligations of Cohabitants Act 2010. For LPT deferral purposes, the required period of cohabitation is at least 2 years where the couple have children or at least 5 years where they do not have children.

Example 9.3

Tessa Lisbon is a single owner-occupier of a residential property worth €230,000. As of 1 November 2015, Tessa earns €22,000 per annum and has projected gross mortgage interest payments of €6,500 for 2015. Tessa's local authority has not adjusted the LPT rate for 2016.

Her liability to LPT for 2016 is as follows:

Market value	€230,000
Valuation band number	04
Valuation band	€200,000–€250,000
Mid-point of valuation band	**€225,000**

LPT:

€225,000 @ 0.18%	€405
LPT 2016	€405

Tessa wishes to opt for a deferral of some, or all, of her LPT as she is struggling to live within her income.

Full Deferral:

Gross income threshold (single person)	€15,000
Plus: Mortgage interest @ 80% (€6,500 × 80%)	€5,200
Adjusted income threshold	€20,200

continued overleaf

Full deferral is not available as Tessa's gross income, €22,000, is greater than her adjusted income threshold, €20,200.

Partial Deferral:

Gross income threshold (single person)	€25,000
Plus: Mortgage interest @ 80% (€6,500 × 80%)	€5,200
Adjusted income threshold	€30,200

Tessa is entitled to a partial deferral as her gross income (€22,000) is less than her adjusted income threshold, €30,200.

For 2016, Tessa must pay LPT of €202.50 and can defer €202.50.

2. Personal Representative of a Deceased Liable Person (Deferral Condition Number 5)

Where a liable person who was the sole owner of a property dies, that person's personal representative may apply for a full deferral of LPT for a maximum period of three years commencing from the date of death. Where the personal representative is in a position to transfer the property to a beneficiary of the estate or where it is sold within the three years, the deferral ends at that earlier time. A deferral can be claimed for any LPT outstanding at the date of death, any LPT already deferred by the deceased person and any LPT becoming payable following death, by submitting an LPT2 form along with the LPT1 return form.

3. Personal Insolvency (Deferral Condition Number 6)

A person who enters into any debt arrangement under the Personal Insolvency Act 2012 may apply for a deferral of LPT for the periods for which the insolvency arrangement is in place. The deferred LPT plus interest will become due when the particular insolvency arrangement ceases to have effect.

4. Hardship (Deferral Condition Number 7)

Where a liable person suffers an **unexpected** and **unavoidable** significant financial loss or expense within the current year, and is unable to pay the LPT without causing excessive financial hardship, then that person can apply for a full or partial deferral. Claims for this type of deferral will require full disclosure of the particular loss or expense and details of the person's financial circumstances and any other information required by Revenue. Following an examination of the information provided, Revenue will determine whether to grant a deferral (full or partial) but **will not** refund any payments made by the liable person up to that point.

In order to be considered for a deferral, the loss suffered by the liable person must reduce the remainder of their income to the **income threshold levels** at 1. above, **or**, the total loss suffered must be at least **20%** of their **gross income**. However, it does not follow that, if either or both of these conditions are met, deferral will be granted automatically. The onus is on the liable person to demonstrate that payment of the tax would cause **excessive financial hardship.**

In considering the question of hardship, the liable person's **personal circumstances** may be taken into account, for example, whether the house is occupied by other household members who, although not liable for LPT, may have income and would be expected to contribute to the payment of household expenses, including LPT.

9.5 Compliance

9.5.1 *Penalties and Interest for Non-filing/Late Payment*

Penalty for Non-filing of LPT1 Return
Where a liable person does not file an LPT return, the penalty is the LPT due, subject to a maximum of €3,000.

Penalty for Undervaluing Property
Where a liable person **knowingly** undervalues the property for the purpose of calculating LPT due, the penalty is the correct amount of LPT subject to a maximum of €3,000.

Interest Due on Late Payments
The rate of interest due on late payments (excluding amounts deferred and amounts payable under phased payments options) is **0.0219%** per day or part thereof (approx. 8% p.a.).

9.5.2 *Additional Sanctions for Self-assessed Taxpayers*

- A self-assessed liable person who fails to submit an LPT return on time may incur a **surcharge** for the late submission of their income tax return, **regardless** of whether or not the income tax return is submitted on time. The surcharge amounts to 10% of the income tax liability.
- Where a self-assessed liable person fails to pay LPT, Revenue will not issue a **tax clearance certificate**.
- Where a self-assessed liable person fails to send back the LPT return form and the assessment of LPT liability, the tax set out in the Revenue estimate will be collected using normal collection/enforcement options – sheriff, court action, attachment orders, etc.
- Where LPT remains outstanding, a charge will attach to that property. This charge will have to be discharged on the sale/transfer of the property.

9.6 Appeals

Where there is a disagreement between an individual and Revenue on matters relating to LPT, such as whether the property is residential, who the liable person is, disputed valuations, denial of deferrals, etc. that cannot be resolved, Revenue will issue a formal **Notice of Assessment** or a formal decision or determination. The individual may appeal to the **Appeal Commissioners** against those notices and request a determination.

As with other self-assessed taxes, in order to appeal Revenue's assessment, the individual must have made an LPT return and paid the assessment of the tax due (even if this is disputed). (See **Section 10.4** for details of Appeal procedures.)

Questions

Review Questions
(See Suggested Solutions to Review Questions at the end of this textbook.)

Question 9.1

Bill and Frida are married and own and occupy their home in Waterford city. Their estimated gross income for 2015 is €37,000 and they expect that their gross mortgage interest payments for 2015 will be €6,000. They have no other properties and are not first-time buyers. Bill and Frida's house was estimated to be valued at €330,000 at 1 May 2013.

Requirement
(a) Calculate the amount of LPT payable by Bill and Frida for 2016.
(b) Establish if Bill and Frida qualify for a deferral of LPT.

Question 9.2

Theo and Emer Rohan are a cohabiting couple who own their own home and are not first-time buyers. They have two children for whom they receive child benefit. They had the following income and expenses for 2015:

Income:	
Gross Case I income	€30,000
Schedule E income	€13,500
Department of Social Protection Illness Benefit	€9,776
Child Benefit	€3,120
Expenses:	
Mortgage interest	€16,000

Theo had a serious accident and incurred unexpected medical expenses of €19,000 in 2015, for which he was not reimbursed.

Requirement
Calculate whether Theo and Emer can make a claim for deferral of LPT for 2016.

Question 9.3

Kevin Ryan's residential property, situated in Carrigrohane, Co. Cork, was valued by an auctioneer as having a market value of €1,400,000 as of 1 May 2013.

Requirement
Calculate the amount of LPT that was payable in 2015 and the amount due in 2016.

10

Administration and Procedures

Learning Objectives

In this chapter you will learn:

- the concept of self-assessment and who is a "chargeable person" for income tax purposes;
- preliminary tax requirements for the self-employed;
- the special tax collection arrangements for certain activities – relevant contracts tax and payments in respect of professional services;
- the taxpayer's right of appeal against Revenue decisions;
- policing the system – how Revenue deal with audits and enquiries; and
- how the Revenue On-Line Service (ROS) works, what returns are required to be filed electronically (mandatory e-filing), and the incentives for using ROS.

10.1 Self-Assessment

10.1.1 "Chargeable Persons"

Self-assessment is a system whereby "chargeable persons" **calculate** and **return** taxes due within the timeframes and deadlines specified by tax law.

Self-assessment applies to people, chargeable to income tax, who are in receipt of income from sources which are **not chargeable** to tax **under the PAYE** system, or where some, but **not all**, of the tax on these sources of income is paid under PAYE.

For income tax purposes, self-assessment applies to the following chargeable persons:

- Self-employed persons (i.e. people carrying on their own business, including farming, professions or vocations).
- Proprietary company directors (i.e. holds or controls more than 15% of the ordinary share capital of the company) **regardless** of whether or not they have non-PAYE income.
- Individuals with gross non-PAYE income of €50,000 **or more** from all sources, even if there is **no net taxable income** from that source, for example:
  - income from rental property and investment income;
  - foreign income and foreign pensions; and
  - trading or professional income.

An individual becoming a chargeable person under this rule continues to be a chargeable person for future years, as long as the source(s) of the non-PAYE income continues to exist, **irrespective** of the amount of the annual gross income.

- Individuals with **assessable** non-PAYE income of **€5,000** (2015: €3,174) **or more, irrespective** of the amount of gross non-PAYE income.
- Individuals with profits arising on exercising various share options/share incentives.
- Where an Irish resident opens a foreign bank account of which they are the beneficial owner, they are to be regarded as a chargeable person for the years of assessment during which the account is open.
- Where a person acquires certain foreign life policies, they will be deemed to be a chargeable person.
- Where a person acquires a material interest in an offshore fund, they are deemed to be a chargeable person.
- Individuals in receipt of legally enforceable maintenance payments.

The following are not chargeable persons for the purposes of self-assessment:

- Individuals whose **only source** of income consists of income chargeable to tax under the PAYE system.
- An individual who is in receipt of income chargeable to tax under the PAYE system but who is **also** in receipt of income from other non-PAYE sources will not be regarded as a chargeable person if the total gross income from all non-PAYE sources is **less than €50,000 and** the net assessable income is **less than €5,000** (2015: €3,174) **and** the income is coded against PAYE tax credits (i.e collected through the PAYE system). Note that a married couple or civil partners, who are jointly assessed, are entitled to earn up to €5,000 (2015: €3,174) and have that income coded before the spouse/civil partner on whom the income is assessed becomes a chargeable person. However, where a married couple/civil partners opt for separate or single assessment, each person will have a limit of €5,000 (2015: €3,174).
- Non-proprietary directors **provided** they are not otherwise a chargeable person and **all** of their income is subject to PAYE.
- Directors of dormant and shelf companies.
- An individual who has received a notice from an Inspector of Taxes excluding them from the requirement to make a return (i.e. an exempt person).
- An individual who is only liable to income tax in respect of tax withheld from annual payments.

10.1.2 Obligations under Self-assessment

An individual who is a "chargeable person" for the purposes of self-assessment income tax must:

- complete a "pay and file" income tax return, which must be filed online using the Revenue On-Line Service (ROS) and, at the same time, pay the balance of tax outstanding for the previous year;
- pay preliminary tax for the current tax year on or before 31 October each year (i.e. preliminary tax for the year of assessment 2016 is payable by 31 October 2016).

Note that, while the due date for both returns and payments is 31 October, returns and payments that are made online qualify for an extension to the due date, which is decided on an annual basis by Revenue. The extended date for 2015 returns is 10 November 2016.

Self-computation of Taxes Due
Section 959R TCA 1997 requires self-assessed taxpayers to **compute the tax due** at the date of filing of the tax return. Revenue no longer computes the tax payable based on the return of income nor does it issue assessments to taxpayers.

Taxpayers, however, are entitled to **rely** on the **calculation of the tax payable** by the Revenue On-Line Service (ROS) when submitting their return. A fixed **penalty of €250** will apply where a chargeable person fails to file the necessary self-assessment with his return.

Those taxpayers that file their returns by **paper** can avoid the preparation of a self-assessment where the taxpayer files their tax return by **31 August**. In these instances Revenue will make an assessment that will be sent to the taxpayer.

10.1.3 Preliminary Tax

Preliminary tax is the taxpayer's **estimate** of their income tax payable for the year and must be paid by **31 October** in the tax year. Preliminary tax **includes** PRSI and USC as well as income tax. Note that a time extension is given when the taxpayer pays and files online using ROS. For 2016 income tax returns the extension is to 10 November 2016. However, the **due date** remains **31 October** and in any event of a default or underpayment, interest and penalties are calculated from the **due date**. To avoid interest charges the amount of preliminary tax paid is not less than the **lower** of:

- **90%** of the final tax liability for the current tax year, i.e. 2016; **or**
- **100%** of the final tax liability for the immediately previous year (see Note), i.e. 2015; **or**
- **105%** of the final tax liability for the year preceding the immediately previous year, i.e. 2014. This option is **only available** where the Collector-General is authorised to collect tax by **direct debit**. The 105% rule does not apply where the tax payable for the pre-preceding year is nil.

Note: any relief claimed under EII must be ignored when calculating the previous year's final tax liability.

Example 10.1

Paul Gasbag is a self-employed confectioner and his accounts for the year ended 31 December 2016 show a tax-adjusted profit of €44,000. The capital allowances due for 2016 total €7,000. He received €450 gross interest on his AIB ordinary deposit account, which he has held for a number of years. His wife Sharon is employed by an insurance company and her gross salary for 2016 was €52,000 (PAYE deducted: €9,962). She received €400 gross interest on her medium-term savings account (opened in February 2016).

Paul's final tax liability for 2015 was as follows:

Case I income	€40,000	Income tax due	€6,520
Capital allowances	€6,000	USC	€1,699
Case IV interest (gross)	€350	PRSI	€1,031
		Total liability 2015	€9,250

Paul's tax liability for 2014 was €7,950 (including PRSI and USC).

Income Tax Computation 2016	€	€
Income:		
Case I	44,000	
Less: capital allowances	(7,000)	37,000
Case IV – Paul (gross)		450
Taxable income – Paul		37,450
Schedule E – Sharon	52,000	
Case IV – Sharon	400	
Taxable income – Sharon		52,400
Total taxable income		89,850
Tax Calculation:		
€67,600 @ 20%	13,520	
€850 @ 41%	349	
€21,400 @ 40%	8,560	
€89,850		22,429
Less: Non-refundable Tax Credits:		
Basic personal tax credit (married)	3,300	
Earned income credit	550	
Employee tax credit (Sharon)	1,650	(5,500)
Tax liability		**16,929**

continued overleaf

Less: Tax Paid		
PAYE deducted (Sharon)	9,962	
DIRT (Paul and Sharon) (€850 @ 41%)	349	(10,311)
Net tax liability		**6,618**
Universal Social Charge:		
Paul:		
€12,012 @ 1.0%	120	
€6,656 @ 3.0%	200	
€18,332 @ 5.5%	1,008	
€37,000		1,328
PRSI:		
Paul: €37,450 @ 4%		1,498
Sharon: €400 @ 4%		16
TOTAL LIABILITY 2016		**9,460**

Note: the deposit interest has no further income tax liability, but is subject to PRSI, though not to USC.

Preliminary tax payment for 2016 will be:

Lower of: Year 2015 @ 100%	=	€9,250	*or*
Year 2016 @ 90%	=	€8,514	

Preliminary tax for 2016 will be €8,514 and is payable by 10 November 2016 through ROS (due date 31 October 2016). The balance of the tax due (€9,460 − €8,514 = €946) is payable by 31 October 2017.

If Paul pays his preliminary tax by way of direct debit, his preliminary tax for 2016 will be as follows:

Lower of: Year 2014 @ 105%	=	€8,347	*or*
Year 2015 @ 100%	=	€9,250	*or*
Year 2016 @ 90%	=	€8,514	

Therefore Paul's preliminary tax for 2016 will be €8,347 and is payable by 10 November 2016 through ROS (due date 31 October 2016). The balance of the tax due (€9,460 – €8,347 = €1,113) is payable by 31 October 2017.

Underpayment of Preliminary Tax

Where preliminary tax paid is based on 90% of the **estimated** liability for the current year and the final tax liability is greater than the estimate, interest will be chargeable on the difference between the preliminary tax amount paid and the final tax liability at a rate of 0.0219% per day.

10.1.4 Self-correction and Expressions of Doubt

Self-correction

Where a taxpayer discovers some errors after the submission of a tax return and wishes to rectify the return, Revenue will allow a return to be self-corrected **without** penalty where:

- Revenue is notified in writing of the adjustments to be made, and the circumstances under which the errors arose;
- a computation of the correct tax and statutory interest payable is provided, along with a payment in settlement.

Time Limits for Self-correction

Income Tax	Within 12 months of the due date for filing the return.
Corporation Tax	Within 12 months of the due date for filing the return.
Capital Gains Tax	Within 12 months of the due date for filing the return.
VAT	Before the due date of the income tax or corporation tax return for the period in which the VAT period ends, e.g. a self-correction of the Jan/Feb 2016 VAT for a company with a 31 December 2016 year-end date must occur before 21 September 2017.
PAYE/PRSI/USC	Within 12 months of the due date for filing the annual return.
Relevant Contracts Tax	Within 12 months of the due date for filing the monthly or quarterly online return.
Capital Acquisitions Tax	Within 12 weeks of the due date for filing the return.
Local Property Tax	Within 12 months of the return filing date.

Note that a self-correction **cannot be made** if Revenue has begun to make enquiries into the return or self-assessment for that chargeable period or if an audit or investigation has commenced in relation to the tax affairs of the taxpayer for the chargeable period involved.

Expression of Doubt

Where a taxpayer has a **genuine doubt** over the particular interpretation of an item in a return, for example, the application of a particular relief, etc. The taxpayer may:

- prepare the return for the chargeable period to the best of the taxpayer's belief as to the correct application of the law to the matter, and submit it to Revenue; and
- include a "Letter of Expression of Doubt" with the return.

The letter of expression of doubt means a written or electronic communication that:

- clearly identifies that the communication is a "Letter of Expression of Doubt";
- sets out in full detail the facts and circumstances of the matter in doubt;
- specifies the doubt and the law giving rise to the doubt;
- identifies the amount of tax in doubt in respect of the chargeable period to which the expression of doubt relates.

An expression of doubt can only be submitted if the accompanying return is delivered to Revenue **on or before** the specified return date. Therefore an expression of doubt cannot be made if the return is filed after the due date. Revenue may refuse to accept an expression of doubt in certain circumstances. However, the taxpayer has a right to appeal against such a decision.

10.1.5 *Notice of Assessment*

For tax years 2013, *et seq.*, self-assessed taxpayers are required to submit **self-computations** of the taxes due at the time of filing. As a general rule, Revenue no longer issue assessments to taxpayers and the taxpayer's self-assessment constitutes the tax payable. This does not in any way preclude Revenue from raising an assessment to tax where:
- a return has not been filed; **or**
- Revenue disagrees with the self-computation.

While most self-assessed taxpayers are obliged to file tax returns through ROS, some returns are still filed by paper. Where such a taxpayer files a return by **31 August**, Revenue will prepare a notice of assessment and send it to the taxpayer.

10.1.6   Interest Payable and Late Filing Surcharges

Interest on Overdue Income Tax
The rate of interest on overdue income tax is 0.0219% per day or part thereof (approximately 8% per annum).

Late Filing Surcharges
If a return of income is **not submitted** by the "specified date", i.e. 31 October, in the year following the year of assessment, the tax liability for that year is **increased** by a **surcharge** on the amount of tax assessed. The surcharge is calculated on the **full tax payable for the year** and does not take account of any tax payments already made (e.g. PAYE). The surcharge is calculated as follows:

1. if the return is submitted within two months of the specified return date, i.e. by 31 December, then the surcharge is 5% of the full tax payable for the year, subject to a maximum surcharge of €12,695.
2. if the return is submitted more than two months after the specified return date, i.e. after 31 December, then the surcharge is 10% of the full tax payable for the year, subject to a maximum surcharge of €63,485.

Where an individual files a return and fails to include on the return details relating to any exemption, allowance, deduction, credit or other relief the person is claiming (referred to as "specified details") and the return states that the details required are specified details, the individual may be liable to a 5% surcharge (subject to the usual maximum of €12,695) **even if** they have filed the return **on time**. However, this surcharge may only be applied where, after the return has been filed, it has come to the person's notice (or has been brought to their attention) that the specified details were not included in the return and the person **failed to remedy** the matter.

Fixed Penalty
The penalty for a 'specified' taxpayer not making an electronic payment or not filing a return electronically is €1,520 (section 917EA(7) TCA 1997). The penalty is charged in each instance where payment or filing has not been made electronically.

The fixed penalty for a self-assessed taxpayer not making a return is €3,000 (section 1052 TCA 1997) rising to €4,000 in certain circumstances. In practice, fixed penalties are rarely applied.

10.1.7   Interest on Overpayments of Tax

Interest is paid by Revenue at **0.011% per day** or part thereof (4.015% per annum) on overpaid tax.

Under section 865A TCA 1997, the **date** from which interest runs will **depend** on whether the overpayment is as a result of **Revenue's mistake** or the **taxpayer's**. Where the overpayment arises because of a mistaken assumption by Revenue in the application of tax law, and a claim for repayment is made within the requisite time limit, interest is paid from the day after the end of the tax year to which the repayment relates or, if later, the date of payment, until the date the repayment is made.

Where the overpayment **does not arise** because of a mistaken application of the law by Revenue, the overpayment will only carry interest for the period beginning on the day which is **93 days** after the day on which a "valid claim" for repayment has been filed with Revenue. A "valid claim" is one where all the information, which Revenue might reasonably require to enable it to determine if and to what extent a repayment is due, has been provided to Revenue.

Interest on the overpayment of tax is **not subject** to withholding tax and is **exempt** from income tax. Interest will not be paid where the overall amount due is less than €10.

10.2 Relevant Contracts Tax

Relevant contracts tax (RCT) was introduced with the primary objective of reducing the perceived level of tax evasion by subcontractors in the construction, forestry and meat-processing industries. The RCT system is an electronic system, all communication between the principal contractor and Revenue being conducted online using the eRCT system. Subcontractors are not obliged to register for ROS but, if they do, they can view all transactions on their RCT account using eRCT (sections 530A–530V TCA 1997).

10.2.1 General Scheme

The general rule is that a **"principal contractor"** is required to deduct RCT from payments made to subcontractors under a **"relevant contract"** at one of three rates **to be advised by Revenue**, as follows:

- **rate of 0%** will likely apply where a subcontractor is registered with Revenue and is fully tax compliant;
- **rate of 20%** will apply where a subcontractor is registered for tax and has a record of tax compliance; and
- **rate of 35%** will apply to subcontractors who are not registered with Revenue or where there are serious compliance issues to be addressed.

10.2.2 Operation of the RCT Scheme

Contract Notification
When a principal contractor enters into a relevant contract with a subcontractor, the principal contractor is obliged to provide Revenue, online, with details of the subcontractor and the contract, including a declaration that the contract is **not a contract of employment**.

Where the **tax reference number of the subcontractor is known, the contract notification** will include the following:

- subcontractor's name and tax reference number;
- details of the contract (i.e. sector, nature and location of work, start/end date, value of contract);
- details of the subcontractor's fixed place of business;
- details of whether the subcontractor will supply materials, plant and machinery;
- details of whether the subcontractor will provide their own insurance; and
- details of whether the subcontractor will engage other people to work on the contract at the subcontractor's own expense.

Where the tax reference number of the subcontractor is **not provided or is unknown**, the following details must be provided in addition to the information above:

- the subcontractor's address, date of birth, country, e-mail address, mobile and telephone numbers;
- if registered for tax outside Ireland, state the country and their tax registration number in that country; and
- details regarding the type of contractor, e.g. individual, company or partnership.

Payment Notification
Prior to making any payment under the contract, the principal contractor must notify Revenue, **online**, of their intention to make the payment and provide details of the gross amount to be paid.

Deduction Authorisation
On receipt of a payment notification Revenue will issue a deduction authorisation, which will detail the **rate of tax** and the **total amount of tax** to be deducted from the payment. The principal contractor can only pay the subcontractor in accordance with this notification and must provide a copy of the deduction authorisation to the subcontractor.

Deduction Summary
The deduction summary is created by Revenue from the payment notifications received from the principal contractor during the return period. Depending on the principal contractor's filing frequency, the summary will be available online to the principal contractor shortly after the end of the return period.

Payment of RCT Deducted
The principal contractor should check the deduction summary and make any amendments necessary and arrange for the RCT to be paid on or before the due date which, as electronic filers, will be the **23rd of the month** following the end of the return period. If the deduction summary is amended after the due date, the return will be late and a surcharge will apply.

For subcontractors any tax deducted will be credited against other tax liabilities which the subcontractor may have. Any excess will only be refunded after the tax return for the chargeable period has been filed and paid.

Penalties for Failing to Operate RCT Correctly
A principal contractor is obliged to deduct tax from payments to subcontractors in accordance with the **deduction authorisation** issued by Revenue.

Where a principal contractor fails to operate RCT on relevant payments to subcontractors, in each instance the principal contractor will be liable to the following penalties:

- Where the subcontractor is liable to an RCT deduction **rate of 0%**, the principal contractor will be liable to a **penalty of 3%** of the relevant payment.
- Where the subcontractor is liable to an RCT deduction **rate of 20%**, the principal contractor will be liable to a **penalty of 10%** of the relevant payment.
- Where the subcontractor is liable to an RCT deduction **rate of 35%**, the principal contractor will be liable to a **penalty of 20%** of the relevant payment.
- Where the subcontractor to whom the payment was made is not known to Revenue, the principal contractor will be liable to a **penalty of 35%** of the relevant payment.

In all the above instances, the principal contractor is required to submit an unreported payment notification to Revenue.

10.2.3 Definitions

Principal Contractor
A "principal contractor" in the construction, forestry and meat processing industries, is a person who takes on a subcontractor and who:

- carries on a business that includes the erection of buildings or the development of land, or the manufacture, treatment or extraction of materials for use in construction operations;
- carries on a business of meat processing operations in an establishment approved and inspected in accordance with the EU meat and poultry regulations;
- carries on a business of forestry operations that includes the processing (including cutting and preserving) of wood from thinned or felled trees, in sawmills or other like premises, or the supply of thinned or felled trees for such processing;
- is connected with a company which carries on any of the above businesses;
- is a local authority or a public utility society, or a body referred to in the Housing Act 1966;
- is a Minister of the Government;
- is a Board established by or under Statute or Royal Charter and funded wholly or mainly out of moneys provided by the Oireachtas;
- carries on any gas, water, electricity, hydraulic power, dock, canal or railway undertaking; or
- is a subcontractor who subcontracts all or part of the contract to a subcontractor.

Note: a principal contractor in the provision of construction services is subject to the VAT reverse charge rules (see **Chapter 11**).

Relevant Contract

A "relevant contract" is defined as a contract (not being a contract of employment) whereby a person is liable to another person:

1. to carry out relevant operations;
2. to be responsible for the carrying out of such operations by others; or
3. to furnish their own labour or the labour of others in the carrying out of such operations, or to arrange for the labour of others to be furnished for the carrying out of such operations.

Where a principal contractor engages the same subcontractor on various or multiple contracts, they will be required to notify each contract separately, unless the contracts can be considered to be part of one ongoing relevant contract with the subcontractor.

Relevant Operations

The main "relevant operations" are:

1. the construction, alteration, repair, extension, demolition or dismantling of buildings, including site preparation and haulage;
2. meat processing; and
3. forestry.

Relevant Operations Carried on Abroad

Strictly, a principal contractor is required to deduct RCT in respect of relevant operations carried out by a subcontractor, whether or not the subcontractor is carrying on business in the State and whether or not the relevant operations are carried out abroad. In practice, however, Revenue accepts that RCT does not apply where the relevant operations are performed wholly abroad. Where a contract is performed partly in the State and partly abroad, RCT will only apply to payments in respect of work carried out in the State.

Section 25 FA 2015 amended this definition to include relevant operations carried out in the State or in areas covered by the **Continental Shelf Act 1968**. Effective from 1 January 2016, this will include businesses in certain sectors such as telecommunications, petroleum and renewable energy to the extent that work is undertaken in the Irish continental shelf.

10.3 Professional Services Withholding Tax

10.3.1 Introduction

Chapter 1, Part 18 TCA 1997 provides for a **withholding tax of 20%** to be **deducted at source** from payments made by certain bodies in respect of professional services. The tax is known as professional services withholding tax (PSWT).

PSWT is deducted by "**accountable persons**" from "**relevant payments**" made by them to "**specified persons**" in respect of "**professional services**".

Accountable Persons

For the purposes of PSWT, the following public bodies are "accountable persons":

- Government departments and offices;
- local authorities;
- the Health Service Executive; and
- commercial and non-commercial semi-State bodies and their subsidiaries.

A list of accountable persons is set out in Schedule 13 TCA 1997.

Relevant Payments

"Relevant payments" are payments made by accountable persons in respect of **professional services**. The payments need not be in respect of services provided to the accountable person. PSWT applies to the **entire payment**, including any element which is in respect of the reimbursement of expenses incurred by the specified person, **except** for stamp duties, Land Registry and Deed of Registration fees, Companies Office and Court fees. **VAT charged by the specified person should be excluded when calculating PSWT.**

Excluded Payments

PSWT should **not be** deducted from the following payments:

- payments which are subject to PAYE;
- payments which come within the RCT scheme;
- payments to other accountable persons:
    - in reimbursement of payments for professional services, **or**
    - where the income of the accountable person receiving the payment is exempt from income tax or corporation tax;
- payments to charities which have been granted an exemption from tax by the Revenue Commissioners; and
- where the payment is made by a foreign-based branch or agency of an accountable person to a person resident abroad.

Specified Persons

"Specified persons" are persons who provide professional services in respect of which relevant payments are made to them by accountable persons. Specified persons can be individuals, companies or partnerships and includes non-residents. PSWT deducted is available for **offset** against the specified person's final **income tax/corporation tax liability** for the period in which the relevant payment is charged to tax.

Tax Clearance Certificate

Suppliers of goods or services who enter into a public sector contract with a value of €10,000 (inclusive of VAT) or more, must produce a tax clearance certificate to the public body with whom the contract is being entered into.

PSWT **must be deducted** from relevant payments made by an accountable person to a specified person, **irrespective** of the fact that the specified person produces a tax clearance certificate.

Professional Services

Section 520 TCA 1997 provides that professional services that are subject to PSWT include:

- services of a medical, dental, pharmaceutical, optical, aural or veterinary nature;
- services of an architectural, engineering, quantity surveying or surveying nature, and related services;
- services of accountancy, auditing or finance and services of financial, economic, marketing, advertising or other consultancies;
- services of a solicitor or barrister or other legal services;
- geological services; and
- training consultancy services, including advice on training requirements and syllabus design and development, but **excluding** teaching or lecturing services.

The above is not an exhaustive list. In some cases a service may not of itself attract PSWT but, where a service forms **part of a wider consultancy service**, it would then come within the scope of PSWT, e.g. where printing a brochure forms part of an overall professional service provided to an accountable person, it is an expense incurred in the **provision** of that service. The **full amount** of the payment (including the printing costs) in respect of the overall service is subject to PSWT.

Services that are not regarded as professional services for the purposes of PSWT include:

- teaching, training or lecturing services;
- translation services, including the services of an interpreter;
- proof-reading services;
- services of stenographers;
- setting and assessing oral, aural or written examinations;
- contract cleaning services; and
- maintenance and repair work.

10.3.2 Administration

Where a person provides professional services to an accountable person, they must supply the following to the accountable person:

1. their income (PPS number) or corporation tax number; and
2. if the payment includes VAT, their VAT reference number.

If the specified person does not reside in the State or have a permanent establishment in the State, they must supply details of their country of residence and their tax reference number in that country.

When the specified person has supplied the above information, the accountable person must, when making a payment, complete **Form F45** which contains the following information:

1. the name and address of the specified person;
2. the person's tax reference number;
3. the amount of the relevant payment;

4. the amount of PSWT deducted from the payment;
5. the date on which payment is made; and
6. the amount of VAT charged.

The specified person also gets a copy of this form (Form F45).

A **Form F45** must be issued in respect of **each relevant payment** made, including a relevant payment to a specified person who has not supplied their tax reference number. Only one form F45 should ever be issued in respect of each relevant payment. If a Form F45 issued to a specified person is lost or destroyed or where the details entered require amendment, a **Form F43** can be issued by the accountable person.

The accountable person must make a monthly return **Form F30** to Revenue, declaring the total amount of PSWT deducted in that month. The return and payment of PSWT due must be made online within 23 days from the end of each income tax month. Where no PSWT is deducted by an accountable person in a month, a "NIL" return should be made. An **annual return Form F35** declaring the PSWT liability for a tax year must be returned online by 23 February following the end of the tax year.

10.3.3   Credit for PSWT

Credit will be given to the specified person for PSWT deducted (as confirmed in Form F45) against their income tax or corporation tax liabilities.

Income Tax

PSWT deducted in the basis period may be set against the income tax liability for that year of assessment. Any excess PSWT over and above the income tax liability will be refunded.

Where the basis period for two tax years overlap, the overlapping period is deemed to form part of the second tax year only.

> **Example 10.2**
> An individual commences to trade on 1 July 2016 and makes up accounts for the year ended 30 June 2017. The period 1 July to 31 December 2016 will form part of the basis period for the tax year 2016 and 2017. For PSWT purposes this period will be deemed to form part of the 2017 basis period only. Accordingly, credit for PSWT deducted from payments included in the period 1 July to 31 December 2016 will be given against the individual's tax liability for 2017.

Where a period falls into a gap between two basis periods, it is deemed to fall into the **later basis period**.

> **Example 10.3**
> An individual makes up accounts annually to 30 September. The individual ceases to trade on 30 June 2016. Actual profits for 2015 were less than those originally assessed; therefore, there is no revision of 2015 profits to actual. The period 1 October 2015 to 31 December 2015 does not form part of the basis period for 2015 or 2016. Credit will be given for PSWT deducted from payments relating to the period 1 October 2015 to 31 December 2015 against the individual's tax liability for 2016.

Where the PSWT deducted refers to two or more persons, for example in the case of a partnership, the PSWT suffered is apportioned in the partner profit-sharing ratios.

The taxpayer must submit Form F45, given to the taxpayer by the accountable person, when making a claim for an interim refund of PSWT (see below). Form F45 no longer needs to be submitted with the taxpayer's annual tax return, but they should be retained as they may be requested by Revenue for verification purposes at a later date.

Preliminary Tax

PSWT can be taken into account as a credit in computing the amount of tax **payable** for the year. However, PSWT deducted may not be treated as a payment (or part-payment) of the preliminary tax that is required to be paid directly to the Collector-General.

Example 10.4

Mary Burns estimates that her income tax liability for 2016 amounts to €54,000. She paid PSWT of €10,000 in 2016. Her figures for 2015 were as follows:

Income Tax Liability	€28,000
PSWT	€15,000

Calculation of Preliminary Tax for 2016:
Lower of:

Year 2016 @ 90% = (€54,000 − €10,000) @ 90%	€39,600 **or**
Year 2015 @ 100% = (€28,000 − €15,000) @ 100%	€13,000

Preliminary tax is calculated by reference to the net amount of tax payable after deducting PSWT.

10.3.4   Refunds of PSWT

Where a taxpayer considers that the amount of PSWT deducted from payments is in excess of their likely final liability to tax, an application may be made to the taxpayer's Revenue office for an interim refund of any excess, instead of waiting to have it credited against final liability. The application is made on **Form F50.**

Ongoing Business

An interim refund of PSWT may be given to a person who satisfies the following requirements:

1. the profits of the basis period for the tax year immediately preceding the tax year in question must have been finally determined;
2. the amount of tax due in respect of the tax year immediately preceding the tax year in question must have been paid; and
3. the individual must provide Form F45 in respect of the withholding tax reclaimed.

The amount of the interim refund that can be made is calculated as

> Tax withheld, according to Form F45
> *Less*: tax liability for previous tax year
> *Less*: any outstanding VAT, PAYE or PRSI due by the individual.

Example 10.5

An individual makes up accounts to 30 September each year. In order for the individual to be able to claim a refund of tax withheld from receipts included in his accounts for the year ended 30 September 2016, the individual must have filed a return for 2015 and paid his tax liability for 2015. The individual files his return for 2015 on 31 October 2016 and pays the balance of tax due for 2015 on the same day. An assessment issues on 1 December 2016 showing a total liability for 2015 of €26,500 which has been paid in full. During the year ended 30 September 2016, the individual received €128,000 after deduction of PSWT of €32,000 in respect of services provided during the year ended 30 September 2016. Provided the individual has no arrears of VAT, PAYE or PRSI and has Form F45 in respect of the PSWT paid of €32,000, he may submit a claim for an interim refund of PSWT of €5,500, i.e. €32,000 − €26,500.

Commencing Businesses

Where an individual wishes to make a claim for an interim refund of PSWT in the year in which they commenced business, they does not have to satisfy requirements 1. and 2. above. Instead, the Inspector of Taxes may make an interim refund to the individual of 20% of an amount calculated using the following formula:

$$E \times \left(\frac{A}{B} \times \frac{C}{D} \right)$$

where:

A = the estimated amount of payments from which PSWT will be deducted to be included as income in the basis period for the tax year;

B = the estimated total receipts to be included in income in the basis period for the tax year;

C = the estimated number of months or fractions of months in the period in respect of which the claim is being made;

D = the estimated number of months or fractions of months in the basis period for the tax year; and

E = the estimated expenses to be incurred by the individual in the basis period for the tax year.

Example 10.6

John commences to trade on 1 June 2016. He intends to make up accounts annually to 31 December. His first set of accounts will be made up for the seven months to 31 December 2016. Up to 30 September 2016, he has received payments of €16,000, from which PSWT of €4,000 was deducted. It is estimated that his accounts for the seven months to 31 December 2016 will include income of €100,000 and expenses of €45,000. €40,000 of his total income will be paid under deduction of PSWT. In October 2016, he makes a claim for an interim refund of €2,057, calculated as follows:

$$20\% \times \left(€45,000 \times \frac{€40,000}{€100,000} \times \frac{4}{7} \right)$$

If the actual PSWT suffered was less than €2,057, his refund would be restricted to the amount of tax withheld.

Cases of Particular Hardship

Where an individual claims and proves particular hardship, Revenue can waive all or some of the conditions outlined above governing the payment of interim refunds. In such circumstances, the amount of the refund to be made to the individual is at the discretion of the Inspector of Taxes.

10.4 Tax Clearance Certificates

A tax clearance certificate (TCC) is a confirmation from Revenue that a person's tax and customs affairs are in order at the date of issue of the certificate. A TCC is required in the following instances:

1. **Public Sector Contracts** Section 1095 TCA 1997 requires a contractor to produce a general TCC in order to qualify for a public sector contract of a value of €10,000 or more (inclusive of VAT) within any 12-month period. Such contracts include the purchase, hiring and leasing of goods, services or property by public authorities. The tax clearance requirement applies even where the provision of goods or services is not the subject of a formal written contract.

2. **Grant Payments** Section 1095 also specifies that an applicant must hold a general TCC in order to qualify for State/public authority grants, subsidies and similar type payments of a value of €10,000 or more within any 12-month period.

3. **Licences and Certain Schemes** A current TCC is required by law for the operation of certain types of business situations, which include:

  - liquor licences for wholesale/retail, cultural and sporting institutions etc.;
  - bookmakers licence;
  - gaming licence;
  - granting or renewal of amusement machine permits;
  - auctioneer's or house agent's licence;
  - mineral oil trader's licence;
  - money lenders licence;
  - Mortgage or Credit Intermediaries authorisation;
  - road transport licence (passengers and merchandise);
  - local authority loans scheme (shared ownership);
  - permits for waste collection activities (including slurry spreading);
  - Waste Management (Collection) permit;
  - employers employing or seeking to employ non-nationals;
  - licences for small public service vehicles, e.g. taxis and hackneys;
  - private security services;
  - authorisation as an authorised warehouse-keeper; and
  - authorisation as a Registered Consignor.

4. **Members of the Houses of the Oireachtas** The Standards in Public Office Act 2001 (SIPO) provides for a tax clearance requirement for members of the Dáil and Seanad. Due to the different legal basis, a specific tax clearance certificate is required for the purposes of SIPO. There is a separate application form (TC SIPO) for tax clearance under SIPO and is available on Revenue's website. A TCC issued under other tax clearance provisions is not valid for the purposes of SIPO.

10.4.1 eTax Clearance

With effect from 1 January 2016 an **electronic** tax clearance certificate system applies that will end the issuing of paper certificates. Paper certificates already issued remain valid until the date of expiry noted on those certificates. The two key changes introduced were:

  - processing of tax clearance applications, issuing of certificates and verification by third parties, is all online; **and**
  - if, upon review, a taxpayer is found to be non-compliant with their obligations, the TCC can be **rescinded** or withdrawn.

eTax clearance is available to businesses, PAYE and non-resident taxpayers with a PPSN/tax reference number. The system provides new online application screens for business taxpayers using ROS and for PAYE taxpayers using myAccount. Taxpayers who are tax compliant will receive a Tax Clearance Access Number which, along with their PPSN/tax reference number, they give to a third party to enable that third party to verify their tax clearance through ROS.

eTax Clearance **does not** apply to Standards in Public Office applicants or those not registered for Irish tax (e.g. non-residents or community/voluntary groups). These applications are processed by the Collector-General's office.

10.5   Appeal Procedures

10.5.1   Introduction

If a taxpayer **disagrees** with a notice of assessment or with a Revenue decision in relation to income tax, the taxpayer has the **right to appeal** against such an assessment or decision and an Appeal Commissioner will hear the appeal. From **21 March 2016** all appeals (with the exception of customs duty appeals and "first-stage" VRT appeals) are made directly to the newly established **Tax Appeals Commission** (TAC) and not through Revenue in the first instance.

The taxpayer **can only** appeal if:

1. they have submitted the return of income form; **and**
2. the taxpayer has paid the correct tax they believe is due, together with any interest or penalties payable.

The appeal to the TAC must be made within **30 days** of the issue of the notice of assessment or the decision by Revenue. A taxpayer cannot appeal against a notice of assessment that is in accordance with the information contained in the return of income or that agreed between Revenue and the taxpayer.

Conditions for a Valid Appeal

For an appeal to be valid the following conditions must be met:

1. it must be in writing, "Notice of Appeal", by post or email; **and**
2. the precise item in the assessment that the taxpayer disputes must be specified; **and**
3. the grounds for disputing the item must be detailed.

After receipt of the notice of appeal the TAC will send a copy of all the documentation to Revenue. Any objection Revenue may have to the acceptance of the appeal must be sent, in writing, to the TAC within 30 days of receipt of the notice of appeal. These objections in turn are copied to the taxpayer who can respond to Revenue's objection within 14 days from receipt. The decision to accept or reject the appeal application is taken by the TAC **only**.

10.5.2   Hearing before the Appeal Commissioner

When an appeal has been accepted the TAC may request that either party provide additional information (a "statement of case") and supporting documentation. Where such a request is made, the party so requested must share their statement plus any associated documents with the other party to the appeal and confirm to the Commissioner that this has been done. In some instances the TAC may adjudicate on a matter under appeal without a hearing, provided that the TAC notifies both parties of their intention to so do and where, within 21 days of such notification, neither party requests a hearing.

The parties to the appeal must be given at least **14 days' notice** of the date for the hearing of the appeal by the TAC. At the hearing the Appeal Commissioner will consider the facts of the case and will determine an appeal, either in favour of the taxpayer or Revenue, as soon as is practicable. The Commissioner will notify the parties, in writing, of their decision within 21 days of the appeal being determined.

All appeal hearings are heard **in public** but the TAC may direct, following a request by the taxpayer, that a hearing or part of a hearing be held *in camera*.

Dismissal or Determination of an Appeal

If an assessment is **dismissed**, as opposed to **determined**, there are serious implications for the taxpayer. In the case of the **dismissal** of the appeal, the original tax, as assessed by Revenue, is **confirmed** and becomes **immediately payable** to the Collector-General, as if no appeal had been lodged against the assessment.

If the assessment is **determined** by the Commissioner, the right of appeal to the **High Court** on a **point of law only** is available to either party. Tax will neither be collected nor repaid by the Revenue on the basis of the Appeal Commissioner's determination and Revenue will not be obliged to amend the assessment under appeal, until the appeal process to the High Court has been **fully completed**.

10.5.3 Taxpayer's/Revenue's Right to Appeal: Hearings before the High Court and Supreme Court

If either party to the appeal is dissatisfied with the determination of the Appeal Commissioner on a point of law, they may request the TAC sign a "Case Stated for the Opinion of the High Court" **within 21 days** from the date of determination of the appeal. This will include details of the Commissioner's findings of fact, an outline of the arguments made and the case law relied on by the parties, the Commissioner's determination and the point of law being appealed.

Any party aggrieved by the decision of the High Court has a **right of appeal** to the **Supreme Court**.

10.5.4 Settlement of an Appeal

An appeal may be settled where:

- agreement has been reached between the individual and Revenue;
- either party withdraws their appeal;
- the determination of the appeal by the Appeal Commissioner, High Court or Supreme Court; or
- by default, i.e. failure to be represented at the appeal hearing before the Appeal Commissioner.

10.6 Revenue Audits and Investigations

10.6.1 Introduction

The Irish tax system is primarily a **self-assessment system** where the taxpayer calculates the amount of tax due and pays it over to Revenue within the stipulated timeframe. (The exception is PAYE taxpayers, who are not generally self-assessed.) For the Revenue Commissioners, it is a fundamental principle of self-assessment tax systems that returns filed by **compliant** taxpayers are **accepted** as the basis for computing tax liabilities.

Revenue police the self-assessment system through the use of:

1. Non-audit compliance interventions;
2. Audits; and
3. Investigations.

10.6.2 Revenue Non-Audit Compliance Interventions

Revenue's "non-audit compliance interventions" are usually an enquiry, by letter or telephone, about a specific issue. An example would be a request for further documentation to support a claim for a particular tax relief. These interventions may take the form of:

- "assurance checks" or "aspect queries" – these are not limited only to self-assessed taxpayers, PAYE taxpayers, for example, can also be subject;
- profile interviews;
- sectoral reviews (e.g. a review of specific trades, professions or economic sectors);

- Joint Investigation Unit visits involving other agencies (e.g. Department of Social Protection or National Employment Rights Authority, etc.);
- unannounced visits;
- a request for a person or a business to undertake a self-review of a tax liability;
- the pursuit of returns from non-filers.

Where Revenue undertake any type of non-audit compliance intervention, the taxpayer is still entitled to make an "unprompted qualifying disclosure" (see **Section 10.6.6**), as an audit or investigation is not regarded as having started.

10.6.3 Revenue Audit

Revenue's *Code of Practice for Revenue Audit and other Compliance Interventions* (www.revenue.ie) states that the primary objective of Revenue compliance interventions is to promote "voluntary compliance with tax and duty obligations" and that the audit programme is mainly concerned with "detecting and deterring non-compliance".

A Revenue audit is an **examination** of:

- a tax return (e.g. income tax (including DIRT and other fiduciary taxes), corporation tax, CGT or CAT (either in whole or in part));
- a declaration of liability, or a repayment claim (e.g. VAT, PAYE/PRSI or RCT);
- a statement of liability to stamp duties; and
- the compliance of a person or business with tax and duty legislation.

Location of Audit

The audit is normally carried out at the taxpayer's place of business, or the principal place of business in the case of multiple businesses or locations. The length of such visits depends on the number and complexity of the points at issue.

Audit Notification

Twenty-one days' notice is generally given, in writing, to both the taxpayer and their agent. In certain exceptional circumstances, for example where it is suspected that records may be removed or altered, a visit may take place unannounced. The notice will clearly state that it is a "Notification of a Revenue Audit". Revenue will specify a date at which it wishes to visit the taxpayer's premises to examine the books and records of the business. Almost all audits are carried out for a reason, i.e. Revenue will have information or indications that the taxpayer may be at fault, though some audits are carried out on a random basis.

The audit notification will specify the tax head (income tax, VAT, etc.) and the year of assessment or period in question. The Revenue Inspector is confined to examining the issues **as notified** and cannot extend the audit without good reason at the time of the visit.

As and from the date of the audit notification, the taxpayer can no longer make an "unprompted qualifying disclosure"; they can, however, make a "prompted qualifying disclosure" **before** the audit examination begins. (See **Section 10.6.6**).

Conduct of a Revenue Audit

At the commencement of any **field audit**, the auditor identifies themselves, shows their authorisation and explains to the taxpayer the purpose of the audit. They will draw the taxpayer's attention to the *Customer Service Charter* and outline the authority vested in them under the various Finance Acts in relation to the inspection of records, documents, etc. The taxpayer is **informed** of Revenue's practice of charging interest and penalties and is offered the opportunity to make a prompted qualifying disclosure. In addition, the auditor advises the taxpayer of the **effects** of a **disclosure** regarding penalties and publication.

Having explained their authority, the auditor will normally proceed to point out that, in the event of any irregularities being found which have led to an apparent underpayment in tax, they will request a **final meeting** with the taxpayer and their agent to:

- discuss and present a report on the results of the audit;
- ask for comments and responses from the taxpayer and their agent;
- if possible, reach agreement on the undercharges (if any) under each tax heading, i.e. income tax, USC, VAT, PAYE, PRSI, surcharges, interest and penalties; and
- invite the taxpayer/agent to make a formal settlement offer in writing in the event of discrepancies not fully explained.

Following the final interview, a **written report** will be sent to the taxpayer or their agent setting out the main points arising from the audit.

The auditor will also normally indicate at the interview the **approximate duration** of the audit and where it will be carried out, and will invite questions from the taxpayer and their agent in relation to the audit.

A **written record** of all requests, replies and other requirements, whether raised at the initial interview or subsequently, should be kept by the taxpayer to ensure that the audit is conducted in an orderly way. If some questions raised by the audit are complex, it may be preferable to request the auditor to submit them **in writing**.

A Revenue audit may require the transfer of electronic data from a taxpayer's computer to Revenue. If such a request is made, the taxpayer or their IT supplier or agent is required to provide the necessary data downloads as Revenue is not permitted to operate the taxpayer's computer systems. Any data requested is stored on Revenue-encrypted storage devices.

In the case of a **desk audit**, the auditor will request records to be submitted for examination and, other than in exceptional circumstances, an auditor will **not retain** records for **longer than 30 days**. If more time is required the Inspector will negotiate this with the taxpayer or their agent. The 30-day period can commence only **from the date** on which the auditor has received **all** of the records requested. If items are omitted, then clearly the auditor cannot commence his audit until he has all relevant documentation.

Revenue **does not**, as a matter of normal practice, **issue assessments** where a settlement is reached and agreed with the taxpayer and/or their agent. An assessment is normally only issued where it is **requested** by the taxpayer to enable them to take the matter before the Appeal Commissioners.

10.6.4   *Revenue Investigation*

An investigation is an examination of a taxpayer's affairs where Revenue has evidence or concerns of **serious tax evasion**. Some investigation cases may lead to criminal prosecution. During the course of a Revenue audit, an auditor may also notify the taxpayer that the audit is ceasing and an investigation commencing.

Where a Revenue investigation is being notified, the letter issued will include the wording: "Notification of a Revenue Investigation". Revenue auditors engaged in the investigation of serious tax evasion may visit a taxpayer's place of business without advance notice.

Note: once an investigation is initiated, the taxpayer will not have an opportunity to make any type of qualifying disclosure and so cannot avail of any mitigation of penalties, avoid publication of final settlement or avoid possible criminal prosecution.

10.6.5 Tax, Interest and Penalties

Tax

Any tax due as a result of any Revenue compliance intervention must be paid.

Interest

Interest is always charged if a failure to pay is identified. Interest **cannot** be mitigated. Interest is charged on a daily basis by reference to the date the tax was originally due and payable.

Application of Penalties

Penalties will apply if, in the course of the audit, tax defaults are identified. Penalties are "tax-geared", which means that the penalty is expressed as a **percentage of the tax** (but not the interest) due.

Penalties will apply in circumstances where there has been:

- "careless behaviour without significant consequences";
- "careless behaviour with significant consequences"; or
- "deliberate behaviour".

1. **Careless Behaviour without Significant Tax Consequences**

   The penalty for this category is **20% of the tax**. This will arise if a taxpayer of ordinary skill and knowledge, properly advised, would have foreseen as a reasonable probability or likelihood the prospect that an act (or omission) would cause a tax underpayment, having regard to all the circumstances, but nevertheless, the act or omission occurred. The tax shortfall must be **less than 15%** of the tax liability ultimately due in respect of the particular tax for that period.

2. **Careless Behaviour with Significant Tax Consequences**

   The penalty here is **40% of the tax**. This category is the lack of **due care**, with the result that tax liabilities or repayment claims are **substantially incorrect** and the tax shortfall **exceeds 15%** of the correct tax liability.

3. **Deliberate Behaviour**

   The penalty for deliberate behaviour is **100% of the tax**. Deliberate behaviour has indicators consistent with **intent** and includes tax evasion and the non-operation of fiduciary taxes such as PAYE and VAT.

Careless behaviour in both instances (i.e. with and without significant tax consequences) is distinguished from "deliberate behaviour" by the **absence** of indicators consistent with **intent** on the part of the taxpayer.

Example 10.7

George and Rinah were both subject to Revenue audits after filing individual tax returns. After their audits, George and Rinah were deemed to have acted without due care and attention – both had under-declared their tax liabilities, for income tax and VAT, respectively. They were not deemed to have deliberately under-declared their respective tax liabilities.

	George	Rinah
	George	**Rinah**
Tax amount due	€61,000	€243,000
Tax payable per return submitted	€48,000	€214,000
Tax underpaid	€13,000	€29,000
As a % of tax actually due	**21.3%**	**11.9%**
Penalty (before mitigation)	**40%**	**20%**

While Rinah underpaid a greater amount of tax, as a percentage of the tax due it was George who was the bigger defaulter.

Innocent Error

A penalty will not be payable in instances where the Revenue auditor is satisfied that:

- the error is immaterial in the context of the overall tax payments made by the taxpayer;
- the mistake was not intentional or frequently recurring;
- good books and records were kept; **and**
- the taxpayer has a good compliance record.

Statutory interest is payable upon settlement of the tax due as a result of "innocent errors".

Technical Adjustments

Technical adjustments are adjustments to liability that arise from differences in the interpretation or the application of legislation. For a technical adjustment not to attract a penalty, Revenue must be satisfied that:

- due care has been taken by the taxpayer; **and**
- the treatment concerned was based on a mistaken interpretation of the law, which could reasonably have been considered to be correct and did not involve deliberate behaviour designed to avoid due taxes.

A taxpayer who takes a position on a matter that has significant tax consequences is expected to take **due care**. Matters that are well established in case law and precedent will not be entertained as technical adjustments.

Statutory interest on any outstanding tax is payable upon settlement.

No Loss of Revenue

The expression "no loss of revenue" is used to describe a situation whereby there is no cost to the State even though tax was not properly charged. Take the example of where a sale was made between two VAT-registered businesses without the addition of VAT. This resulted in no VAT being paid on the sale but, correspondingly, no input VAT credit being claimed by the other party. In this case, there was no loss of revenue to the State. However, in the event of an audit, Revenue is entitled to seek the VAT and interest and penalties due for the non-operation or incorrect operation of the VAT system. Taxpayers may, however, make a "no loss of revenue claim" if:

- the tax involved is either VAT or RCT;
- the taxpayer can provide conclusive evidence to demonstrate, to the satisfaction of Revenue, that there was "no loss of revenue"; and
- the taxpayer's compliance record is good and the default in question wasn't as a result of deliberate behaviour.

Where Revenue accepts "no loss of revenue" claims, statutory interest may be payable but limited to any period where there was a temporary loss of revenue. Reduced penalties are payable, as set out in **Section 10.6.6**.

Revenue will not accept "no loss of revenue" claims in the following circumstances:

- where there is a general failure to operate the tax system (and not just a once-off);
- where the default was as a consequence of deliberate behaviour;
- where "no loss of revenue" has not been proven to the satisfaction of Revenue;
- where the taxpayer has not co-operated;
- where the default is in the "careless behaviour" category and there is neither a qualifying disclosure nor co-operation;

▦ where the "no loss of revenue" claim was not submitted in writing; or

▦ where the "no loss of revenue" penalty is not agreed and paid.

10.6.6 Mitigation of Penalties

Under TCA 1997, Revenue has the power to mitigate the penalties in the following circumstances:

▦ co-operation by the taxpayer; and

▦ "qualifying disclosures" made by the taxpayer.

No mitigation of penalties is available where a Revenue investigation has been initiated.

Co-operation

Co-operation includes the following:

▦ having all books, records, and linking papers available for the auditor at the commencement of the audit;

▦ having appropriate personnel available at the time of audit;

▦ responding promptly to all requests for information and explanations;

▦ responding promptly to all correspondence; and

▦ prompt payment of the audit settlement liability.

Qualifying Disclosures

The taxpayer may elect to carry out a review of their own tax affairs and identify where mistakes were made **prior** to their discovery by the Revenue auditor. This type of review is called a "qualifying disclosure", and Revenue has in place special incentives for taxpayers who wish to make qualifying disclosures. A qualifying disclosure results in the following:

▦ non-publication under section 1086 TCA 1997;

▦ no prosecution – a Revenue assurance that, in certain circumstances, an investigation with a view to prosecution will not be initiated; and

▦ further mitigation of penalties.

Qualifying disclosures can be either "**unprompted**" or "**prompted**": The concept of a prompted or an unprompted disclosure is a **key fact** when determining the level of liability to a civil penalty.

An "unprompted" disclosure is a disclosure that is made **before** the taxpayer is notified of an audit **or** contacted by Revenue regarding an enquiry or investigation relating to his or her tax affairs.

A "prompted" disclosure is a disclosure made **after** an audit notice has issued but **before** an examination of the books and records or other documentation has begun.

Format of a Qualifying Disclosure

A qualifying disclosure is a disclosure of the full particulars of all matters occasioning a liability to tax that give rise to a penalty. It must be made **in writing and signed by, or on behalf of, the taxpayer**. It must be accompanied by:

▦ A **declaration**, to the best of that person's knowledge, information and belief, that all matters contained in the disclosure are correct and complete.

▦ A **payment** of the tax or duty and interest on late payment of that tax or duty. Penalties due do not need to be stated – these are subsequently agreed and paid.

In addition:

- All qualifying disclosures (prompted and unprompted) in the "deliberate behaviour" category must state the amounts of all liabilities to tax and interest, in respect of **all tax heads and periods**, where liabilities arise as a result of deliberate behaviour, that were previously undisclosed.
- In the case of a **prompted** qualifying disclosure in the "careless behaviour" category, the qualifying disclosure must state the amounts of **all** liabilities to tax and interest in respect of the **relevant tax heads and periods** within the scope of the **proposed audit**.
- In the case of an **unprompted** qualifying disclosure in the "careless behaviour" category, the qualifying disclosure must state the amounts of **all** liabilities to tax and interest in respect of the tax heads and periods that are the subject of the unprompted qualifying disclosure.

Preparation of a Qualifying Disclosure

In order for the taxpayer to secure an agreed period of time in which to prepare and make a qualifying disclosure, **notice of the intention** to make a disclosure must be given to Revenue.

In the case of an **unprompted disclosure**, the notice of the intention to make a disclosure must be given **before** a notice of audit is issued **or** the taxpayer has been contacted by Revenue regarding an enquiry or investigation relating to their tax affairs.

In the case of a **prompted disclosure**, the notice of intention to make a disclosure must be given **within 14 days** of the day of issue of the notification of audit.

A person who has given notice, within the time allowed, of their intention to make a **qualifying disclosure** will be given **60 days** in which to quantify the shortfall and make the relevant payment. This period of 60 days will begin from the day on which the notice of intention to make a disclosure was given and will be communicated to the taxpayer in writing by Revenue.

MITIGATION OF PENALTIES ON FIRST QUALIFYING DISCLOSURE
(for defaults occurring on or after 24 December 2008)

Category of Tax Default	No Co-operation	Net Penalty after Mitigation (as a % of Tax Underpaid) where there is:		
		Co-operation Only	Co-operation AND a Prompted Qualifying Disclosure	Co-operation AND an Unprompted Qualifying Disclosure
Deliberate behaviour	100%	75%	50%	10%
Careless behaviour with significant consequences	40%	30%	20%	5%
Careless behaviour without significant consequences	20%	15%	10%	3%

A separate table of penalties applies to a second and subsequent qualifying disclosure made within a five-year period (see Revenue's *Code of Practice for Revenue Audit and other Compliance Interventions* at www.revenue.ie).

MITIGATION OF PENALTIES ON "NO LOSS OF REVENUE" DEFAULTS

Category of Tax Default	Net Penalty after Mitigation (as a % of Tax Underpaid) where there is:			
	No Co-operation	Co-operation Only	Co-operation AND a Prompted Qualifying Disclosure	Co-operation AND an Unprompted Qualifying Disclosure
Careless behaviour	100%	Lesser of 9% or €100,000	Lesser of 6% or €15,000	Lesser of 3% or €5,000

A separate table of penalties applies to second and subsequent "no loss or revenue" qualifying disclosures made within a five-year period (see Revenue's *Code of Practice for Revenue Audit and other Compliance Interventions* at www.revenue.ie).

10.6.7 Tax Avoidance

Section 811 TCA 1997 is a general anti-avoidance provision that deals with transactions that have little or no commercial reality and are primarily intended to avoid, reduce or defer a tax liability. However, where a transaction to avoid tax is undertaken in the way provided for but also **intended** by legislation, then this is not regarded as tax avoidance unless there is misuse or abuse of the legislation. Avoidance should not be confused with evasion; tax evasion is an illegal act, with the intention to not pay tax that is rightfully due.

Tax Avoidance Surcharge and Interest
Where a taxpayer is found to have entered into a tax-avoidance transaction which gives rise to a tax advantage, section 811 TCA 1997 may apply a "tax avoidance surcharge" of **up to 30%** of the tax advantage. The surcharge may be reduced where a "qualifying avoidance disclosure" is made within a certain timeframe. The level of reduction of the surcharge will depend on whether or not the transaction was a "**disclosable transaction**" under the mandatory disclosure requirements below.

Mandatory Disclosure
The mandatory disclosure regime requires advisors or taxpayers to provide Revenue with specified information about a transaction that has certain characteristics. A taxpayer may need to confirm with their advisor whether or not a transaction is a "disclosable transaction" in order to be in a position to determine whether or not this regime will apply to them. If the transaction is a disclosable transaction, the taxpayer is obliged to include a "transaction number" (or Revenue reference number) in their return. Transaction numbers are issued by Revenue to a promoter following the submission of a valid mandatory disclosure (see Revenue's *Guidance Notes on the Mandatory Disclosure Regime* at www.revenue.ie).

10.6.8 Review Procedures

Revenue's *Complaint and Review Procedures* entitle a taxpayer to make a complaint or seek a review of Revenue's handling of their case where there is disagreement. This process **cannot** be used or requested where:

1. There is disagreement over a **point of law** – these matters are adjudicated on by the Appeal Commissioners or the Courts.
2. There is dispute regarding **civil penalties** applicable to audit and investigation settlements – these are determined by the Courts.

3. A settlement involving **publication** in the "List of Tax Defaulters" has been agreed, as publication in these circumstances is a legal requirement.
4. **Enforcement proceedings** have been initiated (e.g. tax referred to the Sheriff or external solicitor), or where Court action has been initiated or where the debt is the subject of an attachment order.
5. The complaint is being used to delay or obstruct an audit or investigation or is considered to be frivolous or vexatious.

A taxpayer's statutory right to make an appeal regarding a Revenue decision to the Tax Appeal Commission, or to make a complaint to the Office of the Ombudsman or to the Equality Tribunal is not affected in any way if the taxpayer avails of Revenue's complaint and review procedures.

The steps involved are as follows:

Step 1 – Make a Formal Complaint

> The taxpayer should submit a formal complaint, in writing, to their local Revenue Office with as much detail and information regarding the case as possible. If the issue cannot be resolved or the taxpayer is unhappy with the response, the taxpayer can request a local review.

Step 2 – Local Review

> This review will normally be carried out by the Manager (Principal Officer) of the local Revenue Office or, if requested by the taxpayer, by a manager in the Regional Office. The request for a Local Review should be made in writing to the relevant manager. Where the issue still cannot be resolved or the taxpayer is unhappy with the response, the taxpayer can request an Independent Internal or External Review.

Step 3 – Review by an Independent Internal or External Reviewer

> A request for an Independent Internal or External Review (but not both) should be submitted within **30 working days** from the date of the local review decision:

- by post to The Review Secretariat, Office of the Revenue Commissioners, Dublin Castle, Dublin 2; or
- by secure e-mail to ReviewSecretariat@revenue.ie.

> The internal or external reviewer will make a **final decision** on the issue and will write to the taxpayer setting out, in detail, an explanation of how the outcome was reached, including reference to relevant legislation and case law.

Revenue is bound by the outcome of the review procedure **unless** they are of the view that the decision of the reviewers is not in accordance with relevant legislation.

If the taxpayer is still unhappy, the decision of the internal or external reviewer does not interfere in any way with the taxpayer's right to take a case to the independent Appeal Commissioners, the Office of the Ombudsman or the Equality Tribunal, where appropriate.

10.7   Revenue On-Line Service (ROS)

10.7.1   Introduction

The Revenue On-Line Service (ROS) is an internet facility that allows taxpayers or their agents to file tax returns, pay tax liabilities and access their tax details online.

Some of the main features of ROS include the facility to:

- file returns and declarations online;

- make payments by laser card, debit instruction or online banking (online banking applies to income tax only);
- calculate tax liabilities; and
- claim repayments.

ROS also provides taxpayers (including PAYE taxpayers) with access to their tax account information, including the facility to view details of returns filed and due, payments made, view and amend tax credits, etc.

10.7.2   Mandatory e-Filing

Since **1 June 2011**, the following categories of taxpayer are **required** to pay and file returns electronically:

- all companies;
- all trusts;
- all partnerships;
- self-employed individuals filing a return of payments to third parties (Form 46G);
- self-employed individuals subject to the high earners restriction (Form RR1, Form 11);
- self-employed individuals benefiting from or acquiring foreign life policies, offshore funds or other offshore products; and
- self-employed individuals claiming a range of property-based incentives (residential property and industrial buildings allowances);
- all stamp duty returns and payments due on or after 1 June 2011; and
- employers with **10 or more employees**, not already covered above, are required to pay and file returns electronically since **1 October 2011**.

Since **1 June 2012**, the following categories of taxpayer are required to pay and file returns **online**:

- all taxpayers who are registered for VAT; and
- individuals who avail of the following reliefs and exemptions:
    - retirement annuity contract (RAC) payments
    - PRSA contributions
    - overseas pension plans: migrant member relief
    - retirement relief for sportspersons
    - relief for AVCs
    - artists exemption
    - woodlands exemption
    - patent income exemption
    - income on which trans-border relief is claimed
    - EII relief
    - seed capital scheme relief
    - film relief
    - significant buildings/gardens relief
    - interest relief: loan to acquire share in company or partnership.

From **1 January 2015** newly registering or re-registering income tax taxpayers are required to pay and file electronically.

10.7.3 Online Returns

The following is a list of specified returns and specified tax liabilities that must be paid and filed using ROS (mandatory e-filing):

Tax Head	Specified Return	Specified Tax Liability
Corporation Tax	Form CT1	Preliminary tax and balance due
Partnership	Form 1 (Firms)	–
Trusts	Form 1	Preliminary tax and balance due
Income Tax	Form 11	Preliminary tax and balance due
High Earner Restriction	Form RR1	–
Employer PAYE/PRSI/USC	Form P30 Form P35 Forms P45 and P46	All PAYE/PRSI/USC due
Value-Added Tax	Form VAT 3 Annual Return of Trading Details (RTD) VAT on e-services Quarterly Return	VAT due Quarterly VAT due on e-services
Capital Acquisitions Tax (Gifts and Inheritances)	Annual Return	Annual payment
Vehicle Registration Tax	Form VRT40 Vehicle Registration Form Vehicle Birth Certificate	Monthly VRT due (current payment method remains unchanged)
Betting Duty	Quarterly Return	Quarterly payment
Dividend Withholding Tax (DWT)	Monthly Return	Payment of DWT deducted from relevant distributions in previous month
Deposit Interest Retention Tax (DIRT)	Annual Return	Interim payment and balance due
Life Assurance Exit Tax (LAET)	Biannual Return	Biannual payment
Investment Undertaking Exit Tax (IUT)	Biannual Return	Biannual payment
EU Savings Directive	Annual Return	–
Environmental Levy	Quarterly/Annual Return	All payments due
Transit declaration and notifications	Monthly Return	–
3rd Party Payments Return (46G/46G company)	Annual Return	–
INTRASTAT	Monthly Return	–
CAP Export Trader Refunds	Monthly Return	–
Air Travel Tax	Annual Return	Monthly payment

The above list is not exhaustive as some other taxes, e.g. registered contractors tax (RCT) can **only** be filed and paid electronically.

An electronic version of **Form 12 (eForm 12)** is available through Revenue's *myAccount* facility. This allows a person whose main source of income is from a PAYE employment or pension to complete a return and claim tax credits, allowances and reliefs electronically. Filing of Form 12 or eForm 12 is not mandatory unless requested by Revenue.

The following services are also available through ROS:

- A facility for ROS business customers and agents to apply for and check if a tax clearance certificate is valid (eTax clearance).
- A facility whereby employers can download tax credit certificates (Form P2C). This data can be exported to the customer's payroll system. Payroll agents can also download the P2C on behalf of their clients using ROS. For this, the employer must be registered for ROS and have elected to receive P2Cs electronically.

10.7.4 Off-line Returns

All returns are also available to **upload** to ROS. These have to be created **off-line** via the **ROS Off-line Application**, which has to be downloaded from ROS. Some of the returns can be created off-line using compatible third-party software. Once created and saved, these files can be **uploaded** to ROS.

10.7.5 Registration

In order to use ROS, the taxpayer must first **register** with the service.

Self-employed individuals, business and practitioners

This is a three-step process, which is completed online on the ROS home page.

Step 1: Apply for a ROS Access Number (RAN)

The taxpayer enters one of their tax registration numbers. If an agent is applying for a RAN, they should enter their Tax Advisor Identification Number (TAIN). Revenue will post the ROS Access Number to the taxpayer at their registered address.

Step 2: Apply for a "Digital Certificate"

The taxpayer enters their RAN and registration number together with an e-mail address. Once processed by Revenue, a password will be generated and posted to the taxpayer who will use this password to retrieve their "digital certificate".

Step 3: Retrieve Digital Certificate

The taxpayer will enter their ROS system password (from Step 2 above) and install the digital certificate on their computer in a password-protected file. The taxpayer becomes a ROS customer once the digital certificate is installed.

Correspondence from ROS

A ROS customer will be provided with a secure ROS Inbox. Correspondence posted to this inbox includes reminders to file returns, copies of returns, statements of account and payment receipts. Customers are notified upon accessing ROS if there are any new items of correspondence that have not been viewed. Approaching the due date for filing relevant returns, ROS issues notification to file to customers and/or tax agents acting on behalf of customers. This notification is issued in the form of an e-mail to the designated e-mail address provided by the customer and/or tax agent.

Registering for myAccount

'myAccount' is the Revenue portal that allows non-ROS taxpayers access to a full range of services, including:

- PAYE Anytime;
- eForm 12;
- local property tax (LPT); and
- the home renovation incentive (HRI) scheme.

In order to avail of the full range of myAccount services, the taxpayer will need to register and have their personal details verified. Registering is a two-step process.

Step 1: Enter personal details on screen and submit these online for verification

Following successful Revenue verification of the personal details, the taxpayer will be issued with a Revenue PIN by post.

Step 2: Enter activation code

Once the activation code is entered correctly, the taxpayer will be fully registered and able to log-in to the myAccount service.

Registering with myAccount will provide the taxpayer with the means to access a range of services such as: PAYE, LPT, HRI and eForm12 services online. However, if the taxpayer is already registered for other business taxes with Revenue (e.g. VAT or self-employed income tax), they will not be able to access these with the myAccount registration. Instead they will require a ROS digital certificate. Note that the ROS digital certificate allows the taxpayer to access services for all taxes in ROS (including all those under myAccount) for which they are registered.

10.7.6 Payments to Revenue using ROS

ROS users may pay their taxes using **a Laser debit card** or **ROS debit instruction** (RDI). Users that are registered for income tax also have an option to make a payment using the **online banking** facility (with Allied Irish Bank or Bank of Ireland only).

Taxes may also be paid by credit card (Visa or Mastercard only), but this is subject to a transaction charge of 1.1% of the value of the payment.

An RDI is not a direct debit instruction. Unlike direct debit, RDI is not a fixed monthly payment amount. With RDI, the taxpayer determines the amount of the payment and when the payment is made. RDI does not confer on Revenue **any right** to take money from a taxpayer's bank account.

To set up an RDI using the ROS system, the taxpayer will be asked to enter the details of the bank account from which the payments will be debited, i.e. account name, sort code and account number. The taxpayer will be asked to indicate which tax type they wish to pay from this account. It will be possible to pay **more than one tax type** from the same account. The taxpayer will be asked to sign the RDI with their digital certificate and send the form using ROS. Once the taxpayer has submitted these details online, they will be permitted to file returns immediately for the relevant taxes.

An existing direct debit customer can continue to have deductions made under the standard direct debit scheme every month.

If a taxpayer files their tax return early, Revenue **will not** debit the payment amount from their bank account **before** the due date for payment provided the taxpayer specifies that date as their payment date.

10.7.7   Incentives for using ROS

ROS taxpayers who are obliged to meet "pay and file" obligations for self-assessed income tax on 31 October 2016, will be entitled to have the due date extended to 10 November 2016 when they **file their 2015 income tax return** (Form 11) **and submit their payment online** using ROS for both the income tax balance due for 2015 and preliminary tax 2016.

If the payment is specified online at any date before 10 November 2016, the taxpayer's bank account will not be debited until 10 November 2016, **provided** the taxpayer **specifies that date** as the payment date.

Note: the extended deadline for return and payment will only apply where the taxpayer files the Form 11 *and* makes the payment online, i.e. it is necessary to do both transactions online. Where only one of these actions is completed through ROS, the extension will not apply.

Taxpayers who pay or file by means **other** than ROS are required to submit both payments and returns on or before 31 October 2016.

Where a return and associated payment are not made electronically by the new extended deadlines, the extended time limits will be disregarded so that, for example, any interest imposed for late payment will run from the former due dates and not the extended dates.

Questions

Review Questions
(See Suggested Solutions to Review Questions at the end of this textbook.)

Question 10.1

The senior partner of your firm has come to you with a letter from one of the firm's clients, John Murphy, who was previously an employee and has set up his own business on 1 July 2016. Mr Murphy will prepare accounts annually to 31 December. Mr Murphy is very worried about the self-assessment system.

Requirement
You are required to write a brief letter to Mr Murphy describing the self-assessment system, paying attention to the procedure for each of the following:
(a)   income tax returns and surcharges;
(b)   preliminary tax; and
(c)   mandatory e-filing.

Question 10.2

John Bricks is a self-employed carpenter who employs two full-time employees. John has recently been employed as a subcontractor on the building of a new office block by OMG Ltd. John is registered for VAT and for PAYE/PRSI and is registered with ROS. For his accounting year ended 30 September 2016, John received the following Deduction Authorisations from OMG Ltd.

Date of Payment	Gross Payment €	Net Payment €	Deduction Amount €	RCT Rate €
28/02/2016	20,000	16,000	4,000	20%
05/05/2016	19,500	15,600	3,900	20%
31/07/2016	12,500	10,000	2,500	20%
12/10/2016	28,950	23,160	5,790	20%

John estimates that his tax liability for accounts year ended 30 September 2016 is €5,500 and he owes €3,500 for VAT and €2,950 for PAYE/PRSI as of that date. John wishes to make a claim for a repayment of RCT and has requested your assistance in processing his claim.

Requirement

Advise John of the position regarding income tax and relevant contracts tax paid.

Question 10.3

Paul Joist is a self-employed architect and his accounts for the year ended 31 December 2016 show a tax-adjusted profit of €40,000. Capital allowances due for 2016 total €6,000. He received €1,275 gross interest on his AIB ordinary deposit account. Paul did some consultancy work for the local town council and has a Form F45 for PSWT of €600, deducted from payments made to him in 2016.

His wife Sandra is employed by a marketing and promotions company, and her gross salary for 2016 was €52,000 (PAYE deducted €11,125). Paul's final tax liability for 2015 was €8,100 and for 2014 was €5,800. Paul and Sandra are jointly assessed.

Requirement

Calculate Paul and Sandra's preliminary tax payment for 2016 and calculate their final tax liability for 2016.

Value-Added Tax (VAT)

Learning Objectives

In this chapter you will learn:

- the general principles of VAT;
- the importance and distinction between the supply of goods and the supply of services;
- how to compute the value of the goods or services on which VAT is chargeable;
- the special rules for supplies cross-border within the European Community;
- the operation of the special scheme known as the Mini One Stop Shop (MOSS);
- the rules for the supplies of goods and services outside of the European Community; and
- the administration of VAT – books and records to be kept and tax payment dates.

The Chartered Accountants Regulatory Board *Code of Ethics* applies to all aspects of a Chartered Accountant's professional life, including dealing with VAT issues. As outlined at the beginning of this book, further information regarding the principles in the *Code of Ethics* is set out in **Appendix 3**.

11.1 General Principles of VAT

11.1.1 Introduction

VAT is a tax on consumer spending. It is chargeable on:

- the supply of goods and services within the State by a taxable person in the course of any business carried on by the taxpayer;
- goods imported into the State from outside the EU (VAT at the point of entry);
- intra-Community acquisition of goods by VAT-registered persons; and
- intra-Community acquisition of new means of transport, e.g. motor vehicles, boats, etc. by either a registered or unregistered person.

VAT-registered persons collect VAT on the **supply of goods and services** to their customers. Each such person in the chain of supply, from manufacturer through to retailer, **charges VAT on their sales** and is entitled to **deduct** from this amount the **VAT paid on their purchases** (input credit). The effect of offsetting purchases against sales is to impose the tax on the **value added** at each stage of production – hence Value-Added Tax. The final consumer, who is often not registered for VAT, absorbs VAT as part of the purchase price.

11.1.2   Legislation and Directives

The main legislation governing the Irish VAT system comprises the:

- Value-Added Tax Consolidation Act 2010 (VATCA 2010 as amended);
- Value-Added Tax Regulations (Statutory Instruments);
- EU Regulations and Directives; and
- annual Finance Acts.

European Union Directives and Case Law

VAT is the only tax where the operational rules are decided by the EU. The State is permitted to set the rates of VAT (within certain parameters) but the rules in relation to the operation of the system and the categorisation of goods and services for VAT charging purposes are set by the EU.

The EU issues VAT Directives to Member States and the Member State must give effect to the intention of EU Directives in their national legislation. As a result, a person may rely on the Directive if their national legislation differs in some way.

Member States may have derogations in certain areas, which would allow them to impose national VAT legislation that is not in line with the Directive. In the event of any inconsistency, **EU law takes precedence**. Any decision from the Court of Justice of the European Union is binding on the Member State.

11.1.3   Taxable Persons and Accountable Persons

A "**taxable person**" is one who independently (i.e. other than as an employee) carries on a business in the EU or elsewhere.

An "**accountable person**" is a taxable person who engages in the supply, within the State, of taxable goods or services. An accountable person may also be someone who is in receipt of certain services or goods **in the State** from a supplier established **outside of the State** and the recipient has to **self-account** for VAT as if they were the supplier, i.e. **reverse charge**.

The State and public bodies are regarded as accountable persons for certain activities.

Note: 'accountability' is a key concept in VAT, as persons who are accountable must register for the tax, submit tax returns and payments, keep records and comply with the provisions of VATCA 2010.

11.1.4   Charge to VAT

VAT is chargeable on the following:

- the supply of goods or services for consideration within the State by a taxable person;
- the importation of goods into the State from **outside** the EU (VAT is usually charged at the point of entry by Customs);
- the intra-Community acquisition by an accountable person of goods (other than new means of transport) when the acquisition is made within the State;
- the intra-Community acquisition of new means of transport by either an accountable or non-accountable person.

11.1.5   Registration

"Taxable persons" are obliged to register for VAT if any of the VAT thresholds outlined below are exceeded, or are likely to be exceeded, in a **12-month** period:

- €**37,500** for persons supplying **services**.
- €**75,000** for persons supplying **goods**, including persons supplying both goods and services, where **90% or more** of sales is derived from supplies of goods.
- €**37,500** for persons supplying goods liable at the 13.5% or 23% rates which they have manufactured or produced from **zero-rated** materials.
- €**35,000** for persons making mail order or distance sales into the State.
- €**41,000** for persons making intra-Community acquisitions.
- A **non-established** person supplying taxable goods or services in the State is **obliged** to register and account for VAT, **irrespective** of the level of turnover (i.e. **nil threshold**).
- Persons receiving services from abroad for business purposes in the State must register irrespective of the level of turnover.

For the purposes only of deciding if a person is obliged to register for VAT, the **actual turnover** may be **reduced** by an amount equivalent to the **VAT borne** on purchases of stock for resale. Therefore a person whose annual purchases of stock for resale are €61,000 (€49,593 plus €11,407 VAT at 23%) and whose actual turnover is €75,000 inclusive of VAT is not obliged to register. This is because the turnover, after deduction of the €11,407 VAT charged on the purchases of stock, is below the registration limit of €75,000.

No threshold applies in the case of taxable services received from abroad and in the case of cultural, artistic, sporting, scientific and educational, entertainment or similar services received from a person **not established** in the State. All such services are liable to VAT on a reverse-charge basis.

Suppliers of goods and services that are exempt from VAT and non-taxable entities, such as State bodies, charities, etc. are **obliged to register** for VAT where it is **likely** that they will acquire **more than** €41,000 of intra-Community acquisitions in any 12-month period.

A taxable person established in the State is not required to register for VAT if their turnover does not reach the appropriate threshold, although they may **opt to register** for VAT.

Registration Procedure

In the majority of cases, VAT registration must be completed online using the Revenue's eRegistration Service (see **Chapter 10**). Applicants who cannot access the eRegistration Services must complete either a **Form TR1** or **TR2**. Those who are already registered for ROS or myAccount are obliged to register online.

Registration is effective from the beginning of the next taxable period of two months after the date on which the completed application is received, or from such earlier date as may be agreed between Revenue and the applicant. In the case of a person not obliged to register but who is opting to do so, the effective date **will be not earlier** than the beginning of the taxable period during which the application is made.

A person who is setting up a business but who has **not yet commenced** supplying taxable goods or services, **may** register for VAT as soon as it is clear that they will become a taxable person. This will enable them to obtain credit for VAT on purchases made before trading actually commences.

11.1.6 Group Registration

When a **group of persons**, such as a number of interlinked companies, are registered for VAT, they may apply for group registration. This means that they are treated as a **single** taxable person. In these circumstances, only one member of the group will submit VAT returns for the taxable period and that return will include **all activities** of all members of the group.

All parties to the group are **jointly and severally liable** for all the VAT obligations of the other group members. The issue of tax invoices in respect of inter-group transactions is not required.

To qualify for group registration, Revenue must be satisfied that:

- no loss of VAT would be involved;
- the persons seeking the group registration are all established in the State;
- they are closely bound by financial, economic and organisational links; and
- it would be expedient, in the interest of efficient administration of VAT, to grant the group registration.

The granting of group registration is at the discretion of Revenue and there is no right of appeal.

11.1.7 Returns and Payment of VAT

An accountable person normally accounts for VAT on a two-monthly basis (January/February, March/April, etc.). The return is made on Form **VAT 3,** and this form, together with a payment for any VAT due, should be submitted electronically (through ROS) to the Collector-General on or before the **23rd day** of the month following the **end** of the taxable period (e.g. a return for the VAT period January/February 2016 is due by 23 March 2016). The VAT return shows the **gross amount** of the tax due by the person, the amount of **input tax deductible** and the **net VAT due** to Revenue or **VAT refund** due to the accountable person.

In addition, accountable persons are required to submit an **annual** "VAT Return of Trading Details" (Form RTD EUR), which gives details of purchases and sales for the year, broken down by VAT rates.

Payment of VAT
VAT is payable through ROS on or before the **23rd day** of the month following the **end** of the taxable period along with the Form VAT 3.

An accountable person may pay VAT by **direct debit** in monthly instalments. If a business is seasonal, an accountable person can vary the amounts paid each month to reflect cash flow. Where a person pays a VAT liability by direct debit, the person is only required to make an **annual VAT 3** return, together with the annual VAT Return of Trading Details. At the end of the year, if a shortfall arises, the balance must be included when submitting the annual return of trading (RTD EUR). Where insufficient amounts are paid by direct debit and, as a result, the **balance of tax payable** with the annual return is **more than 20% of the annual liability for VAT**, then an accountable person will be liable to an **interest charge** backdated to the mid-point of the year.

Reduced Frequency for Filing VAT Returns
Eligible businesses will be allowed to reduce their number of VAT filings as follows:

- Businesses making total annual VAT payments of less than **€3,000** are eligible to file VAT returns and make payments on a **six-month** basis.
- Businesses making total annual VAT payments of **between €3,000 and €14,400** are eligible to file VAT returns and make payments on a **four-month** basis.

VAT Returns on an Annual Basis
There is a provision whereby VAT can be returned and paid on an annual basis. Authorisation to do so is at the discretion of the Collector-General, and this authorisation may be terminated at any time. The VAT returns and payment must be submitted electronically to the Collector-General between the 10th and 23rd days of the month following the end of the year.

Interest on Late Payments of VAT
If VAT is not paid within the proper period, interest is chargeable (as a fiduciary tax) for each day at the rate of 0.0274% per day. This interest also applies where a refund of VAT has been made on the basis of an incorrect return, and where all or part of the tax refunded was not properly refundable. Where a person

fails to make returns, Revenue is entitled to make estimates of tax payable and to recover the amount so estimated, subject to the usual appeal procedures.

11.1.8 VAT Rates

Standard Rate of VAT – 23%

This applies to all goods and services that are not exempt or liable at the zero or reduced rates.

Reduced Rate of VAT – 13.5%

Goods and services which attract VAT at 13.5% include bakery products (excluding bread), certain fuels, building services, insemination services for all animals, newspapers, magazines and periodicals, repair, cleaning and maintenance services generally, holiday accommodation, certain photographic supplies, restaurant services, and provision of commercial sporting facilities, etc.

Second Reduced Rate of VAT – 9%

A temporary reduced rate of **VAT at 9%** was introduced in 2011 and extended indefinitely by Finance (No.2) Act 2013. This rate applies to the following services:

- Catering and restaurant supplies, including vending machines and hot take-away food (excluding alcohol and soft drinks sold as part of the meal).
- Hotel lettings, including guesthouses, caravan parks, camping sites etc.
- Cinemas, theatres, certain musical performances, museums, art gallery exhibitions, fairgrounds or amusement park services.
- Facilities for taking part in sporting activities, including subscriptions charged by non-member-owned golf clubs (excluding green fees).
- Printed matter, e.g. newspapers, brochures, leaflets, programmes, maps, catalogues, printed music (excluding books).
- Hairdressing services.
- The supply of live horses (other than for foodstuffs), the hire of horses and the supply of greyhounds.

Reduced Rate of VAT – 4.8%

This applies to livestock in general, and to horses intended for use in foodstuffs or agricultural production.

Farmer Flat Rate Addition – 5.2%

This applies to the sale of agricultural produce and services by non-registered farmers to VAT-registered persons, effective from 1 January 2015.

Zero-rated Goods and Services

These include exports, certain food and drink, oral medicine, certain books, nursing home services, etc.

Exempted Goods and Services

These include financial, medical and educational activities; and green fees and membership fees charged by member-owned golf clubs.

A full list of applicable VAT rates is available at www.revenue.ie – *VAT Rate Subject Index.*

Difference between Exempt and Zero-rated

These terms appear to have the same meaning, but only to the extent that both exempt and zero-rated supplies do not attract what is referred to as a positive rate of VAT. They are different, however, to the extent that a VAT-registered trader making zero-rated supplies (e.g. a book shop or food store) is entitled to a refund of VAT on the taxable business purchases (e.g. shop fittings, wrapping materials, cash registers, etc.), while normally a VAT-exempt trader is **not entitled** to any refund of VAT on purchases in respect of the business. It is a crucial difference.

11.2 Supply of Goods/Services and Place of Supply

VAT becomes due, or a liability for VAT arises, at the time when a supply of goods or services takes place, or on receipt of payment, if an earlier date.

11.2.1 Supply of Goods

A taxable supply of goods means the **normal transfer of ownership** of goods (including developed property) by one person to another and includes the supply of goods liable to VAT at the zero rate. This includes:

- The transfer of ownership of goods by agreement.
- The sale of movable goods on a commission basis by an auctioneer or agent acting in their own name but on the instructions of another person.
- The handing over of goods under a hire-purchase contract.
- The handing over by a person to another person of immovable goods (property) which have been developed.
- The seizure of goods by a sheriff or other person acting under statutory authority.
- The application or appropriation **(self-supply)** by the taxable person of materials or goods to some private or exempt use, e.g. if a builder uses building materials to build or repair their private house, this is a self-supply.
- The provision of electricity, gas and any form of power, heat, refrigeration or ventilation.
- With some exceptions, the transfer of goods from a business in the State by a taxable person to the territory of another Member State for the purposes of the business.
- The transfer of ownership of immovable goods by way of very long leases is a supply of goods.
- Gifts of taxable goods made in the course or furtherance of business are liable to VAT where the cost to the donor, excluding VAT, is €20 or **more**.
- Where vouchers and tokens having a face value are supplied at a discount to an intermediary with a view to their ultimate re-sale to private consumers, such tokens or vouchers become liable to VAT at the standard rate of 23% at the time the consideration is received. VAT is also chargeable on the re-sale of the vouchers by the intermediary to the private customer. However, this rule only applies where the intermediary who purchases the voucher for resale is VAT registered in Ireland, i.e. they must be an accountable person.
- Gift vouchers are subject to VAT at the rate applicable to goods or services supplied in exchange for the voucher at the time the voucher is redeemed by the customer. The retailer must generally only account for VAT on the consideration received for the sale of vouchers at the time the voucher is redeemed by the customer.

A taxable supply is **not affected** where:

- Gifts of taxable goods are made in the course or furtherance of business where the cost to the donor, excluding VAT, is €20 or **less**.
- Special offers, such as two for the price of one and promotional items given away free with the sale of another item, are not treated as gifts. Rather, they are considered to be simply a reduction in price for the relevant items and regular VAT rules therefore apply to such supplies.
- Advertising goods and industrial samples are given free to customers in reasonable quantities, in a form **not ordinarily available for sale** to the public, even where the €20 limit is exceeded.

- Replacement goods are supplied free of charge in accordance with **warranties** or **guarantees** on the original goods.
- Goods change ownership as **security** for a loan or debt.
- A business is transferred from one taxable person to another.

11.2.2 Supply of Services

For VAT purposes a "service" is any commercial activity **other than** a supply of goods. Typical services include:

- The services of caterers, mechanics, plumbers, accountants, solicitors, consultants, etc.
- The hiring or leasing of goods.
- The supply of digitised goods delivered online as well as the physical supply of customised software.
- **Refraining** from doing something and the granting or surrendering of a right.
- Contract work, i.e. the handing over by a contractor, to a customer, of movable goods made or assembled by the contractor from goods entrusted to them by the customer.
- A self-supply of a catering or canteen service (e.g. a vending machine).

Insurance agents, banking agents and certain related agents are **exempt** from VAT.

Services Taxable as Supplies of Goods (the "Two-thirds" Rule)

A transaction which may **appear** to be a **supply of a service** is nevertheless taxable as a **supply of goods** if the value of the goods (i.e. cost excluding VAT) used in carrying out the work **exceeds two-thirds** of the total charge, exclusive of VAT. For example, where the VAT-exclusive cost of materials used by a plumber in the repair of a washing machine is €120, and the total charge for the repair work is €150, the 23% rate applicable to the materials applies, rather than the 13.5% rate which normally applies to repair services. The repair and maintenance of motor vehicles and agricultural machinery is **not subject** to the "two-thirds" rule.

The two-thirds rule does not apply where principal contractors operate the **reverse charge** rule with sub-contractors (see **Section 11.8**) or to supplies of construction services between **connected persons** to whom the reverse charge rule for VAT applies.

11.2.3 Place of Supply

Goods and services are liable to VAT **in the place where they are supplied** or deemed to be supplied. If the place of supply is outside or is deemed to be outside the State, then Irish VAT **does not** arise.

Place of Supply of Goods

The place of supply of goods is deemed to be as follows:

- Where goods are not dispatched or transported, the place of supply is deemed to be the place where the goods are **at the time** of their supply.
- Where goods are installed or assembled by or on behalf of the supplier, the place of supply is the place where the goods **are installed or assembled**. For example, a French-based company supplies and installs a machine in an Irish company's factory in the State. The place of supply is Ireland and the recipient Irish company self-accounts for the VAT on the supply and can claim a simultaneous input credit if the goods are used for the taxable business.
- Where goods are supplied on board **sea vessels, aircraft and trains** (during intra-Community transport), the place of supply is the place where the **transport begins** (e.g. a person buys goods on

board the Dublin–Holyhead ferry, which leaves from Dublin, the place of supply is the State and Irish VAT arises).

▨ In all other cases, the **location** of the goods at the time of supply determines the place of supply.

Distance Sales Rules

Distance sales into Ireland covers mail order and other distance sales to Irish **non-registered** customers, where the supplier is responsible for delivering the goods. Where the value of distance sales into the State **exceeds €35,000** in a calendar year, the **supplier** must **register** for VAT in the State.

Similar rules apply to Irish mail order businesses and other distance sellers supplying to **non-registered** individuals in other Member States. The Irish business must register in **each Member State** in which the sales threshold is **exceeded**. The threshold is €100,000 for Germany, France, Luxembourg, the Netherlands, Austria and the United Kingdom and €35,000 for the other Member States.

Suppliers may opt to register in any State even if the annual thresholds are not exceeded. If the seller's level of trade to private individuals in each individual Member state is below the relevant distance sales thresholds and the seller does not opt to register in those States, the place of supply is Ireland and the seller has to account for Irish VAT on the sale.

Intra-Community Acquisition of Goods

The basic rule is that the place where an intra-Community acquisition occurs is the Member State where the dispatch or transportation **ends** (see **Section 11.5**).

Place of Supply of Services

There are two general "place of supply" rules, depending on whether the recipient is a **business** or a **consumer**:

▨ For supplies of "**business to business** (B2B)" services, the place of supply is the place where the **recipient is established** (reverse charge).

▨ For supplies of "**business to consumer** (B2C)" services, the place of supply is where the **supplier is established**.

Unless covered by an exception, the position is as follows:

▨ Service suppliers in the State must **not charge** VAT when supplying services to a **business** customer established **outside** Ireland.

▨ Service suppliers in the State must **charge** VAT to **non-business** customers **outside** Ireland. However, many services supplied from Ireland to non-business customers **outside** the EU will not be subject to Irish VAT.

▨ Businesses that **receive** services from a supplier **outside** Ireland will not be charged VAT by the supplier of those services, but the recipient will be required to **account** for Irish VAT unless the services concerned are exempt in Ireland (and the business has notified its supplier that such services are exempt from Irish VAT).

For services received from abroad by a **Department of State, a local authority or a body established by statute in the State**, such entities will **not be liable** for Irish VAT in respect of the receipt of the foreign services, such as consultancy services, legal services, etc., **except** where they act as **taxable persons**. The services should be taxed in the country from where they are supplied.

SUMMARY OF PLACE OF SUPPLY RULES FOR SERVICES (UNLESS SUBJECT TO EXCEPTIONS OR EFFECTIVE USE AND ENJOYMENT PROVISIONS)

Country of establishment of supplier	Country in which customer established	Place of supply	Person liable to account for Irish VAT
B2B			
Ireland	Other EU State	Other EU State	No Irish VAT
Ireland	Outside EU	Outside EU	No Irish VAT
Other EU State	Ireland	Ireland	Customer
Outside EU	Ireland	Ireland	Customer
B2C			
Ireland	Other EU State	Ireland	Supplier
Ireland	Outside EU	Depends on service	Supplier (if VAT occurs)
Other EU State	Ireland	Other EU State	No Irish VAT
Outside EU	Ireland	Depends on service	Supplier (if taxable in the State)

It should be noted that financial services supplied by a supplier in the State to a private individual from outside the EU who avails of them **here** are deemed to be supplied in the State.

Exceptions to the General Rules

There are a number of exceptions to the general rules that more closely **link** the place of supply to **where** the service is performed. Unless covered by a reverse charge arrangement, the supplier will be **required** to register and account for VAT in the **Member State of supply**.

The following table summarises the exceptions and sets out the current place of supply rule that applies from 1 January 2010 onwards.

EXCEPTIONS TO VAT PLACE OF SUPPLY OF SERVICES RULES

Supply	Place of Supply
Supply of services connected with immovable goods (property) (B2B and B2C)	Place of supply is where the goods are located. (When the service provider is outside Ireland and the work is carried out in Ireland, VAT is accounted for by the Irish business recipient on a reverse charge basis.)
Passenger transport services (B2B and B2C)	Place of supply is where the passenger transport takes place.
Intra-Community transport of goods B2C	Place of supply is the place of departure.
Intra-Community transport of goods B2B	Place of supply is the place where the customer is established.
Ancillary transport services, valuations/ work on movable property	Place of supply is where the services are physically carried out. (Reverse charge for B2B.)
Restaurant and catering services	Place of supply is where the services are physically carried out.

Restaurant and catering services for consumption on board ships, planes and trains	Place of supply is point of departure.
Hiring out of means of transport (B2B and B2C) (short-term)	For short-term (≤ 30 days) hiring-out of means of transport, the place of supply is where the transport is put at the disposal of the customer.
Hiring out of means of transport (B2B and B2C) (long-term)	**From 1 January 2013** the place of supply of the long-term (>90 days) hiring of a means of transport (excluding a pleasure boat) to a non-taxable customer is where that customer is established, has his permanent address or usually resides.

Telecommunications, Broadcasting and e-Services (including eGaming)

The place of supply is where the **customer resides**. This means that EU and non-EU businesses will have to register and account for VAT in **every** Member State in which they supply such services to consumers. If the consumer resides or is established outside the EU, the service falls outside the scope of EU VAT. However, this is subject to the use and enjoyment provisions below.

To facilitate the obligations of the suppliers, an optional special scheme known as **Mini One Stop Shop (MOSS)** is in operation that allows suppliers to submit returns and pay the relevant VAT due to the individual Members States through a web portal of **one** Member State. This simplifies the supplier's obligations by removing the requirement to register and submit returns in several Member States. (See **Section 11.9**.)

Cultural, Artistic, Sporting, Scientific, Educational, Entertainment or Similar Events and Services – Changes Effective from 1 January 2011

A clear distinction is made between the **provision** of a cultural, artistic, sporting, scientific, educational, entertainment or similar **service** and the **admission** to a cultural, artistic, etc. **event**.

Provision of a Cultural, Artistic, etc. Service

▨ Where the supply of the services is to a business customer (B2B), the place of supply is where the business customer is established. The customer must self-account for the VAT on the reverse-charge basis.

▨ Where the supply of the service is to a non-business customer (B2C), the place of supply is where the supplier is established, and the supplier charges VAT to the customer at the appropriate rate.

Admission to a Cultural, Artistic, etc. Event

For both business (B2B) and non-business (B2C) customers, the place of supply of the right of **admission** to cultural, artistic, sporting, scientific, educational, entertainment, or similar events, and services ancillary to the admission, is where the **event actually takes place**. Charges for admission to such an event in Ireland will be liable to Irish VAT, **regardless** of whether the person paying the admission is a taxable person or a non-taxable person. Thus, a taxable person from outside the State, attending an event in Ireland, will pay Irish VAT on the admission charge and will not, if they are established in the EU, account for the VAT due on a reverse charge basis in their own Member State.

Use and Enjoyment Provisions

The purpose of the use and enjoyment rules is to prevent double taxation, non-taxation or distortions of competition and to better reflect the place where the service is actually received (which, in turn, is the place of taxation).

The section covers two types of situation:

- The place of supply of services provided in the State but effectively **used and enjoyed outside** the EU is deemed to be outside the EU.
- The place of supply of services provided by persons **established outside** the EU but effectively used and enjoyed **in the State** is deemed to be the State.

There are a number of areas specifically covered in **section 35 VATCA 2010**:

- The hiring out of movable goods – if the actual place of supply is outside the EU but the goods are used and enjoyed in the State, the place of supply is deemed to be the State.
- The hiring out of means of transport – if the actual place of supply is in the State but the goods are used and enjoyed outside the EU, the place of supply is deemed to be outside the EU.
- B2C supplies of telecommunications, radio/television broadcasting or phone card – if the actual place of supply is outside the EU but the services are used and enjoyed in the State, the place of supply is deemed to be the State.
- B2C supplies of financial and insurance services, including reinsurance and financial fund management (but excluding the provision of safe deposit facilities) – if the actual place of supply is outside the EU but the services are used and enjoyed in the State, the place of supply is deemed to be the State.
- Money transfer services supplied to persons in the State by an intermediary on behalf of a principal established outside the EU – if the actual place of supply is outside the EU but the services are used and enjoyed in the State, the place of supply is deemed to be the State.

11.3   Amount on which VAT is Chargeable

11.3.1   General

In the case of the supply of goods or services and the intra-Community acquisition of goods, the amount on which VAT is chargeable is normally the **total sum** paid or payable to the person supplying the goods or services, including all taxes, commissions, costs and charges whatsoever, but **not including** the VAT chargeable in respect of the transaction. However, **section 38 VATCA 2010** provides an anti-avoidance measure, which states that **Revenue** may determine that the **value** on which tax is charged in relation to certain transactions **between connected persons** is the **open market value**.

11.3.2   Other

1. **Imports**
   VAT on imports is charged on the cost, **plus** transport cost, **plus** duty payable of the goods (customs value).
2. **Goods/Services Supplied otherwise than for Money**
   Where a customer agrees to pay the supplier in kind, the amount on which VAT is chargeable is the **open market** or arm's length value of the goods or services supplied.
   In the UK case of *Boots Company plc v. ECJ*, it was decided that money-off vouchers which were given to customers by Boots to enable them to buy other products at a discount did not form part of the consideration for the purchase.
3. **Credit Card Transactions**
   The taxable amount is the total amount actually charged to the customer by the trader. Any amount withheld by the credit card companies from their settlement with the trader forms part of the taxable amount.

4. **Special Schemes**

Special schemes operate in relation to the sale by dealers and auctioneers of second-hand movable goods, works of art, collector's items and antiques. The principal feature of the schemes is that dealers and auctioneers effectively pay VAT only on their margin in certain circumstances.

A **special scheme** also operates in relation to the VAT treatment of second-hand motor vehicles whereby the dealer accounts for VAT under the **margin scheme, i.e. the dealer only accounts for the VAT on the margin or profit**.

5. **New Motor Vehicles**

The amount on which VAT is chargeable on a new motor vehicle is normally the price of the vehicle **before** vehicle registration tax (VRT) is applied.

6. **Intra-Community Services**

The amount on which VAT is chargeable in relation to intra-Community services received from abroad will normally be the **amount payable** in respect of those services.

7. **Packaging and Containers**

When goods are supplied packed for sale and **no separate charge** is made for the packaging in which the goods are contained, the rate of VAT chargeable is that **applying to the goods.** If containers are charged for **separately** from the goods, the transaction is regarded as consisting of separate sales of goods and of packages and **each** such **separate sale** is chargeable at the appropriate rate.

Where containers are returnable and a separate charge in the nature of a deposit is included on an invoice, the containers are regarded as being the property of the supplier and the **deposit** is **not** subject to VAT. VAT **is** payable on the value of containers which are **not returned** to the supplier. This VAT may be accounted for at the time when the containers' account is being balanced and a charge is being raised by the supplier against the customer for the value of containers not returned.

8. **Postage and Insurance**

Where a separate charge is made for postage and insurance and paid over in its **entirety** to the carrier or to the insurer on behalf of customers, suppliers may treat such charges as not being subject to VAT. If, for example, a trader charges an extra €1 for posting an order and such amount of postage is actually paid over, the €1 may be treated as exempt. Similarly, if a car hire company charges €50 for motor insurance, and that amount is actually paid over in full to insurers in the name of the lessee, the €50 may be treated as exempt. However, if a charge is made for posting and/or insurance, and a **lesser amount** is paid over by the supplier to the carrier or the insurer, the charge made to the customer is regarded as part of the total price of the goods/service supplied, and is subject to the VAT rate applicable to the goods/service in question.

9. **Mixed Transactions (Package Rule)**

A "package" comprises two or more elements that attract different VAT rates.

Composite Supply   Where there is a **principal element** and an **ancillary supply** the VAT rate is that attaching to the principal element. The main feature of an ancillary supply is that it has no standalone value or use other than in the context of the principal component. For example, the provision of an instruction booklet (VAT 0%) with an MP3 player (VAT 23%) is an ancillary supply to the principal supply of the MP3 player.

Multiple Supply   Where a number of individual supplies are **grouped together** for a single **overall** consideration, the consideration should be apportioned between the various individual supplies and taxed at the appropriate VAT rate. The main feature of an individual supply is that it is physically and economically distinct from the other elements of the multiple supply. For example, a meal sold at an all-inclusive price that includes food and wine – the food is liable to VAT at 9% and the wine at 23%.

10. Bad Debts

Relief for VAT on bad debts is allowed, subject to Revenue's agreement, where bad debts have been written off after VAT has been accounted for on the supply.

11.3.3 Deductible VAT

In computing the amount of VAT payable in respect of a taxable period, a person may **deduct** the VAT charged on most goods and services that are used for the purposes of their **taxable business**. To be entitled to the deduction, the trader must have a proper VAT invoice or relevant customs receipt as appropriate.

While a deduction of VAT is allowable only on purchases which are for the purposes of a taxable business, a situation may arise where a **portion** of a person's purchases may be for the purposes of the taxable business and the remaining portion for the person's **private use** (e.g. electricity, telephone charges, heating expenses, etc. where the business is carried on from the trader's private residence). It may also arise that inputs may be used for **both taxable and non-taxable** activities. In such cases, only the amount of VAT **that is appropriate to the taxable business** is deductible. Similarly where a person engages in both taxable and exempt activities (dual-use inputs), it will be necessary to **apportion the credit** in respect of these dual-use inputs.

In general, VAT is deductible against a taxable person's liability in any of the following situations:

- VAT charged to a taxable person by other taxable persons on supplies of goods (including fixed assets) and services.
- VAT paid by the taxable person on goods imported.
- VAT payable on self-supplies of goods and services provided that the self-supplies are for business purposes.
- VAT payable on purchases from flat rate farmers.
- VAT on intra-Community acquisitions.
- VAT payable under **reverse charge rules**, provided the goods or services are used for the purposes of their taxable business (e.g. goods that are installed or assembled in the State by a foreign supplier, etc.).
- Reduction in VAT input credit for unpaid amounts – where an accountable person has claimed a VAT input credit in relation to a supply to them but the consideration for such a supply remains partially or fully outstanding six months after the period the initial input credit was claimed, the accountable person must reduce the amount of VAT deductible by the amount of VAT relating to the unpaid consideration.

  Where the accountable person makes a subsequent payment or part payment, they may claim a VAT input credit for the consideration paid (section 62A VATCA 2010).
- **Qualifying Vehicles** – section 62 VATCA 2010 allows any VAT-registered person (other than motor dealers, car-hire companies, driving schools, etc.) to recover **20%** of the VAT charged on the purchase or hire of vehicles **coming within VRT Category A**, subject to the following conditions:

  - The vehicle must have been registered on or after **1 January 2009**.
  - A maximum of **20% of the VAT** incurred on the cost or on the monthly hire/lease charge can be reclaimed.
  - VAT can only be reclaimed for vehicles that have a level of CO_2 emissions of less than 156g/km (i.e. CO_2 emission bands A, B and C).
  - At least **60%** of the vehicle's use must be for business purposes.
  - If the business is exempt from VAT (e.g. taxi, limousine and other passenger transport), then no VAT can be reclaimed. Partly exempt businesses can reclaim some, but not all, of the 20%.
  - If VAT is reclaimed on a vehicle purchased under this provision, some or all of the VAT must be repaid to Revenue if the vehicle is disposed of within **two years**.

- There is no need to charge VAT on the disposal of the vehicle, even though VAT was reclaimed under this provision.
- If the vehicle is sold or traded-in to a motor dealer, the margin scheme for second-hand vehicles will apply.

11.3.4 Non-deductible VAT

No deduction is allowed in respect of VAT paid on expenditure on any of the following:

- The provision of food, drink, accommodation or other personal services supplied to the taxable person, his agent, or his employees, **except** to the extent that the provision of such services represents a taxable supply by the taxable person. For example, where a hotel incurs expense in providing accommodation for its own employees, this would be a taxable supply and the VAT arising would be a deductible input. A taxable person can claim VAT on "**qualifying accommodation**" in connection with the **attendance** at a "**qualifying conference**" by the taxable person or their representative, **except** where it was supplied under the Travel Agent Margin Scheme (TAMS). Where the accommodation is supplied and invoiced **directly** to the taxable person, a deduction for the VAT applies.
- Entertainment expenses incurred by the taxable person, their agent or their employees.
- The acquisition, hiring or leasing of motor vehicles that are not "qualifying vehicles" (as above), **other** than as stock-in-trade or for the purpose of a business which consists, in whole or in part, of the hiring of motor vehicles, or for use in a driving school business for giving driving instruction.
- The purchase of petrol **otherwise** than as stock-in-trade.
- Expenditure incurred on food, drink, accommodation or other entertainment service, as part of an advertising service, is not deductible in the hands of the person providing the advertising service.
- VAT in respect of goods or services used by the taxable person for the purposes of an exempt activity or for the purposes of an activity not related to their business.

11.4 Cash Receipts Basis

An accountable person normally become liable for VAT at the time of the **issue** of **sales invoices** to their customers **regardless** of whether they have received payment for the supplies made. Accordingly, an accountable person must include in their January/February 2016 VAT return VAT on **all sales invoices issued** during January and February 2016. This is known as the **invoice basis of accounting** for VAT. Under the cash receipts basis of accounting, persons **do not** become liable for VAT until they have actually **received payment** for the goods or services supplied.

The cash receipts basis **does not apply** to transactions between **connected** persons. VAT on such transactions must be accounted for on the normal invoice basis. VAT on **property transactions** must always be accounted for on an invoice basis.

An accountable person who opts for the cash receipts basis of accounting is liable for VAT at the **rate ruling at the time the supply is made** rather than the rate ruling at the time payment is received.

For example, Joe, operating under the cash receipts basis, made a supply of goods in December 2011 when the higher rate of VAT was 21%. He received payment of €1,000 for those goods in January 2012 when the higher rate had changed to 23%. Joe accounts for the VAT on the supply at 21% (i.e. €1,000 × 21/121 = €173.55) in his January/February 2012 VAT return.

In addition, where such a person receives a payment from which PSWT or RCT has been deducted, the person is deemed to have received the **gross amount due** and is liable to pay the **full amount** of the VAT due. For example, if an architect receives a payment of €800, being €1,000 less PSWT at 20%, he is deemed to have received €1,000 and must account for VAT on this amount.

Accountable persons accounting for VAT on the basis of moneys received must issue to a VAT-registered customer, or other person entitled to a VAT invoice, a credit note showing VAT if there is a discount or price reduction allowed subsequent to the issue of an invoice. The effect of the credit note is to reduce any VAT deduction available to the customer on the basis of the original invoice. The accountable person accounts for VAT on the money received.

It should be noted that the cash receipts basis of accounting **only applies to sales and supplies** and VAT on purchases is still claimed on an invoice basis.

Entitlement to Cash Receipts Basis

The cash receipts basis of accounting for VAT may be used by persons engaged in the supply of taxable goods or services if:

- at least **90%** of the supplies are to **unregistered** persons; **or**
- the trader's turnover is not likely to **exceed €2 million** per annum.

Formal Election

Any accountable person who finds that they are eligible to use this basis of accounting and wishes to use it should apply to the local Revenue district for authority to do so. Such persons may not change from the invoice basis of accounting to the cash receipts basis, or vice versa, without such authority.

Persons who are applying for VAT registration for the first time, and find that they are eligible for the cash receipts basis, should indicate in the appropriate box on the application form (TR1 or TR2) whether or not they wish to use it.

Change of Basis of Accounting

A person who has been accounting for VAT on the cash receipts basis and now wishes to revert to the invoice basis (or who ceases to be a taxable person) will have to make an adjustment. The adjustment must be made by reference to the **VAT due on outstanding debtors**.

11.5 Intra-Community Acquisition and Supply of Goods and Services

11.5.1 Introduction

Following the introduction of the **Single Market** on 1 January 1993, the way in which VAT was charged on goods moving between EU Member States was changed.

The concept of import and export was **abolished** for such trade and replaced by a system of **intra-Community supply and acquisition** of goods. While the VAT treatment of most services supplied to traders in other Member States did not change, there were important changes relating to intra-Community goods transport and related services.

The terms "intra-Community acquisition" and "intra-Community supply" relate to goods supplied by a business in one EU Member State to a business in another EU Member State where the goods have been dispatched or transported from the territory of one Member State to another as a result of such supply. The terms also apply to new means of transport supplied by any person in one Member State to any person in another Member State and transferred to that other Member State.

11.5.2 VAT on Purchases from Other EU Countries – Intra-Community Acquisitions

VAT is **no longer** payable at the **point of entry** on goods imported from another Member State. The treatment for **VAT** on **purchases** varies, depending on the taxable status of the purchaser.

1. **Accountable Persons**

   When an Irish accountable person purchases goods from a supplier in a Member State and these are dispatched to the State, they must provide the supplier with their Irish VAT number. Upon receipt and verification of this number, the supplier will zero-rate the goods in question. The accountable person then:
   - becomes liable for VAT on the acquisition of the goods;
   - declares a liability for the VAT in the VAT return;
   - claims a **simultaneous input credit**, thus **cancelling** the liability (assuming they are entitled to full deductibility); and
   - accounts for VAT on any subsequent supply of the goods in the normal manner.

   Example 11.1

   A shipment of wood is sold by a VAT-registered trader in France to a VAT-registered business in Ireland for €10,000, and delivered from France to Ireland by the supplier. The supply is charged at the zero rate out of France. The Irish company would then self-account for Irish VAT on the acquisition of the wood as follows:

	€
VAT on sales €10,000 @ 23%	2,300
VAT on purchases @ 23%	(2,300)

   There is no net effect on the VAT liability since the VAT on the wood is recoverable by the trader.

   Contrast this with a situation where the same trader buys a motor car in France for €10,000 and it is delivered from France to Ireland by the supplier. The supply is charged at the zero rate out of France.

   The Irish company would then self-account for Irish VAT on the acquisition of the car as follows:

	€
VAT on sales €10,000 @ 23%	2,300
VAT on purchases	(0)
(assuming the car is not a "qualifying vehicle")	

   In this scenario, the trader is not allowed to claim VAT on motor cars and there is a VAT liability on the transaction as a result.

   ---

2. **Unregistered Persons**

   Persons who are not registered for VAT in the State must pay VAT on their intra-Community purchases in the Member State of **purchase** at the VAT rate applicable there. Where the threshold of **€41,000** in respect of intra-Community acquisitions **is exceeded**, the person must register for VAT in Ireland and account for the VAT in the manner described at (1.) above.

3. **Non-taxable Entities/Exempted Activities**

   In the case of non-taxable entities, such as Government departments, and exempted activities, such as insurance companies or banks, VAT is payable in the Member State of purchase at the VAT rate applicable there. Again, if the threshold of **€41,000** in respect of intra-Community acquisitions **is exceeded**, the entity must register for VAT in Ireland and account for the VAT in the manner described at 1. above. However, as their activities are non-taxable/exempt, these entities **cannot claim input credits** and no Irish VAT is chargeable on a subsequent sale.

4. **Purchases by Private Individuals**

   The private individual pays the VAT charged by the supplier in the Member State and no additional Irish VAT liability will arise. This does not apply to **new** means of transport, e.g. boats, planes, motor cars. These items are liable to VAT in the Member State of the **purchaser**.

   Where a private individual purchases goods through **mail order,** he must pay the VAT applicable in the **place of purchase** (e.g. goods purchased by mail order in Germany will be subject to German VAT). However, such acquisitions may be subject to the distance sales rules.

11.5.3 VAT on Sales to Other EU Countries – Intra-Community Supplies

The treatment for **VAT on supplies** varies depending on the **taxable status** of the customer:

1. **VAT-registered Customers**

   Where a taxable person in Ireland **sells or supplies** goods to a VAT-registered person within the EU, the transaction will be **zero-rated** in Ireland and will be liable to foreign VAT in the Member State of the purchaser.

   A VAT-registered person in the State may zero-rate the supply of goods to a customer in another EU Member State if:

   - the customer is registered for VAT in the other EU Member State;
   - the customer's VAT registration number (including country prefix) is obtained and retained in the supplier's records;
   - this number, together with the supplier's VAT registration number, is quoted on the sales invoice; and
   - the goods are dispatched or transported to that, or any other, EU Member State.

Where any of the above four conditions are not satisfied, the Irish supplier should charge Irish VAT at the appropriate Irish VAT rate (i.e. as if the sale had taken place between two Irish traders). If the conditions for zero-rating are subsequently established, the customer is entitled to recover the VAT paid from the supplier. The supplier can then make an adjustment in his/her VAT return for the period.

2. **Unregistered Customers**

   Where the customer is unregistered, the Irish supplier should charge Irish VAT. If their sales in the customer's home country are above the VAT registration threshold in that country, they will be obliged to register for VAT in that country and charge local VAT to their customers there.

11.5.4 VIES and INTRASTAT

VIES (VAT Information Exchange System)

When an accountable person makes **zero-rated supplies** of goods or services to a VAT-registered person in another EU Member State, summary details of those **sales** must be returned to Revenue on a quarterly or monthly basis. There is no threshold. This return, known as the VIES return, is to enable the authorities in each EU Member State to ensure that intra-Community transactions are properly recorded and accounted for. The VIES return is made to the VAT Authorities in the **Member State of the exporter** and contains the following:

- the VAT number of each foreign Member State customer (this number can be verified with the Irish Revenue); and
- the total € value of sales to each customer in the quarterly (or monthly) period.

The return must be submitted by the 23rd day of the month following the end of the period covered by the return.

Monthly VIES statements are **mandatory** where intra-Community supplies **exceed €50,000 quarterly** for goods. Irish VAT-registered suppliers whose intra-Community supplies do not exceed the threshold may report **quarterly**. Suppliers of services may also opt to submit quarterly statements.

Note: where a trader has no exports to another Member State in a particular period, a "NIL" statement must be submitted for that period.

INTRASTAT VAT Return

This return system is designed to ensure that all **statistical data** relating to purchases and sales of goods (not services) between Member States continues to be available to each Member State and the EU Commission. Depending on the level of intra-Community trade carried out by each taxable person, there are two methods of making the necessary returns:

1. Where a person's **acquisitions** from other EU Member States **do not exceed €500,000** (2015: €191,000) **annually** or the value of goods **supplied** to other EU Member States **does not exceed €635,000 annually** (1 January to 31 December), then the appropriate disclosure can be made by way of the normal VAT 3 return. This form contains two boxes (E1 and E2) in which the trader inserts the value of exports and imports arising in the period covered by the VAT 3 return.
2. Where the €500,000/€635,000 limits are **exceeded**, then a monthly **INTRASTAT** return, **in addition** to the normal VAT 3 return, must be prepared.

Where a person **exceeds both limits**, then a separate INTRASTAT return must be prepared (in addition to the normal VAT 3 return) in respect of **both** supplies and acquisitions.

The INTRASTAT must be submitted to Revenue not later than the 23rd day of the calendar month following the end of the month to which the return relates.

Category	VIES	INTRASTAT
Persons who supply to EU Member States	Complete VIES statement (quarterly or monthly, annually in limited cases)	If value of supplies exceeds **€635,000** annually, complete a detailed INTRASTAT monthly return
Persons who **purchase** from EU Member States.	Do not complete (VIES statement applies only to supplies)	If value of purchases exceeds **€500,000** annually, complete a detailed INTRASTAT monthly return
	A 'Nil' declaration must be made where appropriate for a particular period.	

The information to be included in an INTRASTAT return includes the following:

1. Trader's name and address
2. Commodity code
3. Member State of consignment (if arrival) or Member State of destination (if dispatch)
4. Country of origin
5. Mode of transport
6. Nature of transaction
7. Invoice value (rounded to €)
8. Delivery terms
9. Statistical value
10. Nett mass (in kilograms)
11. Quantity

See Revenue's detailed *VIES and INTRASTAT Traders Manual* at www.revenue.ie

11.6 Imports/Exports from/to Non-EU Countries

11.6.1 Imports from Non-EU Countries

For VAT purposes, "imports" are goods arriving from non-EU countries. In this context, it should be noted that certain other territories (e.g. the Canary Islands and Channel Islands) are regarded as not being part of the EU for VAT purposes, while others are (e.g. Monaco and the Isle of Man).

VAT is due at the **point of entry** on imports.

- VAT is charged **at the same rate** as applies to the sale of the particular goods within the State and is charged at the point of importation. Zero-rated/exempt goods therefore attract no liability on importation.
- VAT is payable **before** the imported goods are released by the Customs authorities, unless the importer is approved for the Deferred Payments Scheme.
- Eligibility under the **Deferred Payments Scheme** will permit payment of the VAT liability in respect of the goods on the **15th day** of the month **following** the month in which the VAT becomes due. Importers wishing to participate in the Deferred Payments Scheme must make an application to the Revenue's Customs division. Under the scheme, Revenue are authorised by the importer to initiate payment of the VAT by the issue of a direct debit voucher drawn on the debtor's bank. To qualify for this scheme, the importer must be able to obtain a guarantee from its bank that the VAT liability demanded for imports will be paid to Revenue.
- The **value** of imported goods for the purposes of assessment to VAT is their **value for Customs purposes**, determined on a delivery to State basis, together with any taxes, duties, and other charges levied inside the State on the goods, but not including VAT.
- A VAT-registered person who imports goods during a taxable period is entitled to **claim credit** in their VAT returns for that period for the VAT paid or payable in respect of the goods imported. A taxable person who qualifies under the Deferred Payment Scheme and who imports goods on, say, 26 February, will pay VAT on 15 March and will recover the VAT on 23 March (date of VAT payment for Jan/Feb VAT return).
- VAT-registered persons who are in a **permanent repayment position** as a result of VAT paid at the point of importation may be permitted to make **monthly** returns.
- Goods imported into the Shannon Customs Free Airport from outside the State are not liable to VAT.
- Persons who **export 75%** or more of their produce are allowed to import raw materials and components **without** payment of VAT at the point of importation (**for persons with section 56 authorisation** – see below).

11.6.2 Exports to Non-EU Countries

For VAT purposes, "exports" are goods directly dispatched to a destination **outside the EU**. In this context, it should be noted that, for VAT purposes, certain territories (e.g. the Canary Islands and the Channel Islands) are regarded as outside the EU.

The **zero rate** of VAT applies to **all exports**. A number of export type transactions and related services are also zero-rated, as are supplies of goods to VAT-registered traders in the Shannon Customs Free Airport.

A VAT-registered person who supplies goods to the domestic market and **also** exports goods is entitled to an **input credit** or deduction for VAT invoiced on purchases for **both domestic and export sales**. The credit may be taken against the VAT liability on domestic sales. Normally a person established in the State is not entitled to receive, from another VAT-registered person, taxable goods free of VAT on the grounds that the goods are intended for export. However, see below for an exception to this rule under the **Section 56**

Scheme. Persons who by virtue of the level of their exports are in a permanent repayment position may arrange with Revenue to submit monthly returns to facilitate earlier repayment of input VAT.

Section 56 Scheme: Zero-rating of Goods and Services

This scheme provides that an accountable person who derives **not less than 75%** of their annual turnover from the supply of goods out of the State can apply to Revenue for the zero-rating of goods and services supplied to them and intra-Community acquisitions and imports made by them. Revenue will issue a certificate, usually for a two-year period, which is sent to all suppliers in order that purchase invoices are zero-rated. The zero-rating does not apply to the supply or hire of any passenger motor vehicles, the supply of petrol or the provision of services consisting of the supply of food, drink, accommodation, entertainment or other personal services and other non-deductible purchases.

11.7 VAT Records

11.7.1 Records to be Maintained

A VAT-registered trader must keep **full records** of all transactions that affect the liability to VAT. The records must be kept up to date and be sufficiently detailed to enable a trader to accurately calculate liability or repayment and also to enable Revenue to check the calculations, if necessary.

Purchases Records

The purchases records should **distinguish** between purchases of goods for **resale** and goods or services **not for resale** in the ordinary course of business. The records should show the date of the purchase invoice and a consecutive number (in the order in which the invoices are filed), the name of the supplier, the cost **exclusive** of VAT and the amount of VAT. Purchases at **each rate** must be recorded **separately**. The same information should be recorded in respect of imports, intra-Community acquisitions and services received.

Sales Records

The sales records must include the amount charged in respect of every sale to a registered person and a daily entry of the total amount charged in respect of sales to unregistered persons, **distinguishing in all cases** between transactions liable at each **different VAT rate** (including the zero rate) and **exempt** transactions. All such entries should be cross-referenced to relevant invoices, sales dockets, cash register tally rolls, delivery notes, etc. Traders who are authorised to account for VAT on the cash receipts basis are also obliged to retain all documents they use for the purposes of their business. Persons involved in intra-Community trade also have requirements in relation to retention of records as regards certain transfers of goods to other Member States.

11.7.2 Retention of Records

An accountable person **must retain** all books, records and documents relevant to the business, including invoices, credit and debit notes, receipts, accounts, cash register tally rolls, vouchers, VIES and INTRASTAT returns, stamped copies of customs entries and other import documents and bank statements. These business records must be retained for **six years** from the date of the latest transaction to which they refer, unless written permission from Revenue has been obtained for their retention for a shorter period.

There is no requirement to retain the paper originals of any third-party record where an electronic copy of the original record is generated, recorded and stored in accordance with Revenue's information technology and procedural requirements.

11.7.3 Information to be included on VAT Invoices/Credit Notes

Revenue imposes strict requirements on the information given on invoices and credit notes. This information establishes the VAT **liability** of the supplier of goods or services and the **entitlement** of the customer to an **input deduction** for the VAT charged.

Accountable persons who issue invoices and credit notes, and persons to whom these documents are issued, should ensure that the documents **accurately represent** the transactions to which they refer. For example, if an incorrect rate of VAT is used on an invoice, both the supplier and the customer are liable for VAT at the correct rate, unless the supplier has **overcharged** VAT and is therefore liable for the total amount of VAT invoiced.

Form of VAT Invoice/Credit Note

An accountable person who supplies taxable goods or services is obliged to issue a VAT invoice where the supply is made to:

- another accountable person;
- a Department of State;
- a local authority;
- a body established by statute;
- a person who carries on an exempt activity;
- a person other than a private individual in another EU Member State;
- a person in another EU Member State where a reverse charge to VAT applies, i.e. where the supplier is not accountable for VAT in Ireland but the customer is accountable for VAT in the other Member State;
- an unregistered person in the State who is entitled to a repayment of such VAT, and it is requested in writing. (Otherwise, an accountable person is not required to issue a VAT invoice to an unregistered person but may do so if they wish).

The VAT invoice should show the following:

- Name and address of the supplier issuing the invoice.
- Supplier's VAT registration number.
- Name and address of the customer.
- Date of issue of the invoice.
- Date of supply of the goods or services.
- Full description of the goods or services.
- Quantity or volume and unit price of the goods or services supplied.
- The amount charged **exclusive** of VAT (in €).
- The rate (including zero rate) and amount of VAT at each rate.
- The total invoice/credit note amount exclusive of VAT (in €).
- A person who makes zero-rated intra-Community supplies is obliged, in addition to the above, to show the **VAT registration number of the customer** in the other EU Member State.

If a VAT invoice is required to be issued, it must be issued **within 15 days** of the end of the month in which goods or services are supplied. Where payment in full is made **before** the completion of the supply, the person receiving payment must also issue an invoice within 15 days of the end of the month in which the **payment** was **received**.

11.7.4   *Allowances, Discounts, etc.*

When the amount of VAT payable, as shown on an invoice, is reduced because of an allowance or discount or similar adjustment, the accountable person who issued the VAT invoice must issue a credit note stating the amount of the reduction in the price and the appropriate VAT. This person may then reduce their VAT liability by the amount credited in the accounting period in which the credit note is issued. Likewise, the customer or recipient of the credit note must increase their VAT liability by the same amount. All credit notes must contain a reference to the corresponding invoices.

Where a VAT-registered supplier and a VAT-registered customer **agree** in respect of a transaction **not to make any change** in the VAT shown on the original invoice, even though the price charged may subsequently be reduced, there is **no obligation** to issue a credit note in respect of the VAT. Such a practice saves trouble for both seller and purchaser. For example, if the discount taken by the purchaser is only on the goods, and the amount of VAT originally invoiced is allowed to stand, no adjustment for VAT is necessary and a VAT credit note is not required.

11.7.5   *Electronic Invoicing (E-invoicing)*

An accountable person may choose to issue an invoice in electronic format, subject to the following conditions:

- The issuer and the recipient of the e-invoices must agree **in advance** to the issue and acceptance of e-invoices.
- The electronic system being used **conforms** to the following specifications:

  - the system must be able to produce, retain and store electronic records in such form and containing such particulars as are required for VAT purposes, and make them available to Revenue on request;
  - the system must be able to reproduce in paper or electronic format any electronic record required to be produced, retained or stored; **and**
  - the system must be able to maintain electronic records in a manner that allows their retrieval by reference to the name of the person who issues or receives the message, or the date of the message, or the unique identification number of the message.

- The issuer and recipient of an invoice or other document have an obligation to ensure the authenticity of origin, the integrity of content and a reliable audit trail between the invoice and the supply for the duration of the period of storage of the invoice. This can be done using business controls and Revenue may require evidence of those business controls.
- An accountable person may choose to issue a simplified invoice where the amount of the invoice is **not greater than €100**. Minimum particulars to be included on a simplified invoice are:
  - the date of issue;
  - a sequential number that uniquely identifies the invoice;
  - the full name, address and registration number of the person who supplied the goods or services;
  - a description of the goods or services supplied; and
  - the tax payable or the consideration exclusive of tax in respect of the supply of the goods or services.

  A simplified invoice cannot be used in relation to a supply of intra-Community goods or services.
- An accountable person who makes **multiple supplies** during the same calendar month to the same customer can opt to issue a **summary** invoice.

■ **Batch invoicing** – where an accountable person is issuing a batch of invoices electronically to the same customer, those invoices may record details that are common to the individual invoices **once per transmission**.

11.8 VAT Reverse Charge

Under the VAT reverse charge rules, it is the **receiver** of the relevant supply and **not the supplier** who accounts for and pays the VAT to Revenue.

Under section 16 VATCA 2010, VAT reverse charge applies to:

■ NAMA and any NAMA entity;
■ a taxable person in receipt of greenhouse gas emission allowances;
■ a principal contractor in receipt of construction operations from a subcontractor subject to relevant contracts tax (RCT);
■ a taxable person dealing in scrap metal;
■ a taxable person in receipt of construction services from an accountable person who is **connected** to the taxable person; and
■ effective from **1 January 2016**, a taxable person in receipt of a wholesale supply of gas or electricity or in receipt of a gas or electricity certificate (section 52 FA 2015).

Procedures Under the VAT Reverse Charge Rule

■ The supplier issues the recipient a reverse charge invoice that includes all of the information required on a VAT invoice, except the VAT rate and the VAT amount. It also includes an indication that it is the recipient who is accountable for the VAT.
■ If there is prior agreement between the supplier and the recipient, the recipient may issue the reverse-charge invoice, subject to agreed procedures being in place for the acceptance by the supplier of the validity of the invoice (e.g. invoice is signed by both parties).
■ The recipient does not pay the VAT to the supplier but, instead, accounts for it in the VAT return for the relevant period in "VAT on Sales" (T1).
■ The recipient can claim a simultaneous input credit in "VAT on Purchases" (T2) for that VAT if the recipient has valid documentation and would have been entitled to an input credit if that VAT had been charged by the supplier.
■ The recipient pays the supplier for the VAT-exclusive value of the supply, less RCT if applicable.

Example 11.2

Allen Ltd is renovating a factory building for a manufacturing company. Allen Ltd invoices the manufacturing company in October 2016 as follows:

	€
Construction services	740,740
VAT @13.5%	100,000
Total	840,740

These services do not come within the reverse charge since Allen Ltd is not a subcontractor to the manufacturing company for RCT purposes.

Burke, a building contractor, supplies services to Allen Ltd. Allen Ltd is the principal contractor and Burke is the subcontractor.

Burke incurred €13,000 VAT on purchases in September–October 2016 for the purposes of his business.

continued overleaf

Burke charges Allen Ltd €600,000 in September 2016 for the building services. Burke does not charge any VAT on this amount.

Allen Ltd VAT Return

Allen Ltd accounts for the VAT on the construction services from Burke. VAT chargeable on the services is €600,000 @13.5% = €81,000.

As the construction services provided by the subcontractor to the principal were invoiced during September–October 2016, the VAT on these services is accounted for by reverse charge.

In its September–October 2016 VAT return Allen Ltd includes VAT €181,000 as VAT on sales (i.e. VAT on its own sales of €100,000 plus reverse charge VAT €81,000 on services received from Burke).

Allen Ltd can claim input credit for €81,000 reverse charge VAT in the same return.

Allen Ltd should pay Revenue €100,000.

Allen Ltd notifies Revenue of the gross payment to Burke (Payment Notification) online. Revenue issues a Deduction Authorisation, which states that RCT @ 35% should be deducted from the payment.

Allen Ltd should deduct RCT from the payment due to Burke (amount deducted €600,000 @ 35% = €210,000) and pay Burke net €390,000.

Burke's VAT Return

Burke does not account for VAT on the services supplied to Allen Ltd. As Burke only does work for a principal contractor, his VAT on sales figure is nil.

Burke is entitled to his input credit of €13,000.

He is entitled to a VAT repayment of €13,000.

Example 11.3

Axel Ltd supplies scrap metal to Breakers Ltd for €1,000 (excl. VAT). Both companies are registered for VAT.

Axel Ltd raises an invoice (or, if agreed, Breakers Ltd may raise the invoice), which shows that the recipient (Breakers Ltd) is accountable for the VAT. The VAT amount or rate is not shown on the invoice.

Breakers Ltd calculates the VAT (€1,000 × 23% = €230) and accounts for it in the VAT return for that period as VAT on Sales (T1). Breakers Ltd, subject to deductibility rules, can claim input credit, in the same return for that VAT (T2).

11.9 Mini One Stop Shop (MOSS)

VAT rules came into operation from 1 January 2015 providing that the place of supply of **telecommunications, broadcasting and e-services to consumers (B2C)** is where the consumer **resides**. As a consequence, every EU and non-EU business (which includes a company, a partnership or a sole trader) has to register and account for VAT **in every Member State where they supply such services**. However, in order to simplify this onerous requirement, an optional special scheme known as Mini One Stop Shop (MOSS) is in place, whereby a business can submit returns and pay the VAT due to the relevant Member States through the web portal of **one** member State, instead of having to register for VAT in each Member State.

Businesses Established in the EU

Businesses can only register for MOSS in the Member State where the business has its place of establishment (the "Union scheme"). This State is known as the **Member State of Identification (MSI)**. The business cannot use MOSS for supplies made in any Member State in which it has a fixed establishment and where all supplies are already declared via domestic VAT returns. A **fixed establishment** is "any establishment, other than the place of establishment of a business … characterised by a sufficient degree of permanence and a suitable structure in terms of human and technical resources to enable it to receive and use the services supplied to it for its own needs … [or] to enable it to provide the services which it supplies".

Example 11.4

SmartPhones Ltd has its head office in Dublin and has fixed establishments in France and Germany. The Dublin office makes telecommunications supplies to private consumers in Ireland, France, Belgium, United Kingdom and Germany.

Declarations under MOSS:
Supplies to Belgium
Supplies to United Kingdom

Declarations in domestic VAT returns:
Supplies to Ireland – in Irish domestic VAT return
Supplies to France – in French domestic VAT return
Supplies to Germany – in German domestic VAT return.

Businesses Established Outside the EU

A business established outside of the EU that has a fixed or several fixed establishments within the EU, can choose to register for MOSS in any Member State where it has a **fixed establishment** (under the Union scheme).

A business with **no fixed establishment** in the EU can choose **any** Member State in which to register for MOSS (the "non-Union scheme").

Operation of MOSS

A business opting to using this special scheme will register for MOSS in its MSI; and will submit a **quarterly return** and the related payment to the MSI. In turn, the MSI will then distribute the VAT due to the various Member States in accordance with the information on the return. The business must identify and calculate the VAT due to each Member State.

MOSS VAT Returns and Payments

The MOSS VAT return covers a calendar quarter commencing 1 January, 1 April, 1 July or 1 October. The return and payment must be made, through ROS, within **twenty days** of the end of the quarter, e.g. the return relating to October–December 2016 must be submitted and payment made on or before 20 January 2017.

Only output VAT is included in the MOSS VAT return, no credit for input VAT can be claimed or deducted. The payment corresponding to the quarterly MOSS VAT return should also be made on or before the 20th day of the month following the calendar quarter. MOSS VAT returns are **additional** to the VAT returns a business normally makes in its domestic Member State. Any credit note issued in a later period must be accounted for by adjusting the MOSS return in which the original supply was declared (within three years of the date of the original return). A negative return can therefore never arise.

Questions

Review Questions
(See Suggested Solutions to Review Questions at the end of this textbook.)

Question 11.1

With regard to VAT, set out:
(a) the criteria for determining the obligation to register, and
(b) the records to be maintained and the information required to complete a VAT 3 return.

Question 11.2

Outline the VAT rules for determining the tax point or time when a supply of goods or services is treated as taking place.

Question 11.3

Michael, a friend of yours, has recently set up business in Ireland selling computers. He has already registered for VAT.

Requirement

Advise Michael on:
(a) what records he should keep for VAT purposes in relation to purchases and sales; and
(b) when VAT returns and related VAT payments should be returned to Revenue and the consequences if he defaults.

Question 11.4

John Hardiman's business consists partly of the supply of VAT-exempt services and partly of services liable to VAT at 23%. He is authorised by the Revenue Commissioners to account for VAT on the cash receipts (money received) basis.

John's records for the VAT period September–October 2016 provide the following information:

		€
1.	Sales and cash receipts:	
	Supplies of services at 23% VAT (gross)	24,000
	Supplies of services exempt from VAT	2,000
	Cash receipts relating to supplies of services at 23% VAT (gross)	30,250
	Cash receipts relating to supplies of exempt services	3,000
2.	Purchases	€
	Purchases of goods and services at 23% VAT (gross)	6,150
	Purchases of goods and services at 13.5% VAT (gross)	2,270

3. It has been agreed with the Revenue Commissioners that 10% of John's input credits relate to his exempt activities.
4. Included in the purchases figures at 2. above are the following items:
   (i) An invoice for the servicing of his motor car amounting to €160 plus VAT at 13.5%. It has been agreed with the Revenue Commissioners that the private use of his car is 25%.
   (ii) An invoice for the lease of the motor car referred to in (i) above. The invoice is for €300 plus VAT at 23%. The car is a "qualifying vehicle".
   (iii) An invoice for the purchase of stationery amounting to €123 was included with purchases at 23% VAT. A closer examination of the invoice revealed that it had no supplier VAT number listed and no details of VAT rates or amounts.
   (iv) An invoice for the building of a new office. The invoice was in respect of an instalment payment and amounted to €1,000 plus VAT at 13.5%.
   (v) A petty cash voucher for postage, amounting to €64, was included with purchases at 23% VAT.

Requirement

On the basis of the above information, calculate the VAT liability/refund of John Hardiman for the VAT period September–October 2016.

Question 11.5

Mr Byte supplies computers to business and retail outlets. You are given the following information in connection with his VAT return for the period July–August 2016.

	€
Invoiced sales July–August (excluding VAT)	100,000
Cash received July–August (including VAT)	75,000
Purchases invoices received July–August (excluding VAT)	40,000
Purchase invoices paid July–August (excluding VAT)	50,000
Other expenses:	
Stationery (excluding VAT @ 23%)	6,000
Wages (VAT-exempt)	20,000
Electricity (excluding VAT @ 13.5%)	2,000
Hotel bills (excluding VAT @ 9%)	1,000
Rent (VAT-exempt)	2,400

Requirement

Compute the liability to VAT of Mr Byte for the period July–August 2016 assuming he is authorised to account for VAT on the cash receipts basis.

Question 11.6

Joe, who is a baker, supplies you with the following information from his books for the months of May and June 2016 (all figures are **exclusive** of VAT).

		May	June
		€	€
Sales of bread	zero rated	10,000	8,000
Purchase of ingredients	zero rated	5,000	2,000
Expenditure on petrol	23%	1,000	1,000
Purchase of mixing machine	23%	–	6,000
Lease rentals – vans	23%	2,000	2,000
Bank interest	exempt	400	400

Requirement

Compute the VAT liability for the period in question, and show the date on which the VAT returns should be submitted.

Question 11.7

State the categories of persons who may apply for voluntary registration for VAT and discuss the reasons why such persons might choose to apply for voluntary registration.

Question 11.8

(a) Discuss the place where goods and services are deemed to be supplied for VAT purposes.
(b) Explain what you understand the term "self-supply" to mean for VAT purposes.

Question 11.9

Andrew opened a coffee shop on 17 March 2016 and the transactions undertaken during the first VAT period March–April 2016 were as follows:

Sales and Receipts

1. Receipts in respect of supplies of goods and services, inclusive of VAT @ 23%, amounted to €1,815 for the period.
2. Receipts in respect of supplies of goods and services, inclusive of VAT @ 13.5%, amounted to €2,837.50 for the period.

Purchases and Payments

1. Purchase of stock for re-sale: €605 inclusive of VAT @ 23%.
2. Purchase of stock for re-sale: €334 @ zero-rate VAT.
3. Purchase of tables and chairs: €440 excluding VAT @ 23%.
4. Payment of rent to landlord: €373. No invoices have been received.
5. Purchases of second-hand cash register on three months' credit. The invoice dated 3 March 2016 was for €665.50 in total and included VAT @ 23%.
6. Payment of €200 plus VAT @ 13.5% to the tiler on 16 March 2016.
7. On 5 March 2016, Andrew signed a lease for shop fittings requiring a monthly payment of €700 plus VAT @ 23%. The monthly payments are debited to Andrew's bank account on the 30th of each month.
8. Payment of €750 on account to a solicitor for legal fees on foot of a bill received for €1,452 inclusive of VAT @ 23%.
9. Purchase for the business of a commercial van for €9,840 inclusive of VAT @ 23%.
10. Purchases of petrol for the van totalling €98 inclusive of VAT @ 23%.

All invoices relating to the above transactions have been received unless otherwise stated. Assume that Andrew was registered for VAT prior to incurring any expenditure.

Requirement

Calculate the VAT liability/refund for the VAT period March–April 2016.

Question 11.10

Hermes Ltd distributes pet food on the home and foreign markets. The following transactions were undertaken by the company during the VAT period March–April 2016:

Sales invoiced to customers within the State	€250,000
Sales invoiced to customers in the US	€10,000

The above amounts are stated net of VAT. The VAT rate applicable to the company's sales is 23%.

During the same period, purchase invoices were received in respect of the following:

	Gross Invoice Value €	VAT Rate Applicable %
Stock purchased from suppliers in the State	233,700	23
Stock purchased from suppliers in the UK	50,000	23

Professional fees	6,150	23
Motor car leasing ("qualifying" car)	3,690	23
Motor car repairs	1,135	13.5
Computer	9,225	23

The amounts stated include VAT where charged.

Requirement
Calculate the VAT due for the period March–April 2016. The computation of VAT return figures should be clearly laid out in your workings.

Question 11.11

Elixir Ltd operates an Irish-based business selling materials for the repair and maintenance of yachts and small boats. During the VAT period of two months ended 31 October 2016, it recorded the following transactions:

Supplies of services (exclusive of VAT)		€
Sales in Ireland		950,000
Sales to Spain (to Spanish VAT-registered customers)		320,000
Sales to non VAT-registered customers in the UK		25,000
Sales to VAT-registered customers in the UK		135,000
Sales to customers located in Singapore		46,000

Purchases (inclusive of VAT where applicable)	**VAT Rate**	
Purchase of materials from Irish suppliers	23%	369,000
Purchase (imports) of equipment from German supplier	23%	200,000
Purchase of machinery locally	23%	246,000
Rent of premises (Note)	23%	18,450
Repairs and maintenance of office and equipment	23%	14,145
Audit and accountancy fees	23%	11,070
Diesel for staff vehicles	23%	5,535
Electricity and gas	13.5%	2,400
Salaries and wages	n/a	167,000
Advertising costs	23%	30,750

Note: VAT at the rate of 23% is included in the amount of the rent paid on the company's premises.

All of the above purchases of goods and services (except for wages, salaries and imports) are supplied by businesses which are registered for VAT in Ireland. The imports are purchased from a VAT-registered business in Germany.

Requirement
Calculate the VAT payable by (or repayable to) Elixir Ltd for the VAT period ended 31 October 2016.

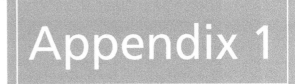

Taxation Reference Material for Tax Year 2016

Table of Contents

Table 1 INCOME TAX RATES AND INCOME TAX CREDITS FOR 2016

Rates

Single/Widowed/ Surviving Civil Partner with Qualifying Children	Rate	Single/Widowed/ Surviving Civil Partner without Qualifying Children	Rate	Married Couple/ Civil Partners	Rate
First €37,800	20%	First €33,800	20%	First €42,800/€67,600[1]	20%
Balance	40%	Balance	40%	Balance	40%

[1] Depending on personal circumstances of a married couple/civil partners.

Credits (Non-refundable)

	Tax Credit
	€
Single person	1,650
Married couple/civil partners	3,300
Widowed person/surviving civil partner (year of bereavement)	3,300
Widowed person/surviving civil partner tax credit – no dependent children	2,190
Widowed person/surviving civil partner tax credit – with dependent children	1,650
Single Person Child Carer Credit (additional)	1,650
Widowed parent/surviving civil partner tax credit – with dependent children	
Year 1 after the year of bereavement	3,600
Year 2 after the year of bereavement	3,150
Year 3 after the year of bereavement	2,700
Year 4 after the year of bereavement	2,250
Year 5 after the year of bereavement	1,800
Employee tax credit	1,650
Earned Income Tax Credit	550
Age tax credit – single/widowed/surviving civil partner	245
Age tax credit – married/civil partners	490
Incapacitated child tax credit	3,300
Dependent relative – income limit €14,060	70
Home carer's credit – income limit €7,200 (lower)/ €9,200 (upper)	1,000
Blind person	1,650
Both spouses/civil partners blind	3,300
Rent tax credit[1]:	
Single person aged under 55	80
Single person aged 55 or over	160
Married couple/civil partners aged under 55	160
Married couple/civil partners aged 55 or over	320
Third-level education fees[2]:	
Full-time course	800
Part-time course	1,100

[1] The tax credit is equal to the lower of the actual rent paid at the standard rate or the "specified limit" at the standard rate of tax. The tenant must have been paying rent under a tenancy on 7 December 2010.

[2] There is a maximum level of qualifying fees, per academic year, of €7,000 per student, per course, subject to the first €3,000 (full-time) or €1,500 (part-time) being disallowed (per claim, not per course).

Table 2 INCOME TAX ALLOWANCES AND RELIEFS FOR 2016

Deduction for employed person taking care of incapacitated person (maximum) – €75,000
Provision of childcare services — – income limit €15,000
Rent-a-Room relief (maximum) — – €12,000

Table 3 INCOME TAX EXEMPTION LIMITS FOR PERSONS AGED 65 AND OVER FOR 2016

	€
Single/widowed/surviving civil partner	18,000[1]
Married/civil partners	36,000[1]

[1] Dependent children: increase exemption by €575 for each of first two, and by €830 for each additional child.

Table 4 MORTGAGE INTEREST RELIEF FOR 2016

Interest Ceilings for Non-first-time Buyers

	Ceiling	Rate of Relief	Maximum Relief
	€		€
Single	3,000	@ 15%	450
Married/widowed/civil partners/surviving civil partner	6,000	@ 15%	900

Interest Ceilings for First-time Buyers

	Ceiling	Relief Years 1 & 2		Relief Years 3, 4 & 5		Relief Years 6 & 7	
		Rate of Relief[1]	Maximum Relief	Rate of Relief[1]	Maximum Relief	Rate of Relief[1]	Maximum Relief
	€		€		€		€
Single	10,000	@ 25%	2,500	@ 22.5%	2,250	@ 20%	2,000
Married/widowed/ civil partners/ surviving civil partner	20,000	@ 25%	5,000	@ 22.5%	4,500	@ 20%	4,000

[1] Rate of relief is increased to 30% for loans taken out to buy a first principal private residence on or after 1 January 2004 and before 31 December 2008 or to buy a second principal private residence in this period where the first principal private residence was purchased on or after 1 January 2004.

[2] Relief only applies to interest on qualifying loans taken out on or after 1 January 2004 and before 31 December 2012 and to loans taken out in 2013 to construct a home on a site where the site was purchased in 2012 or where loan approval was given in 2012 for a loan to repair, develop or improve a home and the loan was taken out partly in 2012 and partly in 2013.

Table 5 PENSION CONTRIBUTIONS

The maximum amount on which tax relief may be claimed in 2016 in respect of qualifying premiums is as follows:

Age	% of Net Relevant Earnings[1]
Under 30 years of age	15%
30 to 39 years of age	20%
40 to 49 years of age	25%
50 to 54 years of age	30%
55 to 59 years of age	35%
60 years and over	40%

[1] The earnings cap for 2016 on net relevant earnings is €115,000.

Table 6 PREFERENTIAL LOANS

The specified rates for 2016 are:

- 4% in respect of qualifying home loans.
- 13.5% in respect of all other loans.

Table 7 MOTOR CAR BENEFIT IN KIND SCALE FOR 2016

Annual Business Kilometres	Cash Equivalent (% of OMV)
24,000 or less	30%
24,001 – 32,000	24%
32,001 – 40,000	18%
40,001 – 48,000	12%
48,001 and over	6%

Table 8 LOCAL PROPERTY TAX VALUATION TABLE

Valuation Band Number	Valuation Band €	Mid-point of Valuation Band €	LPT in 2016/17 (full-year charge) €
01	0 to 100,000	50,000	90
02	100,001 to 150,000	125,000	225
03	150,001 to 200,000	175,000	315
04	200,001 to 250,000	225,000	405
05	250,001 to 300,000	275,000	495
06	300,001 to 350,000	325,000	585
07	350,001 to 400,000	375,000	675
08	400,001 to 450,000	425,000	765
09	450,001 to 500,000	475,000	855
10	500,001 to 550,000	525,000	945
11	550,001 to 600,000	575,000	1,035

Valuation Band Number	Valuation Band €	Mid-point of Valuation Band €	LPT in 2016/17 (full-year charge) €
12	600,001 to 650,000	625,000	1,125
13	650,001 to 700,000	675,000	1,215
14	700,001 to 750,000	725,000	1,305
15	750,001 to 800,000	775,000	1,395
16	800,001 to 850,000	825,000	1,485
17	850,001 to 900,000	875,000	1,575
18	900,001 to 950,000	925,000	1,665
19	950,001 to 1,000,000*	975,000	1,755

*Residential properties valued over €1 million will be assessed at the actual value at 0.18% on the first €1 million in value and 0.25% on the portion of the value above €1 million (no banding will apply).

LPT Local Adjustment Factors: 2016

The local adjustment factor (LAF) increasing or decreasing the basic LPT rate in operation for 2016:

Local Authority	LPT Rate Adjustment
Clare County Council	15% decrease
Cork County Council	5% decrease
Cork City Council	10% decrease
Dublin City Council	15% decrease
Dun Laoghaire/Rathdown County Council	15% decrease
Fingal County Council	15% decrease
Kildare County Council	7.5% decrease
Longford County Council	3% decrease
Louth County Council	1.5% decrease
Monaghan County Council	7.5% decrease
South Dublin County Council	15% decrease

Table 9 UNIVERSAL SOCIAL CHARGE (USC) FOR 2016

Employment Income

The rates of USC (where gross income is greater than €13,000 per annum) are:

Rate of USC	Annual Income	Monthly Income	Weekly Income
1.0%	First €12,012	First €1,001	First €231
3.0%	€12,013–€18,668	€1,002–€1,555	€232–€359
5.5%[1,2]	€18,669–€70,044	€1,556–€5,837	€360–€1,347
8%[1,2]	Balance	Balance	Balance

[1] Persons aged 70 years and over with income of €60,000 or less are not liable at the 5.5%/8% rates but instead pay at 3.0%.
[2] Persons who hold a full medical card and with income of €60,000 or less are not liable at the 5.5%/8% rates but instead pay at 3.0%.

Exempt Categories

- Where an individual's total income for a year does not exceed €13,000.
- All Department of Social Protection payments.
- Income already subjected to DIRT.

Self-assessed Individuals

The rates of USC (where gross income is greater than €13,000 per annum) are:

	Aged under 70/Aged 70 and over with income >€60,000/Full medical card holder with income >€60,000	Aged 70 and over with income of €60,000 or less/Full medical card holder with income of €60,000 or less
First €12,012	1.0%	1.0%
Next €6,656	3.0%	3.0%
Next €51,376	5.5%	3.0% (max. €41,332)
Balance[1]	8%	N/A

[1] An additional USC charge of 3% is payable by individuals on self-assessed income (excluding employment income) in excess of €100,000 in a year, regardless of age.

Surcharge on use of Property Incentives

There is also an additional USC surcharge of 5% on investors with gross income greater than €100,000 where certain property tax reliefs have been used.

Table 10 PRSI 2016

Employees/Employers' Rates

Employee's income	Employee rate	Employers' rate
Income of €38–€352* per week	Nil	8.5%
Income of €352*–€376* per week	4%	8.5%
Income greater than €376 per week	4%	10.75%

* EE PRSI credit applies to earnings up to €424.

Employee PRSI Credit

Effective from **1 January 2016**, a new employee PRSI credit of a maximum of €12 per week is available to Class A employees with gross earnings between €352 and €424 per week. The credit is reduced by one-sixth of gross earnings in excess of €352 per week. The reduced credit is then deducted from the employee PRSI liability calculated at 4% of gross weekly earnings.

Self-employed

All income is subject to PRSI at 4%.[1]

[1] Individuals in receipt of income of €5,000 or less in 2016 will not be subject to PRSI. Where income is greater than €5,000 PRSI at 4% is payable subject to a minimum contribution of €500. For those with an annual self-employed income of in excess of €5,000 but who have no net liability to tax, the minimum contribution is €300 for 2016.

Table 11 CAPITAL ALLOWANCES AND RESTRICTED COST FOR MOTOR LEASE EXPENSES FOR 2016

Restricted Cost of Passenger Motor Vehicle for Capital Allowances and Motor Leases Expenses Restriction Purposes

Specified Limit	€
From 1 January 2007	24,000

Restricted Cost for Motor Vehicles bought on/after 1 July 2008

Category	CO$_2$ Emissions	Restriction
A	0–120g/km	Use the specified amount regardless of cost.
B and C	121–155g/km	
D and E	156–190g/km	Two steps to calculate limit: 1. take the lower of the specified limit or cost; 2. limit is 50% of this amount.
F and G	191+g/km	No allowance available.

Plant and Machinery

Expenditure incurred on or after 4 December 2002:

Plant and machinery	12.5% straight-line
Cars other than those used as a taxi or in car hire business	12.5% straight-line

Industrial Buildings

Expenditure incurred on or after 1 April 1992	4% straight-line

Table 12 VAT RATES FOR 2016

Standard	23.0%
Reduced rate	13.5%
Second reduced rate	9.0%
Flat rate for farmers	5.2%
Livestock	4.8%

The main zero-rated goods and services are:

Exported goods (export, in this regard, means export outside the EU), most food and drink of a kind used for human consumption, sea-going ships of more than 15 tons, oral medicine, fertilizers, animal feed other than pet food, certain printed books and booklets, most clothing and footwear appropriate to a child under 11 years, seeds and plants.

The main exempted activities are:

Certain lettings of immovable goods, medical, dental and optical services, insurance services, betting, funeral services, transport of passengers and their baggage, educational services, certain banking services.

The main goods and services liable at the reduced rate are:

Immovable goods, services consisting of the development of immovable goods, concrete and concrete goods, waste disposal services, repair and maintenance of movable goods, short-term hire of cars, boats, general agricultural and veterinary services, fuel for power and heating, electricity, gas, timber, coal, driving instruction.

The main goods and services liable at the second reduced rate are:

Supply of food and drink (excluding alcohol and soft drinks), hotel lettings, guesthouses, caravan parks, camping sites, admissions to cinemas, theatre, certain musical performances, museums, fairground amusement receipts, hairdressing services, the supply of live horses (other than for foodstuffs), the hire of horses and the supply of greyhounds.

The main goods and services liable at the standard rate are:

Applies to all supplies of goods and services by taxable persons that are not exempt or specifically liable at 0%, 4.8%, 5.2%, 9% or 13.5%. Includes goods such as adult clothing and footwear, office equipment and stationery, drink and certain foods.

Code of Practice for Determining Employment or Self-Employment Status of Individuals[1]

Introduction

This document has been prepared by the Employment Status Group set up under the Programme for Prosperity and Fairness (PPF).

The group was set up because of a growing concern that there may be increasing numbers of individuals categorised as "self-employed" when the "indicators" may be that "employee" status would be more appropriate. The purpose of the document is to eliminate misconceptions and provide clarity. It is not meant to bring individuals who are genuinely self-employed into employment status. The remit of the group is contained in the PPF document at page 18, paragraph 9 as follows:

"The Office of the Revenue Commissioners and the Department of Social, Community & Family Affairs, in consultation with the Social Partners, will seek a uniform definition of 'employee' based on clear criteria, which will determine the employment status of an individual."

The group consisted of representatives from the following organisations:

- Irish Congress of Trade Unions
- Irish Business and Employers Confederation
- Revenue Commissioners
- Department of Social, Community and Family Affairs (now Department of Social Protection)
- Department of Enterprise, Trade and Employment
- Department of Finance.

Considerations

The group considered two approaches in their deliberations. They considered a legislative approach – to define in statute the traits or indicators of "employee" status using criteria established by common law over many years. The other approach was to reaffirm the criteria as a Code of Practice and to distribute the material as widely as possible to a relevant audience.

It was felt by some members that a statutory definition would provide clarity for anyone dealing with or considering the issue of a person's employment status. It was felt by other members that the case law and criteria laid down by the courts over the years provided flexibility and that a statutory approach would interfere with that flexibility, while others felt that a statutory definition might prove detrimental to "employee" status.

[1] *Report of the Employment Status Group* – PPF, available from the Revenue Commissioners, see http://www.revenue.ie/en/ practitioner/tech-guide/

It was decided to issue the report as a Code of Practice, which would be monitored by the Group with a view to reviewing the position within 12 months. While it was accepted by the Group that the Code of Practice does not have legislative effect, it was expected that its contents would be considered by those involved in disputes on the employment status of individuals or groups of individuals.

It was noted that the Revenue Commissioners and the Department of Social, Community & Family Affairs have already jointly produced a leaflet in September 1998 entitled "**Employed or Self-Employed – A Guide for Tax and Social Insurance**". The Revenue Commissioners also produced a leaflet aimed at the construction industry but which would equally have general application. The Department of Enterprise, Trade & Employment has a range of explanatory leaflets which, while not specifically relating to "employee" status, set out comprehensively the rights of employees under different aspects of employment law.

This Code of Practice is also recommended for the consideration of all appropriate adjudication agencies where issues concerning employment status are the subject of a dispute.

Legal Background

The terms "employed" and "self-employed" are not defined in law. The decision as to which category an individual belongs must be arrived at by looking at what the individual actually does, the way he or she does it and the terms and conditions under which he or she is engaged, be they written, verbal or implied, or a combination of all three. It is not simply a matter of calling a job "employment" or "self-employment".

In the Irish Supreme Court case of *Henry Denny & Sons Ltd T/A Kerry Foods v. The Minister for Social Welfare* (1997), the fundamental test as to whether a person who has been engaged to perform certain work performs it "as a person in business on their own account" was considered among other matters. This fundamental test was drawn from the UK case of *Market Investigations Ltd v. Minister of Social Security* (1969), which has received extensive judicial approval in this country as well as in the UK and other common law jurisdictions. This fundamental test in that case was amplified by a series of specific criteria, as follows. Does the person doing the work:

- assume any responsibility for investment and management in the business?
- otherwise take any financial risk?
- provide his own equipment or helpers? or
- have the opportunity to profit from sound management in the performance of his/her task?

From consideration of such tests one is better able to judge whether the person engaged is a free agent and has an economic independence from the party engaging the service.

In most cases, it will be clear whether an individual is employed or self-employed. However, it may not always be so obvious, which in turn can lead to misconceptions in relation to the employment status of individuals.

The *Denny* case, which is an important precedent in the area of whether a person is engaged under a contract of service (employee) or under a contract for services (self-employed), is of assistance because of the atypical nature of the engagement. The main features of the *Denny* case were:

- The facts were fully established and articulated and relevant legal principles applied by the Social Welfare Appeals Officer. The High Court or the Supreme Court did not disturb the decision.
- The employment was atypical – the person engaged was a demonstrator/merchandiser of food products in supermarkets.
- The employment was also casual in nature and would have included a pool of demonstrators to be drawn from.

▨ Because of the casual nature of the employment, "mutuality of obligation" would have been an issue, i.e. whether or not the person engaged had an obligation to take each engagement when offered.

▨ The right of substitution was an issue albeit with the approval of the employer.

▨ The employment included fixed-term contracts.

▨ References were made to imposed conditional contracts.

▨ It was confirmed that the Appeals Officer was correct in deciding not to be bound by an unreported Circuit Court judgment, dealing with a similar issue under an unfair dismissal claim under employment law, with which he did not agree. The Appeals Officer was correct in considering "the facts or realities of the situation on the ground", i.e. to look at and beyond the written contract to arrive at the totality of the relationship. Certain statements included in the contract and other notes of engagement, such as:

  ● "Deemed to be an independent contractor",

  ● "It shall be the duty of the demonstrator to pay and discharge such taxes and charges as may be payable out of such fees to the Revenue Commissioners or otherwise",

  ● "It is further agreed that the provisions of the Unfair Dismissals Act 1997 shall not apply, etc.",

  ● "You will not be an employee of Kerry Foods", and

  ● "You will be responsible for your own tax affairs",

  were not contractual terms but that "they purported to express a conclusion of law as to the consequences of the contract between the parties".

In other words, the fact that such or similar terms are included in a contract is of little value in coming to a conclusion as to the work status of the person engaged.

Code of Practice in Determining Status

The criteria set out in the next paragraph should help in reaching a conclusion. It is important that the job as a whole is looked at, including working conditions and the reality of the relationship, when considering the guidelines. The overriding consideration or test will always be whether the person performing the work does so "as a person in business on their own account". Is the person a free agent with economic independence from the person engaging the service?

Criteria on Whether an Individual is an Employee

While all of the following factors may not apply, an individual would normally be an employee if he or she:

▨ Is under the control of another person who directs as to how, when and where the work is to be carried out.

▨ Supplies labour only.

▨ Receives a fixed hourly/weekly/monthly wage.

▨ Cannot subcontract the work. If the work can be subcontracted and paid on by the person subcontracting the work, the employer/employee relationship may simply be transferred on.

▨ Does not supply materials for the job.

▨ Does not provide equipment other than the small tools of the trade. The provision of tools or equipment might not have a significant bearing on coming to a conclusion that employment status may be appropriate having regard to all the circumstances of a particular case.

▨ Is not exposed to personal financial risk in carrying out the work.

▨ Does not assume any responsibility for investment and management in the business.

▨ Does not have the opportunity to profit from sound management in the scheduling of engagements or in the performance of tasks arising from the engagements.

- Works set hours or a given number of hours per week or month.
- Works for one person or for one business.
- Receives expense payments to cover subsistence and/or travel expenses.
- Is entitled to extra pay or time off for overtime.

Additional Factors to be Considered

- An individual could have considerable freedom and independence in carrying out work and still remain an employee.
- An employee with specialist knowledge may not be directed as to how the work is carried out.
- An individual who is paid by commission, by share, or by piecework, or in some other atypical fashion might still be regarded as an employee.
- Some employees work for more than one employer at the same time.
- Some employees do not work on the employer's premises.
- There are special PRSI rules for the employment of family members.
- Statements in contracts considered in the *Denny* case, such as:
  - "You are deemed to be an independent contractor",
  - "It shall be your duty to pay and discharge such taxes and charges as may be payable out of such fees to the Revenue Commissioners or otherwise",
  - "It is agreed that the provisions of the Unfair Dismissals Act 1977 shall not apply, etc.",
  - "You will not be an employee of this company", and
  - "You will be responsible for your own tax affairs"
  are not contractual terms and have little or no contractual validity. While they may express an opinion of the contracting parties, they are of minimal value in coming to a conclusion as to the work status of the person engaged.

Criteria on Whether an Individual is Self-employed

While all of the following factors may not apply to the job, an individual would normally be self-employed if he or she:

- owns his or her own business;
- is exposed to financial risk, by having to bear the cost of making good faulty or sub-standard work carried out under the contract;
- assumes responsibility for investment and management in the enterprise;
- has the opportunity to profit from sound management in the scheduling and performance of engagements and tasks;
- has control over what is done, how it is done, when and where it is done and whether he or she does it personally;
- is free to hire other people, on his or her terms, to do the work which has been agreed to be undertaken;
- can provide the same services to more than one person or business at the same time;
- provides the materials for the job;
- provides equipment and machinery necessary for the job, other than the small tools of the trade or equipment which in an overall context would not be an indicator of a person in business on their own account;
- has a fixed place of business where materials, equipment, etc. can be stored;
- costs and agrees a price for the job;

- provides his or her own insurance cover, e.g. public liability, etc.; or
- controls the hours of work in fulfilling the job obligations.

Additional Factors to be Considered

- Generally an individual should satisfy the self-employed guidelines above, otherwise he or she will normally be an employee.
- The fact that an individual has registered as self-employed or for VAT under the principles of self-assessment does not automatically mean that he or she is self-employed.
- An office holder, such as a company director, will be taxed under the PAYE system. However, the terms and conditions may have to be examined by the Scope Section of the Department of Social Protection to decide the appropriate PRSI class.
- It should be noted that a person who is a self-employed contractor in one job is not necessarily self-employed in the next job. It is also possible to be employed and self-employed at the same time in different jobs.
- In the construction sector, for health and safety reasons, all individuals are under the direction of the site foreman/overseer. The self-employed individual controls the method to be employed in carrying out the work.

Consequences Arising from the Determination of an Individual's Status

The status as an employee or self-employed person will affect:

- the way in which tax, PRSI and USC is payable to the Collector-General:
  - an employee will have tax, PRSI and USC deducted from his or her income, and
  - a self-employed person is obliged to pay preliminary tax and file income tax returns whether or not he or she is asked for them.
- entitlement to a number of social welfare benefits, such as unemployment and disability benefits:
  - an employee will be entitled to unemployment, disability and invalidity benefits, whereas a self-employed person will not have these entitlements
- other rights and entitlements, for example, under employment legislation:
  - an employee will have rights in respect of working hours, holidays, maternity/parental leave, protection from unfair dismissal, etc.,
  - a self-employed person will not have these rights and protection.
- public liability in respect of the work done.

Consequence for the Person or Company Engaging the Service of an Individual

In most instances, a person's work status will be clear. It is crucial, however, for a person or company to ensure that a person engaged to perform a service is correctly categorised as an employee or self-employed, particularly where there is a doubt. There may, in certain borderline instances, be a divergence of opinion between the contracting parties' assumptions and that of the Revenue Commissioners, the Department of Social, Community and Family Affairs or the adjudication systems established under employment and industrial relations legislation.

While it is accepted that the operation of the PAYE, PRSI and USC systems and compliance with the rights of employees under employment legislation creates an administrative burden for employers, the integrity of the systems very much depends on employers operating them correctly.

Under tax and social welfare law, if the status of 'employee' is found to be appropriate, the person engaging the 'employee' is the accountable person for any PAYE, PRSI and USC deductible while that person was engaged (whether or not any deductions were made), together with appropriate interest and penalties that may arise.

There may also be penalties under various employment legislation for wrong categorisation of a person's employment status.

Deciding Status: Getting Assistance

Where there are difficulties in deciding the appropriate status of an individual or groups of individuals, the following organisations can provide assistance.

Tax and PRSI

The local Revenue office or the local Social Welfare office (a listing of Revenue and Social Welfare offices is in the telephone book and online). Scope Section in the Department of Social Protection may also be contacted for assistance.

If a formal decision is required, relevant facts will have to be established and a written decision as to status issued. A decision by one Department will generally be accepted by the other, provided all relevant facts were given at the time and the circumstances remain the same and it is accepted that the correct legal principles have been applied to the facts established. However, because of the varied nature of circumstances that arise and the different statutory provisions, such a consensus may not be possible in every case.

Employment Appeals Tribunal

The purpose of the Employment Appeals Tribunal is to determine matters of dispute arising under the Acts relating to redundancy payments, minimum notice and terms of employment, unfair dismissals, protection of employees (employers' insolvency), worker protection (regular part-time employees), payment of wages, terms of employment (information), maternity protection, adoptive leave, protection of young persons, organisation of working time, parental leave, and protections for persons reporting child abuse. Disputes in relation to any matter arising under the above-mentioned legislation may be referred either directly, or on appeal (from a Rights Commissioner, where appropriate), to the Tribunal.

Labour Court

The main functions of the Labour Court are:

- to investigate industrial disputes under the Industrial Relations Acts 1946 to 1990, and to issue recommendations for their settlement;
- to make determinations on appeals against recommendations of equality officers, or for the implementation of such recommendations;
- to make orders in cases of dismissal under the Employment Equality Act 1998, and the Pensions Act 1990;
- to decide on appeals against recommendations and decisions of Rights Commissioners under the Industrial Relations and Organisation of Working Time Acts;
- to establish joint labour committees;

- to make employment regulation orders prescribing legally enforceable pay rates and conditions in employments covered by the relevant joint labour committees;
- to register employment agreements, which become legally binding;
- to register joint industrial councils; and
- to approve and register collective agreements under the Organisation of Working Time Act 1997.

Department of Enterprise, Trade and Employment

The Employment Rights Information Unit of the Department of Enterprise, Trade and Employment can also be contacted for information on labour law issues. This Unit has a range of leaflets on employment law that are available on request.

Irish Congress of Trade Unions

The Irish Congress of Trade Unions is the single umbrella organisation for trade unions in Ireland representing a wide range of interests.

Irish Business and Employers Confederation

The Irish Business and Employers Confederation represents and provides economic, commercial, employee relations and social affairs services to some 7,000 companies and organisations from all sectors of economic and commercial activity.

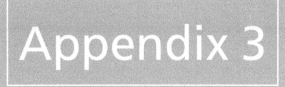

Chartered Accountants Regulatory Board *Code of Ethics*

Under the Chartered Accountants Regulatory Board *Code of Ethics*, a Chartered Accountant shall comply with the following fundamental principles:

1. **Integrity** – to be straightforward and honest in all professional and business relationships.
2. **Objectivity** – to not allow bias, conflict of interest or undue influence of others to override professional or business judgements.
3. **Professional Competence and Due Care** – to maintain professional knowledge and skill at the level required to ensure that a client or employer receives competent professional services based on current developments in practice, legislation and techniques, and act diligently and in accordance with applicable technical and professional standards.
4. **Confidentiality** – to respect the confidentiality of information acquired as a result of professional and business relationships and, therefore, not disclose any such information to third parties without proper and specific authority, unless there is a legal or professional right or duty to disclose, nor use the information for the personal advantage of the Chartered Accountant or third parties.
5. **Professional Behaviour** – to comply with relevant laws and regulations and avoid any action that discredits the profession.

As a Chartered Accountant, you will have to ensure that your dealings with the tax aspects of your professional life are in compliance with these fundamental principles. You will not be asked to define or list the principles, but you must be able to identify where these ethical issues arise and how you would deal with them.

Examples of situations that could arise where these principles are challenged are outlined below.

Example 4.1

You are working in the tax department of ABC & Co. and your manager is Jack Wilson. He comes over to your desk after his meeting with Peter Foley. He gives you all the papers that Peter has left with him. He asks you to draft Peter's tax return. You know who Peter is as you are now living in a house that your friend Ann leased from Peter. As you complete the return, you note that there is no information regarding rental income. What should you do?

Action

As a person with integrity, you should explain to your manager that your friend, Ann, has leased property from Peter and that he has forgotten to send details of his rental income and expenses. As Peter sent the information to Jack, it is appropriate for Jack to contact Peter for details regarding rental income and related expenses.

Example 4.2

You are working in the tax department of the Irish subsidiary of a US-owned multinational. You are preparing the corporation tax computation, including the R&D tax credit due. You have not received some information from your colleagues dealing with R&D and cannot finalise the claim for R&D tax credit until you receive this information. Your manager is under pressure and tells you to just file the claim on the basis that will maximise the claim. He says, "It is self-assessment, and the chance of this ever being audited is zero." What should you do?

Action

You should act in a professional and objective manner. This means that you cannot do as your manager wants. You should explain to him that you will contact the person in R&D again and finalise the claim as quickly as possible.

Example 4.3

Anna O'Shea, financial controller of Great Client Ltd, rings you regarding a VAT issue. You have great respect for Anna and are delighted that she is ringing you directly instead of your manager. She says that it is a very straightforward query. However, as you listen to her, you realise that you are pretty sure of the answer but would need to check a point before answering. What should you do?

Action

Where you do not know the answer, it is professionally competent to explain that you need to check a point before you give an answer. If you like, you can explain which aspect you need to check. Your client will appreciate you acting professionally rather than giving incorrect information or advice.

Example 4.4

The phone rings, and it is Darren O'Brien, your best friend, who works for Just-do-it Ltd. After discussing the match you both watched on the television last night, Darren explains why he is ringing you. He has heard that Success Ltd, a client of your Tax Department, has made R&D tax credit claims. Therefore, you must have details regarding its R&D. Darren's relationship with his boss is not great at present, and he knows that if he could get certain data about Success Ltd, his relationship with his boss would improve. He explains that he does not want any financial information, just some small details regarding R&D. What should you do?

Action

You should not give him the information. No matter how good a friend he is, it is unethical to give confidential information about your client to him.

Example 4.5

It is the Friday morning before a bank holiday weekend, and you are due to travel from Dublin to West Cork after work. Your manager has been on annual leave for the last week. He left you work to do for the week, including researching a tax issue for a client. He has advised you that you are to have an answer to the issue by the time he returns, no matter how long it takes. It actually took you a very short time and you have it all documented for him.

   Your friend who is travelling with you asks if you could leave at 11am to beat the traffic and have a longer weekend. You have no annual leave left, so you cannot take leave. You know that if you leave, nobody will notice, but you have to complete a timesheet. Your friend reminds you that the research for the client could have taken a lot longer and that you could code the five hours to the client. What should you do?

Action

It would be unprofessional and would display a lack of integrity if you were to charge your client for those five hours.

Suggested Solutions to Review Questions

Chapter 1

Question 1.1

Income Tax Computation – Pat and Una 2016

	Pat €	Una €	Total €
Total income	<u>15,000</u>	<u>47,000</u>	<u>62,000</u>
Tax payable: (married persons)			
Una – First €42,800 @ 20%		8,560	8,560
Pat – €15,000 @ 20%	3,000		3,000
Una – Balance €4,200 @ 40%	_____	<u>1,680</u>	<u>1,680</u>
Gross income tax liability	3,000	10,240	13,240
Less: tax credits	_____	_____	<u>(6,600)</u>
Net tax due			**6,640**

Question 1.2

Income Tax Computation – Paul and Jason 2016

	Paul €	**Jason** €	**Total** €
Total income	<u>47,000</u>	<u>41,000</u>	<u>88,000</u>
Tax payable: (civil partners)			
First €67,600 @ 20%			13,520
Balance €20,400 @ 40%			<u>8,160</u>
Gross income tax liability			21,680
Less: tax credits			<u>(4,400)</u>
Net tax due			**17,280**

Question 1.3

Income Tax Computation of Seán and Norah 2016

	Total
	€
Total income	88,000
Tax payable: (married, one income)	
First €42,800 @ 20%	8,560
Balance €45,200 @ 40%	18,080
Gross income tax liability	26,640
Less: tax credits	(5,950)
Net tax due	**20,690**

Chapter 2

Question 2.1

(a) 2014

TEST 1:	Did Hank spend more than 30 days in Ireland in 2014?
ANSWER:	Yes, 226 days. Therefore, go to Test 2.
TEST 2:	Did Hank spend 183 days or more in Ireland in 2014?
ANSWER:	Yes; therefore, Hank is Irish resident for 2014.

(b) 2015

TEST 1:	Did Hank spend more than 30 days in Ireland in 2015?
ANSWER:	Yes, the full year. Therefore, go to Test 2.
TEST 2:	Did Hank spend 183 days or more in Ireland in 2015?
ANSWER:	Yes, the full year. Therefore, Hank is Irish resident in 2015.

(c) 2016

TEST 1:	Did Hank spend more than 30 days in Ireland in 2016?	
ANSWER:	Yes, 121 days. Therefore, go to Test 2.	
TEST 2:	Did Hank spend 183 days or more in Ireland in 2016?	
ANSWER:	No. Therefore, go to Test 3.	
TEST 3:	Number of days in Ireland in 2016 (if more than 30)	121
	Number of days in Ireland in 2015 (if more than 30)	365
	Total days in Ireland in current and previous years	468
QUESTION:	Did Hank spend 280 days or more in Ireland in 2015 and 2016?	
ANSWER:	Yes. Therefore, Hank is Irish resident in 2016.	
	(Note: split-year residence relief may be available. See **Section 2.7**.)	

Question 2.2

(a) 2013

TEST 1:	Did Kenji spend more than 30 days in Ireland in 2013?
ANSWER:	No, 15 days. Therefore, Kenji is not Irish resident for 2013.

(b) 2014

TEST 1:	Did Kenji spend more than 30 days in Ireland in 2014?
ANSWER:	Yes, the full year. Therefore, go to Test 2.
TEST 2:	Did Kenji spend 183 days or more in Ireland in 2014?
ANSWER:	Yes. Therefore Kenji is Irish resident in 2014.

(c) 2015

TEST 1:	Did Kenji spend more than 30 days in Ireland in 2015?
ANSWER:	Yes, the full year. Therefore, go to Test 2.
TEST 2:	Did Kenji spend 183 days or more in Ireland in 2015?
ANSWER:	Yes. Therefore Kenji is Irish resident in 2015.

(d) 2016

TEST 1:	Did Kenji spend more than 30 days in Ireland in 2016?
ANSWER:	No, 16 days. Therefore, Kenji is not Irish resident in 2016.

Question 2.3

Tax Year	Resident	Ordinarily Resident
2015	Yes > 183 days	No
2016	Yes > 183 days	No
2017	Yes > 183 days	No
2018	No – fails 30-day test	Yes, as resident for three preceding years

For the years 2015 to 2018, Aurore is resident in Ireland and will be taxed on both her Irish salary and her salary paid in France if the latter is paid in respect of the performance of her duties as an employee in Ireland. The salary paid in France does not have to be remitted to be liable to tax in Ireland; it must be connected to the performance of Aurore's employment duties in the State. Any other foreign income will only be taxed to the extent that it is remitted to the State.

For the tax year 2018, Aurore will be taxed on her Irish income, and on other income paid into the State, but will not pay tax on her French salary or other non-Irish income where it does not exceed €3,810 in the year. Aurore will continue to be ordinarily resident in Ireland until she has been non-resident for three years, i.e. until 2021.

Question 2.4

As Mr Harris is neither Irish resident nor Irish domiciled, he is liable only on income arising in Ireland and is not entitled to the married persons tax bands and has a reduced entitlement to any tax credits.

	€
Schedule D, Case V	<u>37,000</u>
€33,800 @ 20%	6,760
<u>€3,200</u> @ 40%	<u>1,280</u>
€37,000	
	8,040
Less: tax deducted at source from rent paid	<u>(7,400)</u>
Tax due	<u>640</u>

Question 2.5

SARP Relief 2016:

Is relevant income > €50,000 (€75,000 × 8/12ths)?

Salary €250,000 > €50,000 (€75,000 × 8/12ths), therefore eligible for SARP relief

Calculation of specified amount:

	€
Total income	272,500
Less: lower threshold (€75,000 × 8/12ths)	<u>(50,000)</u>
	<u>222,500</u>
Specified amount @ 30%	<u>66,750</u>
Total income	272,500
Less: specified amount	<u>(66,750)</u>
Taxable income	<u>205,750</u>

Note: as Mr Klaus has paid PAYE on his total income, he will need to make a claim for a tax repayment of €66,750 @ 40% = €26,700.

Chapter 3

Question 3.1

Year of Assessment		Basis	Original Figure €	Final Figure €
2015	1st Year:	Actual 01/06/2015 – 31/12/2015 7/12 × €48,000	28,000	N/A
2016	2nd Year:	12-month accounting period ending in tax year 01/06/2015 – 31/05/2016	48,000	N/A
2017	3rd Year:	12-month accounting period ending in the year of assessment – year ended 31/05/2017	39,000	33,750 Note
2018	4th Year:	12-month accounting period ending in the year of assessment – year ended 31/05/2018	37,200	N/A

Note: amount assessed in the second year (2016)		48,000
Less: Actual profits for the second year (2016)		
	(€48,000 × 5/12) + (€39,000 × 7/12)	<u>42,750</u>
	Excess	<u>5,250</u>
Final 2017 assessment: €39,000 – €5,250		<u>33,750</u>

Question 3.2

Year of Assessment	Basis	Initial Figure €	Final Figure €
2015	1st Year: Actual 01/05/2015 – 31/12/2015 €44,800 + (2/12 × €54,400)	53,867	N/A
2016	2nd Year: 12-month accounting period ending in tax year y/e 31/10/2016	54,400 Note	N/A
2017	3rd Year: 12-month accounting period ending in tax year y/e 31/10/2017	53,600	53,467

Note: amount assessed in the second year (2016)	54,400	
Less: Actual profits for the second year		
(€54,400 × 10/12) + (€53,600 × 2/12)	<u>54,267</u>	
Excess	<u>133</u>	

As the amount assessed for the second year exceeds the actual profits for the second year, a claim may be made for a deduction of €133 against the profits of the third year of assessment (2017):

y/e 31/10/2017	53,600
Excess for 2016	<u>(133)</u>
Final assessment	<u>53,467</u>

Question 3.3

Case II Assessments

		€
1st Tax Year 2015	01/05/2015 – 31/12/2015	
	8/12 × €48,000	<u>32,000</u>
2nd Tax Year 2016	12-month accounting period ending in tax year y/e 30/04/2016	<u>48,000</u> Note
3rd Tax Year 2017	Y/e 30/04/2017	<u>60,000</u>
4th Tax Year 2018	Y/e 30/04/2018	<u>9,600</u>

Note: profits assessable for second year, i.e. 2015: 48,000

Actual profits for second year 2016: (€48,000 × 4/12) + (€60,000 × 8/12) = 56,000

Therefore no reduction for third year, 2017.

Question 3.4

Case I Assessments

		€
1st Tax Year 2016	01/05/2016 – 31/12/2016	
	8/12 × €179,400	<u>119,600</u>
2nd Tax Year 2017	12-month accounting period ending	
	in tax year y/e 30/04/2017	179,400

Donna Ross		**2016**		**2017**
Income Tax Computation for 2016 and 2017		**€**		**€**
Schedule D, Case I		119,600		179,400
Schedule E salary		<u>20,300</u>		–
Total income		139,900		179,400
Tax payable – single parent:				
€37,800 @ 20%		7,560		7,560
Balance @ 40%	(€102,100)	40,840	(€141,600)	56,640
Deduct: tax credits		(4,950)		(3,850)
PAYE paid		<u>(3,902)</u>		–
Income tax due		39,548		60,350

MEMO

To: Donna Ross   **Date: 3 January 2018**

cc:

From: Your Accountant   Re: Taxable Trading

I refer to our meeting last week. I have calculated your income tax liability for 2016 and 2017 at €39,548 and €60,350, respectively. The computations are attached.

I have considered the facts around your eBay activity for 2014 and 2015. To be liable to income tax, your eBay activity must constitute trading. There is no definition of trading in the Irish income tax legislation (TCA 1997), and guidance is available in case law and from the UK Royal Commission Rules. The rules or "Badges of Trade" help determine if your activity constitutes trading for Irish tax purposes. These are:

"Badges of Trade"	Your circumstances
Subject matter – if ownership does not give income or personal enjoyment, then sales indicate trading.	As your sales were of items bought originally for your enjoyment, this is not indicative of trading.
Length of ownership – short period indicates trading.	The 2015 job lot purchase and sale had a very quick turnaround, indicating trading.
Frequency – more over a long period indicates trading.	Transactions appear infrequent and opportunistic, not indicative of trading.
Supplementary work indicates trading.	As you didn't have an eBay "shop" until 2016, there is no indication of an effort to obtain customers.
Circumstances, if opportunistic or unsolicited, refute trading.	Sales until 2016 were opportunistic and the items sold personal in nature. This would counteract the trading suggestion.
Motive.	The evidence suggests the activity was merely a hobby until the business was established in 2016.

In deciding if trading is carried on, all rules are evaluated and the whole picture is taken into account. The overriding evidence in your case suggests that no trading took place during 2014 and 2015, and the activity involved was an attempt to de-clutter your home. However, for 2016 and 2017 you would be considered to be trading and therefore subject to Irish income tax on the income derived from your eBay sales.

Question 3.5

Year of Assessment	Original Basis Period	Original Figures €	Revised Figures €	
2014	Year ended 31/05/2014	64,000	N/A	
2015	Year ended 31/05/2015	72,000	N/A	(Note 1)
2016	Actual 01/01/2016–31/12/2016	16,000	N/A	(Note 2)

Notes:
1. Actual profits 2015
   (€72,000 × 5/12) + (€9,600 × 7/12) = €35,600, therefore no revision.
2. Actual: 01/01/2016−31/12/2016 = €12,000 + (5/12 × €9,600) = €16,000

Question 3.6

Year of Assessment	Original Basis Period	Original Figures €	Revised Figures €	
2014	Year ended 31/07/2014	32,000	N/A	
2015	Year ended 31/07/2015	60,000	N/A	(Note 1)
2016	Actual 01/01/2016–31/05/2016	20,000	N/A	(Note 2)

Notes:

1. Actual profits 2015
    (€60,000 × 7/12) + (€40,000 × 5/10) = €55,000

    Therefore, original assessment will not be revised.

2. Actual profits 01/01/2016−31/05/2016
    €40,000 × 5/10 = €20,000

Question 3.7

			€
Final year 2016	01/01/2016–30/09/2016	9/12 × €240,000	180,000
Penultimate year 2015	01/01/2015–31/12/2015	(Note)	78,000

Note: actual profit 2015: (€24,000 × 9/12) + (€240,000 × 3/12) = €78,000

This figure will be assessed for 2015, as it is higher than the profits for the y/e 30/09/2015 of €24,000 which would have been originally assessed.

Alex	€
Income Tax Computation for 2016	
Schedule D, Case I	180,000
Schedule E salary	15,000
Total income	195,000
Tax payable – single person:	
€33,800 @ 20%	6,760
Balance @ 40% (€161,200)	64,480
	71,240
Deduct: tax credits	(3,300)
PAYE paid	(3,485)
Income tax due	64,455

Question 3.8

As J. Cog retired on 30 September 2016, his last year of assessment is 2016. The requirement is therefore to calculate his assessable income for 2015 and 2016. The tax years 2013 and 2014 don't change.

		€
2016	9/11 × 24,000 (9 months to 30/09/2016)	19,636
2015	y/e 31/10/2015	64,000 (Note)
2014	y/e 31/10/2014	65,000 – no change
2013	y/e 31/10/2013	40,000 – no change

Note: actual profit 2015: (€64,000 × 10/12) + (€24,000 × 2/11) = €57,697. The 2015 assessment will therefore not be revised to an actual basis.

Question 3.9

Distribution of Profits

	Total €	Alex €	Bill €	Colin €
Year ended 30/09/2012	20,000	10,000	10,000	Nil
Year ended 30/09/2013	25,000	10,000	10,000	5,000
Year ended 30/09/2014	30,000	12,000	12,000	6,000
Year ended 30/09/2015	30,000	Nil	15,000	15,000
Year ended 30/09/2016	35,000	Nil	17,500	17,500

Assessments will be raised as follows:

Alex	Yr of Assessment	Final Basis Period	Profits Assessable €
	2012	y/e 30/09/2012	10,000
	2013	Actual (Note)	10,500
	2014 Cessation	01/01/2014–30/09/2014 (€12,000 × 9/12)	9,000

Note: 2013 actual profits: (€10,000 × 9/12) + (€12,000 × 3/12) = €10,500. As this is higher than profits of the original basis period y/e 30/09/2013, the assessment will be revised and actual profits will be assessed.

Bill	Yr of Assessment	Final Basis Period	Profits Assessable €
	2012	y/e 30/09/2012	10,000
	2013	y/e 30/09/2013	10,000
	2014	y/e 30/09/2014	12,000
	2015	y/e 30/09/2015	15,000
	2016	y/e 30/09/2016	17,500

Colin	Yr of Assessment	Basis Period	Profits Assessable €
	2012 Commencement	01/10/2012–31/12/2012 (3/12 × €5,000)	1,250
	2013	y/e 30/09/2013	5,000
	2014	y/e 30/09/2014 (Note)	6,000
	2015	y/e 30/09/2015	15,000
	2016	y/e 30/09/2016	17,500

Note: 2013 actual profits: (€5,000 × 9/12) + (€6,000 × 3/12) = €5,250. As this is greater than the profits assessable for the second year, the third year does not require amendment.

Question 3.10

Allocation of profits

	June €	Mary €	Karen €	Jill €	Louise €	Total €
Y/e 30/06/2012	16,000	12,000	12,000			40,000
Y/e 30/06/2013	24,000	18,000	18,000			60,000
Y/e 30/06/2014	21,600	16,200		16,200		54,000
Y/e 30/06/2015	20,000	15,000		15,000		50,000
Y/e 30/06/2016	9,000	9,000		9,000	9,000	36,000
Six months to 31/12/2016	5,000	5,000		5,000	5,000	20,000

2012		**€**
June:	year ended 30/06/2012	16,000
Mary:	year ended 30/06/2012	12,000
Karen:	Actual (Note 1)	15,000
2013		
June:	Year ended 30/06/2013	24,000
Mary:	Year ended 30/06/2013	18,000
Karen:	Actual (Note 2) (cessation)	9,000
Jill:	Actual (Note 3) (commencement)	8,100
2014		
June:	year ended 30/06/2014	21,600
Mary:	year ended 30/06/2014	16,200
Jill:	year ended 30/06/2014	16,200
2015		
June:	year ended 30/06/2015 (Note 6)	20,000
Mary:	year ended 30/06/2015 (Note 6)	15,000
Jill:	(Note 4)	14,400
Louise:	Actual (Note 5) (commencement)	4,500
2016	(year of cessation – all partners on actual basis)	
June:	01/01/2016 – 30/06/2016 (€9,000 × 6/12)	4,500
	01/07/2016 – 31/12/2016	5,000
		9,500
Mary:	As above	9,500
Jill:	As above	9,500
Louise:	As above	9,500

continued overleaf

Note 1:

Karen:	2012: original assessment: y/e 30/06/2012	<u>12,000</u>
	Actual profits 2012:	
	(€12,000 × 6/12) + (€18,000 × 6/12)	<u>15,000</u>
	Penultimate year revised to actual	

Note 2:

| Karen: | 2013: final year actual: 01/01/2013 – 30/06/2013 | |
| | €18,000 × 6/12 | <u>9,000</u> |

Note 3:

| Jill: | 2013 first year actual €16,200 × 6/12 | <u>8,100</u> |

Note 4:

Jill:	Second year 2014: assessment y/e 30/06/2014	
	Actual profit for second year:	16,200
	(€16,200 × 6/12) + (€15,000 × 6/12)	<u>(15,600)</u>
	Excess	600
	Final third year assessment:	
	€15,000 – €600	<u>14,400</u>

Note 5:

| Louise: | 2015: First year actual: €9,000 × 6/12 = €4,500 |

Note 6:

There will be no revision of 2015 (penultimate year) profits to actual as actual profits were less than those assessed, i.e.:

> June actual 2015 (€20,000 × 6/12) + (€9,000 × 6/12) = €14,500
> Mary actual 2015 (€15,000 × 6/12) + (€9,000 × 6/12) = €12,000
> Jill actual 2015 – as for Mary €12,000

Question 3.11

Income Tax Computation of Maeve 2016

		€
Schedule D, Case IV (Note 1)		13,932
Schedule E SW		11,976
Schedule F dividends (Note 2)		<u>23,900</u>
Total income		<u>49,808</u>
Tax payable:	Deposit interest €13,932 @ 41%	5,712
(widowed without dependent children)	€33,800 @ 20%	6,760
	Balance €2,076 @ 40%	<u>830</u>
	Gross income tax liability	<u>13,302</u>

continued overleaf

Less: tax credits		(2,740)
Less: DIRT paid		(5,712)
Less: DWT paid		(4,780)
Tax due		70

Note 1: Schedule D, Case IV		Gross	DIRT @ 41%
		€	€
PTSB	€6,300/0.59	10,678	4,378
Credit Union	€1,200/0.59	2,034	834
Long-term interest account	€720/0.59	1,220	500
		13,932	5,712

Note 2: Schedule F dividends		Gross	DWT @ 20%
		€	€
Tyson	€17,520/0.80	21,900	4,380
Holyfield	€1,600/0.80	2,000	400
		23,900	4,780

Chapter 4

Question 4.1

Computation of Tax-adjusted Case I Profit y/e 31 December 2016		€	€
Profit per accounts			9,874
	Add: Drawings (Note)	8,500	
	Interest on VAT	1,121	
	Interest on PAYE	1,238	
	Depreciation	13,793	
	Subscription (political, football, old folks, sports)	525	
	Repairs (€6,480 – €2,335)	4,145	
	Bad debts – increase in general provision (€7,975 – €5,100)	2,875	
	Legal fees (capital)	1,009	33,206
			43,080
Deduct:	Dividend from Irish Co.	2,813	
	National loan stock interest	2,250	
	Deposit interest	170	
	Profit on fixed assets	5,063	(10,296)
Case I profit			**32,784**

Note: disallow Mr Murphy's salary of €7,500 and the €1,000 holiday trip as these are drawings.

Question 4.2

Computation of Tax-adjusted Case I Profit y/e 31 December 2016		€
Net profit before taxation		36,050
Add:	**Disallowed Expenses:**	
	Motor vehicles (Note)	2,400
	Depreciation – Equipment	2,500
	– Vehicles	3,000
	– Office Equipment	900
	Construction of garages (capital)	3,150
	General bad debt provision	275
	Drawings	20,000
	Entertainment – Holiday	1,200
	– Tickets (non-business)	300
	– Customer business meals	<u>1,200</u>
Case I Tax-adjusted profit		**<u>70,975</u>**

Note: disallowed motor expenses	€
Expenses for Andy Reilly's car	4,000
Disallow personal element 60% × €4,000	2,400

Question 4.3

(a) Computation of adjusted profit for the 15 months ended 31 December 2016 and the 12 months ended 31 December 2017:

	15 months ended 31/12/2016		12 months ended 31/12/2017	
	€	€	€	€
Net loss per accounts		(4,350)		(7,400)
Disallow:				
Depreciation	3,000		2,400	
General provision for bad debts	2,500		(2,500)	
Entertaining	1,500		700	
Political donations	100			
Charitable donations	50			
Interest on late payment of VAT	250		–	
Drawings	<u>15,000</u>		<u>12,000</u>	
		<u>22,400</u>		<u>12,600</u>
Adjusted profit		**<u>18,050</u>**		**<u>5,200</u>**

(b) Tony's Case I taxable profit for 2016:

2016 is Tony's second tax year of trading. An accounting period for a period in excess of 12 months ends in that year, namely the 15-month period ending 31 December 2016. Accordingly, Tony is taxable on the profits for the year ending on 31 December 2016. Taxable Case I profits for 2016 are therefore €18,050 × 12/15 = €14,440.

Question 4.4

Computation of Adjusted Profit for the 12 Months ended 30 April 2017	€	€
Profit per accounts		2,820
Disallow:		
Drawings (wages to self)	5,200	
Own PRSI	200	
Depreciation	1,250	
Motor expenses (Note 1)	924	
Leasing charges (Note 2)	1,994	
Extension	1,500	
Provision for repairs	1,000	
Interest on late payment of tax	120	
Covenant to church (Note 3)	260	
Covenant to son	710	
Retirement annuity premiums	1,100	
Life assurance	460	
		14,718
		17,538
Less: Interest received		(390)
Adjusted trading profits		**17,148**

Note 1:

		Add back
Motor expenses	1,860	
Less: parking fine	(100)	100
	1,760	
Plus car insurance	300	
	2,060	
Less: private element 40%	(824)	824
	1,236	
Total disallowed		924

continued overleaf

Note 2:

		Add back
Lease charges on car	2,800	
Less: private element 40%	(1,120)	1,120
Lease charges restriction (category D):	1,680	
$1,680 \times \dfrac{(25,000 - (24,000 \times 50\%))}{25,000}$		874
		1,994

Note 3: a donation made to an eligible charity is not a deduction from Case I or Case II income.

Note 4: the accrued bonus for the sales assistant should be added back if it remains unpaid six months after the year end.

Question 4.5

Computation of Adjusted Profit for the Year Ended 31 December 2016	€	€
Profit per accounts		22,000
Disallow:		
Wages to self	8,000	
Light, heat and telephone (5/6 × 1,500)	1,250	
Repairs and renewals (extension to shop and general provision)	3,400	
Legal and professional fees	300	
Bad debts (decrease in general reserve)	(600)	
Travel and entertainment (Note 1)	1,100	
Lease interest (Note 3)	2,000	
Sundries (Note 2)	1,549	
		16,999
Allow:		
Lease repayments (Note 3)		(18,600)
Case I adjusted profits year ended 31/12/2016		**16,999**

Notes:

1. **Travel and entertainment**	€
Motor expenses (private 1/3 × €1,500)	500
Entertaining customers	600
	1,100

2. **Sundries**	
Political party	1,000
Parking fines	49
Charitable donation	500
	1,549

continued overleaf

3. **Lease interest**

	€
Deduct: total repayments for the year (allowable)	18,600
Add back: lease interest deducted from profit	2,000

Question 4.6

Case II Computation of Adjusted Profit	€	€	€
Net profit y/e 30/01/2016		46,000	
Add back:			
Disallowed expenses	26,000		
Partner salaries	41,000		
Partner interest	13,000	80,000	
Assessable profit		126,000	

Partnership Allocation	Total	Jack	John
Salaries (actual)	41,000	20,000	21,000
Interest (actual)	13,000	6,000	7,000
Balance (50:50)	72,000	36,000	36,000
Total	126,000	62,000	64,000
Case II taxable profits for 2016		**62,000**	**64,000**

Question 4.7

Income Tax Computation 2016		Notes	€	€
Income:				
Schedule D:	Case III – Anthony	(1)		900
	Case IV – Anthony	(2)	310	
	Case IV – Sandrine (Dresdner Bank)		2,000	2,310
Schedule E:	Anthony		50,000	
	Sandrine		28,000	78,000
Schedule F:	Gross dividend	(3)		3,125
Total/taxable income				84,335
Tax payable (married, two incomes):				
	€2,310 @ 41%		947	
	€67,600 @ 20%		13,520	
	€14,425 @ 40%		5,770	20,237

continued overleaf

Deduct:	Tax credits	9,900	
	DIRT paid: €310 @ 41%	<u>127</u>	<u>(10,027)</u>
Net Tax Liability			<u>10,210</u>
Deduct:	PAYE paid – Anthony		(5,800)
	PAYE paid – Sandrine		(4,000)
	DWT		<u>(625)</u>
Tax refundable			<u><u>215</u></u>

Notes:

	€
1. Case III income:	
UK dividends net of UK tax	900
2. Case IV income:	
Credit Union interest, ordinary deposit account	80
Credit Union interest, medium-term share account	100
AIB interest, ordinary deposit account	<u>130</u>
	<u>310</u>

Dresdner Bank interest of €2,000 is treated as Case IV and taxed at the DIRT rate of 41%.

	€
3. Schedule F income:	
Dividends net of DWT	2,500
DWT @ 20%	<u>625</u>
Gross	<u>3,125</u>

Question 4.8

David Lee – Income Tax 2016	€	€
Schedule D, Case III		
Interest on Government stock		1,130
Schedule D, Case IV: €500 + €140 + €29 = €669 @ 100/59		1,134
Schedule E salary		<u>42,000</u>
Taxable income		<u>44,264</u>
Tax payable:		
€37,800 @ 20%		7,560
€1,134 @ 41%		465

continued overleaf

€5,330 @ 40%		2,132
€44,264		
		10,157
Deduct: personal tax credits	4,950	
DIRT paid €1,134 @ 41%	465	(5,415)
Tax liability		4,742
PAYE deducted		(4,637)
Tax payable		€105

Note: interest from Post Office Savings Certificates is ignored as these are exempt.

Question 4.9

			Properties		
		A	B	C	D
Case V	Notes	Res. €	Comm. €	Res. €	Res. €
Rent receivable during 2016		6,000	5,000	3,500	52
Premium on lease	(1)		6,000		–
		6,000	11,000	3,500	52
Less: Allowable expenses:	(2)				
Bank interest		(4,125)	(3,000)	–	–
Storm damage		–	(1,400)	–	–
Advertising		–	–	(130)	–
Roof repairs		–	–	–	(160)
Blocked drains and painting		–	–	(790)	–
Net rents		1,875	6,600	2,580	(108)
Summary:	(3)				
Property A				1,875	
Property B				6,600	
Property C				2,580	
Net assessable Case V 2016				€11,055	

Notes:

1. Rent Receivable

    Property A

    Although the rent for December was not received until after the end of the tax year, it is still taken into account in 2016 as Case V is assessed on rents receivable.

    Property B

    Let from 1 August 2016, i.e. 5 months @ €1,000 per month = €5,000

    Premium on lease:

    Assessable portion of premium: $€10,000 \times \dfrac{51 - 21}{50} = €6,000$

    Property C

€6,000 × 4/12 = 2,000	(4 months to 30 April)
€9,000 × 2/12 = 1,500	(2 months to 31 December)
3,500	

2. Allowable Expenses

    Property A

    As the property is registered with the PRTB, a deduction for interest is allowable. However, section 97 TCA 1997 restricts the allowable interest on rental residential properties to 75% of the amount incurred. Therefore, the interest allowable is:

    €5,500 × 75% = €4,125

    Property B

    Pre-letting expenses are not allowable. These include bank interest paid in June 2016 of €1,800 and the interest relating to the period 1 July 2016 to 31 July 2016.

    Interest charge restriction:

    $(€3,600 \times \dfrac{5}{6}) = €3,000$

    Expenses incurred in April and June are also disallowed as those are pre-letting expenses.

    Property C

    Although the property was vacant when the expenditure was incurred, this was only a temporary period of vacancy and the expenditure is allowed in full.

3. Summary

    Losses on one property may be offset against the rental profits arising on other properties. However, the loss arising on Property D is ignored for tax purposes as it is a "favoured" letting.

Question 4.10

(a) Property Income Assessable 2016

Rent Account 2016

	Property 1	Property 2	Property 3	Property 4
	€	€	€	€
Gross rents	16,000	8,000	9,600	4,500
Expenses	(4,300)	(1,200)	(800)	–
Interest	–	–	(1,400)	–
Net rents	11,700	6,800	7,400	4,500
Case V 2016	30,400			

Notes:

1. The rent to be brought into account is that receivable in the tax year 2016 whether or not rent is actually received in the year, i.e. for Property 4 = 6/12 × €9,000.
2. The income from Property 5 is excluded on the grounds that the rent receivable under the lease, taking one year with another, is not sufficient to meet the allowable expenses connected with the property and it is an uneconomic letting. Losses may be accumulated and set off against future rental income from that property only.
3. Because all properties are commercial, there is no restriction to the interest and there is no requirement to register Property 3 with the PRTB in order to claim a deduction for the interest paid.

(b) Tax Effects of Investments

(i) *National Instalment Savings Scheme*
Any bonus or interest payable to an individual under an instalment savings scheme is exempt from income tax.

(ii) *Government Securities*
Interest on Government securities is paid without deduction of tax and, accordingly, is assessable under Schedule D, Case III on an actual basis.

Question 4.11

Tax-free Element of Lump Sum

		€	€
1.	Basic exemption: €10,160 + (€765 × 18)		23,930
2.	May be increased to:		
	Basic exemption		23,930
	Plus:	10,000	
	Less: tax-free lump sum from pension scheme	(3,000)	7,000
			30,930
3.	May be further increased to SCSB, if greater:		

$$SCSB = \frac{(A \times B)}{15} - C$$

A = average of last three years' emoluments

B = number of complete years of service

C = tax-free lump sum from pension scheme

Therefore:

$$A = \frac{(€52,000 + €55,000 + €57,000)}{3} = €54,667$$

B = 18 years

C = €3,000

$$SCSB = \left(€54,667 \times \frac{18}{15}\right) - €3,000 = €62,600$$

As SCSB results in the highest figure, the tax-free element of the lump sum is €62,600.

Therefore the taxable element is €2,400 (€65,000 − €62,600).

Income Tax Liability 2016 – Mr Houghton

		€	€
Schedule E:	Salary €57,000 × 6/12		28,500
	Pension €18,000 × 6/12		9,000
	Termination payment	65,000	
	SCSB	(62,600)	2,400
Total/taxable income			39,900
Tax payable:			
	€33,800 @ 20%		6,760
	€6,100 @ 40%		2,440
	€39,900		
			9,200
Deduct:	Tax credits		(3,300)
Net tax liability			5,900
Deduct:	PAYE paid		(4,940)
Tax due			**960**

Question 4.12

1. Basic exemption €10,160 − (€765 × 18) = €23,930.

2. Increased basic exemption − not available as the tax-free pension lump sum of €19,000 received exceeds €10,000.

3. SCSB

$$A = \frac{37,250 + 34,500 + 32,625}{3} = €34,792$$

$B = 18$ years

$C = €19,000$

$$\left(€34,792 \times \frac{18}{15}\right) - 19,000 = €22,750$$

As the basic exemption is higher than the SCSB, this is the exempt amount.

Lump sum	€30,000
Less: basic exemption	(€23,930)
Taxable lump sum	€6,070

Income Tax Computation 2016 – Mr Moran		€	€
Schedule E:	Salary	28,500	
	Taxable lump sum	6,070	
Taxable income			34,570
Tax @ 20%		6,914	
Deduct tax credits		(4,950)	
Net tax liability			1,964
PAYE deducted			(750)
Tax due			1,214

Question 4.13

Income Tax 2016 – Mr Lynch

		€	€
Schedule E:	Salary		43,000
	Termination payment (Note 1)	30,000	
	Exempt (Note 1)	(27,810)	2,190
Total/taxable income			45,190
Tax payable:	€33,800 @ 20%		6,760
	€11,390 @ 40%		4,556
	€45,190		
			11,316

continued overleaf

Deduct:	Tax credits	(3,840)
Net tax liability		7,476
Deduct:	PAYE paid	(6,600)
Income tax payable		**876**

Note 1. Lump sum: €30,000

Exemption: (a) €10,160 + (€765 × 10)	€17,810
(b) Increased basic exemption	€10,000
Total (a) + (b)	€27,810

(c) SCSB 10/15 × (43,000 + 35,000 + 30,000) ÷ 3

$$= 10/15 \times \frac{108,000}{3} = €24,000$$

As SCSB is lower than the increased basic exemption, the taxable element is €30,000 less increased exemption of €27,810 = €2,190.

Pension contributions refund: these have been taxed at 20% under the usual arrangement and the figures will not impinge upon the computation of liability.

Question 4.14

(a) Taxable Element of Lump Sum

		€
(i)	Basic exemption €10,160 + (€765 × 15)	21,635
(ii)	May be increased by €10,000 less tax-free lump sum from pension scheme	
	Increased exemption	10,000
	Less: tax-free lump sum from pension	Nil
		10,000
	Increased basic exemption	31,635
(iii)	May be further increased to SCSB if greater.	

$$SCSB = \frac{A \times B}{15} - C$$

A = average of last three years' salary	
Year ended 30/09/2016	47,000
Year ended 30/09/2015	54,000
Year ended 30/09/2014	52,000
	153,000
Average (total ÷ 3)	51,000

continued overleaf

B = number of complete years of service = 15 years

C = tax-free lump sum from pension scheme = Nil

SCSB = €51,000 × 15/15   51,000

As SCSB is greater than the increased basic exemption, the taxable
element of the lump sum is: €57,000 – €51,000   €6,000

(b) Mr Flynn Income Tax Liability 2016

Income:		€	€
Schedule E:			
Salary from old job	€47,000 × 9/12	35,250	
Unemployment Benefit (Note 1)	(€188 – €13 = €175 × 8)	1,400	
Holiday pay		2,000	
Salary from new job		2,500	
Benefit in kind	€2,000 × 1/12	167	41,317
Lump sum		57,000	
Less: SCSB exempt amount		(51,000)	6,000
Taxable income			47,317
Tax payable:			
€42,800 @ 20%		8,560	
€4,517 @ 40%		1,807	10,367
€47,317			
Less: Non-refundable Tax Credits:			
Personal tax credits			(4,950)
Tax liability			5,417
Deduct: PAYE paid			(3,030)
Net tax payable			**2,387**

Note 1: the first €13 of weekly benefit is not taxable.

Question 4.15

(a) (i)   Basic exemption €10,160 + (€765 × 15) = €21,635

(ii)   Increased basic exemption not available as tax-free pension lump sum of €22,000 receivable exceeds €10,000.

(iii) SCSB

$$A = \frac{48,900 + 38,000 + 42,100}{3} = €43,000$$

B = 15 years

C = €22,000

$$\left(43,000 \times \frac{15}{15}\right) - 22,000 = €21,000$$

As the basic exemption is higher than the SCSB, €21,635 is the tax-free termination payment that can be made to Dermot O'Donnell.

Calculation of the lump sum:

	€
Compensation payment	40,500
Car	22,500
Lump sum	63,000
Less: basic exemption	(21,635)
Taxable lump sum	41,365

(b) Dermot O'Donnell Income Tax Computation 2016	€	€
Schedule E: Salary to September (Point 2)	37,000	
Holiday pay (Point 1)	1,200	
Salary to year end (Point 3)	4,200	
Taxable lump sum	41,365	
Taxable income		83,765
Tax payable:		
€37,800 @ 20%	7,560	
€46,965 @ 40%	18,386	25,946
€83,765		
Deduct: tax credits		(4,950)
Net tax liability		20,996
PAYE deducted (€3,500 + €100)		(3,600)
Tax payable		**17,396**

Note: statutory redundancy is not taxable.

Question 4.16

(a) Calculation of Taxable Benefit in Kind

Car:

	€
OMV = €35,000	
Rate for 26,400 business km 24%	8,400

Deduct: fuel and insurance reimbursed	(1,300)
Sid's personal contribution €100 × 12	(1,200)
Final benefit in kind	5,900

Free use of apartment:

Annual value 8% × €110,000	8,800
Add: expenses paid by company	890
	9,690

Meals − exempt as provided free of charge to all staff.
Loan − waiver of loan is treated as additional benefit in February 2016 of €1,000.
Loan interest − $1,000 \times 13.5\% \times \dfrac{1 \text{ month}}{12 \text{ months}} = €11$

(b) **Income Tax Computation For 2016**			€	€
Schedule E income:				
Salary 2016				40,000
Round sum expense allowance: €100 × 12				1,200
Benefit in kind:	Car		5,900	
	Apartment above		9,690	
	Meals		Exempt	15,590
Perquisites:	Loan waived		1,000	
	Deemed interest paid			
12 months	$€1,000 \times 13.5\% \times \dfrac{1 \text{ month}}{12 \text{ months}}$		11	1,011
Gross income				57,801
Tax payable (single):	€33,800 @ 20%		6,760	
	€24,001 @ 40%		9,600	
	€57,801			
			16,360	
Deduct: basic personal tax credit			(3,300)	13,060
Deduct: PAYE paid				(13,900)
Tax refund due				**(840)**

Question 4.17

(a) **Benefit in kind – Rich Bank plc**

	€	
Mortgage Loan:		
€125,000 @ 4%	5,000	
Less: €125,000 @ 2%	(2,500)	Actual interest paid
Benefit in kind assessable	2,500	
Preferential Loan:		
Golf Club loan €10,000 @ 13.5%	1,350	
Company Car:		
Cash equivalent percentage	18%	
(Business Km 36,000)		
€30,000 @ 18%	5,400	
Less: reimbursement by employee 10,400 @ 15c	(1,560)	
Benefit in kind assessable	3,840	

Taxable benefits:

Mortgage loan	€2,500
Other loan	€1,350
Golf club membership	€3,500
Car	€3,840
Total benefits assessable in 2016	€11,190

PAYE payable @ 40%   €4,476 = cost of benefits provided

(b) Terry – Income Tax Computation 2016	**New Job**	**Current Job**
	€	€
Schedule E salary	70,000	75,000
Benefit in kind	11,190	0
Taxable income	81,190	75,000
Tax payable (married, one income):		
€42,800 @ 20%	8,560	8,560
Balance @ 40%	(38,390)15,356	(32,200)12,880
	23,916	21,440

continued overleaf

Deduct:

Personal tax credits	(5,950)	(5,950)
Net tax liability	17,966	15,490

Net Pay Calculation:

Salary	70,000	75,000
Deduct: tax	(17,966)	(15,490)
	52,034	59,510
Add: value of benefits:		
– Mortgage interest saved (Note 1)	3,750	0
– Car running costs (Note 2)	9,564	0
Value received by Terry	**65,348**	**59,510**

Note 1: Mortgage

Interest paid @ 5%	€125,000 @ 5%	6,250
Interest paid @ 2%	€125,000 @ 2%	(2,500)
Saving		3,750

Note 2: Car running costs

Estimate current costs	10,500
Less: reimbursed to bank (€1,560 – 40%)	(936)
Saving	9,564

Question 4.18

Mr Stodge – Income Tax Computation 2016

	€	€
Schedule E:		
Salary (actual)	41,600	
Salary (spouse)	5,500	
Sales commission (actual earnings basis)	6,000	
Lump sum expense allowance 12 × €100	1,200	
	54,300	
Schedule E expense claim (Note 1)	(10,675)	
Total/taxable income	43,625	

continued overleaf

Tax Payable (married, two incomes):

(€38,125 + €5,500 = €43,625) @ 20%	8,725	
Deduct: tax credits	(6,600)	
Net tax liability	2,125	
Deduct: PAYE paid (€4,900 + €230)	(5,130)	
Tax Refund due	(3,005)	

Note 1: Schedule E expense claim 2016

Motor car operating costs 2016	6,450	
Less: related to private use (10%)	(645)	
Allowable running costs		5,805
Lease charges:		
Total lease charges	5,700	
Less: personal element (10%)	(570)	
	5,130	

Less: restricted amount:

$5,130 \times (27,000 - \dfrac{24,000}{27,000})$	(570)	4,560

Other expenses tax year 2016:

Total per schedule		910	
Disallow:	Suits	(450)	
	Correspondence course	(150)	310
Total allowable Schedule E expenses			10,675

Note: as Philip's car is a category B car, there is no further restriction to the lease allowances based on CO_2 emissions.

Question 4.19

(a)   **Frank – Income Tax 2016: Current Arrangement**

	€	€
Schedule E		
Salary		50,000
Sales commission		8,000
		58,000
Schedule E expense claim:		
Motor expenses (Note 1)	6,944	

continued overleaf

Lease charges (Note 2)		0	(6,944)
Total/taxable income			51,056

Tax payable (single):

	€33,800 @ 20%	6,760	
	€17,256 @ 40%	6,902	13,662
	€51,056		
Deduct: tax credits			(3,300)
Tax liability			10,362

Note 1: *Allowable motor expenses*

Petrol		4,300
Insurance		1,500
Motor tax		1,480
Repairs and services		1,400
Disallow private €8,680 × $\dfrac{8,960 \text{ km}}{44,800 \text{ km}}$		8,680
		(1,736)
Allowable		6,944

Note 2: *Allowable lease charges*

Total lease charges		6,600
Disallow personal element		
$6,600 \times \dfrac{8,960 \text{ km}}{44,800 \text{ km}}$		(1,320)
Less: restriction (emissions Category F)		5,280
$5,280 \times \dfrac{(51,000 - 0)}{51,000}$		(5,280)
		0

(b) **Frank – Income Tax 2016: New Arrangement**

	€	€
Schedule E		
Salary		50,000
Sales commission (two-thirds)		5,333
BIK (Note)		5,580
Taxable total income		60,913

Tax payable:

€33,800 @ 20%	6,760	
€27,113 @ 40%	10,845	17,605
€60,913		
Deduct: tax credits		(3,300)
Tax liability		14,305

Note:

Benefit in kind – car	€31,000	
18% (business 35,840 Km)	€5,580	

After-tax position	Option (a)	Option (b)
Gross salary	58,000	55,333
Less: tax	(10,362)	(14,305)
Less: car running costs (€8,680 + €6,600)	(15,280)	0
Net cash	32,358	41,028

Conclusion: Frank has more disposable income under option (b).

Chapter 5

Question 5.1

Computation	Motor Vehicles 12.5% €	Plant and Equipment 12.5% €	Total €
Asset cost	*12,000	2,500	14,500
Additions 2016		4,500	4,500
Cost of assets qualifying for capital allowances	12,000	7,000	19,000
TWDV 01/01/2016	10,500	1,875	12,375
Additions y/e 30/04/2016			
(Basis period for 2016)		4,500	4,500
	10,500	6,375	16,875
Wear and tear 2016	(1,500)	(875)	(2,375)
TWDV 31/12/2016	9,000	5,500	14,500

*Cost €35,000 – restricted to €24,000. Wear and tear allowance for the car is further restricted by 50%, i.e. €1,500 as the car is a Category D car for CO_2 emissions.

Question 5.2

Year of Acquisition	Cost €	TWDV 01/01/2016 €	Wear and Tear 12.5% €	TWDV 31/12/2016 €
2013	15,000	9,375	(1,875)	7,500
2014	9,000	6,750	(1,125)	5,625
2016	5,100		(637)	4,463
		16,125	(3,637)	17,588

Question 5.3

Tax Year of Acquisition	Cost	TWDV 01/01/2016 €	Wear and Tear 12.5% €	TWDV 31/12/2016 €
2012	10,000	5,000	1,250	3,750
2016 assets not in use	2,300			2,300
2016	9,920	_____	1,240	8,680
		5,000	2,490	14,730

Note: the printer ink cartridges are not a capital item.

Question 5.4

Computation
First tax year for which business assessed: 2016
Basis period for 2016: 01/10/2016–31/12/2016

Second tax year for which business assessed: 2017
Basis period for 2017: 01/10/2016–30/09/2017

Asset bought and put into use during basis period for 2016.
Wear and tear allowances for 2016 and 2017 computed as follows:

	€	
Qualifying Cost	1,000	
Wear and tear 2016 @ 12.5% for 3 months (basis period for 2016)	(31)	$\left(12.5\% \times 1,000 \times \frac{3 \text{ months}}{12 \text{ months}}\right)$
TWDV as at 31 December 2016	969	
Wear and tear 2017 @ 12.5% (basis period 12 months)	(125)	
TWDV at 31 December 2017	844	

Question 5.5

Computation	€	
Qualifying cost	10,000	
Wear and tear 2016 @ 12.5% for 7 months (basis period for 2016)	(729)	$\left(12.5\% \times 10,000 \times \frac{7 \text{ months}}{12 \text{ months}}\right)$
TWDV 31/12/2016	9,271	
Wear and tear 2017 @ 12.5%	(1,250) (full year)	
TWDV 31/12/2017	8,021	

Question 5.6

Computation

Basis period for 2016: 01/05/2016 – 31/12/2016 (8 months)

Basis period for 2017: y/e 30/04/2017

		Plant and Machinery (12.5%) €
TWDV	01/01/2016	–
Additions (basis period for 2016)	01/05/2016–31/12/2016	9,000
Wear and tear 2016 (8 months)	€9,000 @ 12.5% × 8/12	(750)
TWDV 31/12/2016		8,250
Additions 01/01/2017 – 30/04/2017		1,700
		9,950
Wear and tear 2017 (Note)		(1,337)
TWDV 31/12/2017		8,613

Note: €9,000 + €1,700 = €10,700 @ 12.5% = €1,337

Question 5.7

	Motor Car (12.5% p.a.) €	Allow (3/4) €	
Cost (restricted by 50%) (Category D car)	10,500		
Wear and tear 2016 €10,500 @ 12.5%	(1,312)	984	(75%)
TWDV 31/12/2016	9,188		

Question 5.8

	Motor Vehicles (12.5%) €	Allow (2/3) €
Cost (restricted) 2016	24,000	
Wear and tear €24,000 @ 12.5%	(3,000)	2,000
TWDV 31/12/2016	21,000	

Car cost restricted to €24,000.

As the vehicle is emissions Category C, no emissions restriction applies.

Question 5.9

Allowances Computation for 2016

		Motor Car (12.5%)	Allow (70%)	Office Equipment (12.5%)
		€	€	€
TWDV @ 01/01/2016				7,500
Acquired in y/e 31/12/2016	(restricted)	24,000		1,000
Disposals 2016 @ TWDV				(7,500)
Wear and tear 2016		(3,000)	(2,100)	(125)
TWDV 31/12/2016		21,000		875

Car cost restricted to €24,000
As the car is emissions Category A, no emissions restriction arises.

Balancing Allowance (Charge) assessable:

Office equipment	€
TWDV 01/01/2016	7,500
Proceeds	(3,500)
Balancing allowance	4,000

Capital Allowance Claim	€
Wear and tear	2,225
Balancing allowance	4,000
Total 2016	6,225

Question 5.10

Capital Allowance Computation 2016

		€
Proceeds:	$20,000 \times \dfrac{24,000}{27,000}$	17,778
TWDV @ 01/01/2016 (Note)		(18,000)
Balancing allowance		222
Business use 70%		155

Note:	€
Motor car (Oct 2014) allowable cost	24,000
Wear and tear 2014	(3,000)
Wear and tear 2015	(3,000)
	18,000

Question 5.11

Capital Allowances Computation for 2016

	Plant (12.5%) €	Lorries (12.5%) €	Motor car* (12.5%) €	Total €
Cost at 01/01/2016	52,000	26,000	24,000	102,000
Additions at cost 2016	50,000	20,000	0	70,000
Disposals at cost 2016	(42,000)	0	0	(42,000)
Cost at 31/12/2016	60,000	46,000	24,000	130,000
TWDV 01/01/2016	8,750	0	15,000	23,750
Additions	50,000	20,000	0	70,000
	58,750	20,000	15,000	93,750
Disposals at TWDV	0	0	0	0
	58,750	20,000	15,000	93,750
Wear and tear:				
Allowance 2016	(7,500)	(2,500)	(3,000)	(13,000)
TWDV at 31/12/2016	51,250	17,500	12,000	80,750
Wear and tear:				
Allowance 2017	(7,500)	(2,500)	(3,000)	(13,000)
TWDV at 31/12/2017	43,750	15,000	9,000	67,750

Balancing Charge/Allowance 2016

TWDV of plant sold	0
Proceeds	2,200
Balancing charge	2,200

Cannot be offset as no replacement plant purchased.

Asset sold for €1,500 with a nil TWDV ignored as proceeds < €2,000.

Summary
2016 €

	€
Wear and tear: €7,500 + €2,500 + (€3,000 × 1/3)	11,000
Balancing charge	(2,200)
Total allowances	8,800

continued overleaf

2017

Wear and tear: €7,500 + €2,500 + (€3,000 × 1/3)		11,000
*Motor Car (12.5%)		
Cost 16/07/2012 i.e. y/e		
30/04/2013 (restricted)	24,000	
Wear and tear 2013	(3,000)	(restricted 1/3 for business use)
TWDV 31/12/2013	21,000	
Wear and tear 2014	(3,000)	(restricted 1/3 for business use)
TWDV 31/12/2014	18,000	
Wear and tear 2015	(3,000)	(restricted 1/3 for business use)
TWDV 31/12/2015	15,000	

Question 5.12

Assessable Profits

Tax Year	Basis Period	Profits
		€
2013	01/06/2013 – 31/12/2013	34,417 (7/12 × €59,000)
2014	Year ended 31/05/2014	59,000
2015	Year ended 31/05/2015	38,417 (Note)
2016	Year ended 31/05/2016	120,000

Note: profits assessable for the second year 2014:	59,000
Less: Actual profits (€59,000 × 5/12) + (€46,000 × 7/12)	51,417
Excess	7,583

Final third year 2015 assessment: €46,000 – €7,583 = €38,417

Capital Allowances Computation for 2016

	Equipment (12.5%) €	Car (12.5%) €	Allow (60%) €	Total €
Additions at Cost 2013:				
General equipment	26,000			26,000
Hairdryers	800			800
Additions at Cost 2014:				
Chairs	1,400			1,400
Motor car	0	14,000		14,000
Cost at 31/12/2016	28,200	14,000		42,200

continued overleaf

	Equipment (12.5%) €	Car (12.5%) €	Allow (60%) €	Total €
01/06/2013 – 31/12/2013:				
Additions	26,800	–	–	
Wear and tear (7 months)	(1,954)	–	–	(1,954)
TWDV 31/12/2013	24,846	–	–	
Additions 2014	1,400	14,000		
Wear and tear 2014	(3,525)	(1,750)	(1,050)	(4,575)
TWDV 31/12/2014	22,721	12,250		
Wear and tear 2015	(3,525)	(1,750)	(1,050)	(4,575)
TWDV 31/12/2015	19,196	10,500		
Wear and tear 2016	(3,525)	(1,750)	(1,050)	(4,575)
TWDV 31/12/2016	15,671	8,750		

Question 5.13

(a) Computation of taxable case/income for the year ended 31 December 2016

	€	€
Loss per accounts to 31 December 2016		(310)
Adjustments – add back:		
Wages to self (drawings)	5,200	
Motor expenses 25% × €1,750 (private element)	437	
Light and heat 25% × €1,200 (private element)	300	
Christmas gifts (entertainment – n/a)	300	
Depreciation	900	
Covenant	105	
Cash register (fixed asset)	380	
Deposit on shelving (fixed asset)	1,000	
Display freezer (fixed asset)	600	
Flat contents insurance (private element)	100	
Hire-purchase instalments	1,920	
Notional rent (drawings)	2,000	
		13,242
		12,932
Deduct: Hire-purchase charges		(376)
		12,556

continued overleaf

Deduct: Building society interest received		210		
Sale proceeds of equipment		1,500	(1,710)	
Adjusted profits			10,846	
Case I taxable income for 2016			10,846	

(b) Capital allowances claim 2016

	Plant (12.5%) €	Motor car (12.5%) €	Allow (75%) €	Total €
Cost at 01/01/2016	2,500	14,000		16,500
Additions at cost 2016:				
Cash register 01/02/2016	380			380
Shelving 10/02/2016	5,633			5,633
Freezer 01/03/2016	600			600
Disposals at cost 2016	(2,500)	0		(2,500)
Cost at 31/12/2016	6,613	14,000		20,613
TWDV 01/01/2016	**1,250**	**5,250**		**6,500**
Additions at cost	6,613			6,613
Disposals at TWDV	(1,250)			(1,250)
Wear and tear 2016	(827)	(1,750)	(1,312)	(2,577)
TWDV 31/12/2016	**5,786**	**3,500**		**9,286**

Balancing Charge/Allowance calculation

Proceeds of sale	1,500
Less: TWDV	(1,250)
Balancing charge – ignored as proceeds < €2,000	250
Capital allowances due 2016	
Wear and tear €1,312 + €827	2,139

Question 5.14

Mr Goa

2012   Basis period y/e 30/06/2012:
       Annual allowance of €140,000 × 4% = €5,600 claimed

2013   Basis period 30/06/2013 balancing charge as set out below:

	€
Sale proceeds (€190,000 – €25,000)	165,000
TWDV (€140,000 – €5,600)	134,400
Balancing charge	30,600
Restricted to allowances actually claimed: (€140,000 – €134,400)	5,600

Mrs Statham

Qualifying expenditure	140,000

2013 Basis period: 01/05/2013–31/12/2013

$$\frac{8}{12} \times \frac{1}{25-1} \times 140{,}000 = €3{,}889$$

Basis period is less than 12 months

2014   Basis period y/e 30/04/2014

$$\frac{12}{12} \times \frac{1}{25-1} \times 140{,}000 = €5{,}833$$

2015   Basis period y/e 30/04/2015

$$\frac{12}{12} \times \frac{1}{25-1} \times 140{,}000 = €5{,}833$$

2016   Basis period y/e 30/04/2016

$$\frac{12}{12} \times \frac{1}{25-1} \times 140{,}000 = €5{,}833$$

Question 5.15

Calculate eligible items

	€	
Site purchase cost	0	
Site development costs	5,000	
Construction of factory	95,000	
Construction of adjoining office	0	(Note 1)
Construction of adjoining showroom	0	(Note 1)
Total cost	100,000	

Note 1:

The 10% rule for eligible items applies to the showroom and office as follows:

$$\frac{10{,}000 + 15{,}000}{(135{,}000 - 10{,}000)} = 20\%$$

IBAA @ 4% of €100,000 = €4,000

Question 5.16

Capital Allowances Computation 2016

	Plant (12.5%) €	Motor Car (12.5%) €	Trucks (12.5%) €	Total €
Cost at 01/01/2016	25,500	24,000	18,750	68,250
Additions at cost 2016:				
Office furniture (1)	10,000			10,000
Truck (2)			25,000	25,000
Car (4) (restricted to 50% Category D)		12,000		12,000
New machinery (5)(net of grant)	20,000			20,000
Disposals at cost 2016	0	(24,000)	0	(24,000)
Cost at 31/12/2016	55,500	12,000	43,750	11,250
TWDV 01/01/2016	**15,937**	**9,000**	**14,062**	**38,999**
Additions	30,000	12,000	25,000	67,000
Disposals at TWDV	0	(9,000)	0	(9,000)
	45,937	12,000	39,062	96,999
Wear and tear 2016	(5,742)	(1,500)	(4,883)	(12,125)
TWDV 31/12/2016	**40,195**	**10,500**	**34,179**	**84,874**

Industrial Building Allowance (6)

Original cost €75,000

IBAA €75,000 × 1/15 = €5,000

Extension to Factory Premises (7)

IBAA not due as extension was not in use at the end of the basis period.

Balancing Allowance Charge Computation – car		€
TWDV at 01/01/2016		9,000
Sale proceeds:	$7,500 \times \dfrac{24,000}{26,000}$	(6,923)
		2,077
Balancing allowance	2,077 × 75%	1,558

Summary of Capital Allowances 2016

	€
Plant	5,742
Car (€1,500 × 75%)	1,125
Trucks	4,883
IBAA	5,000
Balancing allowance	1,558
	18,308

Question 5.17

	Plant and Machinery (12.5%) €	Motor Trucks (12.5%) €	Vehicles/ Cars (12.5%) €	TOTAL €
Original cost 01/01/2016	45,000	17,000	24,000	86,000
Additions at cost	25,000		48,000	73,000
Disposals at cost	(35,000)		(24,000)	(59,000)
Remaining cost	35,000	17,000	48,000	100,000
				–
TWDV 01/01/2016	5,000	2,125	11,500	18,625
Additions y/e 31/05/2016	25,000		48,000	73,000
Disposals y/e 31/05/2016			(12,000)	(12,000)
	30,000	2,125	48,000	80,125
Wear and tear 2016	(4,375)	(2,125)	(6,000)	(12,500)
TWDV 31/12/2016	25,625	–	42,000	67,625

Balancing allowances charges:

Machinery:	Sold for	14,000	
	TWDV	Nil	
	Potential balancing charge	14,000	Offset as replacement
Replacement option:	49,000		
	(10,000) Grant		
	(14,000) Replacement option		
Plant addition	25,000		

Balancing allowance charge on sale of car:		
	TWDV	12,000
	Proceeds €12,500 × €24,000/€24,000	12,500
	Balancing charge	500

Wear and tear is not due for the photocopier as it was not in use at the end of the 2016 basis period.

IBAA

Second-hand industrial building: $\dfrac{120,000}{25-11}$ = €8,571 IBAA per annum.

Sale of office building: no balancing charge as the office would not have qualified as an industrial building.

Extension to industrial building: €70,000 × 4% = €2,800 IBAA per annum. The offices qualify for IBAA as they did not cost more than 10% of the overall cost.

Summary

	€
Wear and tear	12,500
Balancing charge	(500)
IBAA	8,571
IBAA	2,800
Total capital allowances due 2016	23,371

Question 5.18

Assessment 2016	€
Case I	–
Schedule E	80,000
	80,000
Less: section 381 loss	(60,000)
Taxable income 2016	20,000

As Linda is involved in the business in an "active capacity", i.e. more than 10 hours a week, there is no restriction on the section 381 relief available.

Question 5.19

Mr Jones Assessment 2016	€
Case I	0
Case III (Government securities)	25,000
Schedule E	55,000
Gross statutory income	80,000
Deduct: section 381 loss (restricted)	(31,750)
Taxable income 2016	**48,250**
Loss available under section 382	8,250

As Mr Jones is only involved in the business for seven hours a week, he is not involved in the business in an "active capacity", i.e. more than 10 hours a week, and therefore the section 381 relief is restricted to €31,750.

Question 5.20

This gives rise to a loss of €7,000 (27,000 – 20,000), which can be claimed under section 381.

	€	€
Profit y/e 31/12/2016		20,000
Less: capital allowances	(37,000)	
Deduct: balancing charge	10,000	(27,000)
Section 381 loss 2016		(7,000)

Note: capital allowances carried forward from previous year cannot be used to create or augment a section 381 loss claim directly. However, they may be used to wipe out any current year balancing charges and to reduce current year profits and in this way may result in increasing a section 381 claim.

Question 5.21

		€
2016	Section 381 claim is computed as follows:	
	Tax-adjusted Case I profit y/e 30/09/2016	9,000
	Deduct: capital allowances forward (limited)	(9,000)
	Net Case I	Nil
	Balancing charge	3,000
	Deduct: balance of unused capital allowances forward (€9,600 – €9,000)	(600)
	Net balancing charge	2,400
	Deduct: 2016 capital allowances claim	(7,500)
	Section 381 loss (available to reduce total income for 2017)	(5,100)

Question 5.22

	2014	2015	2016	Total
	€	€	€	
Case I	Nil	17,000	50,000	
Deduct: Case I losses forward (section 382)	___	(17,000)	(1,000)	(18,000)
Assessable Case I	Nil	Nil	49,000	

Jim is obliged to take relief for the loss forward in the first year in which Case I profits from the same trade are available. This occurs in 2015 and results in a waste of his personal tax credits for that year. Jim would have preferred to defer relief for some of the loss until 2016 to avoid wasting his 2015 tax credits and to avail of relief from the tax that will be suffered in 2016. Unfortunately, this is not permitted.

Question 5.23

Assessments

		€
2014	Case I	80,000
	Case IV	1,000
	Case V	20,000
	Taxable 2014	**101,000**
2015	Case I	Nil
	Case IV	1,200
	Case V	30,000
		31,200
	Less: section 381	(31,200)
	Taxable 2015	**Nil**

2016	Case I	45,000
	Section 382 relief (€37,000 – €31,200)	(5,800)
		39,200
	Case IV	1,200
	Case V	25,000
	Taxable 2016	**65,400**

Chapter 6

Question 6.1

(a) As only one spouse has income, the Joyces are entitled to the married couple, one income standard rate band. Their income tax liability for 2016 is as follows:

Income Tax Computation 2016 – Joyces	**€**	**€**
Taxable income		46,000
Tax payable:		
€42,800 @ 20%	8,560	
€3,200 @ 40%	1,280	9,840
€46,000		
Less: Tax Credits		
Basic personal (married)	3,300	
Employee tax credit	1,650	
Home carer tax credit	1,000	(5,950)
Tax liability		3,890

(b) If the home carer had income of €9,500 in 2017, i.e. above the income limit for the home carer tax credit in 2017, a home carer tax credit can still be claimed as the home carer was entitled to the tax credit in 2016. The maximum home carer tax credit claimable would be the tax credit claimed for the tax year 2016.

 However, it will be more beneficial for the increased standard rate band to be claimed, i.e. the tax saving by claiming the increased standard rate band (i.e. €9,500 @ (40%–20%) = €1,900) will be more than the reduction due to claiming the €1,000 home carer tax credit.

Question 6.2

As both spouses have income, they are entitled to the increased standard rate tax band. As one spouse has income of less than €9,200, they also qualify for the home carer tax credit. If the increased standard rate tax band is claimed, their income tax liability for 2016 will be as follows:

Income Tax Computation 2016 – Roches

	€	€
Schedule E salary		46,000
Schedule F		8,000
Taxable income		54,000
Tax payable:		
€50,800* @ 20%	10,160	
3,200 @ 40%	1,280	11,440
€54,000		
Less: Tax Credits		
Basic personal tax credit (married)	3,300	
Employee tax credit	1,650	(4,950)
Less: refundable tax credit DWT		(1,600)
Tax liability		4,890

* The standard rate band of €42,800 is increased by the lower of €24,800 or the total income of the lower income spouse, i.e. €8,000 in this case.

If the home carer tax credit is claimed instead of the increased standard rate band, their liability will be as follows:

Income Tax Computation 2016 – Roches

	€	€
Taxable income		54,000
Tax payable:		
€42,800 @ 20%	8,560	
€11,200 @ 40%	4,480	13,040
€54,000		
Less: Tax Credits		
Basic personal tax credit (married)	3,300	
Employee tax credit	1,650	
Home carer tax credit: €1,000 – ((€8,000 – €7,200)/2)	600	(5,550)
Less: refundable tax credit DWT		(1,600)
Tax liability		5,890

As their tax liability is lower if the increased standard rate tax band is claimed, they should claim the increased standard rate tax band instead of the home carer tax credit.

Question 6.3

Medical Expenses	€
Mr Murray	80
Michael Murray	200
David Murray	210
Sean Ryan	650
	1,140

Medical expenses allowable for 2016 are €1,140. Relief is at the standard rate of 20% = tax credit of €228.

Mr Murray is also entitled to a deduction from net statutory income in respect of the €1,200 he pays towards nursing home care for his mother. Therefore, if Mr Murray's marginal rate of tax is 40%, tax relief @ 40%, i.e. €480, will be available. If the nursing home did not provide 24-hour nursing care on-site, then no deduction would be available.

Mr Murray should submit a claim either using Form Med 1 or online on PAYE Anytime after the end of the tax year to claim the tax credits available for both the medical expenses and the nursing home charges.

Question 6.4

(a) Rachel will be entitled to interest relief as a charge of €2,250 ((€10,000 × 6/12 × 25%) + (€10,000 × 6/12 × 80/100 × 25%)) in 2016.

Interest on loan taken out before 15 October 2013 allowable @ 25% for 2016.

(b) Rachel's net relevant earnings for 2016:

Net Relevant Earnings 2016 – Rachel	€
Case II	320,000
Less: capital allowances	(10,000)
Less: charges – interest relief	(2,250)
Net relevant earnings	307,750
Premium paid	**75,000**
Maximum claim allowed:	
Net relevant earnings ceiling restricted to	115,000
Relief restricted to €115,000 × 25%	**28,750**

Question 6.5

Income Tax Computation 2016 – Mr Frost	€	€
Salary		46,000
VHI (gross) (Note)		1,160
Taxable income		47,160

continued overleaf

Tax payable:

€33,800 @ 20%	6,760	
€13,360 @ 40%	5,344	
€47,160		12,104
Less: Tax Credits		
Basic personal tax credit	1,650	
Employee tax credit	1,650	(3,300)
		8,804
Tax deducted from VHI €1,000 (max.) @ 20%		(200)
Tax liability		8,604

Note: VHI – 1st €1,000 @ 20% tax credit net   €800

       Balance €160 @ Nil tax credit net   €160

         Gross €1,160   Net   €960

Question 6.6

John's income tax computation for 2016 will be as follows:

Income Tax Computation 2016 – John   **€**

Schedule E: Salary			75,000
Tax payable:	€33,800 @ 20%	6,760	
	€41,200 @ 40%	16,480	23,240
	€75,000		
Deduct:	Basic personal tax credit		(1,650)
	Employee tax credit		(1,650)
	Mortgage interest relief	max: €3,000 @ 15%	(450)
	PAYE deducted		(19,950)
Tax refund due			(460)

TRS does not apply to the mortgage interest paid by John as the residence in question is situated outside the State.

If this was the first mortgage in respect of which John had claimed relief and the loan had been taken out in June 2009, he would have been entitled to mortgage interest relief of €3,000 (€10,000 × 30%). If the mortgage was taken out prior to 1 January 2004, no relief would be available.

Question 6.7

Income Tax Liability 2016 – June	€	€
Schedule E income:		
Salary	43,000	
Retirement annuity premium paid	(2,000)	41,000
Widow's pension		10,062
Total income		51,062
Tax payable:		
€37,800 @ 20%	7,560	
€13,262 @ 40%	5,305	12,865
€51,062		
Less: Tax credits:		
Basic personal tax credit (widowed)	1,650	
Single person child carer credit	1,650	
Widowed parent (third year after year of death)	2,700	
Incapacitated child tax credits × 2	6,600	
Employee tax credit	1,650	
College fees (€3,000 − €1,500) @ 20%	300	
Rent relief €1,600 @ 20% (max.)	320	
Medical expenses €500 @ 20%	100	
Total tax credits due		(14,970)
Tax liability		(2,105)
Restrict as tax credits are non-refundable		0
Less: PAYE paid		(5,000)
Refund due		**(5,000)**

Notes:

1. Medical expenses incurred for David of €500 are allowable. Expenditure incurred on eye test and spectacles for John is not allowable.
2. The income received by John and Mary has no effect on June's entitlement to tax credits.
3. VHI premium paid is ignored. Tax relief is given at source.
4. The first €1,500 of college fees, where all of the students are part-time, is not allowable.

Question 6.8

Income Tax Computation 2016 – John Fitzpatrick	€	€
Schedule E:		
Pension (gross)		<u>29,400</u>
Tax payable:		
€29,400 @ 20%		5,880
Less: Tax Credits		
Widowed person tax credit	(2,190)	
Age tax credit	(245)	
Employee tax credit	<u>(1,650)</u>	
Total credits		<u>(4,085)</u>
Tax liability		1,795
Less: PAYE paid		<u>(1,900)</u>
Refund due		(105)

Notes:

1. Donation to eligible charity is ignored. Charity will claim back tax of €135, i.e. €300 ÷ 0.69 less €300 in respect of the donation (31% rate).
2. VHI premium paid is ignored as tax relief is given at source.

Question 6.9

Income Tax Computation 2016 – Jason and Damien	€	€
Schedule E income/taxable income – pension (gross)		35,000
Tax payable:		
€35,000 @ 20%		7,000
Less: Tax Credits		
Basic personal tax credit – civil partners	(3,300)	
Age tax credit	(490)	
Employee tax credit	<u>(1,650)</u>	<u>(5,440)</u>
Initial tax liability		1,560
Income exemption limit €36,000		<u>(1,560)</u>
Final tax liability		0
Less: PAYE paid		<u>(2,000)</u>
Refund due		(2,000)

Note: it is the older civil partner's age that is relevant.

Question 6.10

	2015		2016
Retirement Annuity Relief – Bob	**€**		**€**
Relevant earnings	20,980		24,480
Less:			
Charges not covered by non-relevant income (€3,000 – €1,160)	(1,840)	(€3,000 – €1,195)	(1,805)
Net relevant income	19,140		22,675
Maximum allowable premium (30% in 2015, 35% in 2016)	5,742		7,936

2015:	Premium paid	6,000	
	Restrict to	5,742	
	and carry balance of €258 forward to 2016:		
	Premium paid		4,000
	+ carried forward		258
	Allow		4,258

Question 6.11

Maria's Income Tax Computation 2016	**€**	**€**
Schedule E salary		35,000
Less: Charges		
Covenant (€4,000/0.8)		(5,000)
Total income		30,000
Tax payable:		
€30,000 @ 20%		6,000
Less: Basic personal tax credit	(1,650)	
Employee tax credit	(1,650)	
		(3,300)
Add: tax on covenant €5,000 @ 20%		1,000
Tax liability		3,700
Less: PAYE tax deducted		(4,400)
Refund due		(700)

Father's Income Tax Computation 2016		
Schedule D, Case IV		5,000
Schedule D, Case V		8,000
		13,000
Tax payable:		2,600
€13,000 @ 20%		

continued overleaf

Less:

Widowed person tax credit	(2,190)
Initial tax liability	410
Income exemption limit €18,000, thus tax liability	nil
Less: tax paid on covenant €5,000 @ 20%	(1,000)
Refund due	(1,000)

Question 6.12

Income Tax Computation 2016 – Robert		€	€
Schedule D, Case IV (€1,600/0.59)			2,712
Case IV shares in lieu			800
Case V (Note 1)			3,019
Schedule E salary		84,000	
Less: pension contribution (max. 20% of Schedule E)		(16,800)	67,200
Schedule F	(Note 3)		6,500
Gross income			80,231
Deduct:	Covenant: brother (€3,200/0.8)		(4,000)
	Covenant: father (Note 2)		(3,812)
Total income			72,419
Deduct:	EII €20,000 × 30/40 (Note 5)		(15,000)
Taxable income			57,419

Tax payable:			
€33,800 @ 20%		6,760	
€2,712 @ 41%		1,112	
€20,907 @ 40%		8,363	16,235
€57,419			
Less: Non-refundable tax credits	Basic personal tax credit	(1,650)	
	Employee tax credit	(1,650)	
	DIRT	(1,112)	(4,412)
Add: tax on covenant paid (Note 4)			1,700
Tax liability			13,523
Less: PAYE tax deducted			(13,780)
Less refundable tax credits: DWT (€6,500 @ 20%)			(1,300)
Less: medical expenses (€845 @ 20%)			(169)
Refund due			(1,726)

Notes:

1. Computation of Case V income for 2016

Rental income	14,400
Less expenses:	
Mortgage interest (€3,200 × 75%)	(2,400)
Management fee	(3,100)
Expenses	(2,600)
Capital allowances (€2,250 × 12.5%)	(281)
Case V income	6,019
Less: loss forward	(3,000)
Net Case V income	3,019

2 Covenant to father is restricted to 5% of total income as follows:

Schedule D, Case IV (€1,600/0.59)	2,712
Case IV	800
Case V	3,019
Schedule E salary	84,000
Less: pension contribution (max. 20% of Schedule E)	(16,800)
Covenant to brother (€3,200/0.8)	(4,000)
Schedule F (Note 3)	6,500
Total income	76,231
Covenant to parent restricted to 5%	3,812

3. Net dividend received from Independent News €5,200/0.8   6,500

4.

Covenant paid to brother	4,000
Covenant paid to father	4,500
	8,500
Tax deducted @ 20%	€1,700

5. EII relief is available @ 30% with a further 10% potentially available after a holding period of four years, subject to certain conditions.

Question 6.13

Income Tax Computation 2016 – Jenny McFee	€	€
Income:		
Schedule D:		
Case IV €1,200/0.59		2,034
Case V – room rental (Note 1)		NIL
Schedule E:		
Salary	55,000	
Pension	12,150	
BIK – VHI (Note 2)	1,740	68,890
Total income		70,924
Less: employment of carer		(12,500)
Taxable income		**58,424**
Tax payable:		
€37,800 @ 20%	7,560	
€18,590 @ 40%	7,436	
€2,034 @ 41%	834	
€58,424		15,830
Less: Non-refundable Tax Credits:		
Basic personal tax credit (widowed)	1,650	
Single person child carer credit	1,650	
Widowed parent (first year after year of bereavement)	3,600	
Employee tax credit	1,650	
College fees (Note 3)	1,148	
Training courses – maximum	254	
		(9,952)
Tax liability		5,878
Less:		
DIRT paid	834	
Tax deducted from VHI €1,000 (max.) @ 20%	200	
PAYE paid (€5,200 + €2,550)	7,750	(8,784)
Refund due		**(2,906)**

Notes:

1. Room rental
   Rent from student letting is not taxable under the Rent-a-Room relief, i.e. gross receipts are less than €12,000 in 2016

2. BIK – VHI

First	€1,000 @ 20% tax credit	800
Balance	€740 @ nil tax credit	740
Gross	€1,740	Net €1,540

continued overleaf

	€
3. College fees	
Maria: fees €8,500 – limited to	7,000
John: fees	1,740
Total	8,740
Less: amount disallowed	(3,000)
Allowable	5,740
Relief @ 20%	**1,148**

Colm's fees are for an approved training course and qualify for relief under Training Courses, maximum amount allowable at the standard rate €1,270 @ 20% = €254.

Chapter 7

Question 7.1

(a)   Joint Assessment

Income Tax Computation 2016	Patrick	Helen	Total
	€	€	€
Income:			
Schedule E	10,500	50,000	60,500
Schedule E – BIK	–	2,100	2,100
Total income	10,500	52,100	62,600
Less:			
Permanent Health Insurance	–	(950)	(950)
Taxable income	**10,500**	**51,150**	**61,650**
Tax Payable:			
€42,800 @ 20%		8,560	8,560
€10,500 @ 20%	2,100		2,100
€8,350 @ 40%	–	3,340	3,340
€61,650	2,100	11,900	14,000
Less: Non-refundable Tax Credits:			
Basic personal tax credit (married)			(3,300)
Employee tax credits (× 2)			(3,300)
Tax liability			**7,400**
Deduct: PAYE paid	(830)	(8,000)	(8,830)
Net tax refund			**(1,430)**

(b)   Separate Assessment

Patrick – Income Tax Computation 2016	€
Income:	
Schedule E	<u>10,500</u>
Tax Payable:	
€10,500 @ 20%	2,100
Less: Non-refundable Tax Credits:	
Basic personal tax credit	(1,650)
Employee tax credit	<u>(1,650)</u>
Excess tax credits transferred to wife	**<u>(1,200)</u>**
Deduct: PAYE paid	<u>(830)</u>
Net tax refund	**<u>(830)</u>**

Helen – Income Tax Computation 2016	€	€
Income:		
Schedule E		50,000
Schedule E – BIK		<u>2,100</u>
Total income		**<u>52,100</u>**
Less:		
Permanent Health Insurance		<u>(950)</u>
Taxable income		**<u>51,150</u>**
Tax Payable:		
€42,800 @ 20% (standard rate band of €24,800 not fully utilised by Patrick)	8,560	
€8,350 @ 40%	<u>3,340</u>	11,900
€51,150		
Less: Non-refundable Tax Credits:		
Basic personal tax credit		(1,650)
Employee tax credit		(1,650)
Tax credits transferred from husband		<u>(1,200)</u>
Tax liability		**7,400**
Deduct: PAYE paid		<u>(8,000)</u>
Net tax refund		**<u>(600)</u>**

Check:	*Patrick*	*Helen*	*Total*
Separate assessment	<u>(830)</u>	<u>(600)</u>	<u>(1,430)</u>
Refund per joint assessment			<u>(1,430)</u>

(c) Single Assessment

Patrick Income Tax Computation 2016	€	€
Income:		
Schedule E		<u>10,500</u>
Tax Payable:		
€10,500 @ 20%		2,100
Less: Non-refundable Tax Credits:		
Basic personal tax credit	(1,650)	
Employee tax credit	<u>(1,650)</u>	
	<u>(3,300)</u>	
Credits limited to tax liability		(2,100)
Deduct: PAYE paid		<u>(830)</u>
Net tax refund		<u>(830)</u>

Helen Income Tax Computation 2016	€	€
Income:		
Schedule E	50,000	
Schedule E – BIK	<u>2,100</u>	
Total income	<u>52,100</u>	
Less:		
Permanent Health Insurance	(950)	
Taxable income		**<u>51,150</u>**
Tax Payable:		
€33,800 @ 20%	6,760	
<u>€17,350</u> @ 40%	<u>6,940</u>	
€51,150		13,700
Less: Non-refundable Tax Credits:		
Basic personal tax credit		(1,650)
Employee tax credit		<u>(1,650)</u>
Tax liability		10,400
Deduct: PAYE paid		<u>(8,000)</u>
Net tax payable		**<u>2,400</u>**

Question 7.2

Assessment as Single Persons for 2016			
Income Tax Computation 2016	**Peter**	**Paul**	**Total**
	€	€	€
Income: Schedule E	50,000	26,000	
Tax Payable:			
€33,800 @ 20%	6,760	5,200	
€16,200 @ 40%	6,480	–	
€50,000	13,240	5,200	
Less: Non-refundable Tax Credits:			
Basic personal tax credit	(1,650)	(1,650)	
Employee tax credit	(1,650)	(1,650)	
Initial tax liability	**9,940**	**1,900**	**11,840**
Deduct:			
Year of registration of civil partnership relief (Note)	(764)	(146)	(910)
PAYE paid	(10,300)	(2,050)	(12,350)
Net tax refund	**(1,124)**	**(296)**	**(1,420)**

Note: notional joint assessment for 2016.

Notional Liability under Joint Assessment for 2016	**Peter**	**Paul**	**Total**
	€	€	€
Income: Schedule E	50,000	26,000	76,000
Tax Payable:			
€42,800 @ 20%	8,560	–	8,560
€24,800 @ 20%	–	4,960	4,960
€8,400 @ 40%	3,360	–	3,360
€76,000	11,920	4,960	16,880

continued overleaf

Less: Non-refundable Tax Credits:

Basic personal tax credit (married/civil partners)	(3,300)
Employee tax credits ($\times$ 2)	(3,300)
Notional tax liability	**10,280**
Total under single assessment	**11,840**
"Saving"	**1,560**

Saving restricted to:

€1,560 $\times$ 7/12 (months)			910
Split:	$910 \times \dfrac{9,940}{11,840}$	$910 \times \dfrac{1,900}{11,840}$	
Year of registration of civil partnership relief	**€764**	**€146**	**€910**

Question 7.3

(a) (i) No change to Deed of Separation

Mrs Thorne Income Tax Computation 2016	€	€
Income:		
Schedule E	35,000	
Case IV (€200 $\times$ 12)(Note)	2,400	
Total income		37,400
Tax Payable:		
€37,400 @ 20%	7,480	
€NIL @ 40%	NIL	
€37,400		7,480
Less: Non-refundable Tax Credits:		
Basic personal tax credit	(1,650)	
Single person child carer credit	(1,650)	
Employee tax credit	(1,650)	(4,950)
Tax liability		**2,530**

Note: maintenance payments specifically for children are ignored (i.e. €800 − €600).

(a) (ii) Deed of Separation changed

Mrs Thorne Income Tax Computation 2016	€	€
Income:		
Schedule E	35,000	
Schedule D, Case IV (€900 × 12)	10,800	
Total income		45,800
Tax Payable:		
€37,800 @ 20%	7,560	
€8,000 @ 40%	3,200	
€45,800		10,760
Less: Non-refundable Tax Credits:		
Basic personal tax credit	(1,650)	
Single person child carer credit	(1,650)	
Employee tax credit	(1,650)	(4,950)
Tax liability		**5,810**

(b) Comparison

If the deed is not reviewed, Mrs Thorne's financial position is as follows:

	€
Maintenance payments (€800 × 12)	9,600
Salary	35,000
	44,600
Less: tax payable	(2,530)
Net income after tax	**42,070**

If the deed is reviewed, Mrs Thorne's financial position is as follows:

Maintenance payments (€1,000 × 12)	12,000
Salary	35,000
	47,000
Less: tax payable	(5,810)
Net income after tax	**41,190**

Mrs Thorne is worse off financially by €880 (€42,070 – €41,190) if the deed is reviewed.

Question 7.4

(a) **Claim for joint assessment made for year of separation (i.e. election under section 1026 TCA 1997).**

As Mrs Lynch has income other than the maintenance payments, the separate assessment rules are used.

Mrs Lynch Income Tax Computation 2016	€	€
Income:		
Schedule E	15,000	
Total income		15,000
Tax Payable:		
€15,000 @ 20%	3,000	
€0 @ 40%	0	
€15,000		3,000
Less: Non-refundable Tax Credits:		
Basic personal tax credit	(1,650)	
Employee tax credit	(1,650)	(3,300)
Excess tax credits transferred to Mr Lynch		(300)
Tax liability		0

Mr Lynch Income Tax Computation 2016	€	€
Income:		
Schedule E	48,000	
Total income		48,000
Tax Payable:		
€42,800 @ 20%	8,560	
€5,200 @ 40%	2,080	
€48,000		10,640
Less: Non-refundable Tax Credits:		
Basic personal tax credit	(1,650)	
Employee tax credit	(1,650)	
Excess tax credits transferred from Mrs Lynch	(300)	(3,600)
Tax liability		**7,040**
Combined tax liability		**7,040**

Note: mortgage interest relief = NIL as loan was taken out before 1 January 2004.
VHI – tax relief given at source.

(b)   No claim made for joint assessment for year of separation

Mrs Lynch Income Tax Computation 2016	€	€
Income:		
Schedule E (01/07/2016 – 31/12/2016)	8,000	
Case IV (€600 × 6)	3,600	
Total income		11,600
Tax Payable:		
€11,600 @ 20%	2,320	
€0 @ 40%	0	
€11,600		2,320
Less: Non-refundable Tax Credits:		
Basic personal tax credit	(1,650)	
Single person child carer credit	(1,650)	
Employee tax credit	(1,650)	
	(4,950)	
Restrict to amount needed to reduce tax liability to NIL		(2,320)
Tax liability		**0**

Mr Lynch Income Tax Computation 2016	€	€
Income:		
Schedule E – self	48,000	
Schedule E – Mrs Lynch (01/01/2016 – 30/06/2016)	7,000	
		55,000
Less: maintenance payments (€600 × 6)		(3,600)
Net income		51,400
Tax Payable:		
€42,800 @ 20%	8,560	
€7,000 @ 20%	1,400	
€1,600 @ 40%	640	
€51,400		10,600
Less: Non-refundable Tax Credits:		
Basic personal tax credit (married)	(3,300)	
Employee tax credits	(3,300)	(6,600)

continued overleaf

Tax liability	**4,000**
Combined tax liability	**4,000**

Note: as the assessable spouse in the year of separation, Mr Lynch is entitled to a married person's tax credits and tax bands.

(c) Claim for joint assessment made for the year following the year of separation
Same as (a) above.

(d) No claim made for joint assessment for the year following the year of separation

Mrs Lynch Income Tax Computation 2016	€	€
Income:		
Schedule E	15,000	
Schedule D, Case IV (€600 × 12)	7,200	
Total income		22,200
Tax Payable:		
€22,200 @ 20%	4,440	
€0 @ 40%	0	
€22,200		4,440
Less: Non-refundable Tax Credits:		
Basic personal tax credit	(1,650)	
Single Person Child Carer credit	(1,650)	
Employee tax credit	(1,650)	
	(4,950)	
Restrict to amount needed to reduce tax liability to NIL		(4,440)
Tax liability		**0**

Mr Lynch Income Tax Computation 2016	€	€
Income:		
Schedule E – self		48,000
Less: maintenance payments (€600 × 12)		(7,200)
Net income		40,800
Tax Payable:		
€33,800 @ 20%	6,760	
€7,000 @ 40%	2,800	
€40,800		9,560

continued overleaf

Less: Non-refundable Tax Credits:		
Basic personal tax credit	(1,650)	
Employee tax credit	(1,650)	(3,300)
Tax liability		**6,260**
Combined tax liability		**6,260**

Question 7.5

(a) Income Tax Computation 2016 – Assessable Spouse Matthew (deceased)

Matthew DuBlanc (deceased) – Income Tax Liability 01/01/2016 to 30/05/2016

	€	€
Income:		
Schedule E		
Matthew	60,000	
Jane (to 30/05/2016)	30,000	
Total income		**90,000**
Tax payable:		
€67,600 @ 20%	13,520	
€22,400 @ 40%	8,960	
€90,000		22,480
Less: Non-refundable Tax Credits:		
Basic personal tax credit (married)	3,300	
Employee Tax credits (x 2)	3,300	
		(6,600)
Tax liability		15,880
Less: PAYE paid (€19,250 + €7,800)		(27,050)
Refund due		**(11,170)**

Jane DuBlanc – Income Tax Liability 31/05/2016 to 31/12/2016

	€	€
Income:		
Schedule E salary		42,000
Taxable income		**42,000**

continued overleaf

Tax payable:

€37,800 @ 20%	7,560	
€4,200 @ 40%	1,680	
€42,000		9,240

Less: Non-refundable Tax Credits:

Basic personal tax credit (year of bereavement)	3,300	
Employee tax credit	1,650	
		(4,950)
Tax liability		4,290
Less: PAYE paid		(10,950)
Refund due		**(6,660)**
Total refund 2016		**(17,830)**

(b)   Income Tax Computation 2016 – Assessable Spouse Jane

Jane DuBlanc – Income Tax Liability 01/01/2016 to 31/12/2016

	€	€
Income:		
Schedule E:		
Jane	72,000	
Matthew	60,000	
Taxable income		**132,000**
Tax payable:		
€ 67,600 @ 20%	13,520	
€ 64,400 @ 40%	25,760	
€132,000		39,280
Less: Non-refundable Tax Credits:		
Basic personal tax credit (married)	3,300	
Employee tax credits (x 2)	3,300	
		(6,600)
Tax liability		32,680
Less: PAYE paid (€19,250 + €18,750)		(38,000)
Refund due		**(5,320)**

Jane would receive an extra €12,510 tax refund if Matthew was the assessable spouse at the date of his death.

Chapter 8

Question 8.1

(a) Net pay receivable by Mary – August 2016

	€	€	€
Gross salary – this employment		2,200	
Gross salary per P45		16,310	
Cumulative gross pay to date			18,510
Cumulative SRCOP to date	€2,817 × 8		22,536
Tax @ 20%	€18,510 @ 20%		3,702
Cumulative tax credits to date	€275 × 8		(2,200)
Cumulative tax due to date			1,502
Less: tax paid per P45			(1,208)
Tax due for August 2016			294
Net Salary for August 2016:			
Gross salary August 2016			2,200
Less:			
PAYE			(294)
PRSI	€2,200 @ 4%		
			(88)
USC: cut-off point 1	€1,001 × 8 @ 1%	8,008	80
cut-off point 2	€555 × 8 @ 3%	4,440	133
Balance	€18,510 − (€8,008 + €4,440) @ 5.5%	6,062	333
Cumulative pay to date		18,510	546
Less: USC paid per P45		485	(61)
Net pay for August 2016			**1,757**

continued overleaf

(b) Total Gross Taxable Pay for Andrew – June 2016

	€
Benefit in Kind Calculation:	
Original market value of car	28,000
% applicable for annual business travel (km): 51,200 – 8,000 = 43,200 km = 12%	
Cash equivalent €28,000 @ 12%	3,360
Less: annual amount paid to employer	(1,500)
Annual benefit in kind assessable	**1,860**
Gross taxable pay June 2016:	
June 2016 salary	4,167
BIK (monthly)	155
Gross taxable pay June 2016	**4,322**

Question 8.2

(a) Value of BIK on Van

	€
OMV of van €17,500	
Cash equivalent 5% of €17,500	875
Less: refunded by Sean	(120)
Annual BIK on van	755
Taxable BIK 2016 (6/12ths)	378

(b) (i) With PPS No. (Emergency Basis)

Gross wages – this employment	500.00
SRCOP	650.00
Tax @ 20% (€500 @ 20%)	100.00
Tax credits (€1,650/52)	(31.73)
Tax due for first week	68.27
PRSI: €500 @ 4%	20.00
USC €500 @ 8% (emergency)	40.00
Total	60.00
Gross salary for August 2016	500.00
PAYE	(68.27)
PRSI	(20.00)

continued overleaf

USC		(40.00)
Net pay for August 2016		371.73

(b) (ii) Without PPS No. (Emergency Basis)

Gross wages – this employment		500.00
SRCOP		0.00
Tax at 40% (€500 @ 40%)		200.00
Tax credits (€nil/52)		(0.00)
Tax due for first week		200.00
PRSI: €500 @ 4%		20.00
USC €500 @ 8% (emergency)		40.00
Gross salary for August 2016		500.00
PAYE		(200.00)
PRSI		(20.00)
USC		(40.00)
Net pay for August 2016		240.00

Question 8.3

(a) Net pay receivable by Paul for w/e 17 October 2016 (Week 46)
Temporary Basis

		€	€
Gross salary – this employment	(39 × €21) + (11 × €21 × 1.5)	1,165.50	
Gross salary per P45 – not used		0	
Gross pay to date			1,165.50
SRCOP to date	€823.07 × 1		823.07
Tax @ 20%	€823.07 @ 20%		164.61
Tax @ 40%	€342.43 @ 40%		136.97
	€1,165.50		301.58
Tax credits this period	€95.19 × 1		(95.19)
Tax due to date (non-cumulative)			206.39
Tax paid per P45 – not used			0
Tax due for week 46			206.39

Net Pay for Week 46:

Gross pay for week 46		1,165.50

continued overleaf

Less:

PAYE				(206.39)
PRSI:	€1,165.00 @ 4%			(46.62)
USC:	€231 @ 1%	€231.00	2.31	
(Week 1 basis)	€128 @ 3%	€128.00	3.84	
	Balance @ 5.5%	€806.50	44.36	(50.51)
		€1,165.50		

Net pay for Week 46   **861.98**

(b) Net pay receivable by Paul for w/e 17 October 2016 (Week 46)
Cumulative Basis   €   €

Gross salary – this employment	(39 × €21) + (11 × €21 × 1.5)	1,165.50		
Gross salary per P45		43,540.00		
Cumulative gross pay to date				44,705.50
Cumulative SRCOP to date		€823.07 × 46		37,861.22
Tax @ 20%		€37,861.22 @ 20%		7,572.24
Tax @ 40%		€6,844.28 @ 40%		2,737.71
		€44,705.50		10,309.95
Cumulative tax credits to date		€95.19 × 46		(4,378.74)
Cumulative tax due to date				5,931.21
Tax paid per P45				(5,724.82)
Tax due for week 46				206.39

Net Pay for Week 46:

Gross pay for week 46				1,165.50
Less:				
PAYE				(206.39)
PRSI:	€1,165.50 @ 4%			(46.62)
USC: cut-off point 1	€231 × 46 @ 1%	10,626	106.26	
cut-off Point 2	€128 × 46 @ 3%	5,888	176.64	
Balance	€44,705 − (€10,626 + €5,888) @ 5.5%	28,191	1,550.51	
Cumulative pay to date		44,705	1,833.41	
Less: USC paid per P45			(1,782.92)	(50.49)

Net pay for Week 46 **862.00**

Question 8.4

Net pay receivable by Charlotte for w/e 6 July 2016 (Week 27)		€	€
Gross wages this week		1,050.00	
Gross wages to 30 June 2016		27,300.00	
Cumulative gross pay to date			28,350.00
Cumulative SRCOP to date	€650.00 × 27		17,550.00
Tax @ 20%	€17,550	@ 20%	3,510.00
Tax @ 40%	€10,800	@ 40%	4,320.00
	€28,350		7,830.00
Cumulative tax credits to date	€63.46 × 27		(1,713.42)
Cumulative tax due to date			6,116.58
Less: tax paid to date			(5,890.04)
Tax due this week			226.54

Net Pay for Week 27:					
Gross pay w/e 6 July 2016					1,050.00
Less:					
PAYE					(226.54)
PRSI:	€1,050 @ 4%				(42.00)
USC: Cut-off point 1	€231 × 27 @ 1%	6,237	62.37		
Cut-off point 2	€128 × 27 @ 3%	3,456	103.68		
Balance	€28,350 − (€6,237 + €3,456) @ 5.5%	18,657	1,026.13		
Cumulative pay to date		28,350	1,192.18		
Less: USC paid to 30 June 2016			(1,148.03)	(44.15)	
LPT deducted (Note)					NIL
Net pay for Week 27					**737.31**

continued overleaf

Note: Jolly Giants Ltd was not in receipt of the revised P2C before the pay date of 6 July and could not deduct any amount for LPT.

Net pay receivable by Charlotte for w/e 13 July 2016 (Week 28)		€	€
Gross wages this week		1,050.00	
Gross wages to 6 July 2016		28,350.00	
Cumulative gross pay to date			29,400.00
Cumulative SRCOP to date	€650.00 × 28		18,200.00
Tax @ 20%	€18,200 @ 20%		3,640.00
Tax @ 40%	€11,200 @ 40%		4,480.00
			8,120.00
Cumulative tax credits to date	€63.46 × 28		(1,776.88)
Cumulative tax due to date			6,343.12
Less: tax paid to date			(6,116.58)
Tax due this week			226.54
Net Pay for Week 28:			
Gross pay w/e 13 July 2016			1,050.00
Less:			
PAYE:			(226.54)
PRSI:	€1,050 @ 4%		(42.00)
USC: Cut-off point 1	€231 × 28 @ 1%	6,468	64.68
Cut-off point 2	€128 × 28 @ 3%	3,584	107.52
Balance	€29,400 − (€6,468 + €3,584) @ 5.5%	19,348	1,064.14
Cumulative pay to date		29,400	1,236.34
Less: USC paid to 6 July 2016			(1,192.18) (44.16)
LPT deducted (Note)			(10.40)
Net pay for week number 28			**726.90**

Note: LPT = €520 − €260 ÷ 25, i.e. remaining number of pay periods to 31 December 2016. Had Jolly Giants Ltd received the P2C before the pay date of 6 July 2016, the LPT payment would be spread out over 26 weeks.

Question 8.5

Gillian Salary September 2016 – Month 9	€	€
Tax Payable:		
Gross salary September Jingo Ltd €6,500 – (€188 × 2)	6,124	
Less: pension contribution	(650)	
Illness Benefit received €188 × 2	376	
Gross salary to Month 8 (€6,500 – €650) × 8	<u>46,800</u>	
Cumulative gross pay to date		<u>**52,650**</u>
Cumulative SRCOP to date (€2,816.67 × 9)		<u>25,350</u>
Tax Payable:		
€25,350 @ 20%	5,070	
€27,300 @ 40%	<u>10,920</u>	
€52,650	15,990	
Less: Cumulative tax credits to date (€275 × 9)	<u>(2,475)</u>	
Cumulative tax due to date	13,515	
Less: tax paid to Month 8	<u>(12,013)</u>	
Tax due for Month 9		<u>**1,502**</u>
USC Calculation:		
Gross salary September €6,500 – (€188 × 2)	6,124	
Gross salary to Month 8 €6,500 × 8	<u>52,000</u>	
Cumulative gross pay to date for USC		<u>**58,124**</u>

USC cut-off point 1 (€1,001 × 9)	€9,009	@ 1.0%	90.09	
USC cut-off point 2 (€554.67 × 9)	€4,992	@ 3.0%	149.76	
USC cut-off point 3 (€4,281.33 × 9)	€38,532	@ 5.5%	2,119.26	
USC cut-off point 4 (balance)	<u>€5,591</u>	@ 8.0%	<u>447.28</u>	
Cumulative pay to date	<u>€58,124</u>		2,806.39	
Less: USC paid to Month 8			<u>2,521.30</u>	
USC due for September				<u>**285.09**</u>

continued overleaf

PRSI Calculation:

€6,500 – (€188 × 2)	€6,124 @ 4%	**244.96**

Net Salary September:

Gross – Jingo Ltd		6,124.00
Less:		
PAYE	1,502.00	
PRSI	244.96	
USC	285.09	(2,032.05)
Net salary		4,091.95
Less: pension contribution		(650.00)
Net salary September Jingo Ltd		**3,441.95**
Plus: Illness Benefit DSP		376.00
Net receipts September		3,817.95

Gillian Salary October 2016 – Month 10		**€**	**€**

Tax Calculation:

Gross salary October Jingo Ltd		6,500	
Less: pension contribution		(650)	
Gross salary to Month 9		52,650	
Cumulative gross pay to date			**58,500**
Cumulative SRCOP to date (€2,816.67 × 10)			28,167
Tax Payable:			
€28,167 @ 20%		5,633.40	
€30,333 @ 40%		12,133.20	
€58,500		17,766.60	
Less: Cumulative tax credits to date	(€275 × 10)	(2,750.00)	
Cumulative tax due to date		15,016.60	
Less: tax paid to Month 9		(13,515.00)	
Tax due for Month 10			**1,501.60**

USC Calculation:

Gross salary October		6,500
Gross salary to Month 9		58,124
Cumulative gross pay to date for USC		**64,624**

continued overleaf

USC cut-off point 1 (€1,001 × 10)	€10,010	@ 1.0%	100.10	
USC cut-off point 2 (€554.67 × 10)	€5,547	@ 3.0%	166.40	
USC cut-off point 3 (€4,281.33 × 10)	€42,813	@ 5.5%	2,354.73	
USC cut-off point 4 (balance)	€6,254	@ 8.0%	500.32	
Cumulative pay to date	€64,624		3,121.55	
Less: USC paid to Month 9			2,806.39	
USC due for October				**315.16**

PRSI Calculation:

€6,500 @ 4%	**260.00**

Net salary October:

Gross – Jingo Ltd		6,500.00
Less:		
PAYE	1,501.60	
PRSI	260.00	
USC	315.16	(2,076.76)
Net salary		4,423.24
Less: pension contribution		(650.00)
Net salary October		**3,773.24**

Gillian Salary November 2016 – Month 11	**€**	**€**
Tax Payable:		
Gross salary November Jingo Ltd €6,500 – (€230 × 4)	5,580	
Less: pension contribution	(650)	
Gross salary to Month 10	58,500	
Cumulative gross pay to date		**63,430**
Cumulative SRCOP to date (Note)	30,063.33	
Tax Payable:		
€30,063.33 @ 20%	6,012.66	
€33,366.67 @ 40%	13,346.67	
€63,430.00	19,359.33	
Less: Cumulative tax credits to date	(2,841.00)	
Cumulative tax due to date	16,518.33	
Less: tax paid to Month 10	(15,016.60)	
Tax due for Month 11		**1,501.73**

continued overleaf

USC Calculation:

Gross salary November				5,580
Gross salary to Month 10				64,624
Cumulative gross pay to date for USC				**70,204**
USC cut-off point 1	(€1,001 × 11)	€11,011	@ 1.0%	110.11
USC cut-off point 2	(€554.67 × 11)	€6,101	@ 3.0%	183.04
USC cut-off point 3	(€4,281.33 × 11) €47,095		@ 5.5%	2,590.20
USC cut-off point 4 (balance)	€5,997		@ 8.0%	479.76
Cumulative pay to date	€70,204			3,363.11
Less: USC paid to Month 10				3,121.55
USC due for November				**241.56**

PRSI Calculation:

€5,580 @ 4%	**223.20**

Net salary November:

Gross – Jingo Ltd		5,580.00
Less:		
PAYE	1,501.73	
PRSI	223.20	
USC	241.56	(1,966.49)
Net salary		3,613.51
Less: pension contribution		(650.00)
Net November Jingo Ltd		**2,963.51**
Plus: Maternity Benefit DSP		920.00
Net receipts November		3,883.51

Gillian's PAYE liability remains the same for the three months, but her liability to USC and PRSI reduces when in receipt of DSP benefits as these are not subject to PRSI or USC.

Note:

Revised P2C from Revenue – effective from 1 November 2016:

SRCOP Month 11	€33,800 × 11/12ths	€30,983.33
Less: Maternity Benefit November €230 × 4		(€920.00)
Cumulative SRCOP Month 11		€30,063.33

continued overleaf

Non-refundable Tax Credits:

Basic personal tax credit	€1,650	
Employee tax credit	€1,650	
	€3,300	
Cumulative tax credits November €3,300 × 11/12ths		€3,025
Less: Maternity Benefit: €230 × 4 @ 20%		(€184)
Revised tax credits		€2,841

Question 8.6

John Wages: Week 32		**€**	**€**
Tax Calculation:			
Gross wages week 32	(€16 × 20)	320.00	
Gross wages to week 31		19,840.00	
Cumulative gross pay to date			**20,160.00**
Cumulative SRCOP to date	(€823.07 × 32)		26,338.24
Tax Calculation:			
€20,160 @ 20%		4,032.00	
Less: cumulative tax credits to date	(€95.19 × 32)	(3,046.08)	
Cumulative tax due to date		985.92	
Less: tax paid to week 31		(1,017.11)	
Tax refund for week 32			**(31.19)**
PRSI:			
Wages €320 – Class A0 – EE PRSI @ NIL%			**0.00**
ER PRSI @ 8.5%			**27.20**
USC Calculation:		**€**	**€**
Cumulative Gross Pay to date for USC		20,160.00	
USC cut-off point 1	(€231 × 32)	€7,392 @ 1.0%	73.92
USC cut-off point 2	(€128 × 32)	€4,096 @ 3.0%	122.88
USC cut-off point 3 (balance)		€8,672 @ 5.5%	476.96

continued overleaf

Cumulative pay to date	€20,160	673.76	
Less: USC paid to week 31		669.76	
USC due for week 32			**4.00**
Net wages week 32:			
Gross			320.00
Less:			
PAYE refunded		(31.19)	
PRSI		0.00	
USC		4.00	27.19
Net wages week 32			**347.19**

John Wages: Week 33		€	€
Tax Calculation:			
Gross wages week 33	(€16 × 25)	400.00	
Gross wages to week 32		20,160.00	
Cumulative gross pay to date			**20,560.00**
Cumulative SRCOP to date	(€823.07 × 33)		27,161.31
Tax Calculation:			
€20,560 @ 20%		4,112.00	
Less: cumulative tax credits to date	(€95.19 × 33)	(3,141.27)	
Cumulative tax due to date		970.73	
Less: tax paid to week 32		(985.92)	
Tax refund for week 33			**(15.19)**
PRSI:			
Wages €400 – Class AL			
EE PRSI @ 4%		16.00	
PRSI credit calculation:			
Maximum credit	€12.00		
Less: 1/6th × (€400 – €352.01)	(€8.00)		
Deduct PRSI credit		(4.00)	
EE PRSI			**12.00**
ER PRSI @ 10.75%			**43.00**

continued overleaf

USC Calculation:

			€	€
Cumulative gross pay to date for USC			20,560.00	
USC cut-off point 1	(€231 × 33)	€7,623 @ 1.0%	76.23	
USC cut-off point 2	(€128 × 33)	€4,224 @ 3.0%	126.72	
USC cut-off point 3 (balance)		€8,713 @ 5.5%	479.22	
Cumulative pay to date		€20,560	682.17	
Less: USC paid to week 32			673.76	
USC due for week 33				**8.41**
Net wages week 33:				
Gross				400.00
Less:				
PAYE refunded			(15.19)	
PRSI			12.00	
USC			8.41	(5.22)
Net wages week 33				**394.78**

John Wages: Week 34			€	€
Tax Calculation:				
Gross wages week 34		(€16 × 23)	368.00	
Gross wages to week 33			20,560.00	
Cumulative gross pay to date				**20,928.00**
Cumulative SRCOP to date		(€823.07 × 34)		27,984.38
Tax Calculation:				
€20,928 @ 20%			4,185.60	
Less: cumulative tax credits to date		(€95.19 × 34)	(3,236.46)	
Cumulative tax due to date			949.14	
Less: tax paid to week 33			(970.73)	
Tax refund for week 34				**(21.59)**
PRSI:				
Wages €368 – Class AX				
EE PRSI @ 4%			14.72	

continued overleaf

PRSI credit calculation:

Maximum credit	€12.00	
Less: 1/6th × (€368 – €352.01)	(€2.67)	
Deduct PRSI credit		(9.33)
EE PRSI		**5.39**
ER PRSI @ 8.5%		**31.28**

USC Calculation:

			€	€
Cumulative gross pay to date for USC			20,928.00	
USC cut-off point 1	(€231 × 34)	€7,854 @ 1.0%	78.54	
USC cut-off point 2	(€128 × 34)	€4,352 @ 3.0%	130.56	
USC cut-off point 3 (balance)		€8,722 @ 5.5%	479.71	
Cumulative pay to date		€20,928	688.81	
Less: USC paid to week 33			682.17	
USC due for week 34				**6.64**
Net wages week 34:				
Gross				400.00
Less:				
PAYE refunded			(21.59)	
PRSI			5.39	
USC			6.64	9.56
Net wages week 34				**409.56**

Chapter 9

Question 9.1

(a) Calculation of LPT

House valuation	€330,000
Valuation Band 6	€300,000 – €350,000
Mid-value Band 6	€325,000

LPT for 2016:

€325,000 @ 0.18%	€585

(b) Deferral

Full Deferral

To qualify for a full deferral, Bill and Frida's gross income must not exceed €25,000 plus 80% of their gross mortgage interest payments:

Gross income threshold: €25,000 + (€6,000 × 80%)	€29,800
Bill and Frida's gross income	€37,000

As Bill and Frida's gross income is greater than the full deferral adjusted income threshold, they do not qualify for a full deferral.

Partial Deferral

To qualify for a partial deferral, Bill and Frida's gross income must not exceed €35,000 plus 80% of their gross mortgage interest payments:

Gross income threshold: €35,000 + (€6,000 × 80%)	€39,800
Bill and Frida's gross income	€37,000

As Bill and Frida's gross income is less than the partial deferral adjusted income threshold, they do qualify for a partial deferral (50%).

LPT partial deferral for 2016: €585 @ 50%	€293

If they wish to opt for partial deferral, they should enter "Deferral Condition Number 4" at Option 6 of the LPT1 return form and select one of the payment options for the balance (€293) of the LPT due. A charge for the deferred amount, including interest at 4%, will be placed on the property.

In order for the couple to qualify for a deferral of LPT in 2017 and subsequent years, they must satisfy the gross income thresholds for each year at the liability date of 1 November of the previous year. To qualify for deferral of LPT for 2017, Bill and Frida must estimate, on 1 November 2016, the amount of their income and mortgage interest payable for the whole of 2016.

Question 9.2

1. Deferral based on income

Calculation of adjusted income threshold:

Full deferral €25,000 + (€16,000 × 80%)	€37,800
Partial deferral €25,000 + (€16,000 × 80%)	€47,800

Theo and Emer gross income:

Gross Case I income	€30,000	
Schedule E income	€13,500	
Child Benefit	N/A	
Department of Social Protection Illness Benefit	€9,776	
Gross income		€53,276

As their combined gross income is greater than both adjusted income thresholds, Theo and Emer do not qualify for a full or partial deferral of LPT for 2016 on income threshold grounds.

2. Deferral based on hardship

Theo and Emer's gross income	€53,276
Less: unexpected medical expenses	€19,000
Adjusted gross income 2016	€34,276

As the unexpected significant expense is more than **20%** of their gross income **and** it reduces their gross income to below the full deferral income threshold of €37,800, Revenue might consider an application for a deferral where appropriate documentary evidence is provided by Theo and Emer in support of their claim that, as a result of payment of the un-reimbursed medical expenses, payment of the LPT would cause excessive hardship.

Question 9.3

Kevin Ryan: Market value (1 May 2013)	<u>€1,400,000</u>

LPT for 2015:

€1,000,000 @ 0.162% (0.18% × 90%)	€1,620
€ 400,000 @ 0.225% (0.25% × 90%)	<u>€900</u>
LPT 2015	**<u>€2,520</u>**

LPT for 2016:

€1,000,000 @ 0.171% (0.18% × 95%)	€1,710
€ 400,000 @ 0.2375% (0.25% × 95%)	<u>€ 950</u>
LPT 2016	**<u>€2,660</u>**

Cork County Council was one of the local authorities who varied the LPT rate in 2015 by a LAF of 15% (decrease) and in 2016 by a LAF of 5% (decrease).

Chapter 10

Question 10.1

ABC
Accountants

Dear Mr Murphy,

I refer to your letter requesting some information regarding the system of self-assessment.

Income Tax Returns and Surcharges

A self-assessed taxpayer must submit a tax return whether or not he has been requested by Revenue to do so. The return must be submitted before 31 October in the year following the tax year; otherwise a surcharge of up to 10% on the tax ultimately due (subject to a maximum of €63,485) is imposed.

A return for 2016 will be available from Revenue to the taxpayer after the end of the tax year. The taxpayer must enter details of income and capital gains from all sources, and claim allowances and reliefs, for the tax year. The return will also request details of all capital assets acquired. An individual within the self-assessment system must submit his return on or before 31 October in the year after the tax year to which the return refers. Accordingly, a tax return for 2016 would normally have to be submitted before 31 October 2017.

However, as you have only commenced to trade in 2016, you have until 31 October 2018, the due date for the filing of your 2017 tax return, to file your 2016 tax return without incurring any penalties.

Note that individuals who enter the self-assessment system because they have commenced to trade have until the return filing date for the second year to submit tax returns for both the first and

second year of trading. However, this does not extend to tax payments, preliminary tax for 2016 must be paid by 31 October 2016 and the balance of the 2016 tax due is payable in full by 31 October 2017, even though your 2016 return is not due for filing until 2018.

Preliminary Tax

All taxpayers within the self-assessment system are required to pay preliminary tax by 31 October in the tax year. Accordingly, preliminary tax for 2016 must be paid on or before 31 October 2016.

If interest charges are to be avoided, preliminary tax must amount to:

(1) 90% of the final liability for the tax year; or

(2) 100% of the final liability for the preceding tax year.

Failure to pay preliminary tax by 31 October will result in interest accruing on the full liability from 31 October to the date the tax is paid. Also, even where a preliminary tax payment is made in time but proves to be less than 90% of the tax ultimately due (or 100% of the preceding year's liability, as adjusted for USC, whichever is lower), interest will run on the full underpayment at the rate of 0.0219% per day.

An individual may opt to pay preliminary tax by direct debit. If he chooses to do this, instead of paying 90% of the current year's liability or 100% of the adjusted previous year's, he has the option of paying instead 105% of the pre-preceding year's liability.

The direct debit payments are made on the 9th day of each month. For the first year in which a taxpayer opts to pay his preliminary tax by direct debit, he can opt to pay his liability in a minimum of three equal instalments in that year. In subsequent years, the taxpayer must pay his liability in at least eight equal instalments. If these conditions are satisfied, the person is deemed to have paid his preliminary tax on time. The Collector-General can agree to vary the number of instalments to be made, or agree to increase or decrease the instalments, after one or more instalments have been made.

Balance of Income Tax

An individual must pay the balance of his income tax due, after payment of preliminary tax, on the due date for the filing of his income tax return. Accordingly, the balance of income tax due for 2016 must be paid on or before 31 October 2017.

For the tax year 2016, as this will be your first year to pay tax and file your return under the self-assessment system, you will not be required to make a preliminary tax payment on 31 October 2016. This is because you had no liability under the self-assessment system for the tax year 2015, so 100% of your prior year's liability is nil. Your total liability for 2016 is therefore due on 31 October 2017. You must pay your entire liability on or before this date if you wish to avoid interest, even though you will not incur any penalties if your return for 2016 is not filed until 31 October 2018.

Mandatory Requirement to File Tax Returns Electronically

Most self-employed individuals are required to submit, electronically, their tax returns and payments of tax due using the Revenue On-Line Service (ROS). Specifically, self-employed taxpayers subject to the high-earners restriction and/or claiming numerous reliefs and exemptions (e.g. EII relief, and property-based reliefs, etc.) are required to pay and file electronically. The advantage is that the taxpayer receives an extension to the filing date, which in 2016 is 10 November 2016 (as opposed to 31 October 2016).

If you require any further information please do not hesitate to contact me.

Yours faithfully,

ABC
Accountants

Question 10.2

ABC Accountants
Main Street
Dublin 2

Dear Mr Bricks,

Re: Relevant Contractors Tax (RCT) – Subcontractors

Under the electronic RCT system you were automatically credited for the deducted tax on the days the payments were notified to Revenue by OMG Ltd. These deductions are available as a down payment against any liability to Income Tax in the period the tax was deducted. Therefore all the deductions to 30 September 2016 are available against your tax liability for 2016. The deduction on 12 October 2016 is not available until the tax year 2017 as it was deducted in your accounts year 30 September 2017.

Repayments of RCT will not be made until your income tax return has been filed. However, the deducted RCT is available for offset against any liability to VAT and PAYE/PRSI as it arises and this may assist you in managing your cash flow.

At 30 September 2016 this situation is as follows:

RCT deducted (to 30/09/2016)	€10,400
Estimated tax liability 2016	€5,500
RCT refundable	€4,900

As you have liabilities of €6,450 for VAT and PAYE/PRSI, it would be in your interest to offset the RCT deducted as this would use up the deduction immediately instead of waiting until the submission of your return for a RCT refund.

If you require any further information, please do not hesitate to contact me.

Yours sincerely,

ABC Accountants

Question 10.3

Income Tax Calculation for 2016 Paul and Sandra Joist	Notes	€	€
Income:			
Schedule D, Case I		40,000	
Less: capital allowances		(6,000)	34,000
Schedule D, Case IV			1,275
Taxable income Paul			35,275
Schedule E – Sandra			52,000
Taxable income			87,275

Tax Payable:

€67,600 @ 20%	13,520	
€1,275 @ 41%	523	
€18,400 @ 40%	7,360	21,403
€87,275		
Deduct:		
Basic personal tax credit (married)	3,300	
Earned income tax credit	550	
Employee tax credit	1,650	(5,500)
Income tax liability		15,903
Deduct:		
PAYE paid	11,125	
DIRT paid (€1,275 @ 41%)	523	(11,648)
Tax due		**4,255**
PRSI due: (Note 1)		
Paul's income €35,275 @ Class S1 (4%)		1,411
USC due: (Note 1)		
€12,012 @ 1.0%	120	
€6,656 @ 3.0%	200	
€15,332 @ 5.5%	(843)	1,163
€34,000		
Total liability 2016		6,829
Less: PSWT paid		(600)
Net tax liability 2016		6,229

Note 1: Sandra is understood to have paid her liabilities to PRSI and USC through the PAYE system.

Preliminary tax due for 2016:

Lower of:	Year 2015 @ 100%	=	€8,100 **or**
	Year 2015 (net of PSWT) €6,229 @ 90%	=	€5,606

Preliminary tax payment for 2016 will be €5,606 and is payable **online** by 10 November 2016.

If Paul pays his preliminary tax by way of direct debit, his preliminary tax for 2016 will be as follows:

Lower of:	Year 2014 @ 105%	=	€6,090 **or**
	Year 2015 @ 100%	=	€8,100 **or**
	Year 2016 @ 90%	=	€5,606

Preliminary tax payment for 2016 will be €5,606 and is payable **online** by 10 November 2016. Balance due of €623 is payable by 31 October 2017.

Chapter 11

Question 11.1

(a) Obligation to register

A person is required to register for VAT if his turnover from the supply of taxable goods or services exceeds, or is likely to exceed, in any continuous period of 12 months whichever of the following limits is appropriate:

- (i) €37,500 in the case of persons supplying services;
- (ii) €37,500 in the case of persons supplying goods liable at the 13.5% or 23% rates which they have manufactured or produced from zero-rated materials;
- (iii) €35,000 in the case of persons making mail-order or distance sales into the State;
- (iv) €41,000 in the case of persons making intra-Community acquisitions;
- (v) €75,000 in the case of persons supplying both goods and services where 90% or more of the turnover is derived from supplies of goods (other than goods referred to at (ii) above);
- (vi) a non-established person supplying goods or services in the State is obliged to register and account for VAT regardless of the level of his turnover;
- (vii) a person receiving services from abroad for business purposes in the State must register irrespective of the level of turnover; and
- (viii) EU and non-EU businesses will have to register and account for VAT in every Member State in which they supply telecommunications, broadcasting and e-services (including gaming) to consumers.

In determining whether or not the relevant turnover threshold has been exceeded, actual turnover may be reduced by VAT on stock purchased for resale.

For example, in a 12-month period a trader purchases stock for €61,767 (including VAT of €11,550) and sells it on for €78,000. For the purpose of determining if the €75,000 threshold has been exceeded, the trader's turnover of €78,000 is reduced by VAT on purchases of stock of €11,550. Accordingly, the trader's turnover is deemed to be €66,450. As this is less than the €75,000 threshold, the trader is not obliged to register.

No threshold applies in the case of taxable intra-Community services received from abroad and in the case of cultural, artistic, sporting, scientific, educational or entertainment services received from a person not established in the State. All such services are liable to VAT.

Suppliers of goods and services that are exempt from VAT, and non-taxable entities such as State bodies, charities, etc., are obliged to register for VAT where it is likely that they will acquire more than €41,000 of intra-Community acquisitions in any 12-month period.

(b) Records and information

A taxable person must keep full and true records of all business transactions that affect, or may affect, their liability to VAT. The records must be kept up to date and must be sufficiently detailed to enable the trader to accurately calculate their liability or repayment, and for Revenue to check if necessary.

The record of purchases should distinguish between purchases of goods for resale and goods and services not intended for resale. The records should show the date of the purchase invoice, the name of the supplier, the cost exclusive of VAT and the VAT. Purchases at each date should be separated and similar records kept for imports.

The record of sales must record the amount charged in respect of every sale to a registered person and a daily total of the amounts charged in respect of sales to unregistered persons. Transactions liable at different rates must be distinguished as must exempt transactions.

All entries must be cross-referenced to the relevant invoices, cash register tally rolls, etc. which must be retained.

The bi-monthly, monthly or annual VAT return to the Collector-General must show the VAT charged on supplies (output tax), the VAT suffered on supplies, self-supplies, and imports used in the business (input tax), and adjustments to previous returns, and the net amount payable or repayable. The return should be on form VAT 3 and should be sent online to the Collector-General within 23 days of the end of each tax period.

Input and output tax figures must be supported by the original or copy tax invoices. Records, including a VAT account, must be maintained for six years. A taxable person must keep a record of all taxable goods and services received or supplied, including any self-supplies and exempt supplies. It is not necessary to submit the supporting documentation with the return, but it must be made available for inspection if required by Revenue.

Question 11.2

(a) Unless a taxable person has been specifically authorised by Revenue to account for tax on the basis of monies received (cash receipts basis), liability for VAT arises at the time when taxable goods or services are supplied. This general rule is, however, subject to a number of qualifications:

    (i) in dealings between taxable persons, tax becomes due on the date of issue of the tax invoice, or the date on which the invoice should have been issued if issue has been delayed;

    (ii) where payment in whole, or in part, in respect of a transaction was received before the date on which the VAT would normally be due, the VAT was due on the amount received on the date of receipt.

(b) Goods supplied on a sale or return basis are treated as supplied on the earlier of acquisition by the customer or when they are invoiced or paid for.

(c) If the services are supplied under a contract over a period during which periodic payments are made, each payment will have its own tax point as, under the general rule, the actual tax point for each payment will be the earlier of the date of the payment received or the issue of the tax invoice.

(d) Tax in respect of 'self-supplies' becomes due in all cases when the goods are appropriated or withdrawn from business stock or when the services are performed.

Question 11.3

(a) Records

A taxable person must keep full and true records of all business transactions which affect or may affect his liability to VAT. The records must be kept up to date and must be sufficiently detailed to enable the trader to accurately calculate their liability or repayment and for the Inspector of Taxes to check if necessary.

The record of purchases should distinguish between purchases of goods for resale and goods and services not intended for resale. The records should show the date of the purchase invoice, the name of the supplier, the cost exclusive of VAT and the VAT. Purchases at each rate should be separated and similar records kept for imports.

The record of sales must record the amount charged in respect of every sale to a registered person and a daily total of the amounts charged in respect of sales to unregistered persons. Transactions liable at different rates must be distinguished, as must exempt transactions.

All entries must be cross-referenced to the relevant invoices, cash register tally rolls, etc. which must be retained.

(b) If filing bi-monthly returns, the return must be submitted electronically (via ROS) by the 23rd of the month following the end of the two-month taxable period, i.e. 23 March; 23 May; 23 July; 23 September; 23 November and 23 January.

If VAT is not paid within the proper time limit, interest will be charged at the rate of 0.0274% for each day or part of a day by which payment is late. In addition, the Revenue offences listed in section 1078 TCA 1997 apply to VAT as they apply to other taxes. They involve, for example, obtaining a refund of VAT on an illegal input credit, or suppressing a VAT liability.

Question 11.4

	€
Sales: cash receipts €30,250 × 23/123	5,656
Less: purchases (Note)	(1,192)
VAT due	4,464

Note:

	€
Total VAT on purchases:	
(€6,150 × 23/123) + (€2,270 × 13.5/113.5)	1,420
Not allowable:	
Item 4 (i) €160 × 13.5% × 25%	(5)
Item 4 (ii) €300 × 23% × 80%	(55)
Item 4 (iii) €123 × 23/123	(23)
Item 4 (v) €64 × 23/123	(12)
	1,325
Less: 10% exempt	(133)
VAT on purchases	1,192

Question 11.5

The VAT liability of Mr Byte for the period July–August 2016 is:

	VAT-exclusive Amount €	VAT €	VAT Rate
Sales	75,000	17,250	23%
Purchases:			
Purchases for resale	40,000	9,200	23%
Stationery	6,000	1,380	23%
Wages	20,000	–	(Note 1)
Electricity	2,000	270	13.5%
Hotel bills	1,000	–	(Note 2)

Rent	2,400	–	(Note 3)
VAT deductible		10,850	
VAT payable		6,400	

*   VAT, if applied for and authorised by Revenue, is payable on the cash receipts basis, as sales are less than €2 million.

Notes:
1.   Services provided by employees are specifically exempt from VAT.
2.   While VAT is payable at the rate of 9% on hotel accommodation, it is specifically not recoverable, except on "qualifying accommodation" in connection with the attendance at a "qualifying conference".
3.   Rents in most cases are exempt from VAT. While a landlord may waive his exemption, it is assumed that he has not done so in this case.

Question 11.6

Since Joe supplies goods at the zero rate of VAT, he will be in a permanent VAT repayment position. This means that he is entitled to submit monthly VAT returns on the 23rd day of each month in respect of the previous month's purchases and sales.

	VAT-exclusive Amount €	VAT €	Rate €
May 2016			
Sales	10,000	–	(0%)
Purchases:			
Ingredients	5,000	–	
Petrol	1,000	–	(Note 1)
Lease rentals – vans	2,000	460	(23%) (Note 2)
Bank interest	400	0	
VAT recoverable		460	
June 2016			
Sales	8,000	–	(0%)
Purchases			
Ingredients	2,000	–	(0%)
Petrol	1,000	–	(Note 1)
Fixed assets	6,000	1,380	(23%)
Lease rental – vans	2,000	460	(23%)
Bank interest	400	–	
		1,840	
VAT recoverable May/June 2016		2,300	

continued overleaf

Notes:
1. VAT arises at the rate of 23% on purchases of petrol but is specifically not recoverable.
2. VAT on the lease of vans is recoverable. VAT on the lease of passenger motor vehicles is restricted to 20% of the VAT if the vehicle is a "qualifying vehicle", otherwise it is not recoverable.

Question 11.7

The following persons are not obliged to register for VAT unless they otherwise formally make an election to register:

(a) Persons whose turnover does not exceed €75,000 per annum, provided that 90% of their total receipts arise from the supply of taxable goods. The €75,000 registration limit is reduced to €37,500 for persons producing goods liable at the 13.5% or 23% rates from zero-rated raw materials.
(b) Farmers.
(c) Persons whose supplies of taxable goods/services consist **exclusively** of the following:
  (i) supplies of unprocessed fish caught in the course of a sea-fishing business;
  (ii) supplies of machinery, plant, etc. which have been used by that person in the course of his sea fishing business.
(d) Persons whose supplies of services do not exceed €37,500 per annum.

A person might choose to apply for voluntary registration if:

(a) they supply goods or services to VAT-registered persons. If the person registers for VAT, they will receive an input credit for any purchases. Although the sales would then be liable to VAT, VAT-registered purchasers would be entitled to an input credit;
(b) they export goods or deal in zero-rated goods, such as food. VAT would not be payable on sales, but a credit or repayment of any VAT invoiced on business purchases can be claimed.

Another category of person who might voluntarily register for VAT is a person who has not actually commenced supplying taxable goods or services but will soon become a taxable person. This will enable the trader to obtain credit for VAT on purchases made before trading commences.

Question 11.8

(a) The place of supply of goods is deemed to be:

  (i) In a case where it is a condition of supply that they are transported, it is the place where such transportation starts.
  (ii) In all other cases, it is where they are located at the time of supply (i.e. when ownership is transferred). Services are generally deemed to be supplied where the business making the supply is located. Where there is a provision of **international services**, the following rules are applied:
    (I) Services connected with immovable goods – deemed to be supplied where the property is located.
    (II) Transport services – deemed to be supplied where the transport actually takes place. This rule applies to the transport of goods only. Passenger transport is exempt. If the transport of goods is part of a contract to export the goods physically outside of the State, then the transport service may be zero rated.
    (III) Admission to cultural, artistic, sporting or entertainment services – deemed to be supplied where the service is physically carried out.
    (IV) Telecommunications, broadcasting and e-services (including e-gaming) – the place of supply of such services, when supplied to consumers (B2C), is deemed to be the place where the consumer resides.

(b) There is a self-supply of goods when a VAT-registered person diverts to private or exempt use goods which they have imported, purchased, manufactured or otherwise acquired and in respect of which they are entitled to a tax deduction.

Where this occurs, the VAT-registered person is liable to VAT at the appropriate rate on the cost of the goods in question.

Valuation rules for the self-supply of services

Where the supply consists of the private use of business assets, VAT is due on the cost to the taxable person of providing the service.

Where the supply is a non-deductible business service, then VAT is due on the market value of the service.

Question 11.9

Calculation of March–April 2016 VAT Return

		VAT €
Sales		
(1)	Sales @ 23% (1,815 × 23/123)	339.40
(2)	Sales @ 13.5% (2,837.50 × 13.5/113.5)	337.50
		676.90
Purchases		
(1)	Stock for resale (€605 × 23/123)	113.10
(2)	Stock for resale (€334 @ 0%)	Nil
(3)	Tables and chairs (€440 @ 23%)	101.20
(4)	Rent (no invoice/exempt letting)	N/A
(5)	Cash register (€665.50 × 23/123)	124.45
(6)	Tiling (€200 @ 13.5%)	27.00
(7)	Shop fitting lease for two months	
	i.e. 30 March and 30 April (€700 × 2 @ 23%)	322.00
(8)	Legal fees (€1,452 × 23/123)	271.50
(9)	Van (€9,840 × 23/123)	1,840.00
(10)	Petrol (non-deductible item)	N/A
		2,799.25
Net VAT refund due		2,122.35

Question 11.10

Calculation of VAT Liability for March–April 2016

VAT on sales	Net of VAT	VAT Payable
	€	€
Supplies in Ireland	250,000	57,500
Supplies to US	10,000	0
Purchases from UK (Note 1)	50,000	<u>11,500</u>
VAT on sales		69,000

VAT on costs	Net of VAT	VAT Claimable
Purchase of stock from Irish suppliers	190,000	43,700
(€233,700 × 100/123)		
Purchase of stock from UK suppliers (Note 1)	50,000	11,500
Professional fees (€6,150 × 100/123)	5,000	1,150
Motor car leasing (Note 2) (€3,690 × 100/123)	3,000	138
Motor car repairs (€1,135 × 100/113.5)	1,000	135
Computer (€9,225 × 100/123)	7,500	<u>1,725</u>
Total VAT on purchases		58,348
VAT on sales	69,000	
VAT on purchases	<u>58,348</u>	
VAT payable	<u>10,652</u>	

Notes:

1. Where goods are purchased for business purposes from another EU Member State, the supplier will not charge VAT, provided they are given the VAT registration number of the EU purchaser. The purchaser must account for a notional amount of VAT in the sales (reverse charge) and the purchases on their VAT return.
2. VAT charged on car lease is allowed at 20%, as the car is a "qualifying car".

Question 11.11

Calculation of VAT Payable

	Net of VAT €	VAT €
VAT on sales (output VAT):		
Supplies in Ireland (@ 23%)	950,000	218,500
Exports to Spain (to Spanish registered customers)	320,000	0
Exports to non-VAT-registered customers in the UK @ 23%	25,000	5,750
Exports to VAT-registered customers in the UK	135,000	0
Exports to customers located in Singapore	46,000	0
		224,250
VAT EU acquisitions	200,000	46,000
VAT on sales		270,250

VAT on costs (input VAT)	VAT inclusive €	VAT content €	
Purchase of materials from Irish suppliers (€369,000 × 23/123)	369,000	69,000	
Purchase of machinery locally (€246,000 × 23/123)	246,000	46,000	
Rent of premises (€18,450 × 23/123)	18,450	3,450	
Repairs and maintenance of office and equipment (€14,145 × 23/123)	14,145	2,645	
Audit and accountancy fees (€11,070 × 23/123)	11,070	2,070	
Diesel for staff vehicles (€5,535 × 23/123)	5,535	1,035	
Electricity and gas (€2,400 × 13.5/113.5)	2,400	285	
Salaries and wages	167,000	N/A	
Advertising costs (€30,750 × 23/123)	30,750	5,750	130,235
	NET	VAT	
EU acquisitions	200,000	46,000	46,000
VAT on costs			176,235
VAT payable			94,015

Index

THANKS FOR JOINING US

We hope that you are finding your course of study with Chartered Accountants Ireland a rewarding experience. We know you've got the will to succeed and are willing to put in the extra effort. You may well know like-minded people in your network who are interested in a career in finance or accountancy and are currently assessing their study options. As a current student, your endorsement matters greatly in helping them decide on a career in Chartered Accountancy.

How can you help?

O If you have an opportunity to explain to a friend or colleague why you chose Chartered Accountancy as your professional qualification, please do so.

O Anyone interested in the profession can visit **www.charteredaccountants.ie/prospective-students** where they'll find lots of information and advice on starting out.

O Like us on **Facebook**, follow us on **Twitter**.

O Email us at **studentqueries@charteredaccountants.ie**

We can all help in promoting Chartered Accountancy to the next generation and in doing so, strengthen our qualification and community. We really appreciate your support.